A CONSUMING FAITH

New Studies in American Intellectual and Cultural History
Thomas Bender, Series Editor

A CONSUMING

FAITH

The Social Gospel and
Modern American Culture

SUSAN CURTIS

THE JOHNS HOPKINS UNIVERSITY PRESS

BALTIMORE AND LONDON

The Johns Hopkins University Press
701 West 40th Street, Baltimore, Maryland 21211-2190
The Johns Hopkins Press Ltd., London

The paper used in this book meets the minimum requirements of American
National Standards for Information Sciences—Permanence of Paper for
Printed Library Materials, ANSI Z39.48-1984.

The photograph of Washington Gladden on page 39 is courtesy of the Ohio Historical
Society. The photograph of Walter Rauschenbusch on page 102 is courtesy of the
Rauschenbusch Family Papers, American Baptist–Samuel Colgate Historical Library,
Rochester, New York.

Library of Congress Cataloging-in-Publication Data will be found on the last
page of this book.

For my parents,

George William Curtis (1923–1989) and Lieselotte Loeffler Curtis

CONTENTS

FIGURES

PREFACE

As an undergraduate at Graceland College, I assiduously avoided studying the social gospel movement. The men and women who gave that movement its life triggered in me a combination of envy and skepticism. I envied the moral courage it took to give up the comforts of middle-class life to minister to an urban underclass. But my Calvinist upbringing made me skeptical of a generation of Christian reformers that seemed to be so unnaturally good and selfless. Graduate school ended by evasion of the subject, and studying for comprehensive exams forced me to confront my ambivalence about the movement. This book is a result of that confrontation.

In the course of my research, I discovered that my initial ambivalence may have been warranted. For these American Protestants, responsible for acts of courage and kindness in the name of social justice, were also men and women bedeviled by private anxieties that impelled them into the arena of reform. Social gospelers were caught in a painful struggle to do what they believed was right at the same time that they tried to find meaning in a rapidly changing world. They tried to emulate and honor the individualism of their elders even as they recognized the barriers to individual success in industrial America. Social gospel reforms eased the burden of an urban underclass, but it also relieved the private fears of the reformers.

Such a dual impulse need not discredit either the actors or their work, but recognizing this complexity of motivation gave me access to a way of understanding social gospelers as people who were as much a part of the late-nineteenth-century social and cultural transformation as critics of it.

A Consuming Faith is an examination of social gospel ideology and its relationship to broader cultural trends in twentieth-century America. As an ideology the social gospel grew out of the social conditions that transformed American culture at the turn of the century. It provides a key link between the Protestant-based Victorian culture of the nineteenth century and the modern, secular consumer culture that emerged in the twentieth century. I argue that the men and women who articulated the social gospel made significant departures from the beliefs of their parents because of the tremendous changes taking place around them. As they formulated a religious ideology that provided comfort and meaning to them, they tapped many of the same sources as the general culture. Thus, their ideology, which began in opposition to industrial developments, eventually mirrored and affirmed important dimensions of the emerging culture.

The first three chapters of this book attempt to show why young Protestants in the 1880s and 1890s became dissatisfied with the beliefs, practices, and expectations of their parents. These chapters identify private sources of the social gospel. The also begin to show how social gospelers' reconceptualizations of key Protestant ideas were derived from secular, sometimes commercial, sources and affirmed a public realm increasingly dominated by an ethos of consumerism. Chapter 1 establishes the context in which the social gospel first appeared and identifies social gospelers as men and women who were not exclusively, or even primarily, theologians. Chapter 2 examines the ways social gospelers redefined the traditional work ethic. Affected by the tension between Victorian expectations and industrial realities, they reconsidered the relationship between work, success, individualism, and salvation. Chapter 3 focuses on the impact of changes in the nature and meaning of work on family life. Challenges to the Victorian ideal of domesticity prompted responses from middle-class men and women that ranged from assisting troubled, impoverished families to offering advice on the religious and moral training of children. Moreover, their evolving ideals of family life appeared in their descriptions of God (the father) and Jesus (the son). In these ways, social gospelers effectively recast both religious and family ideology.

The final three chapters explore the relationship between social gospel ideas and three twentieth-century phenomena: progressive politics, the Great War, and the emergence of consumer culture. Informed by their concerns about work, social justice, and the endangerment of the American family, Protestants influenced by the social gospel became sympathetic toward much progressive reform. Indeed, some became active in politics—Washington Gladden served on the Columbus, Ohio, city council, and Mary Eliza McDowell served as commissioner of public welfare for the city of Chicago—and they supported bureaus established to provide welfare to families and workers dislocated by industrial and urban expansion. Social gospelers' commitment to the kingdom of God on earth became an important ideological support for the emergence of a progressive political culture.

Social gospelers' support of state mechanisms for reform blossomed into confidence that the state would generally provide for and protect the nation during the Great War. Though critical of war, these reformers believed that the United States could use its involvement in the conflict as an opportunity to reshape Europe into a "Christianized," socially responsible society. The war experience had two important results. First, the brutal, impersonal nature of the combat eroded the naive idealism of the prewar social gospel. Second, the war strengthened ties between business and government that produced security and prosperity in the United States. This alliance affirmed social consciousness, efficiency, and cooperation in the culture at large and in social gospel Protestantism. The war simultaneously legitimized and altered the language, ideas, and values of the social gospel.

By the 1920s, social gospel ideology reflected a redefined work ethic, the ideals of companionate families, a commitment to progressive politics, and an emphasis on manly efficiency. Moreover, it was presented increasingly in commercial idiom and images. In an effort to reach a wide audience, social gospelers had begun to use newspapers and advertising techniques before the war; afterwards, many of these reformers became obsessed with mass media. They experimented with radio, films, special services, and advertising, and they increasingly spoke of the "product" they had to sell. While they did not abandon their commitment to social justice, as the decade wore on they came to believe that business strength, governmental oversight, and an ethos of consumption could deliver abundance, justice, and meaning to Americans.

A Consuming Faith attempts to broaden the more traditional institutional and theological studies of the social gospel movement. Indeed, the story of the movement has been well told and does not bear repeating. I am more interested in the social gospel as an ideology and social gospelers as men and women struggling to make sense of their lives in an era of rapid social change. As a result, each chapter contains a general statement of a problem experienced and conceptualized by a variety of social gospelers followed by a series of biographical sketches to show the personal dimensions of these social issues. The vignettes are designed to illuminate particular facets of social gospel ideology through the experiences of individuals whose thinking was shaped particularly by their confrontation with work, family, politics, war, or popular culture.

Because this is a book about the social gospel as an ideology, it does not traverse some of the main-traveled roads in religious history. It is important, therefore, to note what this book does not attempt. It does not chronicle the establishment and activities of reform societies, institutional churches, quadrennial meetings of the Federal Council of Churches, women's organizations, or pastoral relations between social gospel ministers and their congregations. This work does not cite any Catholic social thinkers, who also began to write and act on America's social problems in the early twentieth century. I have focused exclusively on Protestant ministers, writers, teachers, and activists. Moreover, of the thirty-three denominations that endorsed the Social Creed of the Churches in 1908, only a handful receive special treatment through their outspoken advocates of reform. The works of individual Northern Baptists, Congregationalists, Methodists, Episcopalians, Presbyterians, and Disciples of Christ—members of mainstream denominations—form the basis of my analysis of social gospel thought. I should add that while the social gospel was articulated by Protestants from all regions of the country, its most vocal spokespersons—the ones whose work I have examined most thoroughly—lived and worked in the North, the Northeast, and the Midwest.

I have not dealt with a large number of men and women in this book—and the ones I have chosen are not necessarily representative. But they are important and revealing figures. By the early twentieth century, social gospelers held positions of leadership in national and denominational organizations. They edited much of the Sunday school literature used by local congregations, and they wrote books that appealed to educated middle-class readers. Their programs in cities attracted thousands of workers. I will not venture a guess as to the percentage of adherents in each denomination—even those in the mainstream—but I believe the influence of social gospel thought in Protestant circles was pervasive. For a time in the early twentieth century, even those who later broke with the reformers over modernism, evolution, and social reform engaged in efforts to address serious social problems. By the time the fundamentalist-modernist controversy erupted in the 1920s, the war and the ensuing Red Scare had intervened to polarize opinion in Protestant America and obscured the earlier common cause.

Despite their attention to secular trends, popular culture, environmentalism, social psychology, and social reform, social gospelers must not be confused with secular humanists. Many came out of an evangelical background. They devoted their lives to spreading a Christian gospel and hoped to save wayward souls through the power of Jesus' teaching. The effect of their ideas and practices, I argue, was the absorption of social gospel Protestantism by consumer culture, but that was not their intention. As the Rauschenbusch and Macfarland families suggest, however, it was possible for liberal secular humanists to emerge from families immersed in the teachings of the social gospel.

Social gospel ideology initially was the product of a minority of writers and ministers within American Protestantism, but its impact on American culture was far-reaching. It was the product of a generation of Protestant men and women searching for certainty and reassurance in a troubled, changing world. The social gospel conferred meaning on modern work and family relations, and it created an agenda of reform that gave anxious middle-class Americans purposeful work. In the end, it helped ease the transition from Protestant Victorianism to a secular consumer culture.

ACKNOWLEDGMENTS

When my parents regaled their children with stories about growing up during the Great Depression and living through the horrors of World War II, they probably never dreamed that one of their children would one day become a professional historian. They probably also never knew that their stories sparked my interest in the past. As I began to tally the debts I owe to people who have assisted me in this project, I realized that I owe a great deal to my parents, Lieselotte Curtis and the late George William Curtis, not only for their financial and emotional support through the years, but also for inspiring in me curiosity about the past.

Others focused that curiosity, honed the necessary intellectual tools, and provided material assistance to complete this work. I gratefully acknowledge their inspiration, direction, and help.

I thank the Department of History at the University of Missouri for generous research and travel grants to complete the dissertation on which this book is based. It also supported a lively graduate community that included Philip Scarpino, Steven Watts, Kenneth Plax, Robert Hunt, Kenneth Mernitz, Teresa Prados, Mary Ann Wynkoop, and Bonnie Thompson—all of whom read and commented on portions of this manuscript. Of these friends and colleagues I am particularly grateful to Steve Watts and Ken Plax for leading me down intellectual paths I otherwise might have missed and for patiently offering advice and encouragement.

The following friends and colleagues read parts of the manuscript and offered valuable critical comment: David Roediger, Dina Copelman, Kerby Miller, Jonathan Sperber, J. Craig Jenkins, Larry Hunt, William Russell, Dorothy Ross, Steven Stowe, Richard Fox, Gregory Bush, Mark Szuchman, Joyce Peterson, Darden Pyron, Howard Rock, Brian Peterson, and Eric Leed. This work also benefitted from discussions with and critical insights from James Melton. It is with respect and admiration that I acknowledge the intellectual and scholarly influence of Howard Kaminsky. Our conversations during long walks on Miami Beach prompted me to sharpen my arguments, to deepen my analysis of the social gospel, and to try to write history with force and clarity.

Two other men deserve special mention. Jackson Lears consistently has offered an example of sophisticated historical analysis and sensitivity to the unpredictability of human action. David Thelen always has written history with political purpose. Through their comments and direction, they encouraged me to address issues that matter and to examine these social gospelers with a sympathetic as well as a critical eye. I thank them for their support and for their examples as excellent scholars and responsible citizens.

Thanks to wise editorial suggestions from Thomas Bender and Henry Tom of the Johns Hopkins University Press, this manuscript is much stronger than it otherwise would have been. I appreciate the wonderful work done by the press and by Carolyn Moser, a careful, expeditious copy editor.

Finally, it is a pleasure to acknowledge with gratitude the support of a number of good friends. Thanks especially to Hilma Mernitz Moeller and Kenneth Mernitz, who provided much-appreciated support during the years of researching, writing, and revising this manuscript. Barbara Brockman, Virginia Thompson, Hassan Zahedi, and Betty Scarpino did not read a word of this manuscript, but their friendship and hours on the tennis court helped make the years of writing a lot more enjoyable. As I struggled through the final stages of revising, Charles R. Cutter, a colleague and dear friend, helped me keep things in perspective by offering an example of scholarly and emotional equanimity and by providing both advice and support.

A Consuming Faith

1

AMERICAN PROTESTANTISM

AT A CROSSROADS

When Walter Rauschenbusch wrote *Christianizing the Social Order* in 1912, he believed that the social gospel had become the dominant expression of Protestantism in America. He had returned to the United States in 1908 after a year-long stay in Europe to discover that his book *Christianity and the Social Crisis* had won popular approval beyond his "boldest hopes." He marveled at the "social awakening of our nation" that made people receptive to his ideas. Rauschenbusch applauded Americans' "enthusiastic turning toward real democracy" and the increasing intensity of "religious energy" that accompanied it. He discovered a vast array of programs and projects that heartened him. The Federal Council of Churches, the Social Creed of the Churches, an expanding YMCA, the blossoming of institutional churches across the country, the social interests of the Religious Education Association, the Men and Religion Forward Movement, and the Presbyterians' Labor Temple in New York City—all were evidence to him of a dramatic reordering of Protestant America. To his astonishment and delight, long-time defenders and advocates of the social gospel were not the only ones to sing its praises. "Perhaps the most convincing proof of the spread of the social interest in the ministry," he declared, "is the fact that the old men and the timid men are falling in line."[1] By 1912, Rauschenbusch believed that his social message had become the legitimate expression of mainstream Protestantism in America.

From his vantage point as one of the vanguard of the social gospel movement, Walter Rauschenbusch considered the organizations and achievements that he praised in 1912 as evidence of the triumph of a new kind of Protestantism. The social gospel, as this new Protestantism was known, bolstered the age-old demand for individual regeneration with a powerful social message. It was a gospel that did not let the saved languish in smug self-satisfaction while the ills of society kept others from salvation. According to the social gospel, every Christian had a dual obligation: to himself and to society. As a result, the social gospel provided the foundation for social and political reforms designed to eliminate poverty, disease, filth, and immorality. And its advocates evangelized the unchurched. For example, social gospelers launched a campaign to attract the working class by supporting their class interests for fairer working conditions, by easing the discomfort of their lives with material and medical assistance, and by living among them, sharing their burdens and speaking to them as brothers and sisters with a message of hope. Social gospelers wrote hymns and compiled hymnals that reflected their Christocentric theology and their interest in the kingdom of God on earth. They rewrote Sunday school literature to instruct young people to balance individual piety with social responsibility. The social gospel asked Protestants to address the physical, emotional, and material, as well as spiritual, needs of men and women whether they belonged to a church or not.

The social gospel usually is described as the religious expression of progressivism in the early twentieth century. Like the progressive political culture of which it was a part, the social gospel was perceived by participants and observers alike as a departure from the Protestant emphasis in nineteenth-century Victorian America on individualism. Men and women born in the 1830s and 1840s—such as Elizabeth Stuart Phelps Ward, Josiah Strong, Washington Gladden, and Lyman Abbott—increasingly voiced their dissatisfaction with Protestant belief and practice in the 1860s and 1870s. Initially, their ideas met with disfavor, but beginning in the 1880s a rising generation identified more readily with their critique of individualism. By the 1890s Protestants had established a number of organizations devoted to social reform.

In 1908, when the Federal Council of Churches met in Philadelphia, delegates unanimously adopted the Social Creed of the Churches, which signaled the commitment of a significant portion of Protestant America to an agenda of social justice and social reform. By the time this creed was adopted, the "social question" absorbed the attention of many Protestants. Josiah Strong had announced the dawning of "a new era"; Rauschenbusch had alerted thousands to a serious "social crisis";

Washington Gladden had defined "social salvation" and George Herron, the "new redemption." It would have been difficult to avoid confronting the social gospel. Even conservatives, who later joined with fundamentalists in the 1920s, undertook various programs of reform and responded to the needs of society as well as to the souls of individual communicants. Inspired by the hope of ushering in the kingdom of God on earth, men like John Roach Straton attacked political corruption, prostitution, child labor, women's labor, and bad working conditions in the 1910s.[2]

The social gospel is also explained as a response by late-nineteenth-century American Protestants to problems caused by industrialization, massive immigration, and chaotic urban development. The Labor Temple in New York City, the University Settlement House in Chicago, Walter Rauschenbusch in Hell's Kitchen in the 1880s, and Washington Gladden's political crusades on behalf of workers and reform in Columbus, Ohio, are among the treasured memories of the social gospel movement. Protestants in the late nineteenth century turned away from the accepted religious wisdom of their elders by formulating a theology and practice that redefined the categories of belief and that presented a serious challenge to industrial capitalist society. They exchanged the terror of the anxious bench for a commitment to altruism that would ensure their own and their brothers' salvation. In place of unbridled competition, individual responsibility for success, and governmental policies of laissez faire, social gospelers proposed cooperation, social responsibility for justice, and an interventionist welfare state.

While clearly influential in America's urban centers, the social gospel did more than provide stopgap aid to the victims of urbanization. It affected Protestantism in small cities and burgs in the Midwest and the South as well as in the sprawling metropolises of the North and the Northeast. Places like Kalamazoo, Michigan; Sioux City, Iowa; Topeka, Kansas; and Lexington, Missouri, boasted churches devoted to the principles of the social gospel. Furthermore, people from small towns and farms first gave it expression. Rauschenbusch's optimism in 1912 stemmed from his belief that the social gospel was pervasive and popular.[3]

In addition to the well-known accomplishments of the social gospel movement, this major shift in Protestantism also resulted in different church services. Across the nation, Americans witnessed the emergence of "institutional" churches that remained open seven days a week and provided meals, employment, medical services, clothes, child care, and social activities that bound neighbors together in the quest for justice and nurture. Instead of limiting their service to people formally associated with the church or denomination, Protestants who supported the social gospel sought to serve all those in need. By the early twentieth century the majority of Protestants went beyond providing material and spiritual succor to support more fundamental assaults on the system that created inequality. The Social Creed of the Churches, for example, affirmed laborers' rights to organize unions and to bargain collectively with employers. Some congregations lent assistance to striking workers who tried to wrest a better life from a grudging industrial order, and at least one social gospeler arbitrated labor disputes in his community to the satisfaction and with the gratitude of unionists.[4]

One of the most impressive attempts to launch a nationwide experiment in social salvation was the Men and Religion Forward Movement in 1911. All the major denominations joined together to recruit men for the cause of Christian reform. Making the kingdom of God the focus of their message, they challenged men and boys to devote their lives to its establishment on earth. According to Rauschenbusch, "The movement has probably done more than any other single agency to lodge the social gospel in the common mind of the church. It has made social Christianity orthodox." It was the perfect social gospel program: it evangelized individuals and inspired them to shoulder social responsibility. By the following year, Rauschenbusch could count the success of the Men and Religion Forward Movement as part of the same religious impulse that produced the Federal Council of Churches, the Social Creed, and a new Sunday school curriculum. Even Charles Stelzle's success at the Labor Temple in New York seemed to affirm the strength and soundness of the appeal to men begun by the Men and Religion Forward Movement. Rauschenbusch insisted that the social principles that lay beneath all of these accomplishments had become "the common sense of the Protestant Churches of America."[5]

Social gospelers also produced an extensive literature that helped to popularize the commitment to social justice. Novelists like Elizabeth Stuart Phelps Ward and Charles Sheldon created imaginary communities beset by social ills that flourished once they adopted the social gospel. *In His Steps* by Charles Sheldon became a best-seller in the 1890s and appeared in at least a dozen different languages and countries. The Religious Education Association oversaw the publication of new Sunday school texts that reflected the new social interests of Protestants and acquainted young people with the ideas of the social gospel in stories, object lessons, and community service projects. Most ministers in the movement wrote books aimed at the general educated reader concerned with social ills and reform, but many also tried to reach a working-class audience composed of men and women who had fallen away from the church. Their essays, collections of sermons, and blueprints for reform appeared in monographs, literary journals, and inexpensive religious magazines. William Bliss prepared an encyclopedia of social reform in 1897 that pulled together much of the pathbreaking work by men and women in the social gospel movement, and it remains an invaluable source for the ideas and accomplishments of twentieth-century Christian reformers. These writers shared a desire to improve the physical conditions of life for an urban underclass impoverished by industrial development, and they revolutionized the way middle-class adherents to the movement thought about religion.[6]

These social gospel programs and literature reflected an important transformation of Protestant theology. While formal, academic statements of theology did not appear until later in the twentieth century, social gospelers redefined salvation, the nature of God, and religious commitment and in so doing, made an important departure from the Protestantism of the Second Great Awakening in the early 1800s. Eschewing the lonely struggle with sin for a sense of individual assurance, social gospelers insisted that salvation was a social matter—that Christians were responsible for their brothers' and sisters' redemption as much as their own. The social view of salvation required a united Christian attack on the poverty, vice, and filth that prevented many Americans from staying on the road to redemption. If the conditions that encouraged depravity were removed, these reformers argued, believers would be less likely to stray.

Given this commitment to changing the social environment, it is not surprising that social gospelers redefined the meaning of God as well. Instead of the angry Jehovah of the eighteenth century or even the judgmental God of the "burned-over district," the God of the social gospel was "immanent," "indwelling," and indulgent. A kind parent, God befriended man and surrendered to his moral creatures the agency to usher in his kingdom.

The idea of social salvation granted by an immanent God gave rise to a third important shift in Protestant thinking—away from a concern with the afterlife and toward a concern with this life. Social gospelers proposed active involvement in the affairs of the world, an agenda of reform, and a vital commitment to the kingdom of God on earth. Instead of viewing religion exclusively as a private matter to be addressed by each individual, Rauschenbusch and his colleagues believed in paving the way for individual assurance by removing the social barriers to righteousness. Rather than dwelling on future promises of celestial bliss, they occupied themselves with the evils of poverty, depravity, and injustice in this world.[7]

Social gospelers hold a respected place in American history as Christian reformers in urban, industrial America; and many Americans, then and later, have drawn strength from the example they set. But much more can be learned from these Protestant men and women than how to translate Christian commitment into social action. The social gospel appeared at a critical moment in American history—a moment that marked the unraveling of the Victorian culture of the nineteenth century. Consequently, social gospelers were among those who experienced anxiety when the matrix of beliefs and values that had given life meaning in the nineteenth century began to make less and less sense. Struggling to find religious and personal meaning themselves, they gradually developed a social interpretation of religion that contributed to the formation of the new culture that emerged in the twentieth century. An examination of the social gospel can reveal the intersection of faith and culture and demonstrate how social and cultural facts of life impinged on religion. Such an inquiry also demonstrates the way in which an emergent pattern of religious belief conditioned the standards applied to work, family life, politics, individual personality, and social relationships.

Because of its origin in an era of cultural transformation, the social gospel can help explain how a modern, secular, consumption-oriented culture took root and flourished in Protestant Victorian soil. But gaining this understanding requires a fresh approach to the movement and its message. We must grant to the men and women of the social gospel their sincerity and earnestness in seeking religious and cultural certainty. But we must frame the phenomenon in cultural terms rather than narrowly religious ones. We must look at the relation of reverence and faith to their experience as members of families, as citizens, as workers, and as men and women of letters.

As children in the middle third of the nineteenth century, future social gospelers approached maturity with expectations implanted by their elders. They assumed that the key to their success and salvation lay inside themselves and that failure would be the result of inadequate effort or restraint. They looked forward to starting families and living among neighbors whose domestic harmony and order reflected their own. They never imagined that their Protestant world view, liberal political culture, and Victorian respectability would be significantly challenged.

Yet the Gilded Age called their lives and faith into question. An increasingly industrialized, bureaucratized, urban economy thwarted the efforts of many an ambitious individual to strive and succeed on his own. The demands of the market along with greater educational opportunities for women brought more women into the workplace as laborers and professionals, thus eroding the domestic ideal. Thousands of Catholic and Jewish immigrants from southern and eastern Europe began to undermine the Protestant majority and its outlook, and with the rise of urban political machines, they transformed American politics. While these external forces undermined the culture of Victorian Protestantism, the advent of biblical criticism, Darwin's theory of evolution, and Freudian psychology brought religious certainty under direct attack. Men and women raised to believe in individualism, self-restraint, domesticity, liberalism, and moral free agency found themselves in the late nineteenth century in a world that did not sustain their beliefs.[8] They sought and eventually began to articulate a creed that would reassure them both culturally and spiritually.

American Protestants in the late nineteenth century responded to this changed world in a variety of ways, many of which became parts of the social gospel program. Some rejected trends in the economy as destructive of self-esteem and just rewards for labor. They opposed industrial capitalism because they believed it denied justice, fair distribution of rewards, and human dignity. These critics supported labor unions, socialism, or government intervention and regulation. Others looked nervously askance at an increasingly militant and foreign-born working class and escalating class warfare. Their Christian faith in brotherhood, charity, and harmony clashed with the hateful spirit of both labor activists and exploitative employers. Instead, they sought peace and generosity and social harmony. These Christian men and women wanted to ameliorate the conditions that evoked such fierce anger, which in turn elicited harsh repression.

Many American Protestants worried. They sensed that their beliefs were being drowned out by the plethora of voices, cultures, and creeds of an ever more diverse American society. They feared that Protestant beliefs would be swallowed by the creeds of Catholic and Jewish immi-

grants. They worried that family life, necessary to sustain and repro-
duce their values, would be destroyed by people whose circumstances
demanded, by middle-class standards, unwholesome domestic arrangements. They predicted the demise of democratic institutions if the
new immigrants were not tutored in American political practices. They
wanted to combat their fears by reaching a new audience—not the
already converted but the men and women thronging to America's
shores. They groped toward a bigger and more inclusive way of conceiv-
ing a Protestant America.

Most people who embraced the social gospel questioned the beliefs
or practices of their parents. They sensed that the lessons of their youth
would not stand up to the demands being placed on them by a rapidly
changing society. Personal experiences conditioned their reaction to
their society and culture, and their formulation of the social gospel in
its own way answered deeply felt needs to succeed, to help others, to
restore social (Christian) harmony, to earn their birthright as good
citizens, and to help see that justice was done. Protestants who embraced the social gospel did so because they saw it as a way of presenting new ideas, addressing their fears, and achieving their vision of a
godly society.

Ministers of the social gospel at the turn of the century set themselves
against their parents' professions of religion. They questioned the focus
on individual salvation, not because they believed the individual soul
was somehow unimportant, but because they believed it was not the only
concern. They worried that too much attention to the afterlife would draw
attention away from very real problems on earth that would delay the
coming of the kingdom of God. They rejected the explanation of antebellum religion and postbellum liberal political economy, that people
who failed did so on their own. Social gospelers were deeply aware of the
limits of the individual's power, especially among the lower classes. They
wanted religion to engage, even transform, politics and business.
Though liberal Protestants before the Civil War had begun to blur the
distinctions between heaven and earth, and antebellum Protestant reformers had begun to address a wide range of social problems, social
gospelers shifted the emphasis and believed that they were breaking with
the beliefs and practices of the past.[9] Rauschenbusch remembered the
years before 1900 as "a time of loneliness" for social Christians. Their
elders chided Rauschenbusch and his peers for "wrecking" their careers
by taking theological stands outside mainstream Protestantism. He recalled the "happy surprise" every time he met "a new man who had seen

the light."[10] Indeed, while some parents of social gospelers had fought against slavery, intemperance, ignorance, and poverty, they emphasized individual responsibility and individual solutions. Slaveholders were individual sinners, as were drinkers. The children of these earlier reformers, those who became a part of the social gospel movement, sponsored reform campaigns in municipalities and state legislatures that assumed individual responsibility but looked more often to collective solutions, to a socialized humanity. Social gospelers fought for higher standards of public sanitation, health, education, and working conditions; and they sought to abolish child labor, to protect women at work, and to improve the treatment of immigrant laborers. They placed the burden of responsibility on institutions rather than on the individual, and they proposed social, governmental solutions to problems that their parents had treated as individual failings.

Social gospelers' calls for social salvation, commitment to the kingdom of God on earth, new criteria for evaluating personal worth, cooperation, and involvement in the affairs of the world eventually gained wide acceptance. Certainly not every Protestant was a social gospeler, but in *Christianizing the Social Order* Rauschenbusch noted that the "contrast with the early days . . . makes the present situation in the churches . . . amazing."[11] By 1912, many American Protestants accepted a creed of which the generation of the 1880s would have been skeptical.

The generation of Protestants who followed the original pathbreakers found that it was respectable to advocate a social gospel. In places like Grinnell College in the 1890s, they could take courses in applied Christianity. In leading theological seminaries they studied Christian sociology and wrote theses on various dimensions of the "social crisis." They had at their disposal a growing body of scholarship on Christians' responsibility for economic, social, and political reform. Religious literature for children reflected the interest in social salvation. It did not require the same act of courage for younger men and women to declare their support for the social gospel that it had for the first spokesmen. While this represented "progress" of an important source for the movement, it also changed the movement's character. The focus of the second generation would be different—that of broadcasting the movement.

Some social gospelers in the early twentieth century experimented with new ways of attracting adherents. Their aim was to win the adherence of people outside of Protestantism. Some tried innovations in worship services and in church life. Others dabbled in the new mass media—moving pictures and, later, radio. Some believed that advertising would augment the number of supporters for social Christianity. By the onset of the First World War, the social gospel had been transformed. A movement that had originated in the social problems produced by capitalist industrial production took on the coloration of a movement of a piece with an emergent consumer society.

America's involvement in the Great War in Europe illuminated both the achievements and the much-expanded ambition of the social gospel movement. While social gospelers were morally offended by war, many nonetheless saw a chance to influence society in the postwar Western world. They never wavered in their denunciation of the war's destruction and violence, but they believed that the war was a turning point in Western civilization. It was an opportunity to Christianize society, culture, religion, work, politics, and international relations in the United States and Europe. Social gospelers fused their aims with the nation's, and many became proud defenders of the American mission to make the world safe for democracy.[12]

By the 1920s, the commitment of social gospelers to politics and reform as well as to publicity had been validated by their own involvement in the success of the state and corporate organization during the Great War. The shift must be described with some precision. Social gospelers still urged individuals to save their brothers and sisters as well as themselves. They still spoke of the need to redeem society. Increasingly, however, they articulated their beliefs and aspirations in terms drawn from secular society, terms, indeed, of secular society. They proposed to achieve social harmony and social justice by advocating social sensitivity to others, self-realization, and material abundance for all. The qualities of congeniality, inoffensiveness, and team spirit, evident in such secular settings as the college campus and the corporate white-collar world, promised, in the social gospel's terms, success, morality, and spiritual fulfillment. Participating in the modern workplace and marketplace provided material comfort, promised psychological security, involved the individual in something larger than himself, and thereby could invest religious meaning in secular acts. Affirmation through others, transcendence of the individualistic code, and faith in material comfort conferred a sense of well-being, gave people direction and attainable goals, and connected them to a larger social experience, all of which eased nagging fears of personal failure and eternal damnation. When social gospelers insisted that man could achieve salvation on earth, consumer goods and fellow-feeling came to be regarded among the tangible evidence of that salvation.[13]

The reformers' unhesitating appropriation of the techniques of advertising and the language of commerce in their efforts to promote their agenda of social reform demonstrates their intermingling of the sacred and the secular. In the 1920s, some social gospelers, like Charles Fiske, used the corporation as a model of appropriate Christian society. Others, like Mary McDowell, a Christian director of a Chicago settlement house, placed faith in the state for solutions to social problems, while some, like Edward Scribner Ames, claimed for science what their forefathers once had claimed for God. When an obscure social gospeler from Iowa praised his congregation's social programs as the best that money could buy, his assumptions about value were barely distinguishable from those made in secular commercial life.[14] The all-consuming passion for social justice of early Christian reformers like Washington Gladden and Walter Rauschenbusch had become by the 1920s an assertion that the various dimensions of modern life—the corporation, the state, technological sophistication, and an ethos of consumption—could bring about the kingdom of God on earth.

The innovations that led to this change in the social gospel, while evidence of laudable aims, suggest that social gospel Protestants gradually drew upon values dominant in the secular world for their own religious purposes. They were interested in creating an image of religion that would attract "users" and "nonusers" alike, and in the process, they drew ideas from secular sources. They strove for novelty, entertainment, and personal appeal to package, market, and sell their message. They judged their success by such secular standards as popularity—striving to make their religious services *as* entertaining as the movies, *as* well attended as baseball games, *as* successful as modern businesses. They believed in the social gospel in much the same way that merchants believed in their products—with zeal for its power to make the user a better person, with conviction that the same results could not be obtained from an off-brand, and with proof of results from the people who had already tried it.

Social gospelers spoke a language familiar with commercial ideals. Like many other Americans in the early twentieth century, they assumed that the individual should strive to develop his or her talents and abilities to the fullest, in part by getting along well with others and by participating in a group or cause larger than the individual. But most important, many social gospelers by the 1920s advised their audiences to find fulfillment by "consuming" Protestant values and services just as they would the goods of the marketplace. Religion was variously described in terms of entertainment to which the individual was spectator, in terms of a commodity communicants could buy or ignore, or in terms of psychological well-being. Using the corporation as a model, social gospel ministers often encouraged one another to strive for efficiency in proselytization and worship services and to project an attractive personality to the world. In other words social gospelers came increasingly to articulate their message in the terms of language of the dominant secular culture. Among many, though not all, social gospelers, this absorption of secular values so changed the movement that it shifted in impact, if not necessarily intentions, from critic of to supporter of the emergent culture of corporate abundance.

The social gospel, then, is fruitfully studied in a broader cultural frame as cultural history. From its beginning in the late nineteenth century, the social gospel was a matter of men and women in search of cultural truth as well as spiritual fulfillment. For that reason, it was a "consuming faith," a term used in this study to refer both to the social gospelers' profound commitment to justice and reform and to their eventual adoption of secular and commercial language and methods for achieving their goals. Protestants were articulating the social gospel at the same time that they were experiencing a changing economy, the undermining of Victorian domesticity, the challenge of democratic citizenship in the face of widespread corruption, and eventually the horrifying and galvanizing years of the World War I. They lived in the years that marked an important transition from Victorianism to modern culture, and their religion bore the marks of that dramatic reordering. In order to appreciate these social gospelers as the authors of a new kind of Protestantism, we must also understand them as men and women, children and parents, workers and citizens.

Thus the experiences that shaped the beliefs and outlook of social gospelers—work, family, social and political changes, the war—take on a heightened significance in this study. It was the tedium of work in the 1870s and 1880s, for example, that first frustrated their quest for successful individual achievement. Many suffered because of their early disappointments as middle-class and professional workers and began to ask what work should yield in the modern world. Work, it seemed, ought to be more than physical effort or production: it should be, they thought, a source of personal worth and meaning. They came to seek social justice and individual validation in the experience of work. Such an understanding of work pointed to a more general revision of cultural and religious conceptions of both individual and social salvation. By examining the generational experiences of social gospelers as children and later as heads of families, one gains insights into their conception of the fatherhood of God and the brotherhood of Jesus. These understandings, in turn, led them to embrace new child-rearing practices, and it led them especially to value their social and professional peers. All of this was intertwined with the shift in family life and personal behavior from Victorianism to modern ways. As citizens of a nation marked by labor strife and by political ineffectiveness and corruption, these Protestants sought a place for religion in public life, and they looked for leaders who would respond to the social crisis in terms more vital than liberal self-interest. They were among the vanguard calling for political and social reform that culminated in Progressivism in the early twentieth century. All of these factors—work, family, and political culture—were responsible for creating the need for and the appeal of the social gospel. And the war reinforced the resulting changes. Most came out of the war years surer of the social gospel than they had been before the first American troops were sent to Europe.

These developments associated with the social gospel were parallel, even interactive, with similar shifts in the larger culture, as Victorianism gave way to a modern secular culture embracing self-realization, materialism, and consumerism. The approach proposed here is thus a bifocal one, recognizing that one must attend simultaneously to religious and general cultural developments if one is to grasp the qualities of either in this period of transformation. In arguing that the social gospel is a key part of the cultural mix that gave birth to modern American culture I attempt also to shed light on the complex legacy of the United States in the twentieth century. Much of the admirable strength of twentieth-century American culture—its commitments to activism in behalf of freedom, egalitarianism, social justice, and social unity—can be traced to the influence of the social gospel. But it can also be argued that the same social and moral movement furthered less welcome qualities of twentieth-century American culture—a vacuous mass culture; extreme fears of cultural, intellectual, and political decline in the international arena; political apathy; and pervasive materialism. Those who see the erosion of rugged individualism, the rise of a therapeutic ethos, and the embrace of commercialism as key sources of the United States' current problems might indict the social gospel movement as one of the factors responsible for cultural decline in the late twentieth century. Men and women from the social gospel tradition—Walter Rauschenbusch and Mary McDowell, for example—rank among the most committed and heroic citizens of the United States, yet, ironically, their message and values have undergirded the mass culture that many recent critics have denounced.

Finally, the social gospel movement provides some valuable lessons for latter-day reformers. Commitment to justice, equality, and abundance for all has not subsided. Indeed, through much of the past three decades reformers have struggled to remove the barriers to fulfillment that have been erected against minorities like African Americans and against women. The focus has been on personal liberation—the freedom to realize one's full potential. Like their counterparts in the social gospel movement, late-twentieth-century reformers hope to free themselves and others from economic exploitation, social ostracism, poverty, disease, crime, and discrimination. While they recognize that there is a power structure that limits opportunities, they tend to assume that continued economic growth and expansion, as well as a heightened consciousness, will lead to a more equitable, more democratic society.

When social gospelers in the early twentieth century followed the same tack, they gradually adopted the values and criteria for success of the dominant culture. By using the language and ideas of secular culture, they robbed their message of some of its sting; and as time passed, their followers found less disagreement between their religious values and secular formulas for success and fulfillment.

The lesson to be learned here is that by the 1920s, some social gospelers had lost sight of important questions. They no longer asked whether power was distributed equitably or exercised responsibly for the good of the whole society. They did not demand a structure of power in an industrial capitalist society that could achieve individual autonomy *and* the common good. The men and women who dominated the movement in the 1920s were satisfied with an ideology of self-realization, a diminution of private anxieties, and an improved standard of living for many Americans. They did not challenge power relationships that sustained social, economic, and political inequities. Those who had posed such challenges were either dead by 1920 or had been marginalized and denounced within the movement.

In 1912 when Walter Rauschenbusch wrote glowing reports about the triumph of the social gospel, Protestantism in America had reached a crossroads. The movement had produced admirable reformers, a pervasive consciousness of the need for social justice, and programs that would serve as prototypes for later governmental reforms. Nevertheless, the distinctly Protestant character of the movement had been muted by an increasing commitment to worldly affairs, and the influence of secular culture had left an unmistakable impression on both the style and message of the social gospel. In 1912 all of American society seemed to be poised on the brink of transformation. The midwestern writer Floyd Dell called 1912 "really an extraordinary year in America." For proof he offered the election of Woodrow Wilson, the heated woman-suffragist activity, Edna St. Vincent Millay's poem "Renascence," plans for the Post-Impressionist show, and the opening of Chicago's Little Theatre. All were "evidence," he insisted, "of a New Spirit suddenly come to birth in America."[15] American culture and American Protestant faith were in the midst of change. In both Greenwich Village's Bohemia, where Dell now lived and wrote, and in the social gospel movement, the future of this new culture was unclear. Malcolm Cowley, who lived through the period, suggested in *Exile's Return* the ironic proposition that the cultural radicals in fact furthered the development of a consumer-oriented, even a therapeutic, culture in America. The burden of this book is to compound that irony by showing the ways in which the complex and tentative prewar formulation of the social gospel was transformed into a consuming faith.

2

WORK AND SALVATION

IN CORPORATE AMERICA

During a career that spanned more than three decades, Frank Mason North never enjoyed a reputation as a stirring orator. Friends admired the Methodist minister from New York far more for his administration of the Home Missionary Society than for his simple, drab sermons. Thus, on 5 December 1908, when the Reverend North rose to present a report entitled "The Church and Modern Industry" to the first meeting of the Federal Council of Churches in Philadelphia, one can imagine that long-time acquaintances shifted restlessly, expecting a typically colorless presentation.[1] What they heard during his hour-long discourse, however, not only revealed a side of their respected colleague they never before had seen; it also touched some of their most deeply felt concerns about work and personal worth in corporate America. Questioning the plausibility of individual initiative and individual responsibility in an age of vast corporations, North called for "collective bargaining," for "protection against the hardship often resulting from the swift crises of industrial change," and for state-sponsored social insurance. The competition and industrial warfare that had made their fathers' fortunes should give way to brotherhood and cooperation, North insisted. Instead of unstinting toil, this son of a successful New York entrepreneur demanded "one day's rest in seven" and the right to leisure.

In an emotional finale, North summed up the demands for meaningful work that had made orthodox Protestantism troublesome to so many of the men and women of his generation, who had matured in the years of America's rapid industrialization. They wanted "fearless" and "passionate" commitment to reform. They demanded "equality of opportunity" and protection for the weak against the "unscrupulous." In the face of widespread exploitation, young Protestants rose to champion the cause of industrial workers. Perhaps most important, instead of invoking God the Father, they appealed to the Son of God as the "final authority." As young Protestants recast the faith of their elders, they boldly declared: "This day is the Scripture fulfilled."

When the *Christian Advocate* reported the activities of the newly founded Federal Council of Churches, it noted that Dr. North's paper marked the "highest point of enthusiasm" at the conference and that "at its conclusion the applause was loud and long." At the height of the tumult, the Reverend Charles Stelzle had leapt to his feet and had exclaimed, "The statement presented by Dr. North is the greatest paper on this subject that I have ever heard or read." Another witness to the event called North's report "an epoch-making deliverance that was received with profound attention and unanimously approved."[2] In a single speech Frank Mason North succeeded in revising his reputation as a public speaker. But more important, his oration became the rallying cry of American social gospelers. When the applause finally subsided, delegates representing more than 17 million American Protestants voted to approve the report and to adopt it as the Social Creed of the Churches.

The agenda of social justice outlined in the Social Creed addressed many issues raised by Christian reformers. For this reason, historians have marked its adoption as a national endorsement of the social gospel by Protestant America.[3] By advocating labor unions, protective legislation, and the right to expect leisure and vacations, the Protestants who gathered in Philadelphia in 1908 championed the cause of the working class and bent the rigid demands of the traditional work ethic under the pressure of modern conditions. Protestant activists hailed a new era of cooperation, a spirit of brotherhood, and an emerging ethic of social responsibility.

In the immediate flush of enthusiasm for the Social Creed and for the working-class issues it raised, the Federal Council appointed a Social Service Commission to put the sentiments of the convention into effect. In addition to creating programs for more wholesome social life for urban residents, the Social Service Commission arbitrated labor disputes, averted industrial warfare, and attempted to draw workers into the active life of the church. Protestants who acclaimed the Social

Creed in 1908 joined Charles Stelzle's jubilant boast that if he could tell the "workmen of America" that Protestant leaders meant every word of the Social Creed, it would be "the biggest thing that I can say or that I have ever yet said."[4]

. . .

It was not at all extraordinary that a gathering of Protestants should be interested in the matter of work. Protestants traditionally had considered work on earth linked to their salvation. From Puritans in the seventeenth century, with their dictum of hard work to glorify God, to revivalists of the Second Great Awakening, with their admonitions against sloth and unrestraint, Protestants in America placed heavy emphasis on industry and achievement. Work had answered, for Protestants, the questions, What is my purpose in the world? What am I to do? More generally, as James Gilbert, Daniel Rodgers, and others have noted, the meaning of work had become problematic for the American middle class in the second half of the nineteenth century.[5]

While there were many conversations on this subject in America, that initiated by North was one of the most important because of the way it shifted the usual Protestant way of talking about work. First, North and his colleagues saw work as a collective endeavor as well as an individual obligation. This collective vision represented an important departure from individual enterprise, which had assumed control over one's self and individual responsibility for one's success and salvation. The authors of the Social Creed acknowledged that in most modern workplaces—factories, offices, limited liability corporations—man could not take sole responsibility for his wages, hours, success, failure, or the conditions of his work.

Second, the Social Creed reflected the effect of industry on labor. As the Social Creed portrayed it, industrial labor was exploitative rather than uplifting. Social gospelers recognized that "a reasonable reduction" of the working day would create the condition "of the highest human life." As more and more Americans were learning from muckraking journals, realistic novels, and their own daily experiences, work in industrial America was ennervating rather than ennobling. It appeared to be one of the barriers to salvation rather than an expression of man's urge to create and thereby glorify God. As Walter Rauschenbusch noted in 1907 in *Christianity and the Social Crisis*, man "expresses himself" in the work he does. But the modern industrial system does not "produce in the common man the pride and joy of good work. In many cases the surroundings are ugly, depressing, and coarsening.

Much of the stuff manufactured is dishonest in quality, . . . and the making of such cotton or wooden lies must react on the morals of every man that handles them."[6] If modern man was to be saved, he probably would seek salvation off the job.

Finally, the Social Creed demonstrated social gospelers' interest in the working class. Perhaps this concern with industrial workers sprang from the recognition that changed conditions of work meant that a class of people received few material or spiritual rewards for their drudgery. The working class offered living proof that whatever link had existed between work and salvation had dissolved in the twentieth century.

. . .

The working class had become the focus of interest and concern in the late nineteenth century for a number of reasons. Workers became visible to the rest of society when they went on strike in order to receive a living wage. Sometimes strikes led to violence—when owners used the power of the state to enforce their rule or when desperate, unemployed men took jobs as strikebreakers. Unemployment reached alarming levels in the 1890s, and hundreds of thousands of jobless men marched to Washington to demonstrate that they wanted only to make their way by their own labor. These extraordinary acts drew attention to the conditions under which thousands of Americans toiled and lived and to the meager compensation for their drudgery. Labor unrest made middle-class Americans aware of the high cost of industrialization to working-class families. Often women and children supplemented the earnings of the chief breadwinners by taking in sewing and laundry or working in filthy factories and sweatshops. During strikes the supplemental income had to support the family. This bare subsistence contrasted sharply with the outlandish wealth of the captains of industry. Many social critics—working-class and middle-class alike—noted the disparity and began to question the fairness of industrial capitalism.

Middle-class Christian reformers like those who met in Philadelphia in 1908 feared that the gross inequity workers experienced in the marketplace would jaundice their view of religion as well. After all, the same hard work and self-control that was supposed to yield material success was also supposed to prepare men and women for salvation. When they were told by some men of the cloth that their hard lot was the result of their own failings and sins, how could they find spiritual comfort in the church? Workers sometimes took the clergy's silence on the unequal distribution of profits to mean that churches tacitly approved. Accordingly, workers distanced themselves from formal religion. For example, one worker asked Washington Gladden how he could be expected to pray on Sunday with the man who preyed upon him during the week.

In response to workers' alienation and their own concerns, social gospelers tried to rectify the situation. They championed laborers' rights to organize unions and to bargain collectively with their employers concerning wages, hours, and working conditions. Some, like Mary McDowell, Charles Macfarland, and the Men and Religion Forward Movement in Atlanta, became involved directly in labor disputes. Church members in Lexington, Missouri, in the 1890s canvassed the neighborhoods where striking coal miners lived and offered food, clothes, and money to the families of these embattled workers. As late as 1919, social gospelers in the Interchurch World Movement exposed the wages and working conditions that had driven steelworkers to strike. Charles Stelzle opened a Presbyterian church in New York City that catered primarily to working men, and Caroline Bartlett in Kalamazoo prepared inexpensive meals for workers who lived near the People's Church. In all these ways social gospelers reached out to working people to show support and to relieve some of their misery.

As social gospelers provided material assistance to working-class families, they also began to wonder about the work ethic and Victorian Protestantism in industrial America. When they had been children, social gospelers had been taught that hard work and self-control would earn an individual a comfortable, successful living; but in the latter years of the nineteenth century they saw too many people for whom this was not true. As early as the 1880s, Washington Gladden in Columbus, Ohio, observed "multitudes" of "worthy people" who worked and saved and prayed, but who did "not succeed in raising themselves." For Gladden this broken equation constituted the "labor question" that haunted him and his colleagues for decades.[7]

Other social critics shared Gladden's loss of faith in the individual work ethic. In an article for the *Independent* in 1905, for example, the progressive sociologist Edward A. Ross noted that in the past Americans had enjoyed the option "to move up or to move on" if they were not satisfied with their lot, but in the twentieth-century world of monopolies and closed frontiers, "for the ordinary man the circle of opportunity is relatively narrower." A prominent Baptist minister observed disparagingly that many people "tried as hard as possible" to succeed by working hard and by careful budgeting, but they failed to provide "enough bread for the little ones." The result, Henry A. Atkinson feared, would be "impatience" with religion and destruction of manhood.[8]

As part of the middle class, social gospelers felt a certain responsibility for the hardships of the poor. They knew that workers enjoyed neither the educational opportunities nor the financial cushion against poverty available to the middle class. Some felt guilty for their advantages. The authors of a book that aimed to "interpret" the Social Creed, for example, gave readers a glimpse of commingled benevolence, concern, and guilt underlying their work. "Those who love their neighbors as themselves," they avowed, "cannot rest content" while their working-class brothers and sisters struggle. Social gospelers believed that "opportunities for health and education and spiritual development which their own children enjoy" should be open to all—even the children of a poor man, who "through no fault of his own" could not provide them. Social gospelers wanted everyone to have an opportunity for a "more abundant life" and "free access to all that is best in life." They sensed that the "special circumstances" of industrial capitalism outdated the work ethic of their youth.[9]

Indeed, the working-class rejection of formal religion in the waning years of the century made middle-class Protestants acknowledge that both Victorian culture and the work ethic had become brittle and had begun to crack under the pressure of an emerging economy of corporations and large-scale industries. Too often, hard work, self-control, and individual responsibility delivered frustration and failure rather than assurance of salvation. Just as the Reverend Henry Atkinson feared, they resulted in "impatience" with religion. Anxiety, uncertainty, and despair pervaded middle-class as well as working-class families and provided the impetus for redefining the work ethic and revitalizing American culture and faith. The social gospel and the pathbreaking pronouncements of its Social Creed sprang in part from the tension between an evolving world of specialized work and the strained ethic of shops and farms.

North, Stelzle, and others at Philadelphia in 1908 were painfully aware of the disorder of work in the early twentieth century. Industrial development in the second half of the nineteenth century had drastically altered relations of work. Corporations and assembly lines required workers who would be content with a small part of the process of production—"team players," not independent mavericks. The chance of succeeding as an entrepreneur in competition with large-scale enterprises no longer depended on pluck and perseverance. Americans witnessed massive unemployment, low wages, horrendous working conditions, and, in 1894, a ragtag army of unemployed men. Though Coxey's Army and the subjects of Jacob Riis's photography suffered most obviously as a result of modern industrial development, they were not its only victims. Old expectations in new situations made success for everyone difficult to measure. Whether in factory or office or behind the pulpit, the burdens of individual responsibility in an economy over which individuals could exert so little control overwhelmed Americans and rocked the foundations of the work ethic.[10]

Frank Mason North's words stroked not only the heart strings of his audience, but tender nerves as well. Many of the delegates in Philadelphia, raised on Victorian dictates of individual initiative and fierce independence, might have wondered whether their ministries in large Protestant organizations and in agencies of social reform constituted success as their fathers had conceived it. North himself had studied business with plans for taking over his father's business, but a year in the hurly-burly of commerce had driven him to seminary and the refuge of a quiet New York parish. Washington Gladden, one in the enthusiastic crowd of 1908, had moved unhappily from farm to printer's shop to pulpit until nervous prostration impelled him to seek rest in a suburban parish. Others searched for meaning in work that bore but faint resemblance to the red-blooded individual enterprises carried out by their fathers and held up for their emulation.[11] If their efforts fell short, would salvation elude them as well? Self-doubts may have fueled their horror of poverty and made more pressing the need for reform to relieve both the travail of the poor and their own persistent uneasiness. The Social Creed of the Churches sprang from the guilt, fear, and personal quest of middle-class Protestants like these who endorsed it.

One of the most important ways social gospelers hoped to address working-class disaffection was to redefine the work ethic, and the Social Creed was a start. They wanted to move away from the immorality and inconsistency of industrial relations they had decried in the 1890s and early 1900s. At the height of the depression in 1893, Washington Gladden had denounced the economic system that created the "slavery of the toilers in the midst of increased liberty, leisure, luxury, and the increased pleasure and power which wealth in our time confers." Josiah Strong concurred. In *The New Era*, he noted that poverty and reward supposedly were distributed according to effort in industrial America, but that in 1893 "they are becoming. . . a matter of inheritance" with "no shadow of justification in the character of those whose circumstances paint so strong a contrast." He deplored the power of "industrial kings" in a land of democracy. Both Strong and Gladden realized that the actual conditions of industry required cooperation and interdependence, but that, in fact, the industrial system was governed by competition and individual striving. As Walter Rauschenbusch noted a few years later, industry "pits men against one another in a gladiatorial game in which there is no mercy and in which ninety per cent of the combatants finally strew the arena."[12]

In the early twentieth century, social gospelers wanted to help bring peace to industry by exposing the inconsistencies in the system and by advocating cooperation. Cooperation, of course, can imply a wide range of meanings from simple congeniality to collectivity. But in any case, cooperation meant something other than self-interested, cutthroat competition. For some middle-class Christians, cooperation meant brotherly harmony—give and take on the part of employees and employers. For some professionals, the term suggested interdependence and specialization—a celebration of the special skills each worker and manager brought to the workplace. To those inspired by radical politics, cooperation suggested socialist enterprise—ownership and control of work by the people who performed it. The elasticity of the term made it appealing to many Americans from diverse backgrounds and with divergent agendas. Despite the different meanings, the conception of cooperation inspired a commitment by social gospelers to alter the conditions, nature, reward, and meaning of work.

As champions of the working class, these reformers endorsed the right to collective action. Cooperation became the ideal toward which they believed everyone should strive. Washington Gladden called competition the "law of plant and brutes and brutish men" while cooperation was the "highest law of civilized society." Gladden and others insisted that sacrifice, service, and love were the three great laws of life in the twentieth century. They denounced at every turn individualism and competition because these had become destructive and no longer led the way to salvation. "Every joint-stock company, trust, or labor union organized," wrote Walter Rauschenbusch, "every extension of government interference or government ownership is a surrender of the competitive principle and a halting step toward cooperation." And "cooperation," he believed, "means life."[13]

Social gospelers also urged workers to view their jobs as part of a large and important enterprise. Their particular task might not be an independent accomplishment, but it was valuable nonetheless. Charles

Stelzle, for example, wrote an "everyday creed for the man who works" in 1912 in which he told workers to believe in their job as "a peculiar niche in the world's work." Josiah Strong told his readers a parable about a machine that had quit because "a little pin" had fallen out of place. "Our lives may seem very insignificant," he concluded, "but when we remember that because we belong to the Kingdom they are part of a vast plan, they at once assume importance."[14] By accepting a small part in the collective effort, workers could find new bases for reward and salvation.

. . .

From the acceptance of cooperation and specialization emerged a new character ideal: the team player. The concept of teamwork was the perfect expression of the social gospel. Like members of a team, individual believers were expected to perform at their highest level: they were to make a personal commitment to God and his kingdom. But they were also expected to put the interests of society (the team) above their own. They could be saved only if they tried to save others. In the early twentieth century, baseball players typified the character ideal for workers in corporate America and for social gospel Protestants because they balanced individual achievement with cooperation.

The Religious Education Association and the University of Chicago Press, which together produced a great deal of the Sunday school literature in the early twentieth century, drove home the relevance of baseball for the social gospel. Henry Cope, president of the association, urged Sunday school teachers to use baseball as a pedagogical device. "Baseball," he reminded them, "is a part of the boys' experience of life; it is as much life to them as the factory or office to the man." Life on the diamond raised ethical and social questions, tried young consciences, tested adolescent wills, and strained youthful ideals. Most important, team play represented "ideal social relations" because it provided for "personal development" as well as "social training"—"team cooperation" as well as individual "health, strength, and beauty." Erwin L. Shaver, who wrote pamphlets for the University of Chicago series, advised young people to build character by playing in sports. "Clean sport, fair play, self-sacrifice, obedience to rules, team cooperation, skill, initiative, a sense of honor, chivalry, generous appreciation of an opponent," he wrote in *A Christian's Recreation*, "find expression and development" in athletics. His colleague Herbert Gates suggested that the rules and rewards of team sports have for youth "all the authority that work will have later." He reminded youngsters that "many a lad has learned lessons of cooperation with his teammates, of self-denial in training, of persistence, endurance, and courage in turning defeat into victory, only to have the same lessons stay by him in the stern contest of later life and make him a winner there."[15]

The merging of cooperation with sports had several important implications. First, it provided a critical perspective on industrial capitalism. Team competition (rather than individual competition) brought rewards to everyone as long as the contest was fair. Unfair labor practices, for example, denied laborers their just reward and denied capitalists the deserved gratitude of their employees for having built a productive and progressive order. Therefore, fair play among teammates and between competitive companies was paramount. Second, achieving this sense of oneness with employers required workers to make some accommodations of their own. Social gospelers told workers to accept leisure, a reduced workday, and benefits gained through collective effort as part of their reward for drudgery. Finally, this endorsement of leisure, recreation, and a shorter workday implied that work itself did not necessarily hold the key to character, redemption, or success. Rather, the manner of play, following the rules of the game, relationships among teammates, and the development of camaraderie (which could be acquired in leisure pursuits as easily as at work) constituted appropriate sources of a sense of self-worth, reward, and personal meaning in a modern industrial society. Work *and* play could lead to temporal and spiritual satisfaction.[16]

The powerful image of the baseball player as a model for modern work stirred interest simultaneously in working as a part of an enterprise larger than oneself and in the possibility of leisure that was rewarding. The growing popularity of public amusements, spectator sports, and recreational facilities in the dawn of the new century suggests that people had the time and the wherewithal to take advantage of them. These activities also may have addressed a need for social contact and personal pleasure. Social gospelers spoke to these needs as well by celebrating spontaneity, exuberance, and life away from work. Their Social Creed demanded one day's rest in seven to "rescue" the "industrial army from continuous . . . demoralizing toil." It also urged a "reasonable reduction" of the working day. Departing from the norms of nineteenth-century industry, in which the workday occupied nearly all of the waking hours, social gospelers such as Harry Munro lauded the "manifold and rich advantages" of "active play and happy comradeship" made possible by leisure. Hugh Hartshorne argued that the road to a more abundant life would run through the "land of play, not of work." The Social Service Commission of the Federal Council of Churches made an even clearer distinction between life and work: "Man has a right to live as well as to toil," they contended, "unending drudgery is not life."[17] Play not only rejuvenated worn laborers, but it also began to figure prominently in the social gospelers' modern scheme of salvation. For as a team player, an individual put the interests of the group ahead of his own; he used his talents to the betterment of the whole; and he forged bonds with his teammates. In short, he obeyed the three great laws of sacrifice, service, and love. Cooperation and leisure became both means to and ends of salvation.

Working with others eventually became more important than work itself in social gospelers' schemes of salvation. Cooperation and team spirit involved relationships between men and women at work rather than the toil itself. Modern workers might not be able to control their job, but they could control their relationships with others on the job. Henry A. Atkinson wrote that "the pleasure in the work" of a factory "must be secured from the conditions under which the work is performed—the cooperation in the production, and the feeling that the worker is blessed by being a part of the modern industrial system." Such an emphasis on "feeling" as partial payment for work well done gradually became an important goal for modern American Protestants. A graduate student at the University of Chicago in 1914, for example, learned that children enrolled in social service programs because of the strong emotions and sense of purpose they experienced after helping others. The approval and appreciation of the recipients of their charity and assistance, one boy told William Norman Hutchins, "makes the class feel as if they were doing something." One of the girls in his class confided, "In social service one is doing something. You are making yourself felt."[18] Their feeling of purpose and involvement mattered as much to them as the social relief they provided.

For many social gospelers, friendship best characterized the nature of reward in bureaucratic work relations. Henry Cope described the ideal life as the "friendly life." "Friendship," he insisted, "is the final measure of all our living." Washington Gladden, looking back on his career as a Protestant minister, declared in 1909 that "religion is nothing but friendship," and Jesus, "the Great Companion." A year later, he told the graduating class at Ohio State University that their ambition should be to live exemplary lives so that when their working days ended, people who knew them would say: "He has done more than any other man to promote good will and friendship in the countryside and to make it a pleasant place for men and women and boys and girls to live." Shailer Mathews, a theologian of the social gospel, referred to the "vicarious life" as the "noblest life" because concern with the "welfare of others" represented success. "To merge one's own ambition with those of the group," he wrote, "is the aim of every earnest Christian soul."[19] For social gospelers, working with other specialized skilled laborers and professionals offered a chance for emotional reward.

. . .

A novel by Charles Sheldon, an important popularizer of the social gospel, helps show how Protestants had begun to unite work and intense feeling into a single vision of salvation. Sheldon's novel *In His Steps* (1897) catapulted him to national fame, but in a less well-known book entitled *The Reformer* (1902) he explored the themes of work and worth.[20] John Gordon, the novel's protagonist, rejects his father's business and rushes off on a personal quest for purpose with a vague plan to "love the people." Cut loose from family resources, Gordon makes his way to the slums and decides to work in a settlement house. Though Sheldon offers a sparse description of the reformer's duties and daily occupation, he spares no words to depict the vast array of emotional rewards available to him. Tearful affection from the impoverished, sentimental adoration from the disadvantaged, and personal instruction from Miss Andrews, the founder of Hope House, teach Gordon the value of eliciting friendly, loving approval from others. The story moves from one touching scene to the next, bolstering faith in immediate, intense spiritual gratification, until reaching its climax in a destructive fire in the slum. Neglected tenements run by "selfish" businessmen burst into flames, and the fire destroys several buildings, claims dozens of lives, and threatens to consume Hope House. In a heroic effort to save the settlement, hundreds of neighbors turn out to fight the fire and to show their appreciation for the reformers. "Even with all the horrors of that night, and the awful sight out in the hall and library," Sheldon writes, "Miss Andrews felt a thrill at the thought that the people had loved her a little."[21] The work of the reformer remains unclear throughout the story, but the Reverend Charles Sheldon left one thing certain: making others like you is a full-time occupation, and its reward comes in daily doses of appreciation, affection, and approval.

The emotional force of Sheldon's story conveys two other key points. First, while Miss Andrews and John Gordon will not necessarily grow wealthy, their lives will be worthwhile because others affirm their life's work. Sheldon thereby breaks the connection between success and prosperity that had dominated American thinking in the nineteenth century. Second, though Sheldon devotes dozens of pages to setting his drama in a slum, the working-class residents and their labor remains secondary to the middle-class protagonists' struggle for personal meaning. The working class that sat as models for various tenets of the Social Creed fades into the background of this modern portrait of work and salvation. While the working class prompted guilty concern about waning faith and for that reason drew middle-class authors like Sheldon to working-class conditions, these authors found it difficult to transcend their own class background to explore the possibility of salvation for the working poor. It was their own needs that kept surfacing; the working class served primarily to sharpen the doubts of the middle class.

Sheldon's novel demonstrates one further twist in the work ethic of corporate America: the terminology of the "self-made man" persisted long after the conditions for his success had passed. In typical bourgeois fashion John Gordon feels compelled not merely to succeed but to surpass his father in moral action. His rejection of his father's business represents a critique of the competition, greed, and materialism of entrepreneurial capitalism but also implies a desire to assert his superior aims—to transcend his father's attachment to material comfort. Reform, then, involved cooperation, altruism, and idealism, but also served as a surrogate enterprise. The "vocation" of reformer becomes an "opportunity" for Gordon to prove himself at the same time that he helps usher in a new era of brotherhood. Unlike the lone individual striving for achievement and salvation, Gordon finds himself surrounded by grateful beneficiaries and a loving corps of friends willing to clear the path to salvation by offering daily signs of approval. John Gordon, educated professional, member of the team, patterns his life after an older model of commitment and enterprise but experiences reward and salvation on earth.

Sheldon's novel gave Protestant readers an example of an appealing alternative to individual striving and heavenly reward. His vision of working with others and emotional reward betrayed his impatience with deferred gratification and future spiritual blessing. Indeed, many of his colleagues in the social gospel movement, who wrote about work and salvation, also embraced more immediate signs of grace. They cherished expressions of approval from others, and they sought adventure that released them from the monotony of labor. And they sought an acceptable justification for individual efforts within the corporation that served as substitutes for independent individualism as their parents had known it. Social gospelers acknowledged with Edward A. Ross that their generation had witnessed a "change in the standard of human worth." Ross lauded the "trained expert" who accepted his small role in the world of work and whose chief rewards were the gratitude of "Molly and the babies" and "the 'well done, old man!' of his brother experts."[22]

· · ·

While social gospelers criticized the exploitative nature of work in industrial America, they realized that mundane work was necessary in an industrial economy and tried to suggest that such work could nevertheless provide immediate psychic and emotional rewards. They did this by praising the "heroism" of ordinary men and women. While they were not quite as fulsome or as explicitly antimodern as others in American society, who, for example, embraced medieval architecture and chivalry at the turn of the century, the social gospelers looked backward to address an uncertain future. They looked to a premodern language of honor and heroism to ennoble modern work.

Social gospelers identified heroic men and women in all walks of life. Washington Gladden told employers no man could do "knightlier work" than to employ laborers, treat them fairly, and encourage them to form their own unions. Such employers, he insisted, were "chivalrous" and blessed. For their part, laborers were also willing to perform "heroic service." According to Henry Cope, workers were "ready to answer" the call for "a new type of heroism" and would not hesitate "to toil and suffer in order to be technically trained and efficient." Cope commented on his own work in the Religious Education Association (REA) by using crusading hyperbole to describe the commonplace work of writing and distributing Sunday school literature. He recited the "record of sustained, unstinted sacrifice and service" that "cost blood and lives gladly given."[23] Surely he was carried away by his enthusiasm for the commitment to a revised sacred curriculum. But the very unlikeliness of his description illuminates the intensity with which he believed in the rewarding possibilities of viewing work as a crusade and workers (especially religious reformers) as heroes.

One of the most remarkable series of advice literature for young people at the turn of the century addressed the deep vocational uncertainty of the middle class and developed embryonic ideas of specialization, cooperation, and immediate salvation. *Vocations* (1911), edited by William De Witt Hyde, reflected the concern with the heroic and offered the promise of high adventure to those who chose to devote themselves to working with others. In Ernest Poole's parlance, for example, construction mechanics were "cowboys of the skies" who enjoyed "high pay, a free hand, and excitement every minute" and who performed "real jobs."

According to C. M. Keys, the engineer was a "genie" who conquered nature to build a railroad. Ray Stannard Baker believed that scientists could "surprise new secrets from the sun." Each of the ten volumes that made up *Vocations* promised glamor, excitement, and immediate rewards for those who would "serve society." Hyde reported that a teacher once told him that an "investment of one's self in others" yielded personal satisfaction and collective improvement.[24]

As the liberal president of Bowdoin College, William De Witt Hyde probably sensed the anxiety of young men and women who were preparing for their life's work. His series chronicled the transformation of work and reward in the years bridging the two centuries. Specialized professions, expert skills, and backbreaking jobs passed for enterprise, while teamwork and cooperation had become the means for ushering in the kingdom of God. The "new heroism" of efficiency and self-sacrifice, of daring and service, offered an escape from dull routine at the same time that it legitimized bureaucratic work relations. For young men in the twentieth century, efficient work in profession or firm lifted the crushing burden of individual salvation by removing fear of the future and by distributing the responsibility for success and failure among the members of the team.

The redefinition of the work ethic, which included both social and individual imperatives and new kinds of emotional and spiritual rewards, must be understood in the context of social gospelers' longing for the kingdom of God. They believed that cooperation, brotherhood, the nobility of each man and woman, and justice would reign in the kingdom. This vision meant that life would be worthwhile and joy would be physical and temporal as well as spiritual and eternal. Social gospelers' embrace of more tangible signs of salvation, emotional satisfaction in a job well done, and a full life reflected their impatience with a strictly otherworldly vision of Christian reward. The quality of life, not heaven, was at the center of their discussion of vocation.

Social gospelers urged Americans to make a commitment to social salvation in order to make life better for themselves and others. They invited men and women to involve themselves in the lives of others in order to warm the heart of the benefactor as well as his or her beneficiary. In the workplace, this interest in others would take the form of cooperation, which made interdependence rather than independence a virtue. Work and social life became harder to distinguish, and this offered a finer quality of life. The quest for spiritual reward and salvation appeared far less awesome at the gateway of an earthly kingdom of self-sacrifice, service, and brotherly cooperation than it had at the foot of an anxious bench under the threat of fiery destruction.

One social gospeler, Henry Atkinson, argued that the struggle for life was not a means to salvation, but an end in itself. "The true purpose of life is not work," he insisted, "nor wealth, nor anything else that can be gained by human striving, but *it is life itself*." Erwin L. Shaver appealed to an entire generation of young Protestants in a series of discussion literature and Sunday school projects published in the early twentieth century. He affirmed their chance "to discover, to create, and to accomplish." "In your own new way," he explained to young readers, "you intend to make *this* a better world to live in." Shailer Mathews denounced nineteenth-century theology by claiming that salvation was "more than rescue" and more than removal of the sense of guilt and apprehension for the future. "Salvation," he contended, "is newness of life." Washington Gladden summed up many of these sentiments in a commencement address he delivered to the graduating class at the University of Michigan in 1902. As these young men and women turned their faces to the complex world of work, Gladden reminded them that "their business in life is to live. We are here to live; we have no other calling. . . . Nothing larger or higher or finer or nobler is possible to us than just living."[25]

. . .

The problem of work and salvation held slightly different implications for women in the twentieth century. Though the nineteenth-century ideology of "separate spheres" allowed some movement between home and work for literary women, it erected cultural barriers against widespread individual quests by women in other fields of work. Like the ideal of the self-made man, much of the vocabulary of domesticity and "true womanhood" persisted well into the twentieth century, even while the nature of the "woman's sphere" had transformed. Child care, family nurture, and homemaking continued to rank high on the list of feminine duties, but women redefined the manner in which they carried them out. Educated middle-class girls in the late nineteenth century protested against the confines of domesticity. At a time when individual salvation cultivated in a moral home posed great problems for men in a corporate economy, the purpose of Victorian women seemed unclear as well as restricted.

For many middle-class Protestant women, the dilemma of work and home resulted in a crumbling core of self. Women whose books promoted social gospel ideas complained frequently of divided selves—one side striving for a productive and fulfilling career, the other side longing to uphold the older cultural ideal. In 1912, Ida Tarbell termed the phenomenon the "uneasy woman," bored and troubled by diffuse purpose at home and frustrated with the narrow range of satisfying public jobs for women. In *His Religion and Hers* (1923), Charlotte Perkins Gilman explained that work for women in modern America forced women to waver between "old duties and new ambitions." The result was "much confusion, suffering and nervous strain." Doctor Zay, a heroine in one of Elizabeth Stuart Phelps Ward's early novels, believed it was a "fearful thing" for a professional woman to love a man. When she admitted her own love for Waldo York, her cry, "I have lost my self-possession. I have lost—myself," revealed the vapid quality of domesticity and the threat of lost salvation.[26] The meaning of their lives as true women seemed to be evaporating, yet access to purposeful work outside the home remained limited, if not taboo. Neurasthenia, the disease of the age, most profoundly struck a generation of women searching desperately for moral work and personal salvation.[27]

The social gospel appealed to many such women because it seemed to fuse purposeful action and traditional feminine responsibilities, reuniting fragmented identity. Settlement houses, day-care centers, lobbying for anti–child labor legislation, and other social gospel programs offered public employment to well-educated professional women at the same time as they drew on womanly skills of family nurture and homemaking. Public housekeeping, for example, became an attractive "domesticated" profession for women because they could do what they must to be saved—serve as moral guardians for a larger home and reap the personal satisfaction of working with others in public.

So prevalent had the tension between "true woman" and "new woman" become by the 1910s that an advocate of the "renaissance of motherhood" believed that women who intended to marry and have children should first spend a year of social service as "preparation for motherhood." Women who had no intention of having careers were urged nonetheless to view homemaking as a career and to view the community as their "larger home." Ida Tarbell encouraged homemakers to be intelligent consumers and educated companions to their children. She and other writers also urged women to consult experts in special fields so that their families would not suffer from amateurish household decisions based on tradition or instinct. Various Protestant spokesmen endorsed the "healthy" influence of experts. The Men and Religion Forward Movement, for instance, urged mothers to seek aid in raising their sons. "Even the best of them need help," the author insisted. From schools to public health programs mothers could find a host of social agencies "in every line of expert service" to bring helpless children into "efficient citizenship." The specific charge of instructing boys in "social hygiene" required parents' conferences with physicians and teachers so mothers could learn the best way to approach their children. Worried feminine expressions in early-twentieth-century advertisements evinced the uncertain search for approval from figures of authority outside the home.[28]

The goal of many social gospelers continued to be creating a strong American family and home, and they suggested that specialized agencies would provide the information, standards of acceptable homemaking, and reassurance needed to improve family life. Caroline Bartlett Crane's People's Church, for instance, held monthly mothers' meetings so women could learn how to "do the best for their little children with the time and the strength they had." Reverend Crane fondly remembered that in these "friendly conferences" women "seemed to come nearer to each other," and she concluded that "few things seemed . . . more useful" for women in search of assurance.[29] Mutual emotional support and educated advice promised to make domesticity both more professional and more satisfying.

By the 1910s the complexity of meaningful work and salvation for women surfaced in debates over suffrage. One typical discussion noted with alarm the paralyzing indecision of young women in America. "Girls still in school or lately out," declared Edward Sandford Martin in a 1915 essay on the unrest of women, "grope to discover what is expected of them. Are they to be helpers at home or workers independent of their families? Are they to be domestic or extraparietal? Are they to find an outside job for the sake of their own development, or only seek one if they need the wage it will bring them? . . . Most of them seem to feel more or less uncertain about their destiny."[30]

Regardless of the particular solutions different authors offered, most agreed with social gospelers that the key to satisfaction and self-realization in the twentieth century was service to and direction from others. The middle-class housewife anxious to uphold proper standards of nutrition and domestic economy and eager professional women seeking approval from their clients and colleagues enjoyed frequent signs of appreciation and intense feeling. Like Miss Andrews in *The Reformer* they came gradually to seek immediate emotional salvation for professional domesticity and the domesticated professions that invested their lives with meaning. Elizabeth Stuart Phelps Ward's novel *Friends: A Duet* about a young widow working as a social reformer, revealed the intense and immediate reward Reliance Strong experienced in the larger home of her community. "When she found what a light sacrifice arouses the large loyalty of the poor, and what a profuse expenditure of feeling they return for a little outlay," wrote Ward, "she became at first puzzled, then humbled, then grateful, hopeful, comforted."[31]

. . .

Thus, the gospel of social salvation reflected and legitimized the transformed relations of work in corporate America for both men and women. Frank Mason North's historic statement in 1908 focused the diffuse rays of change and illuminated, albeit dimly, the path of salvation for modern American Protestants. By the late 1910s, much of the promise of daily, earthly salvation in service to the kingdom of God prevailed in Protestant America. Not only did the social gospel open up a wide range of "helping" professions for men and women, but it also emphasized a commitment to serving others in return for rich personal reward. It undergirded bureaucratic work relations by imbuing corporate teamwork with fresh spiritual meaning, by affirming play and leisure, and by defining Christian community as efficient dependence on others.

Whether at home or work, in white collar or housedress, middle-class Protestants, at the behest of a transforming culture, were urged to turn to one another for direction and satisfaction was they worked. The abundant life for which they strove kept pace with an emerging mass society based on the automobile, consumer goods, and intense excitement. As Franklin W. Johnson reminded parents in 1914 in *The Problems of Boyhood*, much had changed in Protestant America since the Civil War. "Not long ago," he wrote, "preachers were accustomed to appeal to their hearers on the basis of the future consequences of their acts. . . . Preachers now have much less to say about the hereafter," he went on, "and are telling us how we may secure happiness *now* in the service of those about us."[32]

Social gospelers appealed to Americans with a gospel that promised immediate, tangible rewards because it addressed their physical as well as psychological needs and eased their frustration with individual salvation. They discovered a whole range of emotional assurances available to them, none of them having to do with eternal judgment or life after death. The last item in Charles Stelzle's "everyday creed for the man who works" placed the hope of modern man in life. "I believe in to-day," he wrote. "It is all that I possess. The past is of value only as it can make life fuller and freer. There is no assurance of to-morrow. I must make good to-day."[33]

For many modern American Protestants, the social gospel resolved the most painful tensions that emerged in a generation caught between a nineteenth-century work ethic and a twentieth-century corporate economy. As will be clearer in the individual biographical sketches that follow, they could not continue to cling to an older ethic in an era of rapid socioeconomic change. It would have been too injurious, physically, spiritually, and psychologically. Their outreach to the working class attempted to ameliorate the tension for others less fortunate than themselves. But working men and women were not the only beneficiaries of a revised work ethic. The reformers themselves found aspects of the old work ethic frustrating and unsatisfying. Their devotion to Protestant belief and their consciousness of the spiritual limitations of work in corporate America prompted them to reconsider the place of work in the scheme of the world. Their demand for cooperation, leisure, earthly and emotional rewards, and salvation in life came in part from their commitment to the kingdom of God on earth. These demands also helped affirm the kinds of work relations that were developing in modern industrial America.

. . .

While most of those who became part of the social gospel movement experienced frustrations associated with work and a sense of worth, three people's lives illustrate the issues most clearly. Washington Gladden, a "prophet of the social gospel," was one of the first to call for a more socially conscious Protestant faith when he wrote *Applied Christianity* in the 1880s. He was one of the first to identify a "labor question" and to reach out to working people. Because he was an older man when the social gospel movement began to coalesce at the turn of the century, Gladden's life illuminates the anguish experienced by the sons of Victorian America as they wrestled with individualistic expectations in an increasingly complex society. His efforts to rethink the relationship between work and salvation paved the way for younger men like Shailer Mathews to reformulate even further the work ethic and the conception of salvation on earth. Because part of the theological battle had been waged by the time Mathews came of age, he did not suffer the same intense anguish that Gladden and others did. Mathews incorporated more of the corporate ethos into his articulation of the social gospel, as is evidenced by his adoption of scientific management in church work. Caroline Bartlett Crane confronted the problem of work and salvation in industrial America as a minister in a working-class church in Kalamazoo, Michigan, and as a woman determined to seek a career outside the home. Her experience reveals how the social gospel helped women combine the demands of domesticity and profession into satisfying work that promised immediate spiritual rewards. Washington Gladden, Shailer Mathews, and Caroline Bartlett Crane addressed various aspects of the religious problems posed by work in corporate America. Their lives and work altered the experience and some of the concepts of religion and helped affirm a new work ethic in the twentieth century.

WASHINGTON GLADDEN

The Labor Question in Industrial America

On Monday morning, 27 November 1866, the small community of North Adams, Massachusetts, hummed with rumors about a lecture given the previous evening at the Congregational church. The Reverend Washington Gladden had addressed the young people of his church with a talk he called "Amusements: Their Uses and Their Abuses," and his discourse evoked curiosity, suspicion, and anger from townspeople of every denomination. Within days of the meeting, twenty-seven laymen requested in writing that Gladden publish the sermon because his "teachings are liable to be misconstrued and misrepresented" and "the matter should not be left to hearsay." Gladden himself admitted that the controversial talk had stirred up inaccurate stories among those who had not heard it, and he finally agreed to publish it. Publication of the lecture did little to quiet the fears of the older generation in North Adams. "Clericus," a particularly savage critic, denounced the young minister in a letter for "talking about regulating dancing and card-playing and the like! Why not preach that lechery and gambling be regulated," he exploded. An upholder of Victorian self-control, Clericus reminded Gladden that the real evil in dancing was "provocation and lust." He advised Gladden to fall "on his knees before God."[34]

Though Gladden had presented a reasoned argument for harmless entertainments run by Christian proprietors, he also had questioned the wisdom of hard, unstinted toil and relentless self-control, the twin pillars of Victorian morality. Gladden contended that "recreation . . . is indispensable to bodily and mental health" because no one can keep himself "constantly in working tension. . . . Amusement is therefore as much a part of the divine economy as prayer, and one can glorify God by play as well as by work or by worship." He believed that "it ought to be a part of the religious instruction of the young that sport, glee, fun, not the dismal, repressed, shame-faced variety, but the real hilarious, exuberant sort, is their lawful inheritance . . . by divine appointment." He even confessed his own childhood yearning for "hilarity and abandon," which had delayed his formal association with a church. "If I had become a Christian then," he explained, "I am sure I should have felt bound to repress all my boyish exuberance of spirits." Moreover, he urged Protestants to lift a century-long ban on dancing, bowling, and card-playing— activities his congregation viewed as positively evil rather than simply frivolous. He dismissed admonitions against these activities by describing billiards and bowling as "beautiful exercises" and by suggesting that they and card games served to draw families and friends together in common pursuits.[35]

Despite the furor over his lecture and subsequent pamphlet on amusements, Gladden published a second book two years later outlining an ideal family vacation "from the Hub to the Hudson." Opening with the disclaimer that the book "may be death to my reader, but it has been sport for me," he described in minute detail natural and mechanical attractions in mill towns and rural villages nestled in the wooded hills between Boston and North Adams near the Hudson River. Like the writers of modern travel guides, Gladden pointed out comfortable accommodations, hospitable inns, attractive scenery, and possible sight-seeing tours. Who could afford to miss the awe-inspiring Hoosac Tunnel or the "curious machines" of the Russell Manufacturing Company, which produced fine knives and forks? By following the trail blazed by Gladden and the Fitchburg Railroad, families in North Adams could transform their summer vacations from "the dreariest days of the year" into time "cheaply and pleasantly" spent.[36]

Though composed for different reasons and presented in different contexts, both lecture and vacation guide disclose Washington Gladden's uneasiness with prevailing attitudes toward work and leisure. Though he himself was nourished by a steady diet of work and self-discipline, Gladden feared the result of uninterrupted labor and relentless self-control. In the talk, he warned of "paralysis," "shattered nerves," "feeble health," and death from following too diligently the Victorian work ethic. In his book, he lauded the emergence of a saner economy based on new labor-saving technology, orderly interdependence, and a yearly vacation to reflect on the wonders of human genius. In both works, he celebrated team play and social responsibility in quiet defiance of the individualism dominant in Victorian America. In the late 1860s, Washington Gladden voiced halting concern with values that many of his Protestant countrymen would over the next few decades find increasingly unsatisfying as they witnessed a mushrooming industrial economy. He spoke to a generation that longed for meaningful work, self-respect, and salvation.

Yet Gladden's decision to discuss work and salvation in terms of leisure and amusement suggests an interesting problem. For Protestants, work was supposed to be the center of life, the source of meaning, a way to glorify God. Gladden proposed something different to his contemporaries. He argued that time away from work provided greater reward than toil. He expressed a message that some were not ready to hear: that hard work and self-control did not necessarily deliver salvation. He undercut one of the cornerstones of their faith. By the end of his career, a majority of American Protestants agreed with his view, and frequented amusement parks, spent time with family during vacations from work, went on shopping sprees, and embraced the popular gospel of social salvation. Gladden's life epitomized Americans' dissatisfaction with the orthodoxy of the Second Great Awakening, their doubt about individual salvation, and their growing reluctance to link work with salvation in the late nineteenth century.

As a child, Washington Gladden was no stranger to hard work. Born in 1836 in Pottsgrove, Pennsylvania, Gladden began working at the age of six when his father died. Two years later his mother moved to Owego, New York, where she apprenticed her eight-year-old son to a farmer. This stout Protestant set an example of "ceaseless industry" and taught Gladden how to do "a man's work."[37] In addition to working on the farm, Gladden also attended a country school near Owego, where he enjoyed reading but otherwise left an unexceptional academic record. At the age of sixteen, he left the farm and entered the office of the *Owego Gazette*, where he spent three years learning the printer's trade.

A strong sense of Protestant duty as well as necessity drove Gladden to early, regular toil. Under his mother's supervision he attended an evangelical church that was "wholly individualistic." Located in New York's "burned-over district"—so named because of frequent emotional campfire revivals—churches in Owego hosted revivalists who roared the time-worn message of repentance, hard work, and individual responsibility for salvation. One such revivalist seared terrifying images of eternal punishment on Gladden's impressionable mind. At the age of

Washington Gladden

seventy-four, Gladden still could not forget the exhorter's description of a "burning pit, with sinners trying to crawl up its sides out of the flames, while devils, with pitchforks, stood by to fling them back again." Fear of death without salvation and hell-fire as punishment were "always haunting" the Protestant lad, and he claimed that his "most horrible dreams were of that place of torment." He did not experience conversion at the time, but wrestled with the stern implications of the revivalist's words. From the time he entered the office of the *Owego Gazette* in 1852, Gladden searched for a purposeful life work to help him avoid fiery retribution.[38]

In the intense Protestant atmosphere of western New York, Gladden struggled to focus his ambition on a career that would allay his concern for salvation and would channel his energy and talent on some useful service. He had worked as a farmhand and as a printer's apprentice, but by the time he celebrated his nineteenth birthday, he had failed to find in either occupation an absorbing life's work. With a vague hope of finding something more worthy of his talent, he entered the Owego Academy and, a year later, Williams College. To compensate for the limited background offered by his hometown academy, Gladden applied himself diligently in his college classes. He constantly guarded against unrestrained, self-centered ambition in the hope of finding work for the glory of God. By the end of his senior year he had decided to enter the ministry, but he had not completely controlled his yearning for self-aggrandizement and fame. In a poem entitled "Onward," written during his last year at Williams, Gladden revealed his inner turmoil over ambition and salvation. The principal theme of the poem was "working the deliverance of man," but one stanza exposed the tempting appeal of renown:

> Hast thou never heard its accents
> Never felt the strong desire
> For being far more noble
> For a station somewhat higher?
> Hast thou never in midnight vision
> Seen the monument of Fame,
> Written o'er in golden brightness
> With the letters of thy name?[39]

The early years of Gladden's ministry suggest that he did gaze longingly at the "monument of Fame." His mother worried about her son's health when he wrote her of his long hours of toil. "I hope you will not sacrifice your health to ambition," she wrote in 1859. She reminded her son that his talent was a gift from God and that he should try to avoid excessive striving.[40] A few months later, Gladden reported to his family that he had agreed to preach three Sunday services for one of his friends. "I don't know as that will be as good as I might have done at Boston," he noted, conscious of the low visibility and miserable pay of his friend's parish. Gladden brightened when the Congregational church of LeRoysville, Pennsylvania, offered him a pastorate, and he hurried to accept it. Less than six months later, however, he left the rural community to advance his career at a more prominent urban charge in Brooklyn.[41]

Romantic entanglements in the 1850s exacerbated Gladden's personal quest for success and purpose. Never secure in his pursuit of a meaningful career, the ambitious young divine faced equally troubling choices in his private life. During his year at the Owego Academy, Gladden became emotionally involved with two young ladies whose divergent personalities presented two clear alternatives to the passionate pilgrim. Hattie Hamilton, a charming, fun-loving girl kept up a suggestive, flirtatious correspondence with Gladden up to the time of his wedding in 1860. Frequent apologies from Hamilton for not having written more often suggest that Gladden at least hinted at serious intentions if he did not actually pursue the young lady. The other classmate, Jennie Cohoon, lacked natural beauty, but exuded a simple modest charm and typical morality. These traits made her an attractive candidate for the role of minister's wife. Gladden courted both girls. Shortly after he became engaged to Jennie Cohoon in 1858, he traveled to Auburn, New York, to visit Hamilton. After the brief interlude, Hattie wrote longingly, "It does not seem as though I had actually *seen* you, conversed with you, and even kissed you!" Gladden kept up a gay correspondence with Hamilton even after he informed her of his engagement to their former classmate. Gladden eventually married Jennie Cohoon in December 1860.[42]

Forced to choose between Jennie Cohoon and Hattie Hamilton, Gladden confronted a decision between Victorian respectability and sensual gratification. And his choice coincided with a particular decision he had to make about his career. He had given up a small parish in rural Pennsylvania, reminiscent of the church of his youth, to take over a larger church in Brooklyn. In each case, he made the choice that did more to advance his career but not without wrenching emotional conflict. By the time of his winter wedding, Gladden was near an emotional, spiritual, and physical breakdown.

When Washington Gladden looked back on his long career in the ministry in 1910, he remembered 1860 as "a momentous year for this country."[43] Though the war to save the Union actually began in 1861, Gladden's private struggle for a coherent identity and single-minded purpose peaked in 1860 and etched that year deeply in his memory. In fact, Gladden might have found it difficult to disentangle the national conflict from his own crisis. When he recalled that "hostile forces" made ready for "deadly conflict," he spoke as much for himself as for the country. Rural versus urban, Victorian domesticity versus passionate allure, Gladden's choices mirrored the broad outlines of national alternatives between a southern agrarian past and a northern industrial future. Gladden searched for salvation in a context riddled with conflict. Having achieved considerable renown in rural LeRoysville to receive the call to the First Congregational Methodist Church in Brooklyn in May 1860, Gladden chafed at the despair which replaced reassuring hope as he toiled in his first urban enterprise. Hard work yielded few rewards in a parish where industry was "paralyzed," men were "standing idle in the marketplace," and the "whole work of the church" had "come to a sudden pause." His second step toward conventional Victorian respectability—marrying Jennie Cohoon—proved as troubling as his coveted urban congregation. The added financial burden of a wife and comfortable domestic furnishings while employed at a "financially disabled" church brought the "wolf" to the "door of the parsonage."[44] And the work itself fell far short of his expectations. Church life in 1860, he remembered, consisted of "preparation of human beings for death."[45] Gladden confronted individual salvation in a world over which he, as an individual, had no control. As he reported in his autobiography, "The young pastor found himself struggling with conditions that were hopeless."[46] When seceding southern states left America with a fragmented identity, Gladden sensed his own disjointed self. Early in 1861, when the guns at Fort Sumter signaled the collapse of the United States, Gladden suffered a disabling nervous breakdown.

For Gladden, it was not the first time that private turmoil resulted in physical ailment. When he graduated from Williams College in 1859, he faced the prospect of proving himself in the workaday world. Moments before he was scheduled to deliver a commencement address, Gladden suffered an attack of facial neuralgia that threatened to sideline him from the exercises. The comforting words of a visiting clergyman quieted the young man's fears. He managed to speak his farewell to his alma mater and classmates, and the four-year respite from continuous toil came to an end.[47] His anxiety in 1861, however, was not so easily allayed. Unable to keep pace with the demands of an urban congregation, Gladden tendered his resignation and retreated to a less taxing church in a quiet suburb, Morrisania, New York. He remained in this location, halfway between rural and urban extremes, for the duration of the war, apparently unable and unwilling to identify with either countryside or city—symbols of America's past and future that hung in the balance of the conflict. At the war's conclusion Gladden complained about his salary, and he accepted a call to a burgeoning industrial city, North Adams, Massachusetts. He chose an ideal community in which to recover his equanimity and to contemplate America's emerging industrial identity.[48] The critique of religious individualism he began to formulate in North Adams provided cultural legitimacy for the embryonic corporate order. It eventually conferred unity and meaning on his own work. In North Adams, Gladden began to merge cooperation and self-respect into a single vision of salvation.

Living in a rapidly expanding industrial center, Gladden came to understand the painful quest for self-respect in corporate America. Gladden watched uneasily as violent labor disputes erupted in 1870. Shoemakers resisted the introduction of machines and unskilled labor, which threatened to drive wages down and to devalue their hard work. They organized a secret order of the Knights of St. Crispin to fight collectively for their individual dignity. Factory owners crushed the strikers by transporting trainloads of Chinese immigrants into the Massachusetts community. Gladden later recalled the thick, threatening atmosphere into which the unsuspecting Chinese trod. The defeated Knights stood empty-handed because they had demanded respect and a decent wage for faithful toil; the Chinese earned scorn as reward for their work. By playing the part of mediator, Gladden helped avert violence. He welcomed the foreign strikebreakers into classes and clubs, and he extended sympathy to the shoemakers as well. Gladden's own career took a temporary turn for the better in the field of writing, so lured by the prospect of greater national fame—greater self-respect—he entered a "new field of labor . . . larger and more important" than his ministry in North Adams. In 1871, he joined the editorial staff of the *Independent*.[49] As a good Victorian, he hoped to succeed at this enterprise; at the same time, he hoped to use the journal as an organ of social reform. In 1871, the social gospel had merely begun to take form in Gladden's mind.

For the next decade, Gladden moved from job to job, usually departing with a "sense of failure" or ill will. Two years before he left the editorship of the *Independent* in 1875, he wrote Henry C. Brown, the chief editor of the journal: "I don't like to sit in the office week by week with my hands tied; with no motive to work; because after doing my level best to write something that shall not only advance the interests of the *Independent* but also help on the causes in which I am interested, I am compelled to see my matter crowded out. . . . There is never any encouragement to work."[50] More complaints and finally a letter of resignation followed. Gladden left the *Independent* and took charge of a congregation in Springfield, Massachusetts. While there he founded a new journal under his own management, describing the endeavor as an enterprise he "had chosen for [him]self" and which he "was entirely free to cultivate . . . [his] own way." Like his other efforts in these years, in 1880 Gladden's publication, *Sunday Afternoon: A Magazine for the*

Household, renamed *Good Company* in 1879, folded. For some of his "liberal" ideas, Gladden also met criticism from what he called the "denominational machine." He despaired that unconventional ministers like himself too often found their "paths to promotion obstructed, and their opportunities of service limited." By 1882, Gladden complained of a "sense of failure," described himself as "worn and jaded," and left Springfield for Columbus, Ohio, to accept anew the challenge of a thriving urban congregation.[51]

Gladden's thirty-six-year tenure at the First Congregational Church of Columbus proved to be the most satisfying work of his career. The unanimous vote by which the congregation called him and their overwhelming approval of his ideas not only drew the middle-aged New Yorker to Ohio, but also became the basis for his modern vision of salvation. Gladden's chastening experiences in ventures after the Civil War paralleled those of other striving young men and convinced him of the brittleness of an individual ethic in industrial America. As the older Protestant ethic began to crack, Gladden and others looked nervously to one another for reassurance to forge "a partnership of sweet reasonableness," as he called it in the 1890s.[52] The independent individual of the immediate Protestant past found himself surrounded by co-workers, foremen, managers, and employers whose capacity to work hinged on the reliability and flexibility of others. Individual success counted far less than cooperation and service in the modern workplace. Thus, blessed assurance and hope of salvation pivoted on others because affirmation and approval came from those who were served as well as from the self. As Gladden explained in *Social Salvation* (1902), "The bread and water of the spiritual life are the doing of one's duty and the service of our fellows; and without these elements one can never have the life of fellowship with God."[53] As Gladden wrestled with the work ethic in the late nineteenth century, he found himself blending the individual obligations and responsibilities of his youth with a collective spirit. In the 1880s, the child of the "burned-over district" loosened his hold on individualism and recognized the need for cooperation.[54]

One way to address the problems created by unfulfilling work was to propose reform. In *Applied Christianity* (1886), his first major work after arriving in Columbus, Gladden did this by raising troubled questions about work and self-respect in modern America. The "Christian Moralist" who opened the volume noted sadly that in industrial America people had to be reminded that "the laborer is worthy of his hire." For too often in the United States in the 1880s men worked without receiving their due reward. The elaborate program of private charity and social reform that followed in this book called for dedicated professionals to remedy this "bad state of things" by serving others. Their efforts would help ensure that "the husbandman that laboreth" would be the first to partake of the fruits.[55] As in later books, Gladden's *Applied Christianity* carried a double message. The first was obvious: social reformers should insist that men and women who worked received just treatment so they could gain self-respect. The second message addressed middle-class Protestants like himself who wrestled quietly and painfully with fears of failure: The social gospel could give their lives purpose. Thus Protestant-sponsored reform lifted the cares of all; it granted material aid to the impoverished and purposeful work for the affluent.

In 1893, in a book entitled *Tools and the Man*, Gladden advocated "industrial cooperation" as a way of making work more meaningful for laborers. He described a system of profit-sharing by which laborers would gain more money and a greater sense of self-respect and by which employers would develop "sympathy, consideration, the sense of stewardship, the responsibility of power, the chivalrous regard" for his workers. He also recognized the need for labor unions. In *The Labor Question* (1911), Gladden cited Herbert Croly's *Promise of American Life* to affirm the "new worker" who supported unions. "As a type the non-union laborer is a species of industrial derelict," he quoted from Croly. "He is the laborer who has gone astray, and who, either from apathy, unintelligence, incompetence, or some immediately pressing need, prefers his own individual interest to the joint interests of himself and his fellow laborers." The union man, by contrast, represented "the independence of the laborer, because under existing circumstances, independence must be brought by association."[56]

When Gladden wrote *Social Salvation* in 1902, he demonstrated the parallels between modern work and salvation. The Protestantism of his youth, like its work ethic, had put too much emphasis on the individual. But in the early twentieth century, Gladden argued, "one man can no more be a Christian alone than one man can sing an oratorio alone." Putting the matter more straightforwardly, Gladden declared, "No individual is soundly converted until he comprehends his social relations and strives to fulfill them." A man was not truly saved until he tried to save others. This Gladden called the "law of love." The law of love, Gladden argued, "defines our relations to men not only in the home and in the church, but in industry and commerce and politics."[57] Gladden saw work as a place where men could exercise this law of love both to improve working conditions and to seek salvation. By the time he wrote his *Recollections* in 1909, Gladden believed that it was imperative to alter the conditions of work in order to save men. "Is the man saved, who, in his dealings with his employee, or his employer, can habitually seek his own aggrandizement at the cost of the other?" he asked. "Is not the selfishness which is expected to rule in all this department of life the exact antithesis of Christian morality? Is there anything else from which men need more to be saved than from the habits of thought and action which prevail in places where 'business is business'?"[58]

With these notions, Gladden paved a path to salvation through the avenues of personal relations in the corporation. The "law of love" and its promise of salvation held out a powerful draught for both workers and their employers. As he explained in *The Labor Question* in 1911, our highest spiritual goal requires "patient, heroic, self-denying work." In return for a commitment to others "in the State or in the factory," Gladden envisioned a great emotional reward. "Can any compensation," he queried, "be higher or finer than that of the man who wins . . . the loyal affection of scores or hundreds of thousands of men? No vocation can be more sacred than this," he concluded, "and no reward more satisfying."[59]

The key to the treasures of social salvation was cooperation. Cooperative men sought to identify their interests with those of others. Workers, for example, who wanted self-respect from work in the factory "would do well" to let their employers "see that their temper is such as to promise pleasant and profitable relations."[60] One of Gladden's many commencement addresses in the early twentieth century extolled the ability of modern managers to "marshal men, and lead them, with never a hint of conflict, in the ways of peaceful industry." He advocated strong ties between workers and employers—"identifying their lives" with one another and "finding reward in the privilege of service."[61] A few years earlier he had contributed an essay to a book entitled *Organized Capital and Labor* (1904) in which he predicted a solution to the labor question when employers and their workers came together on a "basis of genuine good will" acting as "friends, comrades, helpers of one another." He insisted that this could be accomplished when the interests of both were "more perfectly and more consciously identified" with each other.[62]

Gladden struck upon the perfect metaphor for explaining the common interests of the individual and the group—the baseball team. Like other social gospelers, Gladden urged Protestants to think of work and salvation as a baseball game. A boy alone may be trained "for any given position on the field," he argued, "but if he undertook to study it out alone it would not be easy for him to understand it. In fact, it would be impossible. No one could learn the game all alone. The team work is the whole of it." So it was with life—to strive alone stripped life and work of their "whole meaning and significance." "The team work," he repeated, "is all there is of it."[63]

In the midst of Gladden's celebration of team spirit and corporate organization, signs of unresolved ambivalence occasionally appeared in his writing. Identification with others, satisfaction through cooperation, and salvation through personal relations all felt pleasant, but for a man concerned with self-respect this dependence on others for self and salvation may have raised fears of diffusion and confusion. In fact, Gladden seemed at times obsessed with images of decay and disintegration in modern life. In the 1890s, when he assessed the effect of corporations on public morality, images of deterioration abounded. Corporations, he warned at various points throughout the text, are "silently sapping the foundations of our vigor" and our "manhood," and bring about the "degradation of our population" and a "deterioration in the morals."[64] In *Social Salvation*, he likened modern society to Jerusalem just before its fall—a body with "wounds, and bruises, and putrefying sores," "morbid conditions," "tendencies to decay," and "ills that call for healing."[65] Finally, when he reviewed his own career in 1910, he recognized the need to identify the interests of others with his own but feared lest he should "degrade or destroy" himself in ministering to others.[66]

For the most part, however, Gladden tried to dispel gloomy apprehension of personal decay. By the end of his career he proclaimed the emotional bounty in catering to those around him. According to Gladden, every profession could deliver psychic well-being and temporal salvation if undertaken in a spirit of sensitivity to others. Indeed, his comments about social Christians like himself revealed the self-serving quality of Christian reform as well as its altruism. "To make a better world of this is the best thing a man can think of," he wrote in *The Church and Modern Life* (1908). "We know that we shall not make ourselves rich or famous in this undertaking; but we shall see the load lifted from many shoulders, and the light of hope shining in many eyes; we shall hear the din of strife changing to the songs of cheerful labor; we shall share our simple joys with those who know that we have always tried to make their lives happier and who cannot choose but love us; we shall find life worth living and we shall die content."[67]

Washington Gladden's struggles as a young man to contend with a frightening vision of individual salvation and to find success in work probably made him particularly sensitive to the deepening crisis of Victorianism in the late nineteenth century. As industry, factories, and bureaucracies crowded out the shops and farms of his youth, he saw how unfair it was to ask men and women to take sole responsibility for either their spiritual salvation or their advancement at work. For the injustice of industry, the moral decay of industrial cities, and the work itself ground down the spirit and obstructed social and economic improvement. It was not easy for Gladden to question the accepted wisdom of his youth; indeed, his first efforts in the 1860s brought disapproval. But Gladden's own anguish had been great, and the situation in the 1880s and 1890s demanded drastic action. The social gospel of Washington Gladden helped him resolve the tension between the demand for individual achievement in an economy that frustrated it and the demand for individual responsibility for salvation in a society that undermined the efforts of Christians. The reform he proposed aimed to improve life for the working class and to give middle-class people like himself meaningful work. Younger social gospelers built on Gladden's foundation. Men like Shailer Mathews refined Gladden's redefinition of the work ethic and subtly altered his cooperative vision. The social gospel of Mathews and others began to lend moral legitimacy to emerging relations of work in corporate America.

SHAILER MATHEWS

"Men must be convinced that you are sincere"

A reporter once asked Shailer Mathews to name the accomplishment that had given him the greatest satisfaction in his life. In a career spanning the years between the Pullman Strike and Franklin Roosevelt's first inauguration, Mathews had many honors and incidents from which to choose. The aging dean of Chicago's famed School of Divinity had fomented dozens of theological controversies in his day as editor of *The World Today* and *Biblical World*. He had helped renovate the curriculum of the divinity school by incorporating principles of the social gospel in the regular course of theological study. And as president of the Federal Council of Churches he had strengthened the foundation for Protestant unity in the twentieth century. The lofty divine pondered the question for a moment, then replied, "After graduating from Colby I played one professional [baseball] game on the Portland team against Providence, that year champion of the National League."[68] Dean Shailer Mathews took greatest pride in playing on a winning team. Though hardly the expected answer, Mathews's choice perfectly reflected his understanding of twentieth-century Protestantism. All his books and articles and his style of administration and instruction embodied a desire to be a well-adjusted member of a smoothly run organization. During his long career, Mathews strove to be an efficient part of the Protestant team.

If social gospel Protestants had instituted a hall of fame, Mathews surely would have been among the early inductees. After earning degrees from Colby College and Newton Theological Institution, Mathews quickly caught the attention of his Protestant colleagues. A grant to study in Berlin for a year followed closely by his first publication brought him an invitation to teach theology at Chicago's divinity school in 1894. By 1908 he had become dean of the thriving school, a position he held for a quarter of a century. Under his direction, the divinity school sponsored numerous series of Sunday school literature featuring social salvation, and it implemented an extension program to involve religious leaders in various dimensions of social life. He edited two major journals and wrote dozens of books and articles that Walter Rauschenbusch later acclaimed as the first serious attempt to provide a biblical basis for the social gospel. From 1912 to 1916, he served as president of the Federal Council of Churches and used his administrative skills to expand that organization's capacity for social service. Though he retired from the divinity school at the age of seventy, he remained active in his profession. For the last eight years of his life, until his death in 1941, he wrote, made speeches, and attended various national Protestant conferences.[69]

Shailer Mathews played a prominent role in the American attempt to revitalize religion in the early twentieth century. Many perceived him as the quintessential modernist. Detractors saw him as "a trifler, a jester of Voltairean pattern" who displayed "cap-and-bells intellectual mannerisms." According to one historian, in spite of Mathews's efforts to "preserve Christianity" in the "contemporary world," Mathews's name "stood for the destruction of the faith."[70] In one sense the conservatives who accused him of such destruction were correct; Shailer Mathews participated in the separation of work from salvation that had been an important dimension of American Protestant faith. But to dismiss him as the "devil incarnate" is to misunderstand him and to avoid an even more important connection between the social gospel and modern culture. While Mathews experienced some of the same tension between individual responsibility and social responsibility that prompted Gladden's critique of Prot-

Shailer Mathews

estant orthodoxy, by the time the younger man came of age in the late 1880s corporate enterprises in work, education, and leisure enjoyed wider appeal and greater social legitimacy. Mathews adopted much of the language of self-realization that had crept into Protestant discourse by the early twentieth century. He helped shift the basis of salvation from productive work and future reward to personal development and immediate gratification. He hoped that making Protestantism more efficient and personally affirming would enable it to survive and thrive in corporate America.

Like most of his colleagues in the social gospel movement, Shailer Mathews began life securely in the evangelical Protestant fold. Born in 1863 in Portland, Maine, the oldest of four children of Jonathan Bennett Mathews and Sophia Shailer Mathews, the lad grew to maturity in a straitlaced Baptist household. His father engaged in the wholesale trade and oversaw the discipline of his family in characteristic Victorian fashion. His "sincerely religious" mother set aside Sunday afternoon for reading "unexciting stores of the doings of abnormally good, small children" from *Zion's Advocate,* published by her father, the Reverend William H. Shailer.[71] Religion played a central role in young Shailer's life. His grandfather, a prominent Baptist minister in Portland and an observer of a "Puritan Sabbath," urged individual responsibility and a lonely conversion experience. From his grandfather's "conventionally pietistic" teaching, Mathews saw "Hell and the devil" as "very real," and early in life he devoted himself to a "culture of the inner life." As an adolescent, Mathews attended a revival led by George C. Needham and in 1877 underwent a conversion experience. He promptly joined the church.[72]

Having taken the first step on the way to middle-class respectability, Mathews expected to find success, like his father before him, in the competitive world of business. Years later he remembered that in the Portland of his youth, "competition was regarded as the life of trade," and that entrepreneurs' success was due to their "superior wealth and ability." Jonathan Mathews's tea and flour trade, however, fell apart in the depression of 1878, and in that year, his son was forced to work in the family business. Shailer Mathews kept his father's accounts, performed various menial tasks around the wholesale house, and for a while contemplated going into the business. But the market's capriciousness and his family's failure to succeed financially in spite of diligent work clouded Shailer Mathews's confidence in the Victorian formula for success. After two years, he left the family home in Portland for Waterville, Maine, to enter Colby College.[73]

As an undergraduate, Mathews escaped much of the private, individual competition that drove his family in Portland. Student government and committee work afforded him opportunities to engage in cooperative endeavor. He also enjoyed popularity as catcher on the college baseball team. In the early 1930s, Mathews's son related the story of his father's "amazing somersault to catch a foul ball," a story Shailer's classmates relished telling fifty years after the fact.[74] Support from classmates and teammates gave Mathews his first taste of success in a cooperative enterprise, nearly blotting out the anguish of failure at home. By his senior year, however, renewed economic hardship disturbed Mathews's idyll at Colby. He was forced to open a small private bookstore in his dormitory room to meet living expenses. At graduation he turned his back on a career in business and entered Newton Theological Institution in Massachusetts to study religion and to prepare for college teaching. By 1884, Mathews had distanced himself physically and psychologically from disappointment in Portland.

Though he chose to pursue religious studies, Mathews did not enter the ministry. His disaffection from the individualism of his youth made the prospect of parish ministry among the hardy down-easters unappealing. Mathews's only experience as a parish minister was a three-month stint as a supply minister in Baring, Maine, during the summer of 1886. An isolated lumbering community, populated by industrious sawyers and river drivers, Baring offered little in the way of entertainment and society for a young theological student. Even for three months Mathews found the community stifling and made frequent trips to nearby cities for relief. When he could not leave, he attempted to create among the rough lumbering families the social atmosphere of his beloved college days. He organized parties, socials, picnics, and a baseball team.[75] Nevertheless, Mathews wearied of the predominantly individual demands of his job. With obvious references to the Reverend Shailer, he later expressed his frustration with the "old gospel," which asked men to be "virtuous by being like their grandfathers." Mathews had learned that private struggle rarely proved as pleasant as collective enterprise. "Grandfather's virtues like grandfather's clocks are in our day not always in good running order," he insisted. "Obligation is set not only by our relations with individuals but by our relations with the groups of which we are members."[76] By the end of the summer, Mathews realized that he was not cut out to be a Baptist minister. When he left Newton the following spring, he accepted a position as professor of rhetoric at Colby College.

As a professor of rhetoric at an established college, Mathews discovered that without interests outside his field, teaching could become a "deadly routine." To combat boredom, he organized special seminars and became involved in directing the athletic program. Shortly after his wedding to Mary Philbrick Eden in 1890, he went to Germany for a year of study. This last diversion made life in Maine even more oppressive to Mathews, and upon his return he found that the security and quiet of a small college in a small town had become "burdensome." He could prepare lectures and lessons "without any necessity of severe study." He complained of isolation and a dearth of opportunities to participate in social reform. Thus, when Prof. Ernest D. Burton invited him to join the faculty of the University of Chicago as an associate professor of New Testament studies, he overcame initial hesitation and "caught" Burton's "enthusiasm for a university in the making." In words that typified the modern work ethic for which he became a major spokesman, Mathews explained his reasons for accepting the new position: "The appeal of an adventure, an opportunity to share in the life of a university, the possibility of escape from limitations of which I was growing daily more conscious pointed to only one decision." In 1894 he and his family left

Waterville, Maine, to make a new home in Chicago.[77]

From 1894 on, much of Mathews's writing concerned getting along in modern America. Books exploring the connection between work and salvation incorporated and elaborated one or more of the reasons he himself had offered for moving to the University of Chicago: "escape from limitations," "sharing," and "adventure." He more or less accepted the structure of work imposed by corporate order. In fact he advocated "scientific management" of churches a year after Frederick Winslow Taylor introduced the idea to owners of large industrial concerns. But his later work, notably *The Faith of Modernism* (1924) and *What Religion Does for Personality* (1932), argued for seeking psychic rewards from interacting with others within large organizations. Less troubled than Gladden by the impossible demands of individual responsibility in corporate America, Mathews asserted the social gospel and looked for ways to make work and life and religion meaningful on earth through others.

Mathews also articulated the social gospel with greater confidence than Gladden. He penned his autobiography, *New Faith for Old*, in 1936 "in response to a suggestion that someone ought to describe the changes which have come over Protestant religious belief during the last half century."[78] He remembered unsympathetically that Baptists in his youth considered church suppers "cooking stove apostasy" and baseball games "frivolous amusements" rather than opportunities to secure strong social bonds as they were seen in a later day. They thought Protestantism was "essentially for the individual," and as a result, old-time Baptists had been "indifferent" and "aloof" to social ills. Mathews also recalled that the "severities of orthodoxy" had demanded a capricious, vengeful God who willed or at least tolerated human suffering. For social gospelers, God "became a father rather than a judge." Finally, Mathews began to realize that nineteenth-century Protestantism offered a narrow vision of salvation. "Orthodoxy was a presentation of how to get salvation in heaven," he declared. "The social gospel proposed the teaching of Jesus as a call and a way to give salvation on earth." Mathews believed that an old faith in individualism, a harsh God, and heavenly reward for repentance had been overturned for a new faith in collective action, an immanent God, and salvation and reward on earth.[79]

Being a part of a generation searching for authentic experiences, Mathews understandably wanted a religion that addressed concrete human problems. Skeptical of the celestial payoff for hard work and self-control, Mathews urged the twentieth-century Protestant to move away from "a world of abstractions" and dive into "the world in which he actually lives and upon which he is dependent." The social gospel, he thundered, must be "realistic." Thus, he and his contemporaries worked to "discover the real world." Like hundreds of other social gospelers in the twentieth century, Mathews urged others to escape the disappointing private realm by plunging into the sordid tangible world of packing towns, tenements, and gambling halls. There they could lose themselves in others' distress and enjoy concrete rewards as well as flight from personal concerns. Mathews argued that "the real world was composed of real people" and that this "discovery made for friendship." For Mathews, work in specialized corporations, professions, or bureaucracies meant a chance to avoid the lonely battle of proving oneself and a way to ease one's own and others' anxieties by daily acts of kindness and expressions of good will, all of which seemed more attainable and comforting than hope for reward in an afterlife.[80]

Work in modern America provided a forum for transcending the limitations of individualism because it gave men a chance to take part in a complex process of production. Just as Mathews anticipated "sharing in the life of a university," white-collar managers, blue-collar assembly-line workers, and scores of clerical laborers "shared" in the work of the firm or institution. In addition to the obvious therapeutic value of drawing strength from others in the performance of a common task, sharing offered a vision of efficient, scientific cooperation. The value of a person's contribution lay not in the originality or riskiness of his endeavor, but rather in its adjustment to the larger process. Mathews found in Frederick Winslow Taylor's theory of scientific management a ready-made model that elevated efficiency above self-centered drive. In *The Principles of Scientific Management* (1911), Taylor argued that division of labor by specialized functions, planned management of the steps of production, and the unquestioning acceptance and repetition of minute tasks would result in a harmonious workplace and greater productivity. In *Scientific Management in the Churches* (1912), Mathews applied Taylor's principles to religion by proposing to help the "Christian spirit" to "prevail in an age of institutions" by making it efficient. He believed that carefully planned interdependence in Christian life would yield "intimate, friendly cooperation." Mathews thus hoped to satisfy twentieth-century man's need to share in a large enterprise at the same time that he made Protestant churches "the most effective agencies of reform."[81]

Though Mathews pursued a noble object—an efficient program for aiding those disinherited by the industrial system—the message of his book is ambiguous. To participate in reform, American Protestants had to be willing to sacrifice their independence and autonomy and adopt the structure and strategy of corporations. Of course, Mathews never bluntly stated the high personal cost of the social gospel. He couched his remarks in oblique bureaucratic language: "Churches which under a definite policy and plan deliberately undertake to organize themselves as significant forces in the social evolution," he explained, "will have tremendous influence in spiritualizing and moralizing the changing order." He wanted to "eliminate [the] waste" in the organization of the church that sprang from duplicated effort, ineffective advertising, and failure to cooperate with other reform agencies. He hoped to reach his goal by stressing "calm business-like planning."[82]

An efficient church, like an efficient business, required a separation of planning from performance, however. In other words, people who planned programs seldom helped carry them out, and those who put them into effect had no hand in preparing them. The manner of work, rather than work as an integrated whole, counted. Using hierarchical corporate language, Mathews told his readers that pastors would serve as heads of a "board of management," paid assistants as "functional foremen" and "specialists," unpaid assistants as "volunteers . . . disciplined into efficiency," and the working church member as a "soldier restrained within well-conceived plans and a proper division of labor." None took independent action.[83]

Mathews asked American Protestants to take comfort in the act of sharing in active reform. As Mathews's work elevated the Christian specialist, it simultaneously transformed the performance of mundane tasks into an "adventure in social service." Protestants who moved beyond a "complacent assurance" of salvation saw that the "very heart of the Christian life is activity." Being a part, however small, of such action placed the individual at the center of spiritual life. Someone else, of course, would plan the activity. Mathews envisioned "management committees," which, after they studied individual church members, would locate them "in such tasks as they are fitted to perform."[84] Individual Protestants were to surrender their wills to the "board of directors" in exchange for a chance to share. "If this seems to make the Church something of a business establishment," Mathews asserted, "it is precisely what should be the case. We have too long regarded the church as capable of performing its possible services to the community without the most elementary means of administration." He believed that powerful spiritual bonds would unite Protestants in common cause, alleviate misery in the community, and relieve the pressure on individuals to strive alone. A scientifically managed church avoided "hysterical committee-making" and became a "cooperating group of spiritual workmen."[85]

The last dimension of Mathews's gospel of social salvation was emotion. The modernist encouraged Protestants to look sensitively to others for direction and to explore their own feelings. "The vicarious life is the noblest life," he declared in *The Message of Jesus to Our Modern Life* (1915). "It finds its ideal, not in its own success, but in the welfare of others as well as of itself." To derive satisfaction from a vicarious life, Mathews explained, the Protestant must merge his own "ambitions with those of the group" and "subordinate apparent personal good whenever it threatens the welfare of others." If Americans listened to his message, Mathews promised they would "feel anew the spell" of Jesus, and they would "serve others even at the expense of discomfort." And this intense feeling in an age anesthetized by bureaucracy and monotony represented part of the divine plan for modern salvation.[86]

Early reformers had lobbied for shorter working days and greater opportunities for leisure for workers to relieve the monotony of factory and office routine. They believed that in recreation and amusements, Americans could revitalize themselves for work and enjoy a real reward in an otherwise meaningless job. By the time Mathews wrote most of his books, baseball and similar pastimes enjoyed wide popularity, and outstanding players like Walter Johnson and Christy Mathewson embodied the ideal of American manliness. The old catcher, who once had heard the cheers for the Colby nine, believed that he could evoke memories in other American men of their own glory days as the "idol of the 'fans,'" and of their team struggling together in a spirit of "adventuresomeness." Mathews concluded that Americans' "real souls are in baseball." He admitted that their souls were not in work, except insofar as work resembled the game. Americans wanted to "win," but they did so on the basis of camaraderie, esprit de corps, the team effort. The scores of the games or the products they made were long forgotten, but the memory of working together lingered to give life meaning. "Yes, you were a part of it all," he fondly sighed. The social gospel of Shailer Mathews took shape in a society interested in teamwork and spectator sports.[87] It not only affirmed that modern society by borrowing one of its most popular mass symbols, but it also made the final separation between work and salvation. It urged American Protestants to be good sports on the job, to work together to get more and richer time off the job, and to find in corporate life that smile or clap on the back that made life worthwhile.

Shailer Mathews found by the end of his professional career that men and women had become interested in developing a "winning personality"—to fit in, to get work, and to elicit warm approval from others. He was convinced that religion played an important role in the "development of well-integrated, wholesome, powerful personalities, capable of enjoying life to the full and of serving the world." Accordingly, he edited a collection of essays in the early 1930s entitled *What Religion Does for Personality*. In his own contribution to the volume, Mathews advocated constant "social contacts" for "stimuli toward reaction and adjustment. As these are multiplied, and a man undertakes intelligently to cooperate with and to get help from relations with his fellows, he grows personally." In this essay, "Religion as the Source of Poise and Power," Mathews attempted to win Americans to Protestantism by offering them a formula for success in corporate society. "Sacrificial social minded-ness," or treating others in the kindly way one wished to be treated, was the first ingredient. Mixed with a portion of "self-realization and self-expression" it yielded social harmony, "Christ-like unity."[88]

The key to "lasting satisfaction," however, came with the decision of "what sort of self is to be realized . . . and expressed." The final step was to weigh the "relative worth" of all the "possibilities of life" against prevailing "social relations." In other words, popular conventions pro-vided the stuff from which men and women fashioned their personalities. In a sense they were "self-made," but ironically, they were largely de-pendent on others. Mathews took the process a step further by investing it with spiritual significance. God, he argued, was the "great person-ality"; and like human brothers and sisters, he let us know in tangible ways of his approval and disapproval. Through "prayer and meditation" men tested the ethereal mood; "inspiration" and "feelings" were divine answers to human pleas for direction. Goals, direction, appropriate work relations, and assurance of salvation all came from external rather than internal sources.[89]

In the 1930s, Mathews recognized that the Depression had revived old tensions between individual initiative and collective effort. He spoke of a "sense of frustration" pervading his generation, whose members "experienced the difficulty of adjusting their ideals to the exigencies of life." Their children faced conditions "which only gradually offer oppor-tunity," and they needed even more encouragement than their parents. Twenty years earlier, in *The Message of Jesus to Our Modern Life*, he had urged Protestants to be themselves "rather than copies of someone else." He reiterated the same sentiment in his autobiography when he declared that he envied a "generation that will be called upon to defend the individual from absorption" into group life.[90] But he also had urged greater dependence on others for direction, security, and personal reward. It is not altogether clear how Mathews thought individuals should define themselves. He clearly denounced the loner who was insensitive to those around him, but without a definition of self arrived at independently, people could become mere reflections of those about them.

Already by the 1910s, Mathews had come to place greater emphasis on the group than on the individual. He had worked on so many university committees and been part of so many ecumenical associations and scholarly teams that he had confidence in collective effort. In *Scientific Management in the Churches*, Mathews urged Protestants in "cooperating groups" to adopt a confessional mode of discourse so that each member could convey and receive clear indications of their "feelings" and attitudes and assist the church machine in operating smoothly. The individual should strive to be "a true brother of his kind" by demonstrating "sympathy" for others.[91]

Within a few years, however, Mathews discovered that such sharing had taken the form of "pathological self-disclosure" among some college students. In his autobiography, the dean recalled dropping in uninvited one evening to a meeting organized by the campus Christian Association. He found himself in a large hall filled with several hundred college students and illuminated by a single candle. On cue the students began simultaneously to pour out "confessions of all sorts and cried out in prayer to God." Mathews noted that the association eventually abandoned this spiritual practice but said that he continued to struggle with its meaning. Mathews and other social gospelers had urged young people to confess, to share, and to cooperate, to be "selfless," but they had not reckoned on the desperate confusion adolescents would experience nor the "high-voltage emotionalism" he witnessed. The college student needed, Mathews admitted, "not only intellectual assurance that God existed and that prayer was not futile, but also some sort of leadership" in preparing to enter the corporate world of work.[92] When their elders failed to supply authoritative tutelage in life, work, and salvation, young Protestants turned dramatically to one another. Mathews grudgingly acknowledged that their unsettling display was but a caricature of an emerging mode of discourse that he and the social gospel endorsed.

Mathews's response to this display of unrestrained self-disclosure shows how much of the standards of secular culture he had incorporated. First, sincerity, or at least the appearance of sincerity, became paramount. "Men must be convinced that you are sincere," he wrote in *New*

Faith for Old.[93] After all, people depended on others' expressions and social signals for identity, for approval, and ultimately for salvation on earth, so they could not afford to be deceived. Second, in his private life, Shailer Mathews began to internalize and reflect an important theme of much personal advice literature: to be perpetually in the process of growing and of becoming. During the last years of his life, Mathews was constantly on the run, traveling to conferences, going on speaking tours, taking vacations. Each summer he traveled to Maine to try to recapture the inner strength of his past and to "restock his enthusiasm for the year to come." As his son wrote in a tribute to his father in 1933, "He can but move on and on."[94] Dean Mathews's quest for meaning was a drive for self-realization achieved through others.

CAROLINE BARTLETT CRANE

Professionalization of Domesticity, Domestication of Profession

On 31 December 1896, members of the People's Church in Kalamazoo, Michigan, gathered in their house of worship at the request of their beloved pastor. The minister had announced a New Year's Eve musicale to celebrate the passing of 1896 and to welcome 1897. When the last of the latecomers arrived, the organ sounded a joyous melody. But instead of playing "Auld Lang Syne," the organist rang in the new year with the wedding march. The Reverend Caroline Julia Bartlett hurried down the aisle, and Dr. Augustus Warren Crane left his place of hiding in one of the anterooms to join his bride at the altar. "Before anyone could interfere," the two were united in wedlock in front of the stunned congregation. Scarcely eager to shout "Happy new year!" the people of Kalamazoo "talked late that night and went to bed with an uneasy mind . . . afraid of the 'never-again-the-sameness' supposed to come when a woman enters married life."[95] As pastor since 1889, Caroline Julia Bartlett had overseen the construction of a seven-day church that, according to one investigative journalist, had "something greatly worth while to do for the community in which it lived."[96] Church members had grown to respect the energetic woman who had been ordained to the ministry shortly after her arrival among them. They had accepted proudly this educated "new woman," who embraced an entire community as her family. They were convinced, however, that Mrs. Augustus Warren Crane never could continue the work that the Reverend Caroline Julia Bartlett had begun.[97]

Caroline Bartlett Crane

The Cranes' surprise wedding and the congregation's response to it exposed an underlying tension about women's work and morality in turn-of-the-century America. American Protestants were growing more willing by the 1890s to tolerate women who devoted their lives to careers in helping professions that bolstered flagging homes and provided services that overworked mothers simply could not supply adequately. They remained skeptical, however, of women who wanted to continue in their profession after marrying. The proper place for women, after all, was in the home.

But as the nature and rewards of work changed for men, men took a somewhat different view of their homes—a view that had the unintended effect of draining women's work of meaning. Still a private refuge, the home lost a measure of the moral intensity that Victorian women so carefully tended and protected. There were, of course, children to be nurtured and instructed. But by the late nineteenth century, children spent much of their youth in schools, under the instruction and influence of an unmarried woman.

Women began to sense that their moral duties as Victorian wives and mothers were evaporating and that, as a result, the foundation of their own salvation was eroding. If work outside the home, appealing in the satisfaction it provided, remained a forbidden source of pleasure, and responsibilities in the home yielded frustration and failure, what was a woman to do? With all of this as an understood background, the Reverend Crane defied convention in the hope of establishing a new basis for assurance for Protestant women like herself. She longed to make women's domestic responsibilities professional and to infuse their professional work outside the home with values of domesticity.

Caroline Bartlett Crane has not been the subject of any full-length biography, nor does she appear in any of the standard works on the social gospel. For nearly seventy years she has escaped the notice of American scholars. In her own day, however, Crane caused quite a stir. After a decade of service in the ministry, Crane turned her attention to civic sanitation. She began examining meatpacking houses in Wisconsin and lobbied for stringent inspection laws. When Upton Sinclair's *The Jungle* created a national commotion over conditions in Packingtown, dozens of cities invited Crane to carry out detailed investigations of their food-processing plants, social institutions, and the general condition of public health. By the end of the first decade of the twentieth century, she enjoyed fame as a "public housecleaner." *Collier's, Hampton's, Good Housekeeping*, and other popular journals all featured the extraordinary woman at least once in their celebration of Progressive personalities.

Known variously as the "girl preacher" and "municipal housekeeper," Crane dazzled American Progressives with her moral commitment to social redemption and her no-nonsense investigations. She perfectly embodied the blend of "true woman" and "new woman" that twentieth-century middle-class Protestant women sought to become. Were it not for the tremendous personal struggle she endured, her story would end here with brief applause for a woman who defied traditional expectations. But Caroline Bartlett Crane writhed in spiritual uncertainty in her quest for meaningful work and assurance of salvation. Like many other middle-class women in the late nineteenth century, she wrestled to free herself from the constraints of the Victorian home while at the same time transferring the moral imperatives of domesticity to a career outside the home.

The early years of her struggle took place within the confines of a respectable Protestant family. Born in Hudson, Wisconsin, in 1858, Caroline Julia Bartlett was the oldest surviving child of Julia Brown and Lorenzo Dow Bartlett. Her father, one of many children in the nineteenth century named for the famous revival minister Lorenzo Dow, predictably espoused staunch evangelical Protestantism. At the time of his daughter's birth, Bartlett called himself a "medical man" but later left that "profession" to become, in turn, an inventor and steamboat proprietor. His entrepreneurial activities eventually took the family to Hamilton, Illinois, where Caroline spent much of her adolescence. At the age of sixteen, she announced that she wanted to be a liberal minister. Her parents disapproved. In an attempt to please her parents, she taught in a public school in Iowa for four years after graduating in 1879 from Carthage College.

Bartlett's conflict with her parents over her life's work fueled a quest for satisfying work and salvation. Her parents, though religious, could not countenance their daughter crossing cultural barriers to become a minister. The daughter, thus thwarted in her goal, continued in a profession she did not enjoy and to which she felt little commitment. The tension between daughter and parents finally took its toll on her health. After four years of teaching, Caroline Bartlett suffered from an unspecified illness that made teaching responsibilities unbearable and forced her to end her association with the public school. In 1883 she boldly set out to rejuvenate her exhausted emotional resources. Bartlett traveled west to Dakota Territory and lived alone for six months on a homestead claim. Establishing a home of her own and distancing herself from her parents restored her capacity to work and revived her spirits. At the end of the period, she prepared to embark on a new career. But the ties of family and culture proved durable. For instead of pursuing her dream of becoming a minister, she moved to Minnesota to join the reporting staff of the *Minneapolis Tribune*.

Newspaper work proved as unrewarding as teaching had been. After two years reporting news for the *Tribune*, Bartlett accepted the editorship of the *Oshkosh Daily Times*. Returning to the state of her birth and working again at "correcting papers" must have reawakened her old discomfort. Six months after accepting the position of editor, she turned her back on newspaper work forever. Once more, she heeded the call of the West when pressure in her career mounted. In 1886 she returned to

South Dakota—but this time to accept a pastorate with an isolated Unitarian congregation in Sioux Falls. With three years of practical experience behind her, Bartlett moved to Kalamazoo, Michigan, in 1889 to accept the call of another Unitarian congregation.

Caroline Bartlett's restlessness gave way to contentment once she stilled her inner turmoil about work. Having finally found the strength to stand against the Victorian restraints of her family, she drew on domestic values learned at her mother's side to infuse her pastoral work with meaning. "She has never been merely a woman who preached," wrote Paul Kellogg in the *American Magazine* in 1909, "but a woman who carried the traditional concerns of womanhood into her pastorate."[98]

From the beginning, Bartlett's work at the People's Church in Kalamazoo merged professional duties of the ministry with the domestic responsibilities left undone by families disrupted by industrial development. Already in her early thirties, Bartlett administered the church with a combination of moral authority and rational planning, much the same as most Victorian women ran their homes. She pored over plans for a new building in the early 1890s, trying to anticipate the congregation's needs and the space required to fulfill them. Like a pleased bride in her first home, Bartlett exclaimed years later that the church family had been happy in its carefully planned abode. As the head of a seven-day institutional church, Bartlett acted the part of surrogate wife and mother for members of the church. Under her direction the church "reared" many of Kalamazoo's otherwise unattended children. The People's Church established a free public kindergarten, classes for boys and girls in manual training and household science, and a gymnasium. On weekday nights, the pastor helped serve ten-cent dinners to working men, and she organized wholesome family entertainment in a choral union, orchestra, literary club, and Audubon Society. For seven years she successfully blended domestic and professional responsibilities.[99]

Bartlett's romantic involvement with Dr. Augustus Crane in the mid-1890s, however, may have aroused old anxieties about work and salvation. She chose for a spouse a man whose profession evoked memories of her father's. Crane, a prominent radiologist, melded Lorenzo Bartlett's inventiveness and his practice as a medical man into a daunting figure of authority. As Bartlett's husband, he represented domestic duty that she feared would diminish her effectiveness as a professional. The congregation magnified her concerns by informing her in myriad ways of their anger at being "abandoned." Unrestrained weeping at the end of her wedding ceremony told her that they "believed the bride belonged to them." When one of the children heard of the event the next day, he burst into tears and sobbed, "Why didn't somebody stop it! What did they let it go on for!"[100] After seven years of harmonious relations with the administrative board of her church, Crane suddenly found obstacles in formerly open avenues of communication.[101] Within weeks of her surprise wedding, the new Mrs. Crane fell victim to another long and debilitating illness. At the age of thirty-eight, she faced a marriage that stirred old worries and a congregation that no longer welcomed her professional labors. Mrs. Crane found herself in the middle of a nightmare—immobilized by fear while exaggerated figures of father, husband, and children hovered above her as terrifying reminders of the difficult choices she had to make. And she knew that to choose any of the alternatives could rob her of mortal or eternal bliss. In 1898 Caroline Bartlett Crane resigned from the Kalamazoo People's Church.

For the next three years, Crane dropped out of public life to wrestle privately with her life's work and her own salvation. Although the first five years of her marriage were marred by illness and inactivity and the last two years of her ministry were ruined by dissension, Crane nevertheless had not succumbed fully to her malaise. In 1897 in an attempt to repair strained relations with women in the church, she organized a cooking class for young women and enrolled in it herself. Moreover, failing to find a teacher for the course, she instructed them in the principles of nutrition and efficient preparation of food. Like her earlier teaching experience, this one was short-lived, ending within a year. But it gave her a new vision of women's possibilities. The course promoted principles of rational homemaking and encouraged housewives to consult expert nutritionists and to raise the level of their haphazard style of cooking to professional standards. Domestic tasks conducted professionally promised greater rewards, such as a healthier family and more free time to cultivate interests outside the home. For unmarried women, it opened opportunities in helping professions to infuse work outside the home with domestic morality. For all women it offered the chance to shoulder social responsibilities in socially acceptable ways, to revitalize domesticity into meaningful work, and to experience tangible emotional and material rewards for labor. Saved from purposelessness, Protestant women, like their male counterparts, could revel in the exhilarating daily doses of approval from others that made life seem worthwhile and salvation near at hand.

When she made her dramatic reappearance, Crane began to forge the two fragments of her life—domesticity and professional ministry—

into a full career as a "public housekeeper." To escape the boredom of routine housekeeping chores, Crane began photographing the back-yards, alleys, and streets in her neighborhood. She shocked middle-class women with pictures of the filth surrounding their respectable homes and won overwhelming support for forming the Civic Improvement League in 1901. The women began a lively campaign of clean-up and sanitation drives that culminated in 1903 with the Kalamazoo city coun-cil's decision to let Crane and the league administer the municipal street-cleaning department. Within weeks the Civic Improvement League dem-onstrated that middle-class housewives managed the service quite effec-tively. As the president of the league, Crane launched an investigation of meatpacking businesses near the city and lobbied for stricter state in-spection laws. The league inspected dairies, orphanages, asylums, hos-pitals, jails, schools, and playgrounds and submitted reports on their condition as well as recommendations for improvement. Under Crane's leadership, the league made Kalamazoo into the "Spotless Town of the Northwest."[102] By the end of the first decade of the twentieth century, Caroline Crane had visited dozens of cities across the country to inspect, assess, and clean.

Crane's fame as a public housekeeper provided a meaningful solu-tion to her problem of inactivity and a salve to her wounded soul. But just as important, it appealed to other middle-class women because it inves-ted their work with larger social purpose. In 1909 one woman explained to Mabel Potter Daggett, a reporter for the *Delineator*, why she and others participated in the Civic Improvement League: "Something seems very hard and difficult, and we say, Oh, this surely we can never do. Then Mrs. Crane talks a little. Pretty soon you begin to feel all buoyed up and, whiff! the difficulties have floated away like thistle down. Then, first you know, you're doing the thing you couldn't do, and suddenly it's done."[103] Her emphasis lay on her state of mind rather than on the task to be performed.

Like their husbands, many middle-class women found that working with others in a common cause "buoyed" them and made the task reward-ing, not so much because it was essential labor as because it stirred up feelings of usefulness. Crane succeeded in inducing "society girls" to serve as volunteer probation officers in Juvenile Court for similar rea-sons. As Daggett put it, "To other of the poor rich girls of Kalamazoo, starving for activity, who have come to her with the plea, 'Can't you find some things for us to do?' she has assigned the work of what she calls 'lifting the mortgage from a child's life.'"[104] The girls' work helped many people, but it was the feeling of purpose that attracted the young ladies to the labor. Still a member of the People's Church, though no longer its pastor, Crane helped organize monthly mothers' meetings for women whose children stayed at the church's day center. There, the women could learn how to "do the best for their little children with the time and the strength they had." Mrs. Crane fondly remembered that in the "friendly conferences," women "seemed to come nearer to each other," and she concluded that "few things seemed . . . more useful" for women in search of assurance. [105] Once again the reward for motherhood came not so much from inner satisfaction as from approval from and cooperation with others.

Crane's example extended domesticity into public professions. She gave helping professions, which had expanded in response to large social needs, moral authority. One of Crane's biographers, Sarah Comstock, noted that "woman has already been robbed of many of her ancient pursuits," but that she had begun "to seek new outlets for her energy" by "attending to such matters as doing away with a city's smoke, putting in order its back yards, sweeping its streets." [106] If homes could not provide a full occupation, then professions outside the home would keep alive the flame of domestic morality. Visiting nurses, not overtired wives, could tend the ill. Public school teachers, not working mothers, spent most of the day with children. Social workers, not ideal "true women," could promote domestic harmony. The professionals performed their tasks as social responsibilities rather than as private duties.

Crane supported both visiting housekeepers and visiting nurses in her recommendations for municipal reform because these professionals would improve the quality of home life among the poor. The visiting housekeeper offered advice, instruction, and assistance in daily chores. The housekeeper—"the somebody who cares"—offered a reason for keeping a clean house to women who despaired, "What's the use? Who cares, anyway!" But she also accustomed the women to expert advice by including it in her friendly visits. By making suggestions for economical marketing, nutritious recipes, and more efficient methods of housecleaning, "her sympathy and advice and instruction gradually raise the woman out of the slough of despond." Likewise, the visiting nurse undertook the care and nurture of the ill or disabled and simultaneously legitimized the authority of professional healthcare specialists. "She makes her rounds like a doctor," one reporter wrote, "stopping here to bathe a fever patient, there to bring clean bed linens for a paralytic, and again to instruct an ignorant mother in the scientific feeding that shall save a baby's life."[107] The specialist educated women in the highest ideals of domesticity. Her reward was gratitude and fulfilling professional work. The housewife could rest assured that she had met her domestic responsibilities by deferring to the appropriate experts. Looking to one another for fulfillment diminished the anxieties of both housewife and professional and thereby legitimized the influence of outsiders in the management of the home.

By the 1920s Crane's rational vision of self-realization for women in the home and outside of it found expression in Everyman's House. In 1925 Crane oversaw the construction of a model home for Kalamazoo—a "space-saving, step-saving, time-saving, money-saving small house which . . . is built around the mother and baby of an average American family." Her goal in building a model home was twofold. First, she wanted to encourage women to work more scientifically and efficiently in their homes. Planned to the last detail, Everyman's House took into account "the happily depleted tasks of domesticity" and made work at home still more efficient. Since few women had "the time, the energy, and the initiative to analyze and reconstruct their methods," Crane believed it was up to experts like herself, businessmen, advertisers, and other professionals to demonstrate more effective homemaking practices. She legitimized the intrusion of specialists into the woman's sphere as an affirmation of the importance of domesticity and, ironically, as an improvement on women's domestic expertise.[108]

Crane's second goal was to open a window to greater rewards for women as homemakers. She wanted to promote the private sphere as an opportunity for women to perform "valuable specialized service" to the nation. Crane had discovered during the Great War that women who volunteered to help in the war effort apologized to registrars, "Well, I am just a housewife!" She praised the "trained registrar" who had made women "feel that being a housewife marked her an important person." Crane went on to acclaim "private talks" with middle-class women "whose lives had become confused and inarticulate to them." She hoped by building and furnishing a model home and by demonstrating modern household procedures, she could renew their "rejoicing" and "self-respect" and show them that their "daily tasks and sacrifices in child care were actually a part of what was going to be the wealth and salvation of America in the next generation!"[109] The social gospeler in Crane designed Everyman's House to grant women the chance for salvation in modern terms.

Everyman's House also stood as a monument to Crane's success in fashioning a satisfying life work from domesticity and profession. She combined the ideals of the "true woman" and "new woman" into an identity that gave her a place in the modern world of work and that promised salvation. During her career as a public housekeeper, Crane cleaned, sanitized, and approved more than sixty cities in the United States. She conducted scientific investigations that probed into the darkest corners of squalid urban centers, and she aired statistics of social and economic life long hidden from public inspection. During one of her campaigns for more strenuous meat inspection laws, Crane substituted peanut butter for lard in a puckish ploy to convince legislators how easy it was to sidestep the current laws. In her model home, she strove for the highest standards of sanitation. She insisted, for example, on "pure white" enamel paint for woodwork so that the housewife would have no doubt about dirt to be removed. She also took inordinate pride in viewing "a trayful of freshly laundered dishes" in her kitchen because they represented her victory over invisible hordes of germs.[110]

Like many Protestant women of her generation, Caroline Bartlett Crane found in reform that was inspired by the social gospel and progressivism a partial resolution of the dilemma facing her. By participating in reform, she and they avoided the empty frustration of remaining cloistered at home and fulfilled—albeit in new ways—the expectations of caring for their families. In ways she probably did not intend, the Reverend Crane helped confer moral authority on an emerging consumer culture. She helped link women's salvation to a culture of professionalism that endorsed a secular ideal of expertise. Thus, the religious formulation gave moral weight to a cultural ideal that made up part of the foundation of bureaucratic life and consumer capitalism. Crane's implementation of social salvation merged moral and cultural imperatives. This merger, while liberating ambitious women from the constraints of domesticity, had implications beyond the immediate fulfillment of individual women. It granted moral legitimacy to an emerging cultural system that made spiritual life dependent on the temporal world.

.   .   .

As young people, Washington Gladden, Shailer Mathews, and Caroline Bartlett Crane quietly rebelled against Protestant individualism, which they had found to be inadequate for making sense of work. Like other middle-class Protestants in the late nineteenth century, they tried to wrest spiritual meaning from work in corporations and professions that were larger and more specialized than the workplaces and trades of their fathers. Their incorporation of work into their vision of salvation testifies to the force of the cultural imperatives of their youth. Gladden, Mathews, and Crane recast those older values and expectations into modern forms because they realized that they lived in an altered social arena.

A heroic social mission had captured their imagination. Work in an institutional church, an urban parish, or a progressive university offered the chance to serve those who needed assistance and to achieve a sense of purpose and reward more compelling than the ethereal promises of evangelical exhorters. Social gospelers demanded tangible signs of salvation and found them, they believed, in Christian missions that yielded approving glances and expressions of gratitude from others. They savored the warm emotional glow that came from helping the disinherited. The mission itself involved instructing the recipients of their good will in middle-class domestic propriety. Careful household economy, proper family nurture, and protection of childhood in working-class homes, social gospelers believed, would narrow the material and spiritual gap between laborers and middle-class Protestants. And it was a gospel to foster progress and harmony in modern society—terms that reflect its bourgeois origin.

Yet under the surface of social mission, barely concealed, were intensely private impulses. Social gospelers encouraged Protestants to seek personal well-being and private morality. They insisted that social involvement yielded great personal reward. They urged their readers to enjoy life rather than to worry about the afterlife because heavenly assurance seemed to have become vague and unattainable. The reassurance of others and the cultivation of temporal rewards shifted spiritual reward from otherworldly to immediate and earthly sources. In an attempt to carry out the social mission and to feel worthwhile in a world grown larger and more organized, they endorsed "team spirit" at work, therapeutic social relations, and a "gospel" of intense feeling.

In their historic statement of the Social Creed, social gospelers affirmed the necessity of leisure as well as a heroic social mission to find meaning in life and work. Their emphasis on play as a means of recreating the vitality for work was readily accepted by workers dispirited by labor in factory and office. Recreation reinforced teamwork and authentic experience to be derived from labor and offered a greater possibility for creativity and control of the situation. Moments of leisure—and accompanying hilarity and excitement—punctuated otherwise humdrum working days. As the authors of the Social Creed had written, leisure represented the "highest condition" of mankind. In their demand for leisure and their insistence that man is truly alive only outside of work social gospelers inadvertently shifted the focus of salvation away from labor and in the direction of play. Recreation, private consumption, entertainment, and team play did more than revitalize workers: increasingly these activities set the standard for appropriate behavior, involvement with others, and personal reward. Time away from work was not idle repose, but a chance to learn how to live, to embrace a team, to feel the spirit. The vision of salvation implicit in the promise of leisure, therefore, undermined the one based on work. The object of work became leisure, not the kingdom of God, and the object of leisure became creative enjoyment, not necessarily devotion to significant work. Indeed, work, social life, and leisure became less distinctly different, at least in ideal terms.

For a generational group unsure of what it meant to be Protestant, middle-class, entrepreneurs, and housewives, work defined by social gospel missions and the helping professions provided a satisfying structure for identity and achievement. The notion of making oneself was transformed, even as it flourished in the twentieth century. Unlike the highly individualistic, self-made man of the Age of Jackson, the self-made man (and now woman) of the twentieth century shared "success" with others on the "team" who made any endeavor possible. Winning involved attaining the object of one's struggle as well as drawing successfully on the personal resources of others in undertaking the struggle. Moreover, a large number of professions that men entered involved work with children, the sick, the unprotected—feminine duties in the guise of manly endeavor, adventurous crusade, fearless action. Work in the twentieth century and the social gospel altered the definition of masculinity. Men who obeyed the great laws of service, sacrifice, and love in their reform activities, in the helping professions, and in the workaday world commanded respect. They fulfilled manly duties, but in ways different from those of their fathers.

Women like Caroline Bartlett Crane set out to break down the wall between separate spheres of work. Since domestic management had lost much of its social base and significance as well as personal reward by the end of the century, women looked to charitable and professional work in the public arena to validate their labor and their existence. They often performed tasks similar to those their mothers had undertaken, as they worked on behalf of children and families. Often their careers ended with marriage or their chance of marital bliss ended with the commitment to a profession. Some like Crane, combined the two roles, and discovered an escape from the "parasitism" of domesticity. Work in the budding helping professions did not necessarily mean freedom from confinement. Instead it meant a new kind of confinement, one in which women and men were bound by the rules of bureaucratic structure, professional standards, and the imperatives of consumer culture. Because these opportunities came in response to an agenda of Protestant reform, women's striving took on moral meaning that helped grant moral authority to the purveyors of secular culture. Thus, for women and men, the reform that had consumed their energy, commitment, and youth helped give strength to a pervasive faith in consumer culture.

The very suggestion that the woman's sphere no longer satisfied women's longing for moral purpose suggests yet another dimension of a vast transformation that occurred at the end of the nineteenth century. Relationships between parents and children, the purpose of family life, and the values passed from one generation to the next came under question, and they showed themselves to be out of synch with modern American life. Families not only provide the locus of social learning, but they also shape the message children will learn. Children of middle-class Protestant families, for example, had begun to think about work and salvation differently, in part because of subtle changes in parental roles and authority in family life. As they formed families of their own, they reshaped the values they imparted to their own children by welding the principles of social Christianity to the ironclad Protestantism of their youth. In this way social gospelers set the terms, however uncertain and ill-defined, of spiritual life for their children. The rich texture of family patterns in the late nineteenth and early twentieth centuries complements and heightens the complicated scheme of a society and culture in flux, for both were woven from the same strands of change. In the tangled filial ties of turn-of-the-century America lie further clues to the origin and appeal of the social gospel.

3

AMERICAN FAMILIES AND

THE SOCIAL GOSPEL

As social gospelers surveyed society in the late nineteenth century, one of the chief problems they observed was the deterioration of family life. They focused on the deplorable living conditions of the urban poor that made family morality virtually impossible to maintain. When Josiah Strong wrote *The Challenge of the City* (1907), for example, he cited a host of problems that undermined the Victorian ideal of domesticity among urban working-class families. Workers rarely owned their own homes because they could not afford the high price of land. They rented apartments and moved frequently, which contributed to the instability of their family life. Many workers lived in crowded tenement buildings, which produced a "rapidly growing class of malcontents." It was no wonder. Strong told of a visit to one tenement where he found "a courtesan," "a former leader in the Salvation Army . . . half-drunk," "a snoring, disgusting negro wench," and "opium-eating, licentious Italian," and a "swarm" of unattended children.[1] Poverty, crowded slum conditions, and the necessity for both parents to work made it difficult for working-class families to duplicate the moral training and respectability of their middle-class counterparts.

In *The Challenge of the City*, Strong went on to explain how Protestants who were committed to social salvation included the uplift of working-class families as part of their program of reform. He cited more than a dozen institutional churches and settlement houses in such cities as New York, Boston, Chicago, Cleveland, and St. Paul that addressed the needs of working-class families. If bathing facilities were lacking in tenement homes, institutional churches tried to provide them. If families failed to keep children from the evil influences of the street, reform-oriented churches organized social clubs, lecture series, and legitimate entertainment to attract them to more wholesome influences. Since working mothers were "ignorant of household economy," social gospelers offered classes in cooking, sewing, and domestic management. "In the great social organism of the city," Strong declared, "when the home fails, the church sometimes takes its functions."[2]

Social gospel programs aimed at shoring up working-class family life were not limited to those outlined by Josiah Strong. Indeed, many institutional churches like the People's Church in Kalamazoo and Walter Rauschenbusch's church in Hell's Kitchen went much further. They provided free or inexpensive meals for families and single working men. They established day nurseries for children of working parents and mothers' meetings to share ideas on child care. Their sponsorship of visiting housekeepers and visiting nurses provided expert sanitary and medical advice and service. One institutional church in Sioux City, Iowa, even administered an unemployment office to find work for heads of households and a clinic with doctors and nurses available around the clock. Social gospelers across the country addressed their concerns over family life by implementing programs and reforms to improve the physical and spiritual well-being of families victimized by industrial exploitation and urban squalor.[3]

Concerns for the working class and for the nation, however, were not the only reasons American Protestants in the late nineteenth century took an interest in family life. Middle-class families also experienced the shocks of social change that altered the Victorian ideal of domesticity. A dissatisfaction with the individualistic religion of their parents, for instance, reflected social gospelers' ambivalence toward their elders as well as toward their beliefs. The social gospelers' experience in the late nineteenth century helps explain why middle-class Americans who embraced the social gospel defined it as they did. As children they learned from their parents about the dominant culture outside their home. Their parents transmitted cultural explanations for life and death, religious beliefs and practices, and the values necessary to make one's life meaningful.[4]

Part of the social gospelers' anguish arose as they found that these explanations, beliefs, practices, and values were not always applicable in the changing social arena of the late 1800s. Their interest in working-class families was but one expression of a much larger concern with the function, organization, and place of families in modern society. Their redefinition of the heavenly family—God, the Father, and Jesus, the Son—suggests that their reform of the family was not limited to the working class. Indeed, as their work suggests, many Protestant ministers and writers in the late nineteenth century were attracted to the social gospel in part because of their frustration as children in Victorian families in the 1870s and 1880s. Understanding American Protestants' articulation and embrace of a social gospel that addressed family matters requires us to comprehend family life as social gospelers experienced it and redefined it.

. . .

In the early nineteenth century, when most social gospelers' parents were born, Americans considered families the moral center of the nation. Home and hearth provided refuge from the brutality of market competition and were relied upon to build individual character. While the middle-class home presented a striking counterpoint to the market, it also prepared men and women to take their places in one of the nineteenth-century American "separate spheres"—work or domesticity. Under the moral tutelage of "true women," Victorian children learned the difference between right and wrong. They learned to place faith in an unseen power in the universe, and they internalized the values of hard work and self-control that were necessary for work in a market capitalist society as well as for gaining salvation. Childrearing practices of moral suasion, of intense nurture, and of individual punishment thus reinforced the inner direction necessary for success in the market. These practices also laid the groundwork for faith in individual salvation. In other words, in their families, children learned what to do in order to survive and to succeed in market capitalist society. Their faith in a well-ordered universe grew out of and supported their understanding of social existence.[5]

When they began families of their own in the 1850s and 1860s, these men and women conveyed many of the same values, ideas and beliefs to their children. Many social gospelers recalled the moral training, repression and discipline, and individualism of their childhoods. Shailer Mathews, born in 1863, described the "Puritan" training he received from his parents. He described Jonathan and Sophia Mathews as "sincerely religious" parents whose "discipline of the family was steady but not severe." Walter Rauschenbusch, also born in the early 1860s, remembered being whipped by his father for having questioned his Sunday school lesson and his father's authority as teacher of the class. He and his two sisters were expected to behave piously and decorously. Francis McConnell's father was a "widely known evangelistic minister" whom his son described as "Puritanic" and "overexacting." McConnell, born in 1871, remembered his youth as a time when "repression was thought to be a mark of genuine religion." Charles Sheldon, born in 1857, recalled the characteristics of his youth as "hard work, self-control, and individual achievement."[6] Many others reported having been raised in Victorian homes and immersed in individualistic, evangelical Protestantism.

Neither the parents nor the children could have anticipated the ways in which social change would undermine the "fit" of such values. Out of the success of individual enterprise, investment, and accomplishment came an economic order of capitalized, highly organized companies that limited the arena for individual action and control. Out of a concern for the spread of disorder caused by intemperance, prostitution, slavery, and other assorted evils came reform bureaucracies that emphasized organization over the individual actor. These developments also created fields of social endeavor and literary avocation for women that began to warp the orderly functioning of the family. The industrial order that weakened the ideal of individual enterprise for men altered the world of women as well. Hospitals, large companies, food processors, public schools, and the helping professions offered services that before the Civil War had been performed almost exclusively in the home.[7]

The middle-class generation that came of age in the midst of this transformation felt pulled in two directions. They tried to live by the Victorian values of their parents at a time when those values were, it seemed, becoming outmoded and unworkable. This tension between expectation and aspiration prompted in those who would articulate and embrace the social gospel a reconsideration of family life. Their religion, entwined as it was with family, was inevitably affected. In seeking a contemporary faith, they developed a more egalitarian and cooperative notion of family life, less differentiated from broader, also increasingly cooperative, social experience.

The social gospel was an effort to address the obvious problems of family life in urban, industrial America. The free meals, nurseries, settlement houses, and ministries of Crane, Rauschenbusch, and others testify eloquently to that concern. But there was more than social outreach at issue; all of this was driven by an inward trouble in middle-class family life. Key tenets of the social gospel emerged out of young

Protestants' painful experiences as men and women coming of age, equipped (or misequipped, as they saw it) with the values of Victorian family life. The social gospel bore the marks of their anguish. It offered advice on appropriate family relations and the process of identity formation; the new gospel that they would address to their own children paved the way for the companionate families, other-directed personality, and social religion that emerged in the early twentieth century.

Families were unable to supply male or female roles fit for emulation in the changed condition of post–Civil War America. Fathers in particular seem to have been distant and daunting examples of achievement who in spite of their success seemed to offer little direction to their children. The children, consequently, felt under great uncertainty as they set out to find their life's work and to secure their own identities. A surprisingly large number suffered nervous collapses, and all suffered the anxiety of being unprepared for the lives they were being called upon to make in industrializing America. Washington Gladden, who experienced a nervous collapse at the outset of his ministerial career, and Caroline Bartlett Crane, who succumbed to a nervous breakdown after four years of teaching school in Iowa, presented dramatic cases of private conflict over cultural expectations. Frank Mason North, Shailer Mathews, Charles Fiske, Charles Jefferson, George Herron, and Lyman Abbott found it difficult to settle on careers and moved from one profession to the next in search of their callings. Charles Macfarland, who later became the general secretary of the Federal Council of Churches, started out as a businessman until he became paralyzed by his conscience. Some women who challenged the stifling expectations for members of their sex found that the exertion robbed them of any power to act. Elizabeth Stuart Phelps, Charlotte Perkins Gilman, Mary Perley Macfarland, and Jane Addams, for instance, all reported lengthy nervous breakdowns that derived from uncertainty about their purpose and goals in life. [8]

Middle-class Protestants' lack of certainty, identity, and purpose in industrial America caused them to suffer in the unappealing separate spheres of home and work, not entirely sure of alternatives. Men and women alike were torn, as Charlotte Perkins Gilman put it, between "old duties and new ambitions." The "confusion, suffering, and nervous strain" that she believed would result from conflicting ideas pervaded the generation that embraced the social gospel and evinces the difficult choices they had to make. [9] Charles Stelzle, for instance, had an opportunity to go to Germany for a prized university education. Setting out on his own to make his way in a foreign land would have approached the ideal of manly endeavor to which he was supposed to aspire. At the last moment, however, his mother refused to let him go. Released from a terrible isolation yet deprived of the chance to prove himself, young Stelzle responded with ambivalence. "I didn't know whether to weep or feel relieved," he later wrote.[10] Another social gospeler remembered his disquiet when the president of his alma mater asked him, "What are you going to do in the world?" As a trembling undergraduate and later as a commencement speaker retelling the story, Charles Monroe Sheldon hoped for "new opportunities in old professions"—opportunities for "winning that horrible thing called success."[11] Neither Stelzle nor Sheldon found satisfaction in competitive endeavor, but they were also unsure of the morality of embracing something softer than rugged individualism. They were part of a generation caught between two sets of expectations.

The generation that uttered and acclaimed the social gospel felt trapped by the demands of Victorian parents. Yet they were determined to breathe life into the roles they had to play. Social gospelers did not intend to make a radical break with the past. They wanted to adapt Victorian expectations to modern reality. Accordingly, they continued to insist on individual regeneration as well as social responsibility, and they accepted the values of domesticity even though they chose to carry them out in different ways. Their anguish is instructive because it alerts us to the power of family, tradition, and residual beliefs among people whose ideology nonetheless affirms an avant-garde culture. They could escape neither their tradition nor their future.

As young men and women, social gospelers began to speak out against the beliefs of their parents. As early as the 1880s, they began to frame social questions that essentially asked how individuals could be held responsible for failures caused by society. Washington Gladden urged fellow Protestants to apply Christian principles to society in the 1880s as labor unrest and industrial exploitation threatened to rend the nation in two. His "applied Christianity" provided a language for other younger critics of industrializing America. Harry Emerson Fosdick questioned many fundamental beliefs as a young collegian, and when he decided to pursue a career in the ministry, he embraced a "social gospel." He later admitted that he harbored a "hidden anger" against the church of his youth because of its "wretched play upon my selfish fears and selfish hopes."[12] Walter Rauschenbusch, who in 1878 wanted to be "respected" and to "become a man" by joining the church, later declared that this conversion was not satisfying. Ten years later, in 1888, while serving a working-class parish in New York City, he underwent a second conversion. This time Rauschenbusch chose to dedicate his life to redeeming humanity rather than to saving himself. As he explained in 1909 to John S. Phillips, "When I entered the theological seminary at 22 I had no outlook except the common evangelicalism. There was absolutely nothing in our Seminary course at that time to turn my attention to social questions or to impart social passion. Nothing in my home life either. But I got somewhere, I don't know where, the idea that I must 'live over again the life of Christ.'" A few years later Rauschenbusch noted that seminarians in the early twentieth century were investigating social questions in their theses because his generation had paved the way for them. [13]

By 1914 Shailer Mathews could remark in *The Individual and the Social Gospel,* "It was not so many years ago that successful men held up as inspiration for the young were those who were warriors or who had made great fortunes." Individual achievement in 1914, however, was "not a guaranty of popularity." Instead, "a man who represents the best social ideals," he argued, "is regarded as the best man of his time."[14] The key words here are "popularity" and "social ideals." By the time Mathews offered this characterization of "the best man of his time," acceptance by others and aspiration to collective goals had replaced inner satisfaction and individual responsibility as the cornerstones of personality and faith. It was not enough to work hard, to control oneself, and to fix one's sights on an individual accomplishment. The individual had to consider those around him and the aims of his society as the context in which he would do his life's work and strive for salvation. Fitting in with others had become the social imperative of Mathews's generation and the basis of religious peace. And the social gospel was an important source of "the best social ideals" of the turn of the century.

Interest in the problems of working-class families was, of course, one example of social gospelers' interest in social questions. Demanding improved living conditions, educational opportunities, and social life for working-class families exemplified the social ideals of which Mathews spoke. In 1904, Charles Stelzle addressed the problem of deteriorating family life in a book called *Boys of the Street: How to Win Them.* "The home no longer influences the average boy as it did in the days when society had fewer claims upon us," he wrote. Stelzle recognized that the lack of parental guidance was "serious enough in the refined home. But what can we say for the boy who has no place that is a real home, but simply a lodge where he spends the night?" Stelzle reached out to the boys whose "homes consist of only one or two small rooms in a tenement house, sometimes back of a dark, dingy alley." "The boy in such a home," Stelzle insisted, "rarely has the sympathy of his father."[15] Stelzle thought that one way to shore up the families of such boys was to organize boys' clubs to keep the boys out of trouble. He urged churches to sponsor these groups to build character, to instill cooperation, and to provide a moral alternative to the evils of the city. The result was that churches and boys' club leaders performed tasks of child nurture once left to the family, helping to instill social ideals that would enable working-class children to survive in urban industrial America.

As Stelzle's allusion to the absence of "parental oversight and training" in the "refined home" indicates, social gospelers did not limit their discussion of family life to the working class. They recognized that middle-class families were not the domestic ideals of Victorian America. In 1912, for example, Clarence Barbour asserted in *Making Religion Efficient* that "the large majority of homes today are merely places in which a boy may eat and sleep. The original prerogatives of the father and mother, so far as they pertain to the physical, social, mental, and moral development of boyhood, have been farmed out to other organizations in the community." Barbour saw that social institutions and helping agencies had altered the American family. Yet he, like many others, did not believe that that was bad. His suggestions for reform legitimized the emergence of companionate families rather than advocating the revival of the Victorian family of his youth. Barbour urged parents to include their boys in "the direction of family life," to make them "partners," and to replace parental authority with a spirit of "comradeship."[16]

Many social gospelers agreed with Barbour that the church had a stake in redefining family ties. "Fathers usually feel unfitted to do much of the personal work with their boys," wrote the architects of the Men and Religion Forward Movement, "and the boy's friends in the church must certainly not neglect it." They urged the formation of "leagues of friendship" to guide young boys the way their fathers once would have helped them. They encouraged Sunday school teachers and ministers to spend one hour each week in "comradeship" to develop "a precious relationship of mutual confidence" with the boys.[17] One author asserted that between churches and schools, professionals outside the home prepared young people for "parenthood and homemaking . . . and the higher life of the home." Henry Cope praised "special organizations created by church and state" to protect the home.[18]

A few years later, another social gospeler proposed a corporate model for family life. In *The Religious Education of Adolescents* (1918), Norman Richardson advised parents across the country to form a "partnership" with their children, "with father and mother as senior members of the firm; each child being apportioned some particular work which contributes directly or indirectly to the comfort of all the others." Instead of direct punishments, common in Victorian families, Richardson suggested using "secret code words" such as "watch your step." He thereby hoped to level authority relationships and to encourage adult behavior in children. He also recommended relinquishing parental authority to a different child each day. One family that followed his advice reported that "the Captain [of the day] took charge of the discipline" and thereby relieved the parents of exercising authority over their children. Richardson's advice made for families with diffuse authority and for individuals dependent on "social ideals" such as "the spirit of the gang" and "partnership."[19] By the 1920s, Harry Munro believed "there is no turning back to the old ways of parental autocracy." In *Agencies for the Religious Education of Adolescents* (1925), he argued that "many home-centered activities" had been "taken over by specialized agencies." He believed that families had to make a "conscious effort" to create "a body of common interests and activities" to give the family any meaning. He proposed a "program of parent training" to be conducted by churches and schools to instill the proper social ideals in families.[20]

. . .

In rethinking appropriate family relations, social gospelers reflected their evolving ideals of fatherhood, individual behavior, and family interaction in their portrayals of God, the Father, and Jesus, the Son, and in their discussions of the Godhead's relation to man. The most remarkable aspect of their work was the emphasis on human agency and the muting of paternal authority. This evidenced growing skepticism of Providential intervention as well as a longing to act independently of parental ideals. God was in many ways much like the earthly fathers who caused so much frustration in social gospelers. He was either omnipotent or absently indulgent. As a result, while social gospelers wrote about both God and Jesus, they more often turned to the Son than to the Father for examples of proper righteous behavior. Over the decades that spanned the two centuries social gospelers recast these two components of family life in ways that reveal a great deal about their conception of appropriate family relations and personal ideals.

Both men and women, of course, supported the social gospel and spoke to concerns of family. But women were not primarily responsible for redefining the roles of God and Jesus. Elizabeth Stuart Phelps's *Story of Jesus Christ* (1897) was exceptional in a spate of works written by men. Women like Phelps, Crane, Mary Perley Macfarland, Mary McDowell, and others who took part in the social gospel as a way to challenge the demands of domesticity approved of the new images of Jesus and God. As a holy exemplar of social reform, the new Jesus validated their efforts at social improvement. As models of a family ideal based on shared authority and responsibility and mutual affection, the social gospelers' God and Jesus helped affirm family life that relieved women of the stifling demands of domesticity. But the new Jesus spoke most powerfully to men. For the images of both God and Jesus were masculine ideals as well as models of family relations. They served as models for young men at a time when emulating their fathers had become problematic. As Albert Schweitzer put it, "There is no historical task which so reveals someone's true self as the writing of a *Life of Jesus*."[21] At the turn of the century, many men thus revealed themselves.

The Jesus to whom many social gospelers had been accustomed as children was largely the product of sentimental Victorian writers. He was neither fully masculine nor feminine: popular illustrations featured a man in a long white gown whose oval face was ringed with wavy locks and a soft brown beard. He was both madonna and man. As such, Jesus represented simultaneously tender nurture and manly endeavor, and this image helped legitimize the commitment to social service as an acceptable replacement for individual enterprise. Jesus was also a son, which made him a peer instead of an unapproachable figure of authority.

Yet social gospelers were not satisfied with the softness of this kind of Jesus. Walter Rauschenbusch insisted that "there was nothing mushy, nothing sweetly effeminate about Jesus. The Christ-face in art, that gentle oval with the long wavy hair, the full mouth, the meek eyes, is an inheritance . . . of more than questionable value." Rauschenbusch portrayed Jesus differently: "He was the one that turned again and again on the snarling pack of His pious enemies and made them slink away. He plucked the beard of death when He went into the city and the temple to utter those withering woes against the dominant class." Jesus, he concluded, was "a man's man."[22]

Washington Gladden wanted others to recognize that Jesus had dominion over economic as well as religious life. "What sort of a King of men is he who is powerless to control the largest and intensest part of their activity?" he asked in 1893 in *Tools and the Man*. "Under such limitations, the Christian vocation becomes largely a matter of sentiment; what wonder that it is handed over to women and children? We shall never win for our Master the allegiance of the strong men of this world until we show them that he has the power and the purpose to rule the shop and the factory and the counting-room as well as the church and the home." When Charles Macfarland extolled the strength and courage of Jesus in 1912, he confessed, "I know it would have been a great help to me in my boyhood and young manhood had I been led to appreciate the manhood of Jesus."[23]

According to Josiah Strong, interest in Jesus had been growing since mid-century. In 1901 he declared, "During the past fifty years, there has been a vast amount of study expended on the life, the character and the teachings of Jesus, the language he spoke, the people he taught, the times and the land in which he lived."[24] With the appearance of dozens of scholarly treatments and imaginative reconstructions of the life of Jesus, American Protestants could follow "in the footsteps of the master" from "manger to throne," or they could stand in the "shadow of the cross" and answer the "call of the carpenter." They longed to know what he had said (or might have said), how he appeared to his contemporaries, the condition of his life, and his attitudes on a wide range of social and political questions. Many even speculated as to what Jesus would do were he confronted by the confusion of modernity.[25] The interest in Christ was not confined to schools of theology. Novels about Jesus abounded and were read by thousands of middle-class Protestants. Churchgoers across the nation in humble country churches and in magnificent urban temples also began to worship the carpenter more directly than ever before. The principal denominational publishing houses produced a spate of new hymnals that banished the vengeful Jehovah of Isaac Watts and featured in his stead the Nazarene of Fanny Crosby. "What a friend we have in Jesus," they joyfully intoned.[26] To Jesus they carried their burdens, and in him they believed.

Between the beginning of the social gospel movement and the 1920s, Jesus underwent a dramatic metamorphosis from the gentle Jesus of Victorianism to the hearty carpenter-reformer of Galilee and finally to the hale organization man of Bruce Barton's imagination. In the late nineteenth century, social gospelers concentrated on making the Savior more robust, muscular, and active than the sweet, sad man in flowing

gowns featured in sentimental literature. In keeping with the trend toward realism in American culture and toward historical criticism in
theology, authors who wrote about Jesus tried to reconstruct his life and
give him more realistic characteristics. For instance, since Jesus was a
Jew who had learned carpentry from his father and later worked with
fishermen, his biographers gave him dark hair and eyes, a well-
developed physique, and rough, calloused hands. The Reverend
Thomas De Witt Talmage traced Jesus' movements from obscure origins
through his ministry in *From Manger to Throne* (1890), describing the
Nazarene as an example of industry. "Work! Work! Work!" he exclaimed.
"The boy carpenter! The boy wagon maker! The boy housebuilder! Let all
the weary artisans and mechanics of the earth see thee."[27] Jesus was a
man who worked with his hands, just like the toiling workmen of industrial America.

Jesus' humanness and altered outward appearance resulted in a
changed demeanor. Instead of sentimentalizing the soft-spoken author of
the Beatitudes, social gospelers noted the activism and reforming spirit
of this working man. Jesus the Carpenter appealed to laborers, progressives, and social reformers. In *The Call of the Carpenter* (1911), Bouck
White, a New York settlement house worker, imagined Jesus as a radical
populist. According to White, Jesus was a reformer who believed in a
social gospel. "His ideal is the civic ideal," White declared. "Its goal is
'the holy city descending from God out of heaven.' Therefore the
Carpenter-Christ is the fit leader of the multitudinous."[28]

At the same time that Jesus acquired muscles and a coarse beard and
showed a passion for justice, he also become more congenial and social-
minded. Authors of books about Jesus referred to him as "the Captain,"
"elder brother," and a friend. The man who emerged from these studies
was more approachable, got along with others, and assumed the role of a
team captain—a leader among equals. Shailer Mathews recounted the
evolution of Jesus in his autobiography, *New Faith for Old*. At first Jesus
was "clothed in a bizarre combination of piety, theology, and rabbinical
exposition." Gradually he became "a mid-Victorian of the liberal type"
who supported idealism as long as it was "polite." Then, Mathews argued, Jesus became a "real character."[29] Once scholars began to understand Judaic literature, the social psychology of early Christianity and its
relation to the ancient world, and Jesus' teaching, they began to appreciate him as an example of righteous activism.

The Jesus of the social gospel was a reformer whose service, sacrifice, and love did not prevent him from being an assertive activist. Jesus

did not accomplish his goals entirely alone: he depended on his disciples and followers for cooperation and commitment. Nonetheless, he was an inspiration for real men. As Harry Emerson Fosdick reminded readers of *The Manhood of the Master* (1913), "The Master appeals to all that is strongest and most military in you."[30] Jesus performed his manly duties, but he did so in ways different from the individualistic examples offered by social gospelers' fathers. Jesus affirmed the social ideal; he relieved the unrealistic burdens of individual success and salvation; but he was not effeminate. The young men who had struggled unsuccessfully to live up to the ideals of their parents in the 1880s helped to create and endorse a new set of masculine ideals that were more appropriate in the large-scale workplaces of turn-of-the-century America. This image of Jesus helped ease social gospelers' fears of effeminacy as they engaged in social reform that addressed the domestic needs of their parishioners through collective programs that embodied the ideals of service, sacrifice, and love.

By 1925 Richard B. Niese, editor of the *Nashville Tennessean*, in a book written to help ministers use newspapers more effectively for spreading the social gospel, noted that "the religion of Jesus Christ is sweeping the world like nothing that has ever gone before. . . . The biggest men in the country to-day are proud to proclaim their faith in the Nazarene—and they do so without a blush or a stammer." Niese remembered when "Sunday school was looked upon as a place only for women and children," whereas by the mid-twenties "we have weekly men's luncheon clubs composed exclusively of Bible class members who gather around the table and have an hour of fellowship where campaigns for building standard Sunday schools are planned."[31]

Charles Stelzle, who had built one of the most effective workingmen's churches in New York City, turned to church advertising in the early 1900s. He urged churchmen to appeal to young men by advertising that churches fostered "the best kind of manhood." In *Principles of Successful Church Advertising*, he outlined social reform that required willing volunteers: "We need the sort of men who can do things and who do them because they like to do them. Are you that kind of man?" The question had but one answer to any self-respecting man in the twentieth century.[32]

This discussion of businessmen's luncheons, planning, standard Sunday schools, and advertising is evidence of a subtle shift in the social gospel movement in the 1910s and 1920s. While still dedicated to the social gospel and social reform, many younger social gospelers began to plead for efficiency and businesslike promotion of their ideas.[33] The

socially responsible, progressive reformer became the basis for the socially responsive man of the 1920s. Under these changed perceptions of
the social gospel, the image of Jesus made some subtle shifts as well. By
the 1920s, Jesus' charm, glowing good health, and physical strength,
which had emerged in the progressive portrayals of him, made him an
effective leader of men.

In 1920 Frederick Anderson, in his discussion of "Jesus and his
career," insisted that "the personality of the Man of Nazareth . . . is the
power behind Christian history." Two years later, George Fiske offered
young people "a religion of youth" in which Jesus was "the Peerless Ideal
of Youth." In 1926, Rufus Jones insisted in a *Life of Christ* that
Christians would respond to the "charm of his personality." In these and
other books, the ideal Jesus reflected personal traits that were valued by
corporate America: charm, youth, personality, the ability to work with
others. Charles Fiske and Burton Easton's "real Jesus," for example, was
"impressive in appearance and of great physical strength." Jesus, they
wrote, "was not demonstrative and gushing. Nor, on the other hand, was
he narrow and censorious; no true man is. He was not sad and somber,
but natural and spontaneous. He was glad and free, an out-of-doors man
who loved people, was genial and companionable, unaffected, fond of
the society of his day, meeting people of all sorts in the hearty comradeship of life, likable and lovable, genuine, generous, large-hearted,
straightforward, and strong." Others, such as Bruce Barton and Walter
Denny, emphasized his career as a leader of men. His success in both
cases derived not from his skill as a fisherman, carpenter, or rabbi, nor
even from his relationship to God, the father. Rather, his success depended on his ability to organize and manipulate men.[34]

. . .

The image of God underwent no less dramatic transformation than
Jesus. The God of social gospelers' youth had been a stern and unyielding judge, not unlike the strong men who were their fathers. As the boys
grew to manhood and came to terms with both their fathers and their
faith, they modified this God. As Henry Cope put it in *The Friendly Life*
(1909), "God has grown in our thinking from a giant who makes worlds to
a heart that suffers with ours, a soul that seeks ours, a being who is man's
friend, and who cannot be satisfied until all humanity is embraced in that
friendship." In the same year, William Dawson, remarking on the fatherhood of God, declared: "Take the Old Testament through and through
and the general impression given us of God is of purity, not pity; of
majesty, not compassion; of supreme ineffable righteousness and power

and wisdom—the God of the roaring sea and the live lightning, and the tremendous thunder, not the Parent of little children who claim His love and render in return their filial service. The Old Testament pictures God as a King, not God as a Parent."[35] Dawson preferred God as a parent.

One of the consequences of this portrait, however, was to diminish the importance of the Almighty to his children on earth. Josiah Strong noted in 1910 that in the late nineteenth century "God was gradually and rather unceremoniously bowed out of his universe."[36] God's disappearance was due in part to historical criticism, which attempted to authenticate and verify the historical accuracy of biblical events. God eluded verification. Advances in science had offered an alternative explanation for the creation and development of man that challenged God's power. Confidence in human ability to control and exploit the natural world made some men less dependent on and less attracted to the idea of divine intervention.

The judgmental God of the early nineteenth century was ushered out of his universe also because he was too daunting and inaccessible to men who had rejected their father's stern individualism in religion and vocation. Lyman Abbott explained his aversion to the domineering God of his youth in 1921 in *What Christianity Means to Me*. "Suppose that all your life you dreaded an awful god," he wrote, "or in fear submitted to a fateful God, or hesitated between defying and cringing before a hated God . . . and suddenly the curtain were rent aside and you saw the luminous figure of the living Christ, and over his head were written the words, 'This is thy God, O man.'" Abbott rejected God and embraced the son "Who is upon earth" and who lived a "life of love, service, and sacrifice." Similarly, Walter Rauschenbusch explained why he rarely wrote about God. "The God of the stellar universe is a God in whom I drown," he wrote. "Christ with the face of Jesus I can comprehend, and love, and assimilate. So I stick to him."[37]

In part social gospelers' response to God may have been a subtle, half-conscious response to their fathers, who impressed upon these sons seemingly unfulfillable demands for individual achievement. Young Protestant men rebelled at this ideal even as they tried to surpass their fathers' achievements. In that regard, Fayette L. Thompson, a prominent Methodist who helped organize the Men and Religion Forward Movement in 1911, declared that it meant much more to be a Christian in his time of industrial and social strife than it had when his father was alive: "If the manhood of this generation does not awake to the fact that in order to be a true disciple of Jesus Christ in these days it must be responsive to a bigger program than any program of the past, it will fail utterly to realize the glorious opportunity of the present. It will not do merely to measure up to the programs of our fathers. If we are to meet the expectations of God Almighty, we must match a vaster program than our fathers ever dreamed, because our vision of what constitutes a religious life is a greater vision than the fathers ever had."[38]

This passage, while at one level a straightforward call to faith and religious commitment, illuminates a number of private tensions that characterized family relations in late-Victorian America and that informed religious belief. Phrases like "to measure up," "to realize opportunity," and to "match" programs with their fathers resonate with a yearning to reach and exceed the standard set by fathers. It is revealing that Thompson chose to speak of the "manhood of this generation" rather than simply addressing the young men of his day. Manhood implies the quality and essence of being masculine. Furthermore, he refers to the awakening of this manhood in connection with Jesus, the son of God. Opportunity, manhood, and religion came together for this generation in the person of Jesus. This reference takes on greater significance in light of the two sentences that follow it. The first calls on men to do more than measure up to their fathers, and the second asks men "to meet the expectations of God." By following Jesus, men could realize themselves. God, however, like earthly fathers, made known his expectations, which men then strove to meet or surpass, and in this case, Thompson insists, "our vision of what constitutes a religious life is a greater vision than the fathers ever had." Once troublesome paternal expectations were out of the way, men could pursue their real interest, and for that, they looked to Jesus.

When social gospelers became fathers themselves, they tried to define the relationship with their children in terms of equality and friendship, in keeping with their ideal of Jesus. Perhaps in order to prevent the frustration they had felt toward their fathers, they befriended their children and in their advice literature urged other parents to treat their children as "chums." Charles Macfarland, for example, romped with his growing family, joined the Boy Scouts with his sons, and played baseball with all his children. Walter Rauschenbusch told his son Hilmar: "There is no love available to you which is so unvarying and always trustworthy as the love of your mother and father. . . . You must help us make the transition from parenthood to friendship."[39]

This "friendship" changed the nature of the parent-child relationship, and it served the younger people well in a society increasingly based on interdependence. Instead of the old model of individual drive, social gospelers offered an example of cooperation and teamwork. This new model broke down the older relationship based on paternal authority. Identity depended in part on the individual's relationship to a group. Thus, individualism had meaning only in collective endeavor.

By addressing the problems of working-class family life, by offering new advice to both working- and middle-class families, and by redefining the nature of God and Jesus, social gospelers helped instill social ideals in American Protestants attracted to their movement. Their frustrations with Victorian family life, their respect for their parents, and the actual disarray of families in urban America all contributed to their reconsideration of family morality and individual piety. The social gospel arose from deep personal impulses. Their reform programs eased both the burdens of working-class families and the psychological burdens of the reformers. The social gospel proved to be an essential link between the dominant Protestant middle-class culture of the nineteenth century and the secular corporate culture of the early twentieth century.

The biographies of Elizabeth Stuart Phelps, Walter Rauschenbusch, and Charles and Mary Perley Macfarland exemplify the family tensions that many social gospelers experienced and that gave rise to their creed. Both Phelps and Rauschenbusch wrestled with the place of paternal authority and appropriate family relations in their private lives and in their work. Both completed memoirs for their fathers, toward whom they felt a combination of admiration and frustration. Both devised imaginative alternatives to Victorian family life. The relationships of the Rauschenbusches and the Macfarlands with their children was an outgrowth of their social gospel. The social gospel that all of them helped articulate found expression because of their relationship with their parents. Their later ideas of parenthood took form because of their religion. Their lives illuminate private impulses that energized the social gospel and help explain how secular culture took root and flourished in Protestant America.

ELIZABETH STUART PHELPS

"Half the meaning of the gentle scene is hidden"

When Elizabeth Stuart Phelps wrote her autobiography, *Chapters from a Life*, in 1896, she gave her father a prominent position in it. According to the writer, Austin Phelps provided impetus for his daughter's literary career, serving as reader and critic of her first attempts at fiction, and it was to him that Elizabeth Phelps dedicated her first book. She wrote that her father represented "the ideal of fatherhood" that gave her "the best conception . . . of the Fatherhood of God."[40] The novelist—whose books explored the meaning of life, the promise of death, and appropriate family arrangements in the late nineteenth century—found inspiration for her religion in her father. To understand her novels, her life, and the social gospel she espoused in both, one must appreciate the bond between parent and child.

Modern scholars who read Elizabeth Stuart Phelps's novels, especially the novels inspired by the social gospel, cannot miss the benevolent God who dwells in her fictional universe. She and her readers understood at least half-consciously that their reasons for constructing a gospel of social salvation lay buried in the complicated patterns and unresolved tensions in their Victorian families. But the process was not that apparent. Like the fog that made the familiar landscape of Gloucester Harbor indefinite and distorted, modern American religion obscured the private anguish within the middle-class American families that produced it. What Phelps wrote of the mists of Gloucester is equally true of her embrace of the social gospel: "Half the meaning of the gentle scene is hidden."[41]

Elizabeth Stuart Phelps loved her father. Born in 1844 in Boston, Massachusetts, Phelps lost her mother eight years later and understandably invested a great deal of emotion in her father. Moreover, she spent much of her adult life near or with Austin Phelps, whose position as a professor of theology at Andover Theological Seminary kept him in the small New England community. When she finally left home, Phelps and her father corresponded regularly. And near the end of his life Austin Phelps asked his devoted daughter to complete his *Memoir*, a task she lovingly undertook and finished in 1891.[42]

At a casual glance, the Phelps family appears to conform to the ideal evoked by liberal Protestantism. The adoring child loved and respected her father, who encouraged all his children to do well and who spared threats of eternal punishment. Austin Phelps inspired his children to love one another, commanded respect for his tender mercy, and "would go out of his way to save a crawling thing from death, or any sentient thing from pain."[43] Indeed, by her testimony, Elizabeth Phelps understood God because she had her father as a model. But bonds between parents and children, between the Almighty and his creatures, are seldom as simple as they might at first appear. Closer examination reveals that

Elizabeth Stuart Phelps

Phelps never felt sure of her father's affection and felt isolated from him even though they occupied the same house for decades. Despite her great adoration, she questioned her father's authority.

The writer's early life provides the first clue to the complicated nature of the Phelps family. Austin and Elizabeth Stuart Phelps celebrated the birth of a daughter in 1844, and they named her Mary Gray Phelps. Mary, named for her mother's sister, took her mother's name when her mother died in 1852. She did not make the name change casually. She had been the last person clasped in her mother's arms before she died and she must have known that her mother's principal "argument" against death was "her first-born." Mother and daughter had been quite close during their eight years together. Both must have been unsettled by the changes in their lives when Austin Phelps gave up a thriving pastorate in Boston to accept a professorship in sleepy Andover. The theologian described the move as "an occasion of unhappiness, and at times a positive affliction." Indeed, the morning he received notice that his congregation had accepted his resignation, Phelps suffered blindness in one eye that lasted for four years—until his wife's death. Once in Andover the chief source of unhappiness between the couple was the young wife's inability to accept God's grace and assurance. In fact, Elizabeth Stuart Phelps turned to writing for solace. She began to write stories about ministers' wives and domesticity, themes that her daughter later explored with greater sophistication. Her daughter attributed her mother's early death to the combined pressures of childbearing, domestic management, and a budding writing career.[44]

Thus in 1852, Austin Phelps was the sole source of love and authority in the girl's life. Later attempts to win her father's affection suggest that young Elizabeth Phelps hoped by taking her mother's name, to take her mother's place in her father's life. She showered her father with love, tried to care for him when he began suffering from insomnia, and remained by his side through much of her adult life. She probably did not miss the irony, however, when her father's next two wives bore the name Mary. Austin Phelps's second wife, Mary Stuart, was the aunt for whom the girl originally had been named, and she died within months of the wedding. His third wife, Mary Johnson, wed Phelps in 1858. Mary Johnson Phelps tried to provide motherly guidance for her stepdaughter, but Elizabeth Phelps rejected her and entered an institute in Andover that was run by a professor's widow.[45]

For his part, Austin Phelps was a member of what Ann Douglas has called a "feminized" clergy in the mid-nineteenth century. Born in 1820, the son of an abolitionist minister, Austin Phelps was described as a "most unpromising" baby. Despite his apparent weakness, young Phelps became a prodigy, reading by the age of two and working advanced mathematical problems at the age of eight. Phelps entered college at the tender age of thirteen after an emotional conversion at one of Charles Finney's revivals in Geneva, New York. In 1840, he graduated with the valedictory from the University of Pennsylvania and immediately earned a license to preach. "I have never ceased to regret that I entered the pulpit in such a juvenile state of culture," he wrote in his memoir. "My mind was in a chaotic state of growth."[46]

After his remarkable intellectual achievements, Austin Phelps produced a mediocre professional record. At the prominent Congregational church in Boston which had called him to its pulpit, he came to despise writing sermons, delivering them, and having "personal conferences with men on the subject of religion." Upon deciding to go to Andover Seminary, over which his father-in-law presided, Phelps burned three hundred of his sermons. "My sermons were—what they were," he wrote, unable to characterize six years of labor. Yet he viewed the removal to Andover as a "revolutionary change," one for which his "tastes and training" were not adapted. He had taken the position to avoid a nervous breakdown. He suffered instead a debilitating affliction of one eye, and his doctor ordered complete cessation of work. An indulgent Andover faculty, undoubtedly prompted by the seminary's president, lightened the young professor's teaching load and let him work at his own pace. For the next three decades, Phelps complained of ill health, insomnia, and overwork. He retired in his early fifties, an age when many other men are at the pinnacle of power and accomplishment. Austin Phelps, however, as a "nervous invalid."[47]

The death of his wife in 1852 left Phelps with three children to raise. His oldest son, Stuart, became "the staff of life to the shaken man" and Phelps's favorite—a "treasure" and "well-beloved son."[48] His second son, Amos Lawrence, a newborn when his mother died, required immediate and constant attention. His first-born, Elizabeth, proved most trying. The child refused to conform to an acceptable mode of womanly domesticity. The tomboyish girl romped outdoors and refused to learn the fundamentals of cooking and sewing from her two stepmothers. And at the age of ten, she began to write stories for religious weeklies— portending a literary career reminiscent of her mother's. Phelps did not discourage the girl, but he did little to facilitate her work. He let the boys have the run of the house despite his daughter's pleas for some part of the spacious New England house for composing in private. For a time she rented a room with a friend, Dr. Mary Harris, so she could labor in peace. Later, she moved most of her notes and writing supplies into an unheated summerhouse, where she toiled for much of the year. Elizabeth Phelps's confidence had been dampened so thoroughly by the time she published her first story in *Harper's Magazine* that she was afraid to tell anyone about it until it had been accepted and appeared in print. She published her first book under the same secretive circumstances. When Austin Phelps read the poignant dedication, his daughter saw that he noticed a grammatical error instead of noting with appreciation that she had written it for him.[49]

Actually, none of the children saw much of their father while he was a professor in Andover. Austin Phelps secluded himself in his study regularly each day to prepare for classes and to write. Though remembered as a kindly parent, he was nonetheless distant, demanding quiet hours in the morning while he wrote. Insomnia ruined his nights; he refused to let children ruin his days. The Phelps children considered it a treat to be allowed in the study to play quietly while the professor worked. He also left much of the daily round of child care to his wife except in extreme cases. The titular head of the household, Phelps rarely disciplined his children. He represented an ambiguous authority figure, for though he demanded that the household operate to further his work, he seemed as much out of place at home as he was at the seminary. He did not assume command of the family. Rather, he cajoled affection and respect from his sons by indulgence, and from Elizabeth by withholding his affection. He manipulated the family's sentiments for his own purposes, but he and they knew the limits of his authority. [50]

When Phelps intervened in the extreme cases that demanded his attention, his punishments failed to make clear impressions of strength and authority. Elizabeth Phelps included a revealing anecdote in both her autobiography and her father's memoir. She had told a lie and was sent to her father for punishment. Liars go to hell, he told her. But before she could respond or repent, she remembered, Austin Phelps "bowed his face and wept bitterly." He informed the child of her eternal fate, then weakly began to weep—eliciting tender feelings for her wounded father rather than evoking fears of ultimate godly authority. In general, she remembered that "when he did speak a little too soon, he was so afraid that he had wronged the child . . . that nothing could undo the possible mistake quickly or kindly enough." He followed harsh words with "little signs of love"—a kiss, a gift, a note, or treats. [51]

An additional exchange between father and daughter illuminates the complicated nature of their feelings for one another. Elizabeth and Austin Phelps corresponded regularly after she left Andover. He answered her letters promptly, if unemotionally. His memoir included a few of the surviving letters from Phelps to his children. Those to Stuart and Francis, one of two sons born to Mary Johnson Phelps, overflowed with affection, concern, and interest in their careers. The letters he sent to "one of his children"—the one who eagerly completed the story of his life—were strikingly impersonal. He wrote only of his own activities and did not inquire about her health, her writing, her husband, or the state of her soul. In fact, a letter dated 20 July 1889 closed absently with, "I write, not because I have anything to say, but to keep up the habit." [52] Even then, just months before his death, he found it impossible to express genuine love for his only daughter.

Elizabeth Stuart Phelps loved her father, but with a love misshapen by fear, doubt, and at times contempt. Austin Phelps was everything and nothing to her. He was the primary object of her deepest affection, and yet she seems to have regarded his authority over her rather skeptically. She embraced social gospel theology in blatant opposition to her father's conservative orthodoxy. She added a disclaimer to her dedication in *The Gates Ajar* (1868), for example, because she did not want her father wrongly associated with the liberal cause, nor her own work linked with her father's tradition. He wanted a daughter skilled in the accomplishments and graces of a Victorian lady; she longed for an independent existence. Austin Phelps refused his little girl the full shower of emotion that she demanded, and Elizabeth Phelps, like other middle-class children who read her books, looked to others for satisfaction and reward.

The social gospel promised Elizabeth Stuart Phelps much that her father denied her. Its adherents greedily read her books, fueling the career for which she had spent many years preparing. Social involvement with impoverished fishermen in East Gloucester in the 1880s sharpened her critique of orthodox Protestantism and broadened her conception of a liberal faith. It won her the approval and affection of hapless fishing families—approval that she had failed to earn from her father. The social gospel gave her an identity as a socially responsible women who wrote for a living. The social gospel also took shape at the deft touch of her pen. The experiences and family environment that drove her to imagine and depict a religion with meaning compelled other Protestants in her class to embrace the social gospel that she articulated in dozens of books and stories and poems. She sanitized death, elevated life, and properly distanced the paternal Almighty from his skeptical children, all in such a way that middle-class Protestant children could escape the stifling confines of a paternal culture that denied them purpose, direction, and faith to order their lives.

Elizabeth Phelps's novels were quite simple stories. As works of literature, they featured flimsy plots and trite denouements. In his doting old age, Van Wyck Brooks celebrated many sentimental stories, but even he ranked Phelps's work among the second rate *fin-de-siècle* novels.[53] She set most of her stories in tension-ridden Victorian homes and populated them with anxious middle-class Protestants in desperate search of identity and salvation. The value of her writing lies not in its artistic merit but in its power to explain the emergence of modern Protestantism.

In some ways her books chronicle her own quest for faith. Indeed, she drew a great deal of material from her own background. The line between her past and her fantasy world appeared blurry throughout her literary career. Her novels explored—albeit sometimes facilely—the complicated connections between family and faith, connections that bound her to the past and simultaneously propelled her into modernity. Like her life, her novels were attempts to find meaning in incomplete pictures and to forge an identity from disconnected parts. The story of her family reveals the complicated reasons behind her quest for revitalized faith and salvation; her stories uncover the difficulty of the search. Together, they illuminate an ambivalent faith.

The most important contribution of Phelps's work to the emerging twentieth-century religion and culture was to undermine the authority of evangelical Protestantism and Victorian culture. Her first book, *The Gates Ajar*, challenged the accepted wisdom about sin and eternal retribution. Instead of an afterlife of torment for the unrepentant, Phelps pictured universal salvation from a deity who as "a living Presence, dear and real," presided over a heaven that reproduced blissful middle-class family life. Undoubtedly prompted by the loss of her mother in 1852 and of her sweetheart in the Civil War, Elizabeth Phelps told the story of Mary Cabot, whose brother Royal was killed in battle before he had had a conversion experience. Mary knew, and staunch believers confirmed, that unless he had repented in his dying gasp, Royal was doomed to perdition. Unable to accept a view of religion that condemned her brother, showed God to be a heartless tyrant, and left no comfort for the mourners of a good man, Mary with the help of her Aunt Winifred Forceythe articulates a more appealing hereafter. Winifred's daughter Faith, for example, tells one of her playmates that heaven is "splendid" because she will meet her dead father, who will greet her with a cheery "Here's my little girl." She explains that they will "live in the prettiest house," and she will have all kinds of toys among the candy clouds. The child adds eagerly, "I have dreadful hurries to go this afternoon sometimes when Phoebe's cross and won't give me sugar."[54]

Critics of *The Gates Ajar* accused Phelps of cheapening salvation by making concessions to human comfort rather than accepting God's justice, wisdom, and uncompromising authority. Her father and others denounced her as a heretic, but thousands of men and women who had lost loved ones in the Civil War wrote to thank her for the comfort her book had given them.[55] Letters from her enthusiastic readers suggest that she had captured the sentiments of a generation that wanted a religion that provided security in an insecure world. When hard work, self-control, and patriarchal families produced both success and salvation, the assumption that underlay unqualified godly authority troubled few Protestants. But as the industrial expansion, spurred by civil war and the war experience itself, made the individual an insignificant cipher, many American Protestants longed for the kind of psychic comfort that Phelps's book promised.

Critics also objected to the immediacy of gratification that the book represented. Instead of allowing the uncertainty of salvation to promote diligence and dedication to hard work and self-scrutiny, The Gates Ajar promised readers instant satisfaction—both as a reward for a good life and as a hedge against unpleasantness. Little Faith Forceythe had the "hurries" to go to heaven when her elders denied her the treats she wanted. Moreover, the heaven that Phelps envisioned scarcely represented a different realm over which God had full command. God made the delights available, but once inside, people could live their afterlives as a continuation of their earthly lives. Once again, God was the jovial, indulgent father not the omnipotent judge whose authority could not be questioned.[56]

The Gates Ajar served to raise doubts about the plausibility of the Victorian emphasis on hard work and self-control. Neither of these seemed to be the keys to heavenly bliss or earthly comfort. Instead, sentimental relationships and instant gratification provided a sense of security in a world turned upside down. Likewise, Phelps undercut the orthodox faith of an older generation by circumscribing the Almighty's authority on earth and in the universe and by denying the discontinuity between life and death. These theological shifts unleashed a kind of relativism that diluted religious salvation. Phelps's challenge to the cultural and religious imperatives of her youth sprang from profound personal sources and represented her conception of authority in mid-nineteenth-century America. Authority for Phelps rested in the purveyors of material and psychic security, not in her father.

Her later works further challenged the core of Victorian culture and evangelical Protestantism. Most of her stores about families, for example, featured families that were fragmented rather than the unified domestic ideal. Like Mary Cabot, Reliance Strong in Friends: A Duet (1881) and the protagonist in Doctor Zay (1881) had lost their parents in their youth. Other characters, such as Avis in The Story of Avis (1877), Marna Trent in Confessions of a Wife (1902), and Emanuel Bayard in A Singular Life (1894), grew up with just one parent—the parent of the opposite sex. These incomplete families reflect not only the objective reality of Phelps's life but also a deep uncertainty about the role of families in modern America.

Even when Phelps wrote about whole families, as she did in the

Gypsy Breynton series of the late 1860s, the parents fade nearly to invisibility in most of the stories. Gypsy's is a world of children learning from each other the difference between right and wrong and the social graces necessary to make their way in the world. The very name Gypsy reminds readers of one who is defiant of established custom and authority. Gypsy challenges the Victorian convention of womanly domesticity with her tomboyish romps in the orchard and field and by exclaiming of her teacher's impending marriage: "Now she'll have to stay at home and keep house all day, —I think she's really silly, don't you?" Her brother Tom adopts a feminized nurturing attitude toward his younger sister. He, rather than their mother, admonishes Gypsy to "learn to apply" herself to housework. It is Tom who clucks, "I don't know what's going to become of you."[57] Mr. and Mrs. Breynton scarcely figure in the plot of the books. They seem merely to provide the arena in which the children act out their lives, exercise authority, and establish identities.

Except for presenting what Phelps considered be to moral behavior, books like *The Story of Avis, Confessions of a Wife,* and *Donald Marcy* (1893) had little formally to do with religion. In books like *Friends: A Duet, A Singular Life,* and *The Story of Jesus Christ,* however, she began to outline the social gospel. Phelps's social gospel novels, the logical outgrowth of earlier works like *The Gates Ajar* and the Gypsy Breynton series, focused on life and other people rather than on an afterlife and God as the sources of salvation. In *Friends: A Duet,* for example, Charles Nordhall wins the hand of Reliance Strong and a sense of peace only after he begins to participate in reform activities among the disinherited of his community.[58] In *A Singular Life* and *The Story of Jesus Christ,* Phelps rooted her social gospel message in the tradition of Jesus in hopes of lending it credence and as a way of expressing her interpretation of the Christ story for modern Protestants. Her message conferred authority on the sons and daughters rather than on the fathers, and it placed hope of fulfillment in this life rather than in heaven.

A Singular Life, written in 1894, was Phelps's single most important statement of the social gospel, and its protagonist, Emanuel Bayard, represented the principal social gospel figure in her writing. A thinly veiled Christ story, *A Singular Life* borrowed holy names (Emanuel's parents were Mary and Joseph Bayard) as well as places (Bethlehem, Galilee, Caesarea) to make Bayard more than a mere man of the cloth. Shunned by the respectable Congregationalists in Windover, Massachusetts, because he refused to accept the doctrine of eternal damnation for the repentant, Bayard establishes an institutional church among the fishermen of the seaside town. He organizes social clubs, sets up reading and smoking rooms, establishes a lecture series, and builds a gymnasium and bowling alley for wholesome recreation. He challenges the saloonkeeper's belief that individuals alone have responsibility for their personal habits and ultimate destiny. Bayard soon realizes that his life is in jeopardy. Angry henchmen of the saloonkeeper have begun to plot his demise, and on the day he dedicates his chapel called Christ Love, one of them stones him to death. His fishermen disciples vow at his deathbed, however, to continue his work.

Phelps's modern gospel incorporated her perception of the diminished authority of paternal figures and the attraction of intense emotional reward as a synonym for salvation. Phelps scoffs at the authority of the tired orthodox men in Windover who fail to see the miraculous spirit of Bayard. Only young men and women who renounce the individualism of their elders and make sacrifices to usher in the kingdom of God act in Bayard's community. Instead of cowering before the Jehovah of the Old Testament, the young divine worships an indulgent, loving, and distant God—a figure much like the familiar Victorian fathers after whom Phelps and her generation understandably modeled the deity. And throughout the book, the minister who defies the old-timers in Windover reaps a harvest of fellow-feeling from the fishermen. They are attracted to his "elect personality"—his sincerity, intellect, spirituality, manliness, and mystical charm that create an aura of kindness. As Phelps put it, "The fishermen loved him because he loved them."[59] It is this mutual regard that gives Emanuel's life meaning.

Bayard's quest for meaning and purpose and authority mirrors Phelps's. Seemingly unloved by her father and unmarried, she lacked the endorsement of respectable Victorian society, and she longed for peace. As a result, she threw herself into her literary career in the 1870s and 1880s. From her post in Andover, she anxiously cultivated the approval of literati in the Boston area. Throughout the seventies, Phelps corresponded with Henry Wadsworth Longfellow, who kindly agreed to read and to comment on her work. Most of the letters from her aging idol assumed a patronizing tone, interrupted by genuine astonishment when she produced pieces of fine quality. When she began to complain of sleeplessness and exhaustion, she told Longfellow of her affliction. His tender reply carried a dual message. "I am sincerely sorry that you are so sleepless and suffering," he wrote on 7 March 1879. "Why will the busy brain go on all night, swinging its anvils about like a windmill, when it has nothing to grind but itself?"[60] She needed her rest, but he implied that she had no grist for her intellectual mill. By the 1880s, Phelps had written several novels, numerous articles, and essays, but her insomnia worsened, and she had come no closer to gaining the approval she craved.

Sometime in the 1880s, Phelps met a struggling young author, Herbert Dickinson Ward, who was seventeen years her junior. She began writing Ward's father to inquire about "the boy." The two writers began to see one another socially, undoubtedly raising many proper eyebrows. Phelps's anxiety overwhelmed her and took a familiar form: she fell ill with insomnia. Nevertheless, in October 1888, Elizabeth Stuart Phelps married Herbert Dickinson Ward. Austin Phelps did not attend the wedding. With this marriage, Elizabeth created a new family and broke her tie with the old in hopes of finding peace. Herbert Dickinson Ward represented for Phelps the young man she had not been able to marry and the child she had thus been denied. She was forty-three years old when she married Ward, and the age difference with her husband meant that he would be the only "son" she would ever have. Her addressing him as "the boy" suggests that she realized it.[61]

The Wards' marriage failed. Phelps's lifelong quest for salvation ended in illness, discomfort, and isolation. The couple collaborated on a pair of ill-conceived novels and gradually drifted apart. Though Phelps insisted that her husband was her "best friend" and "best critic," it was not long before Herbert Ward took a separate residence. In the 1890s, he moved to South Carolina, where he stayed for the remainder of Phelps's life. She remained in Gloucester for a time, then moved to Newton, just outside of Boston.[62]

In the 1880s, before she became involved with Ward, Phelps had devoted much of her time and energy to helping fishermen in the village near her seaside home. One very moving episode occurred when Phelps and a companion came upon an East Gloucester family in mourning. The man of the house had been murdered. Entering the tenement apartment uninvited, Phelps witnessed anguish and despair such as she had never before seen. In the midst of the wife's seemingly inconsolable lament, Phelps went to her and embraced her until her sobs subsided and until the poor woman saw Phelps's snow-white gloves and suit. From that moment on, Phelps hurled herself into the reform efforts of the village so she could help people like the bereaved woman and her twelve children. Phelps organized temperance meetings and arranged religious services in the local tavern to take the gospel to the men she believed most needed to hear it. For three years she participated in the activities of the social gospel to which she had already made important ideological contributions. Phelps acknowledged in her autobiography the "great happiness" that "serving the people" had given her. "There and then, if ever, I became acquainted with life," she wrote in 1896. "I learned more from my Gloucester people than I ever taught them, and I shall hold them gratefully and lovingly in my heart as long as I live."[63]

In the years of her disappointing marriage, Phelps returned to her "Gloucester people" only on the printed page. Between 1891 and 1910, she wrote such novels as *A Singular Life, The Story of Jesus Christ, Fourteen to One* (1891), and *A Chariot of Fire* (1910), which explored themes of the social gospel as she understood it. The tragedy of Phelps's life lies in her inability to summon the energy to participate in her own solution to the problem of faith in a dying culture. Throughout the 1890s, she wrote testily to organizations and acquaintances that requested her work or her participation in social events. In 1890, she explained to a Mrs. Lothrop, "I am not well enough even to earn my living! And I cannot send you anything worth writing." Two years later she answered another woman who requested work by asserting, "I am far from well and by no means strong enough to undergo the strain and loss of vitality involved in the stage."[64] When the new century dawned, Phelps stayed in seclusion, writing whenever she could. In 1910, she penned her last collection of stories, *The Empty House*, and died alone.[65] Friends notified Ward in South Carolina of his wife's death.

By the time she died, Elizabeth Stuart Phelps had dismantled the appealing life beyond the Gates that she had imagined in her youth. She, like most other Protestants in the 1910s, no longer could afford to consider death, because *life*, not afterlife, held the promise of salvation. Phelps's social gospel, however, was not as fully formed as the statements made by churchmen and churchwomen who would follow her. Hers contained mostly the cry of discontent with the orthodoxy of nineteenth-century Protestantism—the orthodoxy of her father. Elizabeth and Austin Phelps make it easier to understand why children modeled their God after their fathers and then, disappointed, found it hard to worship him. Their complicated bonds of affection, commitment, and habit demonstrate the simultaneous urge to honor and to abandon the past. Phelps's tortured novels about confused women, desperately seeking to know what it meant to be modern Protestants in modern families, speak forcefully of the personal reasons behind dissatisfaction with nineteenth-century Protestantism. Her statements pertaining to social reform, social salvation, and personal well-being are the logical emotional conclusion of her quest for meaning in an era when she and many of her contemporaries could take no refuge in the roles of Victorian manhood and womanhood that had sustained their parents. The challenge to paternal authority that Phelps and her generation posed served to undermine the foundation of Victorian culture and orthodox Protestantism in late-nineteenth-century America.

Phelps's books and ideas helped set the stage for later developments in the social gospel movement. She was among the first to offer criticism of nineteenth-century American Protestantism. Younger Protestants, like Walter Rauschenbusch, channeled Phelps's inchoate critique of American families and religion into an agenda of reform, a Christocentric theology, and a reconsideration of American domesticity. Rauschenbusch's childhood prepared the way for his embrace of the social gospel, and his articulation of the social gospel helped redefine God, Jesus, and ideals for American family life.

WALTER RAUSCHENBUSCH
"Bound Up by a Thousand Ties"

On 16 February 1897, Walter Rauschenbusch sat down in his study to compose a letter to one of his parishioners in defense of a sermon he had given the previous Sunday. In that sermon, he had denounced opulence and had urged his congregation to labor for the kingdom of God and for the well-being of the entire community. He had chided the wealthy for ignoring those in need while they coddled themselves and their families. He abhorred inherited wealth. On this last point, Rauschenbusch had offended a middle-class matron, who asked that the minister explain the correct Christian stance toward riches and family obligations. In the course of his response, Rauschenbusch paused to reflect on the complicated nature of man's inheritance. He could not deny the powerful, irrational family bond that sometimes deterred people from acting on their rational convictions. In fact, he recognized the impossibility of discarding the legacy of one's past, whether that legacy was material or spiritual. He finally softened his defense by concluding his letter with a confession. "I am well aware," he wrote, "how hard it is to extricate [oneself] from a position in which one is born and bound up by a thousand ties."[66]

A few years later, Rauschenbusch acknowledged the departure that the men of his generation had made from the beliefs of their fathers. In an

Walter Rauschenbusch

interview with Ray Stannard Baker that appeared in the *Independent,* he observed: "Within our own memory the fear of hell and the desire for bliss in heaven have strangely weakened, even with men who have no doubt of the reality of heaven and hell. On the other hand, the insistence on present holiness and Christian living has strengthened. Good men give less thought to their personal salvation than our fathers, but their sympathy for the sorrows of others is more poignant."[67] Rauschenbusch contrasted the older fear of hell with a new emphasis on righteousness in life—personal salvation with social salvation. In its broadest outlines, he accurately characterized the shift in Protestant thinking that was taking place in the late nineteenth century.

Yet the recurring reference to "our fathers" suggests that the transformation of Protestantism was neither as impersonal a process nor as clearly defined as the young social gospel ministers made it seem. Ideas did not simply change; men like Rauschenbusch participated in personal ways in that change. As he hinted in his letter to the troubled church member, fathers affect the "position in which one is born" and thereby limit the horizons of the imaginable and debatable. They also serve as springboards from which young men launch their new ideas and as standards against which the young measure their departure. Thus, fatherhood and family ties were inextricably bound up in the origin of the social gospel as well as in young men's anguish over it.

Rauschenbusch's childhood, like his contemporaries', provides an important clue to the emergence and powerful attraction of the social gospel. As a pioneer in the budding social gospel movement in America, he blazed new theological trails as much to escape his confining past as to carry that past into the uncharted territory of the future. His childhood, and especially the evocative figure of his father, energized the social gospel of his manhood. His father, August Rauschenbusch, an eminent scholar at the Rochester Theological Seminary and a Baptist missionary to the American West and to Germany, influenced his son in profound ways. The domineering parent inspired admiration as well as disrespect, longing as well as revulsion. Like Elizabeth Stuart Phelps, Rauschenbusch modeled the God of his religion after his earthly father. Indeed, his ambivalent regard for his father manifested itself in a similarly ambiguous Almighty Father in his theology.

Perhaps it was August Rauschenbusch's accomplishments that daunted his son. Born in 1816 in Germany, the elder Rauschenbusch traveled in 1846 to a new world with little but his faith and mastered an alien tongue and culture. His first mission took him to the relative wilds of Missouri, where he took a courageous and often dangerous stand against slavery. When he refused to offer the elements of the Last Supper to slaveowners in his congregation, prudent sympathizers spirited Rauschenbusch and his young family safely into Illinois. From there he eventually moved to German settlements in New York State. A man of strong convictions and persuasive prose, Rauschenbusch quickly earned the respect of prominent churchmen with this writings and sermons. Theologians in Rochester asked him to give up his pastorate to establish a new German department at their seminary. With little hesitation, he consented. "Teaching was in his bones," his admiring son later remarked. In addition to a distinguished teaching career, Rauschenbusch maintained strong ties with pietistic Protestants in Germany and crossed the ocean on several occasions to minister to struggling congregations. He wrote numerous religious treatises as well as translating a half dozen hymnals.[68]

It is no surprise that young Rauschenbusch longed for his father's approval. Born in 1861 in Rochester, New York, Walter Rauschenbusch was the only son of August and Caroline Rauschenbusch to survive infancy. His father stood sixth in an unbroken line of Rauschenbusch ministers dating back to the seventeenth century, and the lad never doubted that he, too, would pursue a career in the ministry. He slavishly followed most of his father's professional advice. Thus, he spent several years in Germany to take advantage of the exceptional *Gymnasium* system of education and later, at his father's insistence, enrolled in the University of Berlin to study with Adolf von Harnack, one of the premier church historians of the day. Rauschenbusch earned high marks in all the German schools he attended and waited anxiously to see whether or not his father would allow him to combine his senior year with his first year in seminary. Upon his return to Rochester, Rauschenbusch agreed to perform "amanuensis duties" for his father; in return, the aging theologian allowed his son to accelerate his study. When he finally graduated from the seminary, he applied for a home missionary post in Illinois, to follow in his father's footsteps. The congregation refused him when they learned that he did not believe in eternal damnation. The disappointed young divine took a position in downtown New York City instead, and within a few years, he, too, rose to prominence among professors of religion. He eventually followed his father to Rochester, where he launched a courageous and highly publicized career as a theologian for the social gospel.[69]

Rauschenbusch's reverence for his father had never been completely free from generational competition, however. As one of his father's colleagues, F. W. C. Meyer, put it, Walter Rauschenbusch "simply did not take everything for granted," and August Rauschenbusch did not like to have his authority challenged. In the Sunday school class that the boy attended and his father taught, for example, August Rauschenbusch whipped his son for what he called "disseminating thoughts of unbelief among the boys." Walter apparently had asked his father questions and had refused to accept automatically the orthodox replies. Had it not been for the intervention of his mother, young Rauschenbusch would have run away from home to protest his father's arbitrary authority. As it was, he remained, continued to pose embarrassing queries, and barely escaped expulsion from the class.[70] Another family anecdote reveals Rauschenbusch's veiled hope of surpassing his father in some endeavor. August Rauschenbusch was a superb swimmer and, against his parent's wishes, swam frequently in the Rhine. When a cousin drowned in the mighty German river, he swam across at the exact location where the boy had died to demonstrate his defiance of the treacherous current. Years later, Walter Rauschenbusch went to the Rhine, found the same location, and swam to the opposite shore *and back*, to demonstrate his determination to surpass his father's accomplishment.[71]

In spite of his admiration for his father, Rauschenbusch and his father were not particularly close. The son's recollections of the older man reflect ambivalence and unfamiliarity. In completing his father's memoir, Rauschenbusch described his father as "autocratic" and influenced by the "old school" in Germany. "Had he been born in England," his son declared, "he would have been among the sturdiest Puritans."[72] He was quite strict with all his children but especially demanding of his only son. Yet for all the language connoting steadfastness that Walter Rauschenbusch used to describe his father, he intimated that August Rauschenbusch was not exactly a pillar of strength for his family. He recounted a frightening tale of life on the frontier in the 1850s in which his mother, who had been left alone with two small children for several weeks, had to defend the home against "savage strangers" and "poor footloose families" who prevailed on her for food and assistance. At least one, friendly slaves from a nearby plantation rescued her from peril. Rauschenbusch left unspoken his conviction that her husband should have been with her.[73] In later years, a nervous condition left August Rauschenbusch shaky and sleepless. "A slammed door or a dropped book upset him so thoroughly that his hands trembled, and he lost his train of thought," his son reported. He often suffered from insomnia, headaches, and stress, with the result that he did not want to be disturbed by the everyday troubles of his family.[74]

The peculiar nature of the relationship between father and son resulted in large part from circumstances over which Walter Rauschenbusch had no control and which he could not comprehend fully until he reached adulthood. Walter had not been the first son born to the Rauschenbusches. Their first child, Winifred, had been his father's delight, but he had died before he was two. Two daughters followed before, at long last, another son was born. His father, therefore, placed a heavy burden on the lad to work hard and to carry on the Rauschenbusch name with pride. The father understandably expected a great deal from the long-awaited son; the child understandably chafed under the constant pressure to be a model child.

Rauschenbusch also suffered from a situation that he only later appreciated: his parents' marriage was bitter and unsatisfying. Having been rejected by his first love, Frida, August Rauschenbusch married

Caroline Rhomp on the rebound and learned too late that he did not love her. Their first daughter, whom he named Frida and whom he "loved devotedly," served as a constant reminder of his lost love and continued unhappiness. For years, the children knew only that Papa stayed away from home as much as possible and, when forced to be with his wife, either quarreled with her or drank to excess. Rauschenbusch vowed to behave differently from this father. [75]

The greatest barrier to Rauschenbusch's intimacy with his father was the old theologian's frequent absences, which made him nearly unapproachable. For years at a stretch, Walter Rauschenbusch lived without a father. When he was about three and a half years old, for example, his father sent the family to Germany and promised to join them to escort them back to Rochester. Three years later, he traveled to Germany but spent time in Bavaria instead of immediately joining his family in Westphalia. When the family finally was reunited, August Rauschenbusch disposed of his paternal responsibility by taking his children on long walks. Rauschenbusch remembered how his father's nature hikes often resulted in misunderstanding or humiliation. On one occasion, the impatient father sent his son to the back of the procession, forbidding him to utter a sound as punishment for talking too much. On another, he chastised the boy for dangling his feet in the Danube and likened him to the fool who believed that his feet cut off the flow of water to Vienna. [76] Both incidents probably resulted from unfamiliarity rather than from rancor. Nonetheless, the distance between the two widened. When he completed his father's memoir, Rauschenbusch noted in a surprised tone that "much of what my father had done was completely unknown to me" and undoubtedly "much will remain undiscovered." [77] The object of his admiration and envy was shrouded in mystery.

The Rauschenbusches were a caricature of the ideal Victorian family. The father assumed ultimate authority over his moral, self-abnegating wife and over his children. Like many middle-class fathers in the mid-nineteenth century, August Rauschenbusch rarely spoke of his work at home, left much of the daily family administration to his wife, and took up gardening as a pastime. His children, especially Walter, looked to him for guidance and approval—and only sometimes found the former and seldom the latter. The father's lengthy absences and arbitrary punishments did little to breed the deep affection between children and parents that constituted the Victorian ideal. In fact, Rauschenbusch tried to escape his father's authority by running away from home several times and by joining a gang of rowdy boys, for whom he became the

"leader in profanity."[78] Though the Rauschenbusch children seem to
have been protected from many of the harsh realities of industrializing
America and the vagaries of the market, their home did not always
provide a safe haven from tension, disappointment, and frustration.
Marital unpleasantness, unspoken competition between father and son,
and dicta to the children to succeed on their own with little latitude for
individual action all worked to close the domestic walls around them.

Aside from the intimidating figure of August Rauschenbusch, the
Rauschenbusch children were also caught up in a "feminizing" American culture that was reinforced by the pious women in their family.
Rauschenbusch insisted that he "learned religion at his mother's knee"
as well as from the eminent scholar his father. Walter and his sisters
learned well the lessons of service, self-denial, and family nurture from
Caroline Rauschenbusch. All three took refuge in religion in their adult
lives. Frida, the eldest, married George Fetzer, a theologian like her
father; she moved to Hamburg, Germany, with him and tried to make a
home for him like the ideal toward which her mother had strived. Emma,
known as a "wild bumblebee" in her girlhood, married Dr. George
Clough, and together they served as missionaries in India. Emma provided constant inspiration for Walter, who tried to become a missionary
before he went into the Baptist ministry.[79]

The contradictory signals from his domineering father and loving
mother combined with the natural anxiety of adolescence to produce in
Rauschenbusch a severe identity crisis. After a youth of mixed rebellion
and dependence, Rauschenbusch looked to manhood fearfully, not certain that he was adequate to the demands placed on adults. An odd
collection of memories reveals a curiosity and disquietude about sexuality and his own power to create. The man remembered lying on the
porch floor at a neighbor's house to peer curiously beneath the petticoats
of his mother's friend. He also recalled his anxiety shortly thereafter at
seeing a yard full of writhing worms that he had mistaken for twigs. And
he recorded a dream that conveyed his sense of lonely impotence. In the
nightmare, he chased after people who had tried to poison him and
managed to catch two of them. When he called for the police to help him,
however, no one came. He awoke, hoping never again to "dream such a
dreadful dream." His nocturnal adventure suggests his fear of being
destroyed and of being abandoned by traditional figures of authority.
Years later, after he had married, Rauschenbusch worried about his own
sexual capacity. Though the young Rauschenbusches had five children,
their relations were occasionally marred by his fear of impotence.[80]

This anxiety about himself found its greatest expression in religion. Rauschenbusch was seventeen when he first had "a vital religious experience." Bound up with the trauma of maturing sexuality, he experienced conversion at a "time of [physical] awakening" for him. Changes in his body seem to have driven home his need for a developing spirituality as well. In 1878 he declared, "I want to become a man; I want to be respected," and after praying for help Rauschenbusch experienced a sense of relief and comfort. He turned away from his rebellious behavior and determined to devote himself to a Christian life. When he spoke of the conversion, he could not hide the intense emotion out of which it had emerged nor his strange response to it. "It was a tender, mysterious experience," he wrote. "Yet there was a great deal in it that was not really true."[81]

Additional circumstances help explain Rauschenbusch's ambivalence toward his new religious life. In 1878, while Rauschenbusch was feeling the first flush of manhood, his father began to decline in health and mental vigor. Beginning with a severe cold, August Rauschenbusch lost much of his strength of "body and soul" and sank into a deep "sadness and depression."[82] He also began to lose the terrifying grip on his son's imagination. The father's ill health seemed to signal the younger Rauschenbusch's chance at physical and spiritual self-determination. Thus, Walter's desire to become a man coincided with his father's debility and found expression in a declaration of religious faith.

Rauschenbusch's conversion partially unchained him from his father. He no longer felt compelled to act out his father's fantasy, under his father's direction, with his father's dogma. But it was not until 1888 that he broke completely free of his father's faith. In that year, Rauschenbusch plunged into parish work in Hell's Kitchen by initiating numerous social programs to meet the needs of his impoverished parishioners. Daycare centers, soup kitchens, and public bathing promoted the values of family nurture and cleanliness inherent in Victorian domestic morality. At the same time, he deplored harsh messages of eternal punishment and a lonely struggle for salvation.

During the autumn of his first year of pastoral work, an epidemic struck the community, and Rauschenbusch, like many others, fell seriously ill. Before he had recovered completely, he went out to minister to his ailing flock—like a mother caring for her sick children—and in so doing, he lost his hearing. The loss of this sense proved to be a sore trial to the naturally gregarious man; he frequently misunderstood people and responded to their queries and comments in a fashion that baffled, sometimes angered them. But his sacrifice also generated a second conversion experience that was more lasting than his adolescent change of heart. At twenty-seven, the deaf minister suddenly felt compelled to "live over again the life of Christ."[83] As he put it, he wanted to "do hard work for God" and "to participate in the dying of the Lord Jesus Christ." When he declared that he would "die over again his death," Rauschenbusch saw in Jesus a chance simultaneously "to redeem humanity" and to give his life its "fundamental direction."[84]

In his devotion to the appealing, approachable Jesus, Rauschenbusch founded one of the most important organizations for advancing the social gospel and for drawing young Protestants to a fulfilling cause: the Brotherhood of the Kingdom. Begun in 1892 as an informal association of radical Baptists, the Brotherhood eventually became an ecumenical body for advancing social religion. It was premised on the idea that modern men should worry less about the next life and concentrate instead on establishing a righteous kingdom on earth.[85] Accordingly, Rauschenbusch chose Jesus, whose mission had been on earth and who as God's son was man's brother, as the exemplar of the Brotherhood. In the organization as well as in the accompanying theology, he shied away from stifling authority relationships and even avoided referring to God as the rallying captain for latter-day Christian soldiers. Jesus the brother evoked no fear of failure and disappointment as did God the father. In the late nineteenth century, Jesus offered the best model for young men to unite a fragmented sense of self into a coherent identity. He became a model for Protestant virtue in the twentieth century: the man of action with a sentimental commitment to service. Moreover, Jesus inspired service that promoted cooperation and resulted in approval among friends. Jesus legitimized the emotional dependence on others so comforting to middle-class Americans.

Rauschenbusch's continuing efforts in the Brotherhood of the Kingdom, his parish in New York City, and various ecumenical associations gave him the opportunity to work out the complicated ties between his own psychic well-being and a theology for the generation drawn to the social gospel. He became an intimate friend of two young theologians who encouraged him in his work, provided counsel, and poured out their aspirations to their young friend. The "spiritual triumvirate" of Leighton Williams, Nathaniel Schmidt, and Walter Rauschenbusch became the inspirational nucleus that inspired like-minded Protestants to engage in wide-ranging cooperative endeavors. These three men, and others who followed their example, seemed disenchanted with the individual career-making of their fathers and chose instead to work jointly in their scholarship and practical programs. All three nonetheless went on to enjoy distinguished professional lives in prominent schools of theology and as authors of widely read books; the years of Victorian training never could be entirely smudged out. But their simultaneous search for peer approval and individual achievement paralleled a restless search among other turn-of-the-century American men, who nervously appealed to others for guidance, direction, and reward at the same time that they strove for robust masculine adventure and sturdy accomplishment. The Christocentric theology of the social gospel, then, offered a model that wove the competitive and domestic strands of late-Victorian childrearing into the fabric of identity, faith, and action for men in the late nineteenth century. It softened the unyielding demands of individual responsibility and achievement with cooperation and mutual approval. Thus, the theology both derived from, and began to shape, a new ideal in public and private social relations.

Jesus, a loving carpenter, embodied the new ideal. He continued to earn the name "brother" and "son of God," and he inspired a generation to generous acts of conviction and conscience. By the twentieth century, however, Jesus himself had undergone a dramatic transformation in the work of Rauschenbusch and other social gospelers. In their quest for a revitalized personal ideal, these young churchmen found comfort in the qualities of love, self-giving, and cooperation expressed by the nineteenth-century vision of Jesus, but they took the dewy-eyed slip of a savior and endowed him with muscles, calluses, and athletic manliness. "There was nothing mushy, nothing sweetly effeminate about Jesus," Rauschenbusch wrote. "He was the one that turned again and again on the snarling pack of His pious enemies and made them slink away." Jesus was, concluded the adoring social gospeler, a "man's man." And as a manly example, the son of God offered modern man "a life of real adventure" as well as a reassuring life of service and approval. For in the act of service, man could "match himself against superior odds" as he battled to create "the Kingdom of God on earth"—a dominion of brotherly love. Moreover, Jesus never asked his followers to rush into the fray unflanked and unaided. The ideal of the twentieth century revolved around the association of peers to achieve individual and social excellence.[86]

Rauschenbusch urged his congregation, students, and audiences in the 1910s to "realize [them]selves" by participating in social gospel programs. He promised that social salvation put "more meaning in life" because it gave American Protestants the "chance of winning love" and of gaining "fine memories and fame."[87] In saving others, men and women in the twentieth century could secure the affirmation that they had been denied as children and as young adults. In *A Theology for the Social Gospel* (1917), Rauschenbusch elaborated the connection between personal well-being, salvation, and the social gospel. There, he contended that a religious experience was not Christian unless it "binds us closer to men." Rather than fearing God, modern Christians should "lean back on the Eternal" and "draw from the silent reservoirs" for comfort.[88] The Almighty stood on a par with everyone else as an object of love and service and as a source of reassuring strength and reward.

Rauschenbusch's vision of salvation simultaneously fed and tapped deep pools of uncertainty and longing among his generation of American Protestants. Like him, many young people abhorred the frightful atomistic scramble for success and salvation in which their fathers scurried and which triggered anxiety in their own lives. If they did not reject alcoholism and a failed marriage as Rauschenbusch did, they shrank from the corrosive tendency of nineteenth-century individualism with its attendant frustrations. In his presentation and in their embrace of social gospel theology, Rauschenbusch and his peers seemed determined to energize their identity with a powerful image of fatherhood that they wanted to reject. Rauschenbusch, for example, trained in the domestic virtues of love, service, and sacrifice, nevertheless followed his father's lead by studying theology, entering the ministry, teaching at Rochester, and translating a collection of American hymns into German. Despite vigorous protestations to the contrary, Rauschenbusch, at some level, wanted to be like his father—a confident and capable man of God. He wanted to transcend his father's orthodoxy and to supersede the older man's contribution to religious worship and thought, and he succeeded in his object by incorporating his father's spiritual will in a plan of action that promised emotional and spiritual reward. In other words, he became and succeeded his father; and in his theology, Jesus became and succeeded God.

As a result of the psychological sources of his work, Rauschenbusch could not eliminate his continuing ambivalence toward family relations in social gospel theology. It persisted in his writing about the heavenly family as well as in his private experience. While he avoided writing about God because he "drowned" in the greatness of the Almighty, Rauschenbusch nevertheless continued to struggle with the place of the Father in his theology. As he wrote in one of his prayers for the social awakening, "Jesus compels us to clasp hands in spirit with our brothers and thus approach the Father together. This rules out all selfish isolation in religion," he went on significantly. "Before God no man stands alone."[89] In light of the complicated influences of late-nineteenth-century family life, this seemingly simple admonition against Protestant individualism barely conceals his relief in the strength of numbers. Approach the Father, man must—but not alone.

As he formulated this theology of social salvation, Rauschenbusch also adopted a twentieth-century mode of family relationships based on cooperation, companionship, and accessible parents. In the early 1890s, he met and fell in love with a schoolteacher from Milwaukee, Pauline Rother, and by 1892 the couple was engaged to be married. They did not, however, make the decision lightly. Walter feared that his deafness would interfere with open channels of communication with his wife and any children they might have, and Pauline worried about giving up a fulfilling career and independence and becoming a traditional pastor's wife. Within a year, the two were married and the new bride soon discovered that "housekeeping was not to be her major role." Rauschenbusch saw her as a "counselor and constant companion" who participated as his "interpreter" to the rest of the world.[90] Neither tried to dominate the other in the domestic or professional sphere: a rich correspondence between the pair survives to document a tender romance that deepened each of the thirty-three years they were married.

When their five children arrived in the first decade or so after the wedding, Rauschenbusch eagerly became friends with them. He tried to become the ideal father about which he had written in his theology—an indulgent, loving companion rather than a wrathful judge. Parents and children romped in the woods near their home in Rochester and their summer home in Canada, played games together, and corresponded when they were separated. As he wrote to his son Hilmar in 1917, "There is no love available to you which is so unvarying and always trustworthy as the love of your mother and father. . . . You must help us make the transition from parenthood to friendship."[91]

Even Walter Rauschenbusch's family had its darker side. Because he refused to assume ultimate authority over his children, Rauschenbusch never felt certain of their respect and affection. For example, he was away from home for several weeks each year when his first child, a daughter, was small. Named after Rauschenbusch's older brother, who had died in infancy and had been his father's favorite, Winifred prompted separation anxiety in her father. He wrote her small notes in infantile lisps and contractions and instructed Pauline to impress on his daughter that "she must love her Papa. I want her to."[92] Normal misunderstandings between parents and children occasionally mushroomed out of proportion in the Rauschenbusch household because of the theologian's deafness. He worried that he did not understand his children— verbally or emotionally. Shortly before his death he fretted that his children had no idea how much he loved them. He completed instructions for the disposal of his papers and estate with a sad confession: "I cannot expect to be happy again in my lifetime, I go gladly, for I have carried a heavy handicap for 30 years, and have worked hard."[93]

In his young adulthood, Rauschenbusch had believed that cooperation was a plausible alternative to competition in the modern world. The Great War in Europe raised new doubts. While many of his colleagues saw the war as a grand opportunity to save the world and to erect in the truest sense a kingdom of God on earth, Rauschenbusch mourned the passing of his cooperative vision. The man who had spent a career insisting that social salvation required peer approval, brotherly affection, and rewarding lives of service soon discovered that the reservoir of human kindness ran dry during time of war—especially for a man with a Hunnish name like Rauschenbusch. For years he had turned to a small circle of colleagues and a wider circle of admiring audiences for gratifying support in his Christian endeavor. Now Rauschenbusch saw friends and acquaintances withdraw their affection. Long-time friends and neighbors in Rochester, distrustful of his German heritage and outspoken advocacy of Christian socialism, turned from him and refused to attend his services and lectures. An old friend and colleague, Dr. Algernon Crapsey, sent Rauschenbusch a formal letter that included four questions to determine the soundness of his ideology and his theology. Just a little over a decade earlier, Rauschenbusch had been one of Crapsey's few defenders when he was tried for heresy. The Saskatchewan Conference of the Methodist Church cancelled an invitation to him to preach, claiming that he was "undesirable." Neighbors in Bobcaygeon, Ontario, where the Rauschenbusches had spent many pleasant summers, threatened to burn his cottage to the ground if he went there during the war. Others accused him of being part of the German propaganda machine. His oldest son volunteered to go to Europe as an ambulance driver, and afterwards, friends relentlessly urged Rauschenbusch to support the war.[94]

The cumulative effect of severed friendships and social ostracism for Rauschenbusch was an extremely serious illness. A vigorous man in his

late fifties during the war years, Rauschenbusch nonetheless fell myste-
riously ill when the United States began inching its way to war. He
developed a case of pernicious anemia, which doctors could not correct,
and in the end his heart simply gave out. It would be only a slight
exaggeration to conclude that Rauschenbusch died of a broken heart.
For the emotional and spiritual reserves he would have needed to rally
the failing organ had been drained by the agony of war and personal
rejection. In March 1918, he wrote, "I leave my love to those of my
friends whose souls have never grown dark against me, I forgive the
others and hate no man. For my errors and weaknesses I hope to be
forgiven by my fellows."[95] Two months later, he died.

In a sermon Rauschenbusch delivered on numerous occasions in the
last five years of his life, he insisted that religious faith "creates dissatisfaction with our past, repentance, and disillusionment" with the ways of
the world.[96] Walter Rauschenbusch, the beloved pastor and teacher from
Rochester, New York, spent much of his life trying to escape a past that
had denied him fatherly affection and direction and that muted his
devotion to the Almighty Father. In his religious quest, he attempted to
shape a rewarding family life for himself and his struggling parishioners
in Hell's Kitchen. His social gospel, based on that ideal of family,
eventually replaced the orthodoxy of his father's theology. Families—
both impoverished working-class families and his own—laid the foundation of Rauschenbusch's social gospel.

While Rauschenbusch ended his career sad and disappointed by the
outcome of his struggle for a companionate family and a brotherly society, others were more comfortable with the changes. Indeed, the
careers of Charles and Mary Macfarland—both impelled into social-
gospel activities because of family life—show that the social gospel
could inspire commitment to social reform and cultural change outside
the churches. The story of the Macfarland family shows how some Americans could embrace the social gospel and participate in an increasingly
secular, commercialized world.

THE MACFARLANDS

A Social Gospel Family

In the 1930s, near the end of his career, Charles Stedman Macfarland received a letter from a college student asking him to state the
fundamental principles of a Christian life. The aging minister thought

about it, consulted some old seminar notes from his years at the Yale Divinity School, and finally replied. He told the youthful questioner that courage and loyalty underlay Christian life. "I have devoutly prayed that I might be delivered from the sin of cowardice, that I might never be utilitarian or neutral when men were being wronged." As to the second principle, he asserted in his autobiography that he had always tried to be loyal "to friends, to fellow-men, to institutions and to principles."[97] Whether or not Macfarland's response satisfied the student, it accurately reflected the most important principles underlying his contribution to the social gospel. Charles Macfarland's devotion to social justice propelled him into numerous battles against the exploitation of labor by large companies, the destructiveness of war, and the shame of poverty and misery in one of the richest countries on earth. And it was through his loyalty to the institutions he helped to create that Macfarland hoped to carry out his social mission. The Federal Council of Churches, four years old when he became general secretary, provided the institutional framework in which Charles Macfarland promoted the social gospel.

When Macfarland related the incident of the student questioner in his autobiography, he went on to tell of a still "finer human light" that had affected his life, devoting two long chapters to his wife and his family. Neither Charles Macfarland nor his wife, Mary Perley Macfarland, lacked courage or loyalty in their careers as Christian reformers. But for both of them the social gospel sprang from private sources and reflected their reconciliation of Victorian roles, expectations, family arrangements, and salvation with the demands of modernity. Because they were younger than Rauschenbusch and Phelps, the Macfarlands did not face the same anguish. Already by the time of their marriage in the early twentieth century, the strictures of Victorian culture and evangelical Protestantism had been loosened, and alternatives to domesticity had begun to appear.

The story of the Macfarlands, however, can illuminate a dimension of the shift from Victorian culture and religion to consumer culture and the social gospel that the experiences of predecessors like Rauschenbusch and Phelps could not make as clear. The values that informed their social gospel help to explain their children's commitment to and involvement in secular institutions. Their life together underscores the centrality of Victorian family relations to the appeal of the social gospel. It also shows how developments in modern family life in response to that gospel contributed to its transformation.

Like Rauschenbusch and Phelps, the Macfarlands were children of

The Macfarland family. Left to right: *Perley, James, Charles, Jr., Lucia, and Charles, Sr.*

Victorian America. Charles Macfarland, born in Boston in 1866 the son of Daniel and Sarah Macfarland, learned the lessons of hard work and self-control. His father, a Scottish sea captain, demanded discipline and obedience from his son. Macfarland described him as being "stern and impatient" and ambitious for his son. The younger Macfarland was taught at the age of five to recite Bible verses and prayers in Greek, Hebrew, and Swedish, and then taken from Sunday school to lecture series to display his talent. Daniel Macfarland, whose own interest in the

Bible and ancient languages led him to subject his son to such rigorous study, took pride in the boy's accomplishments, but Charles Macfarland disliked the "imposed intellectual discipline" and objected to the public recitations.[98] His father did not relent. Indeed, as the years went by, Daniel Macfarland's devotion to orthodox Protestantism deepened. In 1878, he became involved in a project to erect a statue at Plymouth to honor the seventeenth-century Pilgrims, whose strength of will and strict faith he shared. While working on the monument, he contracted pneumonia and died. Macfarland, just twelve at the time of his father's death, later remembered that every time he "looked up at the Pilgrim Monument," he realized that his father "gave up his life for it." Like so many other fathers of his generation, Daniel Macfarland left his son with a firm impression of his orthodoxy. But near the beginning of his autobiography, Macfarland confessed, "I never really knew him."[99]

It was natural after the death of his father for Macfarland to cleave to his mother. But before long the adolescent lad tried to replace his father. The boy had suffered keenly when his mother had to ask her husband's employer for funeral expenses, so he began to work hard in order to spare his mother further embarrassment. Macfarland, who had begun earning money by collecting and selling driftwood from the Charles River at the age of ten, worked as a cash boy in a drygoods store for a while. Then he established a printing office in his home for custom commercial printing as well as to issue a regular publication called *Our Boston Youth*. To further supplement the family's income, he shoveled coal and snow in season and delivered bundles of clothing from a tailor in the neighborhood. Time and again his employers found him in a dead faint from the "excessive toil." Despite the high physical cost, Macfarland shouldered the burden of earning the family's keep, and together, mother and son overcame many hardships. They moved from one tenement to another, each a bit worse than the one before, and remained only until they had worn out the patience of the local grocer. One winter, their only food came from free soup kitchens and politicians; neighbors gave them patched hand-me-downs to wear.[100]

As the years passed, Sarah Macfarland became the focus of her son's life. Because his mother had been "given up for dead" on a number of occasions during Macfarland's youth, he was determined to work so his mother would not endanger her life. Despite his early training in the Scriptures, Macfarland did not undergo an emotional conversion experience and did not join a church until his mother urged him to do so. He confessed that his decision to join a church resulted "above all" from the "feeling that I should join the church of my mother." Not long after his embrace of religion, Sarah Macfarland cemented her son's place at her side by giving him her wedding band. Macfarland wore it until he was over thirty years old.[101] One can only speculate on the psychological dynamic of the relationship between the Macfarlands. A man who takes his father's place as completely as Charles Macfarland seems to have done must have suffered from nagging guilt about his father even as he succeeded him. He found himself tied to his father's role and values at the same time that he was unbound from paternal domination. The tension between honoring and transcending the past gave Macfarland's religious quest its focus.

The hardships he faced as a child and his relative disadvantages make Macfarland's rise to prominence and his embrace of the social gospel remarkable. Determined to provide well for his mother, he entered the business world and bought into the firm T. O. Gardner and Company, a manufacturing and commission mercantile house. For a time, he played out the familiar American success story. Through diligent work he became the only partner of an ailing elderly man in a thriving business by the time he was twenty-four. Within a few years Macfarland would have enjoyed full ownership. Guilt, however, began to overtake him. He later recalled that "inhuman business competition . . . seemed to force me to win my own living at the expense of men and women" who had to settle for "the miserable pittance" that he paid them.[102] He realized that his comfort depended on someone else's hardship.

Macfarland soon matched his rapid rise to wealth with a precipitous decline in health and in enthusiasm for the demands of the marketplace. Believing he had only months to live, he gave up business in 1892 and began to work for the YMCA. Five years later, however, he had completed Yale Divinity School, had been ordained as a minister, and was a devoted advocate of the social gospel. His decision to enter Yale Divinity School to prepare for the ministry made him see the shortcomings of individualism. For all his diligence as a high school boy in Boston and as a rising businessman, his preparation fell short of the rigorous demands of Yale. Without sympathetic professors who were drawn to the young man's pluck and cleared his academic path of otherwise insurmountable curricular obstacles, Macfarland would have found it difficult to succeed on his own.[103] The realization of his need for others as well as his continued skepticism of traditional authority drew him to a gospel of social salvation. The challenge of embarking on an uncharted journey toward social reform satisfied his longing for heroic manliness, while the cooperative spirit that pervaded the social gospel movement at the turn of the century relieved his fear of drift and failure. Like many of his contemporaries, Macfarland felt rooted in this world rather than the next, and religious certainty for him took the form of social reform.

The social gospel also appealed to the particular circumstances of Macfarland's youth. Jesus, the son, served as an example of morality and as a master whose action and advice led to salvation. For Macfarland, Jesus offered the kind of peer direction to which he and other young men at the turn of the century could respond. God, the father, however, remained a problematic figure, evoking ambivalent memories of Daniel Macfarland. The immanent God of the social gospel—indwelling and obscure—thus suited Macfarland's emotional inclination. His "fatherless" theology, like his fatherless youth, regarded a cooperating group of activists—brothers with Jesus—as the ideal Protestant family of Christians. With mutual assurance and Jesus as the leader among equals, Macfarland believed that social gospelers could sail fearlessly toward the kingdom of God in the twentieth century.

While Macfarland was making his way toward the social gospel and renouncing the orthodox Protestantism of his father, Mary Perley Merrill was on her way to an independent professional career. Unlike the man who would become her husband, Mary Perley Merrill grew up in a home where her father and her family heritage were focal points in her life. Born in 1875 in Davenport, Iowa, Perley (as she was called) was the daughter of two transplanted New Englanders, Louisa Wadsworth and James Griswold Merrill. The Reverend James Merrill came from a long line of churchmen who first came to the New World in the seventeenth century. His wife descended from an equally long and distinguished line of ministers. Perley and her siblings were conscious of the seven generations of clergymen of which they were products, and they grew accustomed to frequent relocation because their father served as a missionary for the Congregational church. After graduating from Smith College in 1897 and earning an advanced degree by 1899, the young woman taught Latin and history at Fisk University, where her father recently had been named acting president. Father and daughter served the same institution for several years before Perley Merrill traveled to Hannover to study German and to make the fashionable tour of the Continent and England. [104] By the time she met Macfarland, Merrill had completed her formal education, had begun a career as an academic, and had made a break with Victorian domesticity.

Charles Macfarland and Mary Perley Merrill, though shaped by different childhood experiences and endowed with completely different dispositions, shared dissatisfaction with Victorian expectations and eventually embraced the social gospel. Where Merrill was fun-loving and expansive, Macfarland was dour and grudging toward those who had humiliated him. He took pleasure in preaching to men in positions of authority who had doubted that the scruffy lad would amount to anything respectable in his manhood. She inspired love and loyalty through her modesty, self-sacrifice, humor, and personal charm. But both Macfarland and Merrill discovered the limits of the roles they were expected to play, and both rejected the religion of which their elders were stalwart defenders. Macfarland shed the individualism of his youth and became an exemplar of cooperative endeavor within large institutions. As a young woman, Merrill refused to be limited to the moral haven of home and family, and when she did marry, she refused to remain in the shadow of her husband. She became a reformer and leader in her own right who was mourned after her untimely death as a "valuable and energetic personality in the great work of the world's redemption."[105]

Coming of age in the 1890s, Merrill perceived alternatives to the endless round of homemaking and child-rearing that made up the domestic ideal for Victorian women. Increasing numbers of middle-class women were attending colleges and universities and were beginning careers as academics, writers, social workers, nurses, and journalists by the time Merrill entered Smith College. While attending this distinguished women's college, she made a host of friends who were drawn to her "pluck," "cheerfulness," "conscientiousness," and "love of good clean fun." Her years as an undergraduate seem to have made a great impression on her. She became a lifelong defender of Smith College and later helped to organize the New Jersey chapter of the American Association of University Women. Her husband admitted that she was not an exemplary traditional minister's wife and that she was "bewitchingly wayward in keeping files and finances."[106] Her appointment to Fisk University's history faculty reflected both her determination to support herself and her interest in helping those less fortunate than herself. Her husband later recalled fondly that she tutored some "backward negro boys" with "unending patience" to help them succeed in the black university. Her visit to Hannover was designed to broaden her cultural and intellectual horizons as well as to further her study of German. Even after Charles Macfarland proposed marriage, Perley Merrill refused to abandon her career to become a minister's wife, and she returned to Fisk University to resume teaching and research.[107]

Macfarland's persistent pursuit of the spirited young woman, however, eventually won her over. Despite her protest that "she was not fitted to meet the requirements of a pastor's wife," Perley Merrill agreed to marry Charles Macfarland. But her decision precipitated a crisis she had previously avoided: choosing between profession and domesticity. As soon as the couple announced their engagement, Merrill suffered a nervous collapse that left her disabled for two years. She gave up her teaching position and indefinitely postponed the wedding date. For nearly three years, she lived in a kind of limbo, unable to continue teaching or to embrace the new role of wife and homemaker. Her paralysis continued until a friend finally intervened, urging Merrill to set a date and go through with the ceremony. The couple took her friend's advice, and on 9 March 1904, they married.

As it turned out, marriage did not impede Perley Macfarland's interest in reform. Indeed, her husband's ministry opened up opportunities for both of them. While they lived in New England, for example, Charles Macfarland battled saloon interests in one community and unfair employers in several others. He helped settle contract disputes for the Buck Stove and Range Company and for the Danbury Hatters union. He celebrated with the printers when they won an eight-hour work day. He remembered with pleasure that leaders of the Hat Trimmers' Union, who asked for his counsel, introduced him at a shop meeting as "our pastor."[108] Macfarland championed the cause of the small man against the intimidating firm. His fearlessness attracted the attention of the men and women who had met in 1908 to organize an ecumenical body of Protestant churches. They saw in Macfarland a dedicated social gospeler unafraid to stand up to powerful interests. In 1912, they asked him to take over the general secretaryship of the Federal Council of Churches. He accepted and held the position until 1931.

Meanwhile, Perley Macfarland responded to the needs of people in her husband's parishes by calling on and assisting "certain needy people" and by caring for others who were "sick, infirm or aged." While they lived in South Norwalk, Connecticut, she noted that many mothers worked in factories but had no adequate facility to care for their children. She established a day nursery. Within five years, Macfarland bore three children, but the responsibilities of motherhood did not prevent her from taking an active interest in matters outside her home and community. She

organized and presided over a division of the American Association of
University Women; she helped found the New Jersey Conference on the
Cause and Cure of War; and she served as a member of the national and
state World Court Committees. Over the years she prepared numerous
papers and addresses on war and peace, became a director of the New
Jersey League of Women Voters, became a member of the Board of
Education in Mountain Lakes, New Jersey, and during the Depression
organized a voluntary unemployment relief agency.[109] Social justice
became her primary goal in life, just as it had become the basis of her
husband's national reputation.

The Macfarlands' adoption of a gospel of social salvation shaped
their family life in the twentieth century. Their reactions against the
stifling individualistic demands of Victorian family life had made the
social gospel attractive in the first place. Their interest in others
prompted their commitment to diverse forms of social service. The language of the private sphere crept into Macfarland's communications as
general secretary of the Federal Council of Churches. In one of his first
reports, for example, he referred to the ecumenical body as "thirty
families of Christ's followers."[110] This cooperative view of the larger
Christian family helped the young couple affirm an emerging middle-
class family ideal of indulgent, youthful parents and independent
children in their private life. Charles Macfarland guided his children
with none of the stern impatience of Daniel Macfarland. He took time to
know his children and to create an open, friendly family environment.
Together they enjoyed winter skiing and summer baseball and frequent
nature hikes. When his two sons reached adolescence, he involved them
in the Boy Scouts of America, to which he became a national field scout
commissioner in 1916. His wife believed that marriage and career need
not necessarily exclude one another. She pursued outside interests while
she raised her family, and she must have made the social responsibility
that she and her husband cherished the point of departure for their
children. The Macfarland home seems not to have been overburdened
with oppressive rules and destructive power plays between the parents
and their children. In fact, it appears to have approached the ideal family
espoused by social gospelers—a cooperative unit, swaddled in friendship, clothed in self-fulfillment, and conscious of its social mission.

Sharing in the care of babies and watching over his nervous wife
tempered Macfarland's defensiveness about his masculinity and colored
his work on religion. He had learned from experience that individual
effort frequently failed to yield success, that service and sacrifice—

traditionally associated with womankind—enhanced both family life and social programs. [111] Shortly after his first son was born, Macfarland began a work entitled *The Infinite Affection* (1907), which, as the title suggests, described the unselfish love of the immanent God of the social gospel. It was to be his only work that focused primarily on the Fatherhood. Most of his twenty-eight books were about Jesus the Son. Macfarland urged his Protestant audience to look to the Son of Man as a peer for guidance and direction. In *The Christian Ministry and the Social Order* (1913), for example, he wrote: "One of the great needs of your church men will be a closer contact and a larger personal allegiance to Jesus Christ, a great affection for him as the sovereign possession of the human mind. Talk to them a great deal about Jesus of Nazareth, make him become to them the symbol of a great unutterably noble life."[112]

Perley Macfarland never fully recovered from the breakdown that preceded her marriage, but she made every effort to combine her professional and domestic roles into a rewarding identity. Macfarland confessed in his autobiography that his wife suffered occasional breakdowns for the rest of her life, but he wrote them off to the "intensity with which she met her obligations in life." In the traditional sense, Perley Macfarland failed as a pastor's wife. Involved with her own activities, she had little time for ladies' luncheons or piano-playing in the parlor. She succeeded, however, in offering twentieth-century women an example of socially responsible womanhood that fused domestic concerns with professional action. Her example beckoned women into social gospel programs that could put their concerns about children, service, and peace into effect. While it is true that she often stayed behind while her husband forwarded his career in Protestant administration and with war work, she did more than keep the home fires burning. When her children were nearly grown and the Great War called Macfarland to Europe, the former professor "revealed qualities that even [her husband] had never discovered during the earlier years." After the terrible carnage of the war to end all wars, she became an outspoken peace advocate, uniting even more perfectly her social action with the responsibilities of motherhood and domestic morality. [113]

It is fairly clear that the messages the Macfarlands conveyed to their children were as different from those of their own upbringing as the social gospel was from the orthodoxy of their elders. They encouraged their children to be outgoing and social-minded rather than introspective and rugged loners. Like others in the social gospel movement, the Macfarlands placed value on leisure, sport, and team spirit rather than on hard, unstinting toil. They also cultivated many friends, acquaintances, and valuable associates who helped them further their own causes. Perley Macfarland consulted William Allen White in Kansas, several officers in the United States Army, and prominent churchmen like Bishop Francis J. McConnell when she exposed the undemocratic and libelous practices of the Daughters of the American Revolution, of which she was a member. Her dependence on cooperation and friendship with others permitted her to clear herself of unjust accusations of subversion that the organization leveled against her, even if it did not prevent the DAR from terminating her membership. [114]

Charles Macfarland adopted much of the language and sensibility of bureaucratic life during his administration of the Federal Council of Churches. By 1916 the "thirty families of Christ's followers" had become, in the general secretary's words, the "constituent bodies" of the ecumenical association, the language itself denoting his adjustment to the reality of managing the largest organization of Christian churches in the early twentieth century. [115] His use of the new bureaucratic language demonstrated his growing confidence in trained professionals, specialized experts, and committees to perform the work of Christian social reform. From a band of social gospelers committed to efficient ecumenical social service, the Federal Council of Churches moved, under Macfarland's leadership, in the direction of more specialized agencies, greater publicity work, and wider influence.

The Federal Council of Churches was Macfarland's greatest legacy to modern Protestantism. In this organization, to which he devoted much of his career, Charles Macfarland institutionalized the principles of cooperation, service, and interdependence, all so deeply rooted in his private life. As one of the chief spokesmen of official American Protestantism, he also urged ministers to convey their message of social salvation by using the most modern methods available: advertising and personal manipulation. He encouraged the establishment of a committee on advertising and publicity in 1916 and furthermore proposed that clergymen develop a "cult of personality" to draw workers into the church. "Get their confidence," he insisted and "get them en masse. . . . If they love you as their pastor, respect you, believe in you, and have a warm personal allegiance for you," you can "stir their consciences."[116] From champion of the underdog, Macfarland himself gradually came to embrace the manipulative ethos of the large-scale corporation that dominated America by 1920.

All three of the Macfarlands' children came to understand the world as a vast arena for playing out one's part in an organization and realizing one's full potential as their father had done in the Federal Council of Churches and their mother had done in numerous organizations.[117] But none felt compelled to follow in their parents' footsteps. They defined success in the bureaucratic terms their parents had come to employ: effective personal skills, loyalty to an organization, and results. Their faith lay not so much in religion as it did in corporate America and in secular culture. Facing none of the financial and cultural barriers that their parents overcame in the late nineteenth century, Charles, Jr., Lucia, and James all attended excellent colleges—Princeton, Smith, Columbia—to prepare for professional lives. All three went on to enjoy successful careers in secular pursuits. Their character and morality were above reproach, and in one way or another, they became important purveyors of modern cultural values. But none of them furthered the specifically *Protestant* character of their parents' social gospel. They acted in a secular world, they embraced the values that underlay corporate capitalism, and they defended the interests of consumerism. However their parents' devotion to the social gospel affected them, they seem to have perceived no contradiction between the religion of their parents and their own worldly endeavors.

Upon graduation from Columbia University, Charles Stedman Macfarland, Jr., began working as an advertising and publicity agent. He and a classmate formed the firm of Macfarland & Heaton in New York City. His younger brother, James Merrill Macfarland, studied at Princeton and earned an advanced degree in business administration at New York University. He took over the Northern New Jersey News Bureau, which his brother originally had developed, and then became a newspaper correspondent for the Associated Press, the New York dailies, and other regional newspapers. Their sister, Lucia Merrill, came the closest to embracing the social gospel. After two years at Smith College, she transferred to the social work program at the Scudder School and spent several months at the Morristown Memorial Hospital to gain practical experience in her profession. Upon completing her training, she became deputy director of the Morris County Welfare Board and began supervising the "problem" cases in the county. She married an accountant.

In their own way, the Macfarland children, like their parents, participated in the making of modern values and in setting the limits of permissible debate and behavior in America. Two worked activity to shape the attitudes, desires, and interests of Americans by creating advertising copy and news. The third, moved by a desire to help those less fortunate than herself, made a commitment to state-sponsored welfare. Her religious motivation found expression in an agency of the state and thereby helped endorse the changing character of American culture and the location of cultural authority. The Macfarland children, like many Americans in the 1920s, accepted as given the importance of social life, the need for others, and the existence of bureaucratic welfare. They pursued the bounty of a consumer culture through their positions in large organizations. But what should be clear is that their faith in corporate America grew out of their parents' devotion to the social gospel.

.   .   .

American Protestants like Elizabeth Stuart Phelps, Walter Rauschenbusch, and Charles and Perley Macfarland who found the social gospel appealing in the late nineteenth century did so because of the turmoil of their private lives as well as the chaos and poverty of industrial America. Their motives for joining the movement were clearly more complicated and mixed than inspired Christian altruism. Their need for direction and purpose and their longing for acceptance drew them toward an emerging gospel of social salvation whose adherents rewarded them for helping others and whose creed glorified an approachable brother named Jesus. Given the combination of rebellion, respect, and guilt that Phelps, Rauschenbusch, and the Macfarlands felt toward their earthly fathers, it is small wonder they embraced a Christocentric theology that protected them from an encroaching heavenly father and affirmed Jesus, whom they saw as a peer. Their longing for the rarefied atmosphere of reform outside their stifling Victorian homes made the social gospel the basis of their hope for a living faith and a life of meaning in modern America.

Their experiences as children in Victorian America influenced their understanding of both God and Jesus. Phelps spoke what the others privately believed: her father symbolized God. However, as the immanent God of the social gospel faded from the world, writers like Rauschenbusch and Macfarland betrayed their complicated attitudes toward their own parents and their need to expiate the pain and guilt of wishing to be rid of their unapproachable earthly and heavenly fathers. Their religion exonerated their own sonship at their same time that it raised questions of authority that would haunt them in the twentieth century. Their religion gave them psychic relief to do what they must in modern America without completely abandoning their tradition and yet without allowing the full force of their commitment to autonomy. The bond of family—in one's past and of one's creation—proved durable and frustrating. As the Phelpses, Rauschenbusches, and Macfarlands learned, no person lives unanchored to a past; no person can escape generational obligation.

As Walter Rauschenbusch found in the early twentieth century, the obligations of fatherhood were demanding. The last two decades of his life brought the sad realization that friendship with his children resulted in a decline in paternal authority that was only partially offset by their displays of affection. Other parents in the early twentieth century experienced Rauschenbusch's dilemma and lived to witness an even more shaking change—the transfer and legitimation of authority from Protestant faith to the secular corporation. Charles Stedman Macfarland and his wife embraced the social gospel for many of the same reasons that Walter Rauschenbusch decided to relive the life of Jesus and Elizabeth Stuart Phelps worked among the fishermen of East Gloucester. The social gospel gave the Macfarlands' lives purpose. As participants in national organizations that institutionalized their beliefs, they participated unwittingly in the glorification of bureaucracy, expertise, and self-realization that proved to be the cornerstones of corporate power over the American imagination. Their children exemplify the connections between the Protestant social gospel and the emergence of corporate America.

The choices and opportunities available to the Macfarland and Rauschenbusch children are evidence of a profound change that had transformed middle-class family life at the turn of the century. As the social gospelers began to recognize the deficiencies of Protestant churches in supporting family life, they began to rely on secular agencies to secure the physical and moral well-being of middle- and working-class families, and they helped to forge an alliance between government and the helping professions to provide the needed social services and moral guidance. Refusing to accept the reigning liberal conceptions of political culture, these Protestants joined in the development of the political culture of progressivism in the hope that the state could become an instrument of Christian leadership. But when social gospelers themselves tried to occupy the bully pulpit of American politics, they sacrificed the independent authority of their religion to the social dynamic of the state. In this way the social gospel became a gospel of social salvation, and the authority of Christian religion was absorbed into the authority of secular culture.

4

MINISTERS AND THE

BULLY PULPIT

In *Christianity and the Social Crisis*, which was completed in 1907, Walter Rauschenbusch included a brief portrait of Theodore Roosevelt as an example of the kind of man who should hold office in the United States in the twentieth century. He recalled the strike by workers in the anthracite coal fields in 1902, when "the country was on the verge of a vast public calamity." Without some interference, Rauschenbusch reported, thousands of Americans would have died from cold and exposure. The bully president decided he had a moral obligation to settle the dispute, so he "set his face grimly" and declared: "Yes, I will do it. I suppose that ends me; but it is right, and I will do it." Roosevelt's intervention failed to cause the anger and political defeat he feared. Instead, according to Walter Rauschenbusch, it earned him the "thanks of every man, woman, and child in the country." President Roosevelt had acted because he thought it was morally correct for the government to ensure peace in the coal fields and to prevent suffering by those who depended on coal for fuel.[1]

A few years later, Washington Gladden echoed Rauschenbusch's sentiments in his autobiography. As he reviewed the fifty years of politics since 1860, Gladden insisted that "no man since Lincoln" had been such a "vitalizing influence" on the life of the nation as Theodore Roosevelt. He spoke of Roosevelt's service to the nation and his "awakening the conscience of the land" against injustice at the hands of unregulated corporations. "To disentangle piratical business from honest business to protect legitimate enterprise and prevent and punish predatory schemes," wrote Gladden, "this was the task set before him."[2] By 1910, Americans had begun to expect such service and morality from their public leaders. Theodore Roosevelt, the "Christian soldier," had become the symbol of a new age of politics.

The new age of politics was more than progressivism, though progressives played a large role in the shift away from nineteenth-century liberalism. Party competition and self-interested politicians—standard fare of nineteenth-century political experience—did not disappear in the twentieth century but became parts of a different political culture. In terms of the expectations of government, public values, and the articulated goals of the state, political culture in twentieth-century America included an expanded sense of social responsibility and public welfare, governmental regulation of business in the interest of democracy, and greater popular participation in government. Progressive legislation protected American consumers from adulterated products and introduced the first programs of social insurance. Direct primaries and direct elections of senators as well as the initiative and referendum permitted citizens to take part in the process of government more directly than in the past. Americans had begun to move away from a stern belief in self-reliance and laissez faire and in the direction of public provision in the case of emergency or disaster. Progressives' vision of an active government prompted social reform. Because they believed in the essential goodness of man, progressives wanted to create a society that would allow individuals to develop their talents. Many progressives also wanted government to guard morality. This set of beliefs, expectations, and reforms demanded more of government.[3] Indeed, an elaborate collection of agencies and commissions were formed by those in power to implement the progressive agenda.

Progressives believed that the government should ensure the public good by creating the conditions for economic growth and stability. This dimension of the progressive agenda demanded government regulation of and cooperation with business. Responsibility for economic health required bureaucratic developments, the recruitment of experts in various fields, and efficiency. Often the government's cooperation with business is perceived as antithetical to social legislation associated with progressives like Robert LaFollette, but the progressive commitment to both social reform and economic strength contributed to a redefinition of state responsibilities. Both agendas expanded the role of government in twentieth-century American political culture. Theodore Roosevelt and Woodrow Wilson were exemplars of this new political culture in the United States in the twentieth century. The two men have often been contrasted, but they emerged out of the same political reordering that began at the turn of the century. Growing intolerance of a politics of self-interest and partisan competition, exemplified in its worst form by a corrupt and "treasonous" Senate and "boss" politicians, had called into being a new view of politics—one based on service, morality, and regulation.

.   .   .

This political transformation did not take place in a vacuum. It was part of larger changes in social relations and cultural values that swept the nation at the dawn of the new century. And it was tied securely to the social gospel. Because social gospelers and Christian social reformers had begun to make demands on government agencies to provide protection and assistance to families buffeted by industrialization and the urban environment, they supported the erection of the machinery of the welfare state that first appeared in the progressive period. Because their programs were designed to shore up domestic morality, these men and women of Christian principle helped to create the "politics of morality" that marked American political culture after 1900. Politics, under the influence of people like Theodore Roosevelt, became an arena for right action—a bully pulpit to defend public morality. For Woodrow Wilson, it demanded "ministers of reform" who would use the machinery of government to build the kingdom of God on earth. The political culture of progressive reform gave ministers of the social gospel hope that they could "Christianize the social order" and thus save the nation.

Progressivism and the Protestant social gospel seemed to sustain one another in the early 1900s. Social gospelers supported progressive politics believing that it would usher in the kingdom of God. In *Christianity and Socialism* (1905), for example, Washington Gladden contended that "if the kingdom of heaven ever comes to your city, it will come in and through the City Hall." Samuel Zane Batten insisted that politics had "at heart" the establishment of a "social order in which the great ideals of the kingdom shall be realized," and the noted social gospeler believed that the state was "a potent agency" in the creation of the "Kingdom of God in the earth." Another social gospeler, Charles R. Henderson, believed that religion reinforced the view of the state as service by "inspiring" churchgoers to "devote them[selves] to the public welfare." Henderson went on to applaud the good work done by groups like the Municipal Voters' League of Chicago, whose success at promoting progressive legislation, he argued, "would have been impos-

sible without the moral education given by the churches and their ministers."[4] Thus, at the prompting of Protestant ministers and reformers,
a transforming politics of service and morality began to take shape.
Men of the cloth gave the bully pulpit of politics both respectability and
an agenda of reform.

Similarly, however, revitalized politics promised new life to religion
as social gospelers conceived it. A political system responsible for social service and public morality extended the influence of churches into
the secular arena and restored the relevance of religion to everyday life.
Most important, progressive politics demanded social gospel Protestantism. In an article for the *Independent* in 1916, Shailer Mathews
suggested that "a religion for democracy" needed a conception of God
that was democratic instead of autocratic. "Our inherited orthodoxy,
shaped up as it was under the influence of political practices and theo-
ries of empire and monarchy," he wrote, "is already with difficulty
appreciated and understood by men . . . of democratic ideals." The
result of transformed politics, he believed, would be a democratic God
and a more believable faith. Others believed that no matter how many
services the state provided, it still needed the spiritual leadership of
churches to perpetuate public morality. The Reverend Paul M. Strayer,
for instance, wrote in the *Biblical World* at the end of 1910 that "government regulation and economic readjustment" would be effective
only with an infusion of "the religious spirit."[5] Even a politician like
Woodrow Wilson affirmed the expanded role of religion. In a 1914 commencement address, the president told ministers that "the Christian
church stands . . . at the center of politics" and that it was their duty
to "show the spiritual relations of men to the great world processes" and
to offer a "complete and satisfactory explanation of life." He concluded
that a religion of service and personal devotion was "more widespread
and dominant than ever before."[6] Wilson and social gospelers believed
that religious leaders should play a vital role in the life of the community.

Social gospelers also believed that the sacred pulpit was as crucial
as the bully pulpit in the program of reform. They did not fear—at
least, not at first—that the state would assume the functions and responsibilities of churches, nor did they view politics as a surrogate for
Christian idealism. Social gospelers involved in politics were *not* the
"ministers of reform" described by Robert Crunden, crusaders who
found fulfillment in progressivism because the pastoral calling seemed
lifeless and out of the mainstream of twentieth-century events. The

social gospel movement, of course, included the dedicated young men and women of the cloth who thought that their efforts would make Protestantism vital and vibrant. Because they conceived of a *social* gospel with a wider impact than the religion of their forefathers, turn-of-the-century Protestants saw in the politics of Roosevelt and Wilson their chance to influence the course and direction of American history. They considered the politics of morality and service as both an arena for and evidence of the social gospel. Their reasons for helping to create progressive politics and for enthusiastically supporting it sprang from optimism about the role religion could play in society as well as from dissatisfaction with the social and cultural underpinnings of nineteenth-century liberal politics and evangelical Protestantism.

Both the social gospel and twentieth-century American politics arose from massive social and cultural changes at the turn of the century. Both were products of a dissolving faith in strict individualism and in a Victorian code that seemed frustrating and unworkable in late-nineteenth-century incorporating America. Both were also results of social changes that disrupted Victorian families and interfered with their capacity to care for their members. And both emerged from a profound psychological dynamic—a shift in the basis of identity, goals, and direction from inner to other sources and a shift in the goals of personality formation from the self-controlled, self-made man to the self-realized team player. Ministers and politicians alike eschewed the individual ethos, which had become nearly impossible to fulfill. They increasingly took responsibility for the nurture, protection, and moral guidance of family members—once considered private tasks left to true women and Christian gentlemen. Social gospelers and political reformers hoped to provide the environment and tools necessary to allow Americans to fulfill their potential and find meaning and purpose in a cause larger than themselves.

. . .

As the nineteenth century drew to a close, the main concern of social gospel Protestants who examined liberal American politics was rampant corruption. Scandals at all levels of government from city hall to the White House prompted intense dissatisfaction with the nature of politics in the late 1800s. The self-interested competition that had run amok in the economy plagued politics as well. In the view of many social critics, liberal politicians had little regard for the general welfare of the community or nation and viewed public office as an opportunity to compete and prosper on their own behalf. One of the early Protestant critics of corrupt politics, Josiah Strong, complained in *Our Country* (1886) that one of the perils facing the nation was "boss" politics— uncontrolled pursuit of self-interest at the expense of good government. Fifteen years later, Strong still blamed "maladministration" of government on public officials who "have carried over into these new and complex social conditions the old individualistic spirit expressed in the motto, 'Every man for himself.' They are in politics," he insisted in *The Times and Young Men* (1901), "for what they can get out of it," sacrificing "the public interest" to serve "their private interest."[7]

Strong was not alone in this critique. Dr. Charles Brown, pastor of the First Congregational Church in Oakland, California, and a popular lecturer in the early twentieth century, addressed the National Council of Congregational Churches in 1904 on "the supreme need of the churches." Brown indicted America's pursuit of "unmodified self-interest," which threatened to usher in the "kingdom of hell" instead of the "kingdom of heaven." In place of unbridled competition in politics and economics, the Californian insisted on "social responsibility" and the "cooperation of trained specialists and Christian preachers" in order to serve one another. In 1907 Charles R. Henderson demanded a "social policy" from American lawmakers that would reflect a "nobler subordination of selfishness to the largest good." He explained that "the 'individualism' of which many boast often means no more than 'die you, live I'; 'every man for himself, and the devil take the hindmost.'" Anyone "who does not enter into the wider sweep of social goodness," he went on, "never makes much of himself. The typical 'individualist' who remains egoistic is a criminal." And as Henderson and others in turn-of-the-century America could see, individualism in politics often *did* result in criminal activity by machine politicians. George Washington Plunkitt's self-styled epitaph, "I seen my opportunities and I took 'em," confirmed Americans' association of political self-interest and corruption.[8]

Competition between parties also worried these Protestant critics of liberal politics. Competition between individuals in the economy and at the workplace had lain at the base of their critique of work and salvation and had inspired the Social Creed of the Churches. Competition between party machines proved equally menacing because the critics could see even more clearly than in the workplace how little control they could exert over the political process as lone individuals. In *The New Era* (1893), Josiah Strong insisted that "if all good citizens would declare their independence of party politics" and then organize to find the "best men fitted for the desired service," the problem of "rabble-ruled cities" would soon disappear. Washington Gladden recalled in his autobiography that the municipal elections in Columbus, Ohio, in 1904 found decent people asking, "Men and brethren, what shall we do?" Party machines seemed determined to fleece the people and to provide little in the way of public service. More than two thousand "good citizens" decided to form a pact, and they endorsed candidates who showed integrity. The result, Gladden remembered, was "a better list of candidates to select from than we should have had otherwise."[9]

Theodore Roosevelt borrowed the language and sentiment of these social gospelers in his plea in *The Conservation of Womanhood and Childhood* (1912). "I shall ask you to think not of yourselves—I do not ask you to do anything for your own benefit," he asserted at the climax of his address. "I ask you to remember, each of you, that each of you is and must be his brother's and sister's keeper." If left in the hands of selfish politicians and unrestrained large interests, Roosevelt predicted, the United States would be "a mighty poor country in which to live."[10] Like in the economy, collective efforts in politics promised reward, whereas concentration on individual interests threatened to result in failure, exploitation, and corruption.

.   .   .

For some social gospelers the anxiety about individualism and competition at work became linked to the same fears about politics, as the case of William D. P. Bliss reveals.[11] Born in 1856 in Constantinople, the son of American Congregationalist missionaries, Bliss grew to young manhood steeped in the evangelical tradition of his parents and of mid-nineteenth-century Protestant America. He traveled to the United States in the 1870s to complete his education. Upon ordination, Bliss decided to remain in the United States and accepted calls to Congregational parishes in Denver, Colorado, and South Natick, Massachusetts. He found his duties in the United States markedly different from his parents' mission to the Turks, and before long, Bliss became disenchanted with what he saw as Congregationalists' unresponsiveness to social problems in "factory villages." He eventually left the church of his parents and joined the Protestant Episcopal church. In 1886, Bliss took charge of an Episcopal parish in Lee, Massachusetts.

While he was in Lee, Bliss's practice of the social gospel took an increasingly political turn. He joined the Knights of Labor and became an active member and delegate to their national meetings. In 1887, after moving to Boston, Bliss and a colleague, Frederick Dan Huntington, co-founded the Church Association for the Advancement of the Interests of Labor (CAIL). An Episcopal organization, CAIL exerted widespread influence in the 1890s. It was one of the first associations to advocate arbitration of industrial disputes and to attack the sweatshop system in New York City. Working on behalf of laboring men and women, Bliss and other members of CAIL also found themselves increasingly confronting a liberal political system that cared little about the interests of labor.

In 1887, the Labor party nominated Bliss for the office of lieutenant governor in Massachusetts. After an unsuccessful campaign for this office, Bliss organized the Society for Christian Socialists in the United States, hoping to transform American politics and to ease the anxiety of workers who met with one failure after another trying to live up to the Victorian work ethic in an age of large corporations. After establishing the Church of the Carpenter in Boston in 1890, Bliss became an active spokesman for socialist politics in America both on the lecture circuit and as a political propagandist. While socialism did not make significant inroads among American voters until 1912, Bliss's *Handbook of Socialism* (1895), his *Encyclopedia of Social Reform* (1897), and his journal, *The Dawn* (1889–96), as well as his leadership of the National Social Reform Union, helped to promote a collective politics of morality and service. For William D. P. Bliss, the impossibility of the Victorian ethic made both work and liberal politics problematic. As a social gospeler he worked to redefine them both.

While other social gospelers shared Bliss's disenchantment with individual responsibility at work and with individual self-interest in politics, few enjoyed the intimate contact with workers and the impoverished that Bliss knew in South Boston. Nevertheless, as their commitment to social reform drew them to the underside of American cities, they began to discover the need to experience the horrible conditions in urban America in order to foster real political and social change. As Samuel Zane Batten put it, "Our modern Christianity, if it would command the allegiance of men, must be real and must deal with real problems. It must prove its courage by probing the wounds of society to the bottom and it must prove its ability to cure the ills of society."[12] A deepening involvement in reform brought a new edge to life for middle-class Protestant Americans because it challenged them to go places they had assiduously avoided, to work with alien people, and to take action that threatened their own personal security. Their "new citizenship" demanded authentic confrontation with social problems and added meaning to their lives. Toward the end of his career, Josiah Strong found municipal politics to be invigorating. It "shook" him "body and soul," he reported, and Strong hoped that greater political action would "shake millions of men out of their lethargy" and involve them in the "vast cosmic transformation" of civic life.[13] Bliss, Batten, and Strong discovered that political reform drew them out of the safety of their middle-class existence into an exhilarating arena of action.

In keeping with their political activism, social gospelers envisioned a new role for the state—a role that was taking shape in the minds of other Americans outside the church as well. They came to view government as a source of security in a world of insecurity. Washington Gladden asserted in 1893 in *Tools and the Man* that the "strength of the state" should "shelter" and "succor" its citizens—especially those who could not survive alone. In *The Message of Jesus to Our Modern Life* (1915), Shailer Mathews declared that the state had an obligation to protect Americans from "exploitation by selfish, ignorant, and evil men" who ran the parties.[14] Samuel Zane Batten, chairman of the Social Service Commission of the Northern Baptist Convention, told his readers that politics was the "science of social welfare," and that good American citizens would "exercise the sovereignty of the state" in order to remove the "handicaps and hindrances" that harmed its citizens. "If conditions are unsanitary in the city, they will organize a Board of Health and will endeavor to make them sanitary," he continued. "If they find that children are growing up in vicious ways they will establish Juvenile Courts and probation officers and will thus save the young from a criminal life."[15] In every case, Batten invoked the state to rectify wrongs, to protect citizens from exploitation and injustice, and to reduce anxieties about success and failure. Theodore Roosevelt acknowledged in an address in the early twentieth century that it had become the "duty" of the state to "safeguard the worker" against "inhuman toil" and exploitation by large factories and corporations, and Edward A. Ross insisted that "administrative bureaus and commissions" in the state should "shield the public from the sharp corners and rough surfaces of the public service corporations."[16] On this issue social gospelers and progressives concurred: the state should protect citizens from hardship and exploitation. Like religious leaders, public officials wanted to improve conditions of life in this world.

·   ·   ·

Part of what prompted social gospelers and politicians to promote a protective state was the disarray of family life at the turn of the century. Middle-class Protestants hoped to impose their domestic values on families whose poverty and incessant toil disrupted healthy family relations. Institutional churches and social service commissions attempted to shore up immigrant and working-class families that could not provide material sustenance and spiritual nurture for their members. From the earliest day-care programs and free meals, at places like Caroline Crane's People's Church in Kalamazoo, social gospelers evinced their concern for urban families. But it was not merely cultural imperialism that drove Protestants in the social gospel movement to demand protection from the state instead of from families. For, as has been demonstrated, middle-class families themselves had been affected by changes in the workplace and by disintegrating Victorian culture. The declining authority of parents, the blending of gender roles, and the growing reliance on teachers, peers, and social experts for identity and direction made middle-class Americans receptive to new forms of protection and nurture in the state. Ostensibly, social gospel reformers began to redefine the government on behalf of poor people who required assistance and reassurance. But they also helped to create and enthusiastically embraced a "domesticated" state for themselves as well.[17]

The participation of Protestant reformers in the domestication of American politics began in the 1880s when Washington Gladden's call for "applied Christianity" generated an interest in the solution of urban social problems. As early as the 1890s, Josiah Strong lamented the "venomous filth and seething sin" of tenement homes. In *The New Era* (1893), Strong identified a list of targets for reform that began with the unhealthful living conditions in slums. He spoke of children "born of drunkenness and lust," "whose lullabies are blasphemies," "whose admonitions are kicks," and "whose examples are vice and crime." Strong concluded that "people cannot be elevated while their environment remains unchanged." Evangelical missionaries in the cities, though well-meaning, he argued, might just as well try to bail out the Atlantic Ocean with a thimble. What was needed, insisted the old man of the social gospel, were public investigation and regulation as well as permanent agencies of reform. In the same year, Washington Gladden wrote in *Tools and the Man* that "good sense and good Christian morality" demanded education, sanitation, protection of women and children, public health and welfare, and limits placed on the wealthy—all functions that could be performed by the state. "The state would be stronger, and the individual members of the state would be richer and happier and better," he contended, "if power and discretion were taken away from the family and lodged with the government."[18] Thus, almost from the beginning, social gospelers' interest in families demanded new services from the government.

Indeed as the progressive spirit began to pervade American political life, social gospelers began to envision an entirely new role for the state. The government itself, they hoped, would become the head of the American family and household. As Lyman Abbott put it, mankind belonged to "one great family," and "the Nation, the State, the town are a household."[19] Others spoke of a political revolution in the early twentieth century that involved a "new faith in human brotherhood," "a great brotherly endeavor," and the creation of a "brotherly society on earth."[20]

Some of the more explicit comparisons between the state and the family came from women authors. For instance, Imogen Oakley and Lucretia Blankenburg, members of the Civic Club of Philadelphia, described the ideal city as "private housekeeping on a larger scale." The utopian embodiment of reformers' dreams promised appropriate "training" of children through the "cooperation of manufacturers and school boards," "pure food, pure water and unlimited fresh air" to all citizens, and a "filial and self-denying affection between citizens and their municipal government." Mary McDowell echoed Oakley and Blankenburg's sentiments in her "civic code" for the citizens of Chicago. Insisting that God had made men and women in the city "brothers and sisters all," McDowell went on to say that "Chicago does not ask us to die for her welfare; she asks us to live for her good, so to live and so to act that her government may be pure, her officers honest, and every home within her boundaries be a fit place to grow the best kind of men and women to rule over her."[21] McDowell and others like Caroline Crane did their part by becoming "municipal housekeepers." The consequent domestication of the state resulted in more opportunities for women in politics. It simultaneously demonstrated the willingness of American Protestants to make the family both the object of and the model for reform.

As the ideas of brotherhood and filial obligations between citizens and government found expression in social gospelers' discussions of political reform, the language of Victorian domesticity crept in as well. More than rhetoric, however, the language signified an important change in the nature of American society and political life. Social gospelers who advocated progressive politics used traditional Victorian domestic values of service, sacrifice, and nurture to define the state they envisioned, and the leaders they elected eventually became the caretakers of these values. The most important value was service. Social gospelers helped to legitimize the idea of government as "public service" instead of pursuit of self-interest. Josiah Strong, for instance, told readers of *The Times and Young Men* (1901) that men who obeyed the "law of service" and who knew "how to serve" would make municipal government "clean and wholesome."[22] Gladden, Rauschenbusch, Mathews, and Batten all echoed Strong's sentiment in their respective works on the church and politics. Their appropriation of domestic responsibilities in political life helped affirm the emerging ideal type for men to which they had contributed: the man devoted to both action and nurture, service and achievement. As Paul Strayer put it in an article for *Biblical World* in 1910, "Government regulation and economic readjustment will be effective only when the religious spirit has created a new form of competition—the competition in service." The masculine drive for contest and the feminine virtue of service produced a "new measure of success, a new standard of greatness."[23]

For many social gospelers, Jesus became the embodiment of this new standard in American politics. After all, Jesus had instructed the disciples that he who would be greatest among men must be their servant.[24] Charles Brown told the National Council of Congregational Churches in 1904 that "Jesus would found the social order on the basis of human brotherhood in the service of one another."[25] The teachings of Jesus helped social gospelers locate the domestic virtues of service and self-sacrifice in the state, which they believed was a reliable vessel capable of being influenced by Protestant citizens. The domesticated government did not mean the domination of politics by women: Jane Addams complained that despite the compliments women received for their work in organizing charity and reform, they rarely had the chance to run the agencies they helped to create because it was considered "very unwomanly."[26] But it did mean that the politics of reform contributed to a blurring of cultural distinctions between men and women that placed new responsibilities on both. Men accepted their new role more readily because as the new century dawned, the figure of Jesus took on a more traditionally "manly" aspect. Walter Rauschenbusch, who in the early twentieth century admired Jesus for his compassion and his manliness, also urged "statesmen, prophets and apostles" to see the "highest self-assertion in self-sacrifice."[27] In other words, he and others in the social gospel movement saw the feminine virtues of service, sacrifice, and nurture, personified in Jesus, as manly traits of public service, heroism, and a passion for justice.

. . .

One of the most important ways the new public servants chose to fulfill their responsibilities was in the promotion of public health. Both health care and sanitation had fallen under the administration of women in Victorian America, and only gradually had women turned to experts in both fields for direction in carrying out the two tasks.[28] Social gospelers seemed obsessed with abolishing disease and cleaning the environment. Their concern seems to have stemmed from at least two sources. The first was related to their commitment to the kingdom of God on earth. Social gospelers' interest in matters of the temporal world instead of other-worldly concerns compelled them to make this world better, a fit kingdom. They moved toward the world instead of away from it and applauded efforts to "fight tuberculosis" and "secure parks and playgrounds" because such endeavors were, as Walter Rauschenbusch put it, evidence of the "power of religion" to "flow out in the service of justice and mercy."[29] Washington Gladden's faith in the eventual emergence of God's kingdom on earth impelled him as a minister and as a city councilman in Columbus, Ohio, to lobby for "good streets, good water, good sewerage, good schools and libraries, good parks and playgrounds and public baths"—all furnished at a reasonable cost—in order to preserve the "health of the city."[30] Health and sanitation, once the responsibilities of the home, fell easily enough under the jurisdiction of a revitalized government according to Protestant advocates of the kingdom of God.

A second, equally compelling reason for supporting public health, however, arose from a deeper psychological motive. For a society whose members were increasingly dependent on one another for identity, direction, approval, and realization of personal goals, a high standard of public health became necessary if each individual was to make the most of his talents and develop his personality. Society could not, perhaps, guarantee individual success, but collectively Americans could ensure that none would be handicapped by bad health, unnecessary accidents, and hazardous living conditions. Just as unemployed workers sparked both guilt and anxiety in the sons and daughters of the middle class, the crippled, dwarfed, and unhealthy children of urban slums reminded middle-class Protestants of their own dependence on good health care, proper nutrition, and basic sanitation for success. Part of Theodore Roosevelt's appeal was his dogged determination to overcome a sickly childhood and live a robust, successful life. The warm embrace of an ideal of "self-realization" and the unspoken acknowledgement of people's needs for the approval and support of others prompted the collective commitment to ensure public health.

The career of Samuel Zane Batten illuminates some of the private impulses to extend governmental and public health services. Batten received a bachelor's degree in 1885 at the age of twenty-six and the following year was ordained as a Baptist minister. For the next quarter-century, Batten's peripatetic ministry took him from Tioga, Pennsylvania, to Lincoln, Nebraska, and several other places in between, and brought him into contact with some of the leading social gospelers in the country. Having made himself visible in his own denomination at the national level in the 1890s, he became involved in such ecumenical movements as Rauschenbusch's Brotherhood of the Kingdom at the turn of the century. He served on various Baptist and ecumenical commissions of social service and boards of church federation, and eventually the Federal Council of Churches selected him to act as an associate secretary. His recognition in Protestant leadership came from his participation in team projects. As he rose to prominence in his profession, Batten came to rely on the help of friends. As he acknowledged in the foreword of *The Social Task of Christianity* (1911), his comrades in the Brotherhood of the Kingdom "had clarified his thought and intensified his conviction," and to them he owed an "immeasurable debt." In turn, Batten offered his book as a means of providing assistance to others in the society. "The great need," he declared in the same foreword, "is a sense of direction of the day's march, a definite idea of the day's task, and a clear understanding of the factors and forces of social progress."[31] Samuel Zane Batten hoped to provide some guidance in his work.

Thus, his concern for public health, as expressed in several of his books on the Christian state and the social gospel, should be understood in the context of increasing social interdependence. In *The Christian State* (1909), Batten argued that the government should "provide conditions for every soul which make possible a worthy human life" and "should provide each man free scope for his talents and encourage him to make the most of his aptitude." A Christian state, he concluded, would be the "conservor of human well-being and the promoter of the good life." In *The Social Task of Christianity*, Batten focused his remarks more directly on the issue of health. "Questions of fresh air, sufficient food, pure water, sanitary conditions, social atmosphere, and clean literature," he wrote, "are . . . of concern to the spiritual worker," for without these essentials of good health, "millions of men are really disbarred from the heights of life."[32] He believed that a domesticated state could play a part in the efforts of men and women to live up to prevailing ideals.

The state as "conservor of well-being" would take partial responsibility for Americans' fulfilling their promise as individuals.

Batten was not alone in his interest in public health and individual fulfillment. Lyman Abbott considered it one of the "rights of man" to grow up in a healthy environment with good education "to give men the ability to take advantage of a chance." Abbott encouraged every American "to be what you can." Walter Rauschenbusch described part of America's "social crisis" as inadequate attention to public health. Nervous disease, malnutrition, and tuberculosis "cripple our children," "snuff out the life of our young men and women," and "leave the fatherless and motherless to struggle alone in their feebleness." If Americans had "sense," Rauschenbusch scolded, they could enlist the state to "eradicate" these blights on the health and future of the country and its citizens. In *Jesus and Politics* (1915), Harold Shepheard contended that political action alone could "plan healthy towns"—private charity was not enough: "Only the common will can ensure that all shall be well-born. Only by political action can we give every soul its perfect opportunity."[33]

.   .   .

The demand for more services, for an environment to fulfill individual potential, and for social responsibility for the good life eventually revealed the appeal of consumerism. In the marketplace, Americans demanded products and services that helped them realize their full potential. They placed a great deal of confidence in experts to create the latest improvements and to advise them on which products to select. Similar trends also appeared in political life. The shift from city mayors to city managers, the emergence of federal agencies like the Bureau of Mines to disseminate technical information, and the skillful manipulation of the press by Theodore Roosevelt and Woodrow Wilson all indicate the importance of expertise and mass marketing in early-twentieth-century American politics. Nor were social gospelers immune to these tendencies. In their promotion of social responsibility in public affairs and in their own institutional development, twentieth-century Protestant reformers incorporated the terms of management, bureaucracy, and expertise into their strategy for success. Both progressive politicians and ministers of the social gospel reflected the hegemony of corporate America.[34]

The evolution of the Federal Council of Churches best illustrates social gospelers' growing reliance on corporate strategies. Until the council was founded in 1908, involvement in programs of reform had been determined by individual inclination and opportunity. The Labor party nominated Rev. Bliss for lieutenant governor of Massachusetts in the 1880s; Charles Macfarland settled some labor disputes in the 1890s; Washington Gladden ran for councilman in Columbus, Ohio, in the early 1900s. After 1908, however, while these individual, idiosyncratic efforts continued, most of the contact between church and state came through leaders of the national body. Bishop Francis J. McConnell, considered to be one of the most effective of the Methodist reformers, earned his reputation for social reform in national committees sanctioned by denominational and ecumenical bodies. His authority as a spokesman for Protestant churches came from the endorsement of church bureaucracy.

In the years immediately preceding World War I, the Federal Council of Churches began to assume the roles of spokesman for mainstream Protestant America and of liaison between socially active churches and a progressive government. In 1913, for example, the council told Woodrow Wilson that the "political forces of the nation" and the "moral forces of the church" could work "together for the social and spiritual well-being of the people." Later that year, the body urged the president and Congress to recognize the republic of China, and it asked the San Francisco municipal government to curb vice and crime during the Panama-Pacific Exposition. In 1915, the council secured the assistance of the government in beginning war relief in Europe. The following year, Charles Stelzle marshalled the resources of the council to conduct a campaign for improved public health care. As he wrote in his report to the general secretary, if public health agencies applied "the science of preventing disease and accidents, according to the experts" misfortune could be reduced and "human life may be extended fifteen years." He proposed a "campaign for the conservation of human life" that would harness the "cooperation of recognized authorities and existing agencies" in a "united national attack" on "disease and death." This and other recommendations called for work with secular organizations and the government. By the 1920s, the Federal Council of Churches had its own lobby in Washington and through it tried to influence public policy.[35] The ministers and churches of America had become one of the many interest groups that tried to influence the "associative state" that was coming into place in the decade of Hoover and Babbitt.[36]

. . .

From the sporadic reform attempts of the 1890s and early 1900s to the efficient lobbying of the Federal Council of Churches, Protestants had influenced American politics in profound ways. The demands for assistance to those in need had called into being the language and structure for expanded government service and had encouraged the halting growth of a progressive ethos. In a sense the politics of progressivism had been a product of both sacred and secular forces. Indeed, progressive political culture and the social gospel grew in strength and popularity together as means of restoring a sense of authentic action to late Victorians, of helping families, and of incorporating domestic values into a collective vision of society.

The social gospelers' spiritual enthusiasm for and legitimation of the progressive ethos infused it with a moral burden. As the "promoter of the good life," in Batten's words, the government, through its agents, had to make choices and policies that were deemed "right" and "best" for the citizenry. Writing legislation thus became more than addressing someone's selfish interest—it was a moral act. Interest groups long had existed to press legislators to enact laws to curb vice and immoral conduct, but they had most often worked for punishment of crimes already committed or reformation of individual evildoers. The moral mission of the progressive period and of the welfare state that followed it was more encompassing. Protestant Americans under the leadership of social gospelers asked that public officials display exemplary moral behavior and that they transform society to eradicate the social bases of immorality. In 1912 Walter Rauschenbusch rejoiced that "the old leaders are stumbling off the stage bewildered" and that a "new type of leader," who responded to a popular "stiffening of will, an impatience for cowardice, an enthusiastic turning toward real democracy," was taking their places. "Were you ever converted to God?" he asked in *Christianizing the Social Order*. "Is not this new life which is running through our people the same great change on a national scale?"[37]

Progressivism, like the religious revivals of old, reaped a harvest of souls in the 1910s. And it prompted Americans to expect moral leadership and personal integrity from their leaders. Theodore Roosevelt had remarked a few years earlier, in the presidential campaign of 1908, that Americans were entitled to know whether a candidate was a "man of clean and upright life, honorable in all his dealings with his fellows" and fit to make moral decisions in the "great office" he pursued.[38] As the emerging welfare state provided more services and protection to citizens and as its agents felt compelled to address the demands of interest groups and the general welfare, the government increasingly became the guardian of national morality.

In the midst of the enthusiasm for this emerging "politics of morality" and a budding welfare state, a few social gospelers who had helped legitimize progressive politics began to raise some concerns. If the state assumed increasing responsibility for the welfare of the American people, what role would churches play? As early as 1907, Shailer Mathews used the pages of *Biblical World* to ask, "Will the state displace the church?" While he believed that the social gospel had made Protestantism a vital force in the twentieth century and that the world needed the spiritual power of churchmen, he conceded that the state "has been and still is absorbing the functions formerly discharged by the church." He went on to declare: "Education, the relief of poverty, the defense of the weak against the strong both in matters of affording asylum to the accused and in the protection of employees against employers, and now at last the 'cure of souls,' to the extent at least of seeking reform and reinstatement of the criminal—all these originally belonging to the church and in large part its creation, are now in the process of passing over into the hands of the state."[39]

A few years later, *Biblical World* published an article by Paul Strayer which pointed out that "the church of the city is losing its former prestige" and that "statesmen are speaking more plainly on great moral issues than clergymen." Strayer insisted that he was not "jealous of state agencies like schools, hospitals, and settlements," but he believed that if any further progress were to come, it should proceed on the "initiative of the church."[40] Even Samuel Zane Batten, who had been instrumental in giving reform a language and a moral foundation, noted that in the twentieth century, one "activity after another was broken away from all control by the Church." Education, charity, social service, and reform, he wrote, "now engage the attention and claim the devotion of many people who are not members of the church. To many people religion is losing its centrality and is becoming simply one interest among many other interests." And worse, many Americans regarded religion as a "somewhat incidental interest."[41]

By the time younger Protestants who had not been at the vanguard of the social gospel came of age in the early 1900s, politics reflected these initial concerns. Protestant Churches *had* given up many social functions to the state. They *had* lost cultural authority in their communities. They *had* become but one interest among many in the associative state. Americans looked to experts in the state and in the marketplace for well-being, protection, and purpose. Science explained life and death, and secular agencies of the state harnessed the knowledge of science to become "promoters of the good life."

Churches in the years following the expansion of the Federal Council of Churches during and after the Great War in Europe lobbied and tried to influence men and women in power in the United States. At best they were gadflies, at worst supplicants. Relief from social misery came about through legislation unaccompanied by Protestant belief. The effect in public life was to focus attention on the state as the provider of protection and assistance and to ignore the role played by churches in inspiring the commitment to reform in the first place. This amounted to a subtle, but significant shift. The credit for social welfare went to the state instead of churches. Churchmen were free to continue to speak out for social justice and ameliorative legislation, but the general public took notice when the government took official action. Suffering citizens eventually could expect assistance from the state and less often looked to churches. Ministers who believed that the bully pulpit of politics would revitalize Protestantism discovered, in time, that politics ultimately was devoid of religion.

The emergence of an ethos of social responsibility in American political life took place slowly and barely perceptibly, as the lives of Lyman Abbott, Mary Eliza McDowell, and Francis John McConnell show. Yet between Abbott's halting critique of nineteenth-century liberal politics and McConnell's leadership of the American Association for Social Security in the 1930s, a vast transformation of politics had occurred. Lyman Abbott was the longtime editor of and contributor to *The Outlook*, which commented on national and international politics. Mary McDowell was a Christian settlement house worker in Chicago who worked to reform city politics and held public office in the 1920s. Both Abbott and McDowell helped to domesticate the liberal state of the nineteenth century, and they helped ease fears about identity and success in their reforms. McConnell fell heir to the relationship between church and state that they had helped develop. All three hoped to revitalize American religion and politics. All three contributed to a growing faith in the state to provide well-being. All three show how the social gospel and progressive politics arose from the same sources, sustained one another, and contributed to the emergence of a secular dominant culture in the United States.

LYMAN ABBOTT

From the "Barbarism of Individualism" to "Fraternal Government"

In January 1890, friends and supporters of Henry George gathered in New York City to honor the reformer on the occasion of his forthcoming journey to Australia, where he planned to promote the single tax and free trade. Among the well-wishers was Lyman Abbott, a Congregational minister and editor of the *Christian Union*. At the end of the banquet, Abbott delivered a speech in which he offered a "true interpretation" of the political beliefs of "a growing body of progressive democrats." The aging editor opened his remarks with a simple declaration: "We are believers in democracy." He then went on to proclaim his faith in "political democracy," "educational democracy," "democracy of wealth," and the partnership of capital and labor. "We do not believe that government is a necessary evil and the less we have of it the better," he insisted. Nor did he wish to retreat either to a "paternal government" or to "the barbarism of individualism." Lyman Abbott and like-minded Americans looked forward to a "fraternal government" where people lived by their "common will" and "common industry" to produce their "common well-being." This "new" view of government placed the burdens of opportunity, justice, protection, and well-being on the state rather than solely on the individual. When Abbott finished, the crowd thundered its approval. The speech had been "continually punctuated with applause," and at its conclusion, one of the guests called for "three hearty cheers," which were promptly and "heartily" given.[42] Lyman Abbott had become one of the bellwethers of a changing view of American politics and government.

Like many of his contemporaries in the middle class who endorsed the progressive tendencies in both major parties, Abbott developed his creed out of disenchantment with self-interested political liberalism that so often ended in bossism and corruption in the years after the Civil War. Fearing individual failure and seeing examples of unsuccessful men and women below them, late Victorians like Abbott questioned the role of government in a world seemingly ungoverned. More and more American Protestants began to question their purpose in life as well as the authenticity of their existence, embraced the ideas of the social gospel, and plunged into the underworld of poverty, vice, and disease in an effort to regain their connection to the real world and to revitalize their faith. Concern with establishing the kingdom of God prompted a reexamination of political belief. For the state became one of the chief agencies through which social gospel Protestants began to work for social salvation. Thus, even moderate social gospelers like Lyman Abbott helped engender expansion of government obligation and service as they committed themselves to the task of redeeming society. Their social gospel demanded a "Christianized" state.

Lyman Abbott

The language of Abbott's speech, however, suggests that his political ideals sprang from private sources as well. His refusal to embrace "paternal" government and his longing for a "fraternal" government and the "brotherhood of man" found their origin in a world of peers and sibs that was beginning to emerge from the transformation of the domestic ideal of family at the end of the nineteenth century. Abbott's own family life was disrupted by death, market demands, and separation. His revulsion against the "barbarism of individualism" revealed hidden wounds and disappointments faced by striving young men in an era of incorporation. Lyman Abbott and the audience who warmly approved his speech in New York City had begun to rethink the nature and role of politics in the United States at a time when social change and cultural transformation had turned their lives upside down and had shaken the solidity of their Victorian faith. An examination of Abbott's life and career helps explain why the progressive view of government had such wide appeal and why many men of the cloth became ministers of reform.

Born in 1835 in Roxbury, Massachusetts, Lyman Abbott was the third son of Jacob and Harriet Vaughan Abbott. Before he was three, the Abbotts moved to Farmington, Maine, where Lyman and his brothers spent much of their childhood. In 1843 Harriet Abbott died in childbirth, leaving her husband with four small boys to raise. Overcome with grief, Jacob Abbott left his sons with a sister and moved to New York City to open a school for girls. Over the years the Abbott boys lived with different relatives—grandparents, aunts, and uncles—and eventually followed their father to the city when they were old enough to enter New York University. Upon completing his studies, Lyman Abbott practiced law for six years before he began to study for the ministry. In 1860, he took his wife of three years to Terre Haute, Indiana, to his first parish. During the Civil War, Abbott offered a moderating influence to a community divided in its sympathies between antislavery and secession, and at the war's end, he served in the American Union Commission to aid families, both black and white, that were dislocated by the war. From 1866 until his death, he divided his time between duties as pastor in various New York Congregational churches and as editor of several religious weeklies. He was best known as the editor of the reformist journal *The Outlook*. Lyman Abbott died in 1922.[43]

Two patterns emerge from the details of his life that help explain Abbott's embrace of the social gospel and his advocacy of reform in politics. Most important, Abbott lived in a world of brothers rather than in a more conventional Victorian domestic circle. In 1849, six years after their mother's death, Abbott and his two older brothers, Benjamin and Austin, shared an apartment in New York. From the moment he joined his brothers and entered New York University, Abbott led a life of "absolute freedom." His brothers advised and assisted him but exerted little authority over him. He confessed to leading a "quasi-bohemian" life in the city, attending the theater, minstrel shows, Barnum's circus, and special attractions as well as enjoying informal drinking. Once out of college, the three brothers opened a law firm together. Each specialized in one dimension of the business, creating perfect coordination, efficiency, and harmony between the partners. In the 1850s, they collaborated on a novel called *Cone Cut Corners*, which proved to be a financial success for "Benauly," the *nom de plume* they constructed from their names. When Lyman Abbott left the firm to enter the ministry in 1859, "their comradeship did not cease." Abbott regarded his brother Austin as his "guardian," "friend," and "counselor" and admired his other brother Benjamin.[44] Even after their marriages to various Abbott cousins, the three men remained close friends and confidants.

When phrases like "the brotherhood of the kingdom" gained wide coinage, and when Congregationalists, Methodists, and Baptists began to form Brotherhood organizations, those groups held special meaning

for men like Lyman Abbott. Any authority that had influenced him had
come from his brothers, not from his father. Like other children who grew
up in a universe of peers and siblings because their parents had outside
interests and obligations in a demanding marketplace, Abbott clung to
his brothers because he had no other choice.

This first pattern—brotherhood—in part prompted his sympathy for
the social gospel.[45] In his spiritual autobiography, *What Christianity
Means to Me* (1921), Abbott wrote that his discovery of Jesus had made
his spiritual life much more comforting and real. "Suppose that all your
life you had dreaded an awful God," he wrote, "and suddenly the curtain
were rent aside and you saw the luminous figure of the living Christ, and
over his head were written the words, 'This is thy God, O man.'" That had
happened in Abbott's youth. Jesus became his "friend" and "Great
Companion." Abbott embraced the Son "who is upon earth" and who
lived a "life of love, service and sacrifice."[46] This "revelation" of brotherhood and camaraderie eventually led to a commitment to "making a
new world out of the old world" and to developing a new "art, literature,
philosophy, government, industry, and worship" with a new social spirit.[47] A religion of brotherhood appealed to him in a way that the orthodox
puritanism of his ancestors could not, because his own family life never
had required reverence for and strict obedience to his father.

Besides brotherhood, another pattern shaped Lyman Abbott's world
view. Ambivalence toward individualism tormented him through most of
his life. The Abbotts had been steadfast Congregationalists for generations by the time Lyman was born. The lad's grandfather had helped
build the "old-fashioned brick Puritan meeting-house" that the Abbotts
attended in Farmington, Maine. Each of the old man's sons had stood
behind the pulpit on various occasions, and two of his grandsons were
ordained there. Thus, it is not surprising that Lyman Abbott anxiously
awaited a religious awakening that would signal his salvation from eternal damnation. Indeed, he writhed in anguish for more than a decade
without a conversion experience. As a child he spent many anxious
nights in his dark room trying to remember all of his sins, drawing on the
memory of his mother in heaven and his father in New York to produce a
sense of guilt.[48] When he finally did join a church as an adolescent, he
suspected that he was accepted "not on his very imperfect confession of
faith" but because members of his family belonged to the church and he
was seen as "a young man without bad habits."[49] His struggle to achieve
individual salvation thus ended in a partial victory. Furthermore, he felt
the tension between individual and social religion in these early years of

faith. Two members of his grandfather's church, who stood out in his memory, represented opposite poles in religious life. One refused to sing any hymns except those by Isaac Watts. The other shunned the angry God of Watts and Jonathan Edwards by opening his prayers with one of two salutations: "kind parent" or "indulgent parent." The boy probably wavered between the two statements of faith.[50]

In addition to religious individualism, individual enterprise and success in the secular world worried Abbott. Shortly after he proposed marriage to Abby Francis Hamlin, he wrote her a stream-of-consciousness confession of anxiety. "I am twenty years of age," he began. "To say that I do not realize it, would not begin to express my want of conception of who I now am and who I used to be. Even now as I walk the room I cannot conceive who I am that am twenty years old." He sensed that his life had become fragmented. His life, he insisted, did not seem "connected together—one whole. There are disjointed pictures here and there." In spite of his unpromising self-portrait, Abby Hamlin agreed to become Mrs. Lyman Abbott in 1857. The Abbotts set up housekeeping in New York, and he worked in his brothers' law firm, which, he realized, "might be anything we had the ability to make it." He worked in the firm for two years, making his contribution but gaining little extra notice. "I was restless," he later complained, "ill at ease."[51] He had not carved out a place of his own, nor had he found individual spiritual peace. In 1859, Lyman Abbott left the law firm and embarked on a career in the ministry.

Whenever the subject of the ministry had come up during the first two years of their married life, Abby Abbott had not taken her husband's aspirations very seriously. Indeed, Abbott wrote uphappily to his father-in-law, "Abby laughs at my ministerial dreams sometimes." As a boy he had considered the ministry to be his "great ambition," and observing Henry Ward Beecher, one of the masters of the American pulpit in the 1850s, renewed his interest. After attending seminary he took over a parish in Terre Haute, Indiana, where the debate between unionists and secessionists raged. Lyman Abbott managed to remain true to his convictions, but he realized that he "had accomplished so much less" than he had hoped that his pastorate seemed to be a "failure." After four years in Terre Haute, he moved his family back to New York City, where he labored in an experimental Congregational church and served on the American Union Commission—"a rare opportunity to take some part both in an individual and a social gospel." In spite of his best efforts, the experimental church failed. It had been an opportunity to succeed, but

the result had been "an invalid wife, a discouraged church, a disheartened minister." Lyman Abbott admitted that "my ambitions were too
great for my abilities. I had not the capacity to do what I had hoped to do,
nor to be what I had hoped to be. My ambitious hopes were ended." In
1870, he left the pulpit and resolved to become a "useful citizen" by
joining the editorial staff of the *Christian Union*.[52]

Abbott's record of individual disappointment made him question the
stern doctrine of individual responsibility and salvation and attracted
him to the language of the social gospel when it began to appear in
popular religious publications in the late 1870s and 1880s. His sense of
failure combined with pleasant memories of brotherly support make it
easy to see why a gospel of social salvation, a Christocentric theology,
and a Protestant commitment to the immediate transformation of this
world appealed to Abbott. By the time he had recovered sufficiently from
his early discouragement to accept another call to a church, the young
people in his congregation appreciated his dissatisfaction with individualism in religion because of their own frustrations with work in corporate
America, and they helped make his ministry and his moderate social
gospel a popular, lasting success. In the meantime, however, Abbott's
decision to be a "useful citizen" as editor of a Christian journal gave him
a chance to articulate the social gospel, which had important implications for American political culture.

From 1870 on, Abbott's work reflected the values of the social gospel. As an editor of the *Christian Union* under Henry Ward Beecher, he
became part of what he called the "new journalism" of the late nineteenth century. New journalists used their publications as forums for
discussing issues of social concern. He and Beecher urged a greater
spirit of "unity" and "cooperation" among Protestant churches in order
to inspire the "Christian life" in all aspects of American society. Abbott
insisted that Protestants devote themselves to ushering in the kingdom of
God on earth. When Abbott became the sole editor of the *Christian
Union*, he redesigned it, renamed it *The Outlook*, and instituted cooperative management practices. Instead of writing "almost entirely" alone,
as he had for the *Christian Union*, Abbott relied on "a number of minds
acting in cooperation" and "joint deliberation" to produce the journal.
"Each issue of 'The Outlook,'" he declared, "is essentially the product of
team work."[53] The new journalism, of which *The Outlook* was a part,
eventually spawned the muckrakers of the early twentieth century. Abbott's work thus simultaneously helped to legitimize a new social ideal of
success and to politicize the social gospel.

In 1887, in addition to editing *The Outlook*, Abbott became pastor of Plymouth Church in Brooklyn. For more than eleven years, he directed this "working church," one that ministered to the needs of its neighbors. Similar to Rev. Bartlett's institutional church in Kalamazoo, Plymouth Church responded to the problems of poverty, unemployment, and family nurture that arose in the 1890s. Abbott's "church of workers" became an employment agency, an educational center, and a source of relief for the poor. In addition to establishing reading rooms, a penny bank, social clubs, gymnasiums, and community health services, the church, under Abbott's guidance, accepted a new test for membership. Rather than passing a doctrinal examination, new members had to explain to a committee the kind of community service they planned to perform and then commit themselves to one of several service departments in the church.[54]

In his parish, Abbott saw extreme poverty, overworked parents, little security against disaster, and a breakdown of family and community life. He saw that problems of disease and sanitation simply could not be handled on an individual basis. Yet municipal government provided few safeguards against any of these social and moral ills. Corrupt bosses and their ward heelers lined their own pockets as "entrepreneurs" within the city government and carried away the spoils of each election. But none regarded the city's collective needs as his interest. The result, from the Protestant's point of view, was that families could not maintain the moral and physical health of their members. Churches could provide some relief and guidance. But both church and family found themselves looking increasingly to a hodgepodge of secular agencies to furnish and coordinate security.

Beginning in the 1880s, Abbott began including critiques of American politics in *The Outlook*. Not surprisingly, the chief complaint he leveled against the political system was the bankruptcy of the two major parties. Without principle, both Democrats and Republicans had become "corpses," and Abbott believed the country needed "live" parties. Parties had become vehicles for self-interested politicians to use office as a way to make money and to gain power. Abbott decried "bosses" and their "selfishness, greed, low ambition, petty intrigue."[55] The editor of *The Outlook* advocated direct primaries so that more people would have a voice in the selection of candidates, and he began to articulate a new view of government. Office holders should be civil *servants*, he averred, making the state an arena of service rather than an arena of competition.

For Abbott, America's involvement in war with Spain in 1898 embodied the mission of a Christianized state devoted to public service. When Dewey's fleet sailed into Manila Bay, Abbott believed that America should be "stirred to a higher sense of national duties within our own borders." The United States' victory signalled the triumph of "the kingdom of conscience, the kingdom of justice, the kingdom of equal chance, the kingdom of universal education, the kingdom of free religion, . . . the kingdom of God on earth." Abbott took the opportunity of the war to expound on the United States as a Christian nation. Battling against "evil within itself" and "evil without itself," the United States struggled toward "a higher and better ideal of justice, mercy, truth, and reverence." Unlike the tyrants defeated in the Spanish-American War, leaders in the United States showed "consideration for the poor, the ignorant, the oppressed and the suffering," and embraced the ideal of "the commonwealth." The United States, Abbott believed, was a nation that "God had built up" because it gave its citizens "more than a fair chance" and provided "something like an adequate education." While Abbott's comments are an Anglocentric, imperialistic justification of the "splendid little war" of 1898, they reveal his sense of the moral achievements and responsibilities of the government.[56]

Abbott recognized that the expanded role in moral leadership that he had hailed in 1898 demanded a concomitant decline of the "authority of ecclesiastical religion." The "moral and religious influences which a hundred years ago went almost exclusively from ministers," he wrote in The Rights of Man (1901), now found expression in a variety of secular public agencies. Abbott celebrated the commitment of the government in the twentieth century to take greater responsibility for the care, nurture, and advancement of its citizens. "We have not only opened the door," he wrote, "but we have gone to the very cradle and said to every child, You shall have an education that will fit you to enter into this door, to take advantage of this chance to be what you can." The "political cooperation" of American citizens made it the right of every man to have "a free and full development of all his powers, physical, intellectual, moral, and spiritual."[57] Citizens should expect the state to help them realize their full potential. Abbott affirmed the new state with religious zeal.

In 1902 when Theodore Roosevelt delivered a series of addresses entitled "Big Corporations Commonly Called Trusts" near the end of his first term, Abbott was "delighted" with the president's proposal to regulate the trusts and eagerly sought permission to publish the lectures in The Outlook. Thus began an association that led to Abbott's ever-increasing involvement in American political life. At the end of his term of office, Roosevelt joined the editorial staff of *The Outlook* and became, in Abbott's words, "an ideal exemplar of the spirit and value of team work." Under Roosevelt's influence Abbott used the pages of his widely read journal to promote government regulation of corporations. In 1912 the U.S. Senate summoned the aging editor to testify before a committee investigating the effectiveness of government regulation of business. "Congress tried regulation in the case of food and drugs and . . . succeeded," he reminded the legislators, "and tried disorganization in the case of the Standard Oil Company and the Tobacco Trust and . . . failed."[58] The implication was clear: the government had a charge to intervene for the welfare of the people.

In the presidential election of 1912, Abbott welcomed the Progressive party, not just because his friend, Theodore Roosevelt, was its creator and candidate, but because he believed it was a party of principle that would conduct a moral campaign and would serve the people if its candidate was elected. In his autobiography Abbott noted, "In my lifetime I have seen the American Government become a great builder of public works, a great financial institution, a great educational institution, a great benevolent institution, a great administrator of public utilities, and a protector of the rights and property of the public as well as of the rights and property of private individuals." The state was becoming the "fraternal government" he had idealized nearly twenty-five years earlier.[59]

Abbott's enthusiasm for a transformation of American politics had been in part a result of private disappointment with liberalism and with family. As a spokesman for "cooperation," "brotherhood," and a "welfare state" (though he probably never used such a term) Abbott answered some of his own needs for assurance, identity, and protection. He knew in a personal way what it meant to be left alone with no one but brothers to give advice and nurture; he also knew what it meant to fail as an individual in an incorporating world. Thus his dissatisfaction with a politics of self-interest came in large part from the frustrations of his childhood and young manhood. And yet Abbott could not slough off entirely an inheritance of values. It was more difficult to uproot the individualistic political expectations in a man of sixty than it was for the generation of men who came of age in the 1890s and 1900s. They used the language provided by older men like Abbott to consolidate the changes in American political culture that had begun to appear.

Because politics had such deep roots in Abbott's past it is little wonder that he returned to the theme of fraternal government as he addressed students at Yale in 1910. "Mankind constitutes one great family," he told them, and "in a more intimate sense the Nation, the State, the town are a household; and . . . as in the family brothers and sisters though of unequal ability and sometimes enjoying unequal advantages are yet equally children of their father and equally brethren and equally concerned in the welfare of the home, so in the Democratic State all races, all classes, all men constitute one household."[60] Abbott spent most of the later years of his career making it his religious duty to redefine and reform the process of government. In so doing he helped transform both Protestantism and liberalism. His commitment to brotherhood, Jesus, and social salvation helped legitimize and promote the social gospel. The more devoted to the social gospel he became, the less concerned he was with ecclesiastical authority. A Christianized state became the basis of his success and hope. By the 1910s, Abbott had crossed a great political divide—from the "barbarism of individualism" to a "fraternal government."

While Abbott hailed the advent of a more activist government at the end of his life, younger social gospelers helped set the agenda for the progressive state. Mary Eliza McDowell was one such socially conscious Christian, who demanded more service for working-class families from the municipal government in Chicago. She and others who came of age in the late nineteenth century helped domesticate American politics by urging the government to shoulder responsibilities once accepted by families. McDowell's understanding of the social gospel led her to take direct political action. And her evolving confidence in the state led to her religious zeal for reform.

MARY ELIZA MCDOWELL

Cleanliness, Godliness, Reform

Mary Eliza McDowell, a social settlement worker in Chicago, spent most of her career in the shadow of Jane Addams. The University of Chicago Settlement, where she spent more than forty years of her adult life, received far less publicity and praise than the more famous Hull House on Halstead Street. While McDowell shared top billing with Addams in 1906 as one of Chicago's "five maiden aunts" active in reform, she never quite earned the nationwide love and respect that her friend in Hull House enjoyed. Indeed, her support of unions and labor strikes in the stockyards brought her contempt and discredit in 1904 and

cost her many friends. Nevertheless, Mary Eliza McDowell can illuminate a dimension of the past upon which her sister Chicagoan can cast
but dim light.

While Addams acknowledged the influence of her Quaker father and
then rarely, if ever, mentioned religion again, Mary McDowell never
forgot the religious roots of her secular service. She was a laywoman who
accepted the Protestant social gospel. The career of this settlement
worker in the stockyards provides an example of how the social gospel
and progressive political culture became intertwined in the early years of
the twentieth century. McDowell's story also helps clarify the process by
which the state began to act as the caretaker of domestic morality. As the
"Duchess of Bubbly Creek," the "Garbage Lady back of the yards," and
the "municipal housekeeper" of Chicago, McDowell provides an angle of
vision for understanding how social gospel Protestantism and progressive political culture arose from and affirmed both social changes and
cultural transformation. McDowell, in her capacity as a social worker
and later as commissioner of public welfare, participated in the transfer
of moral authority from the True Woman to the public servant. Mary
McDowell's embrace of the social gospel helped her to link cleanliness,
godliness, and reform.

Born in Cincinnati, Ohio, in 1854, the oldest of six children born to
Malcolm and Jane Welch Gordon McDowell, Mary learned at an early
age the importance of taking a political stand.[61] From her vantage on the
northern side of the Ohio River, the child witnessed the oppression of a
people in the South and the valiant efforts of the soldiers in blue to end it.
She remembered seeing Union soldiers tramp through the river city en
route to the battlefields. Her father's distinguished service during the
Civil War and his devotion to the "man in the president's house" cemented both her faith in firm political conviction and her adoration of
Malcolm McDowell.

The war brought more than political idealism to the McDowells. It
brought traumatic social changes as well. At the war's conclusion, Malcolm McDowell moved his family from his wife's ancestral home near
Cincinnati to follow the burgeoning railroad industries. He left his
father-in-law's shipbuilding business to superintend iron foundries in
Columbus, Ohio, and Providence, Rhode Island, before he finally made
his way to Chicago. There he opened and managed a steel rolling mill.
Finally, in a move of great significance to his daughter, Major McDowell
left the Episcopal church and joined an "old-fashioned Methodist
chapel" where he sought a "consciousness of relations with God" which

Mary Eliza McDowell

he believed came to "men beneath him in education and social standing." In other words, McDowell hoped to find a vital religion among the
working class. His daughter, only months away from being confirmed in
the Episcopal church, announced firmly, "If Father's going to heaven, so
am I," and joined the Methodist church.[62]

Mary McDowell dated her "consecration" to "social service" from
the moment a Methodist working man performed the laying on of hands, a
ceremony that welcomes new members into the church. Following her
father's lead, she took great pride and comfort knowing that a "carpenter
who built boats on the Ohio River" rather than a "bishop of the apostolic
succession" had blessed her. She remembered that her "social faith" had
been nurtured by the old carpenter who blessed her as well as by the
servants of the city such as the "captain of our fire department" and by
"the immigrant and the Negro" who were a large part of her life. Weekly
visits to the humble chapel with her father reinforced her devotion both to
Malcolm McDowell and to the common people he chose to address as
brother and sister. She gave up dancing lessons, declaring simply, "I'm
not going to dance any more. I'm going to Heaven." In the evangelical
fold, McDowell found that religion "became real" because it involved her

"everyday life," not mere "theological doctrines." As she answered the
lay leader's inquiry after her soul, the devout child realized that her soul
was a "reality" to the old carpenter, and she admitted that it became, "to
the wee girl, a precious something that had to do with my every-day
actions and life with the folks."[63] Her membership in the Methodist
chapel initiated McDowell into the hurly burly of public affairs because
everyone was expected to make a public confession of faith and to
participate in testimonial services.

The McDowells' new religion as well as the other political and social
changes profoundly altered their family life. While she still lived just
outside Cincinnati in the spacious house built by her father, Jane Gordon
McDowell made her home the social center for their community. Her
benevolent care of domestic servants combined with charity to needy
neighbors made Jane McDowell a model of Victorian true womanhood.
She tried to provide her only daughter an example of appropriate womanly behavior and arts to "finish" her education. She saw to it that her
daughter studied dancing and music—necessary accomplishments for a
well-bred young lady. Jane McDowell even oversaw her child's religious
education in the Episcopal church.

With the sudden changes after the war, however, Jane McDowell
became what her daughter later described as an "invalid mother."
Wrenched from the only home she ever had known and thrust into a world
of industry and railroads destined to supplant the workshop of her father,
Jane McDowell may well have felt uncomfortable and out of place. When
her husband and only daughter abandoned her church, she lost one of
the last strands of continuity with a happier past. By the late 1860s, Jane
McDowell no longer could care for her family, and much of the responsibility for her five young sons fell on the shoulders of her daughter, Mary.
The girl remarked years later, "I was under the impression that the whole
McDowell family depended upon me."[64] As a young girl, Mary
McDowell rarely saw glimpses of the domestic ideal in her mother. In the
aftermath of the Civil War, the well-ordered family life of the McDowells
became deranged and the model of womanhood available to Mary
McDowell unappealing. As the years went by, McDowell relied on and
learned from her father.

During their first few years in Chicago, McDowell and her father
became partners in a number of social and religious enterprises. In
1871, for example, when the Great Chicago Fire left thousands of people
homeless, Malcolm and Mary McDowell facilitated the evacuation of the
refugees by furnishing and driving wagons, transporting people and their

belongings, and helping them settle in a makeshift tent camp that sprang up near the McDowell home. When aid came to the homeless from Ohio, Mary McDowell became the "guiding hand" in the relief effort. The father later encouraged his daughter to accept an invitation to visit President Rutherford Hayes at the White House, where she saw a "constant stream" of politicians promoting their ideas. When the McDowells moved to Evanston in the 1880s, father and daughter conducted a church young people's class that discussed the practical application of Christian principles made famous in Washington Gladden's popular *Applied Christianity*. Malcolm McDowell insisted that religion must "express itself in the everyday actions of those who professed it." The discussions he led attracted people like Frances Willard, founder of the Women's Christian Temperance Union, as well as students from Northwestern University, interested citizens in Evanston, and longtime friends from Chicago. His daughter "welcomed new members," "made them feel at home," and added "wit and activity" to the meetings and discussions. As she approached her thirties, Mary McDowell had gained a "breadth of social experience and service" by working and worshiping with her father.[65] She was his partner and protégé.

In the 1880s and 1890s a number of events propelled Mary McDowell into public life. After having met Frances Willard at her father's Sunday meeting, she began to work for the WCTU. While doing temperance work, she met Elizabeth Harrison, whose school for the training of teachers eventually prepared her for a job at Hull House. McDowell organized a kindergarten and woman's club under the supervision of Jane Addams and Ellen Gates Starr. Within a few years she had become acquainted with the most prominent professional women in the Chicago area. McDowell shared these women's aspirations for experiences different from their mothers' lives, but unlike them, McDowell continued to be driven by family obligations and by religious zeal. It took one final event for her to dedicate herself to the social gospel and a life of public service: the Pullman Strike of 1894. The strike highlighted a tension between older Victorian values that lay at the foundation of her faith, on the one hand, and the ideals of the social gospel, on the other. McDowell could not fathom "wage-earners who had work" going out on strike. How could these workers refuse to work when jobs in Chicago had become so precious? Yet, how could workingmen be wrong? After weeks of inner turmoil, McDowell met the Reverend Carwardine, pastor of the Methodist church at Pullman. She later reported that he "helped me to see that the Pullman strike was only typical of a great world unrest which

must be understood." She found herself "more dissatisfied" than ever
with the comfortable ignorance of her sheltered community and determined to learn more of the "drab parts of industrial life" too often
"ignored by an uncertain society."[66]

Members of the faculty at the recently established University of
Chicago shared McDowell's concerns. They organized a Christian Union
to find the cause of the unrest described by Carwardine and to create a
"laboratory of social service" in Chicago. They chose the stockyards for
the location of a settlement house, and, on the recommendation of Jane
Addams, they chose Mary McDowell to serve as the settlement's director.
McDowell moved to a small flat back of the yards, where she began a
decades-long career putting the ideas of the social gospel into practice.
Settlement work is "objective Christianity," she wrote in an unpublished
essay. "It is one of the many expressions of the social conscience that is
slowly but surely feeling its way into action."[67]

The decision to accept a position in the university's settlement house
came quickly for McDowell, and her commitment to social work deepened as she discovered that the people behind the stockyards gave her
life meaning and direction that it lacked in comfortable Evanston. In
time she moved her parents into the house so that her mother's illness no
longer would call her to Evanston. Her father had always told her that
workers could "teach the cultured" about the "life abundant." McDowell
found that life among the impoverished assured her that her middle-class
existence need not insulate her from the authentic struggles of life. As
she wrote after seven years of work, "The Settlement brings to the University the problems of real life—vital problems that need the thinkers
as well as the doers to solve them." As a "laboratory of human experience," the settlement introduced students hoping to enter professional
life as ministers or social scientists to "all kinds of questions and people"
of which they otherwise would be ignorant. It reminded them of the
earthier side of life from which they had become removed.[68] One of her
biographers noted that McDowell was not an "effete" idealist "afraid to
face the realities of existence," the "drunken women and idiot boys of
life." Rather, wrote Howard Wilson, she was "made of sterner fiber."[69]

McDowell acknowledged, decades after she moved into the small flat
on Ashland Avenue, that being among the immigrants and workers had
revitalized her religion and had given her life purpose. "Thirty odd years
of living near to those in the struggle for existence," she wrote in an
autobiographical article for *The Survey*, "have made my early impressions freshly important for me and brought to my religious life a meaning

that grows in value."[70] The settlement gave her life meaning at a time when rapid social change had made true womanhood unfulfilling. McDowell was grateful for the work with humble and gritty immigrants that connected her to an authentic experience. As the years passed, the social gospel that brought her to a new neighborhood in the stockyards of Chicago would propel McDowell into a world of politics that ultimately redefined both the responsibilities of citizenship and the locus of moral authority.

In a memorial tribute to Mary McDowell published in 1938, one of her close friends and colleagues, Dr. Graham Taylor, recalled that the eminent social worker had been asked by the compiler of a local directory to state her occupation. Taylor declared that "she might have mentioned any of the occupational positions she had held," but her response was merely "citizen." Whatever her jobs were, he continued, "she evidently considered them all to be expressions of her all-inclusive calling—citizenship."[71] Taylor's observation shows how McDowell was shaped by her involvement in the social gospel. Her "calling" was public rather than private. She took her civic responsibilities with religious seriousness. For her, a career meant adopting an entire community as a family and overseeing the morality and well-being of the "larger home." She found that she required the machinery of politics to carry out her mission even though officially women were banned from the political arena. For women such as McDowell, citizenship and political activism fused the fragments of moral purpose, expertise, and social usefulness into a single identity. One of her biographers explained that McDowell's was "the story of that new kind of *neighbor* who gossips in statistics and uses the facts of her neighbors' lives to better their living conditions."[72] McDowell and others used state agencies and commissions staffed by experts to carry out their mission.[73]

McDowell's participation in politics began almost the moment she entered the University of Chicago Settlement. She spent more than a decade trying to rouse public outrage over unsanitary conditions in the neighborhoods near the stockyards. Open garbage dumps and a dangerously polluted drainage sewer known as Bubbly Creek spread filth, disease, and noxious odors throughout the stockyards district. These two hazards represented an entire neighborhood's problems and, seemingly, no one's responsibility. "It was not a delectable cause for a woman to embrace," she admitted, but the health and well-being of her larger home hung in the balance. McDowell considered health to be the principal concern, but she believed that the city rather than families

must ensure proper sanitation. Women could "inject into politics
. . . housewifely virtues," but she believed that the municipal government should accept the responsibility for carrying out the work of cleaning the city. By 1911, she secured an injunction against dumping garbage in her neighborhood and forced Chicago politicians to confront the
problem of garbage disposal. After arming herself with information gathered on a trip to some of Europe's model garbage-disposal plants,
McDowell convinced the city fathers to appoint a commission to study
the problem. The commission, under McDowell's leadership, recommended the construction of a reduction plant and several incinerators,
which were considered the most sanitary means of destroying waste.
"The important lesson learned by this excursion into the field of city
sanitation," she concluded, "showed that the municipal government
needs trained scientific experts to run the bureau."[74] Scientific experts,
she hoped, would become the guardians of public health.

Health itself had begun to take on a new significance in these years
that bridged the centuries. Advances in medical practice gave people
greater control over their physical condition. The shift from an other-
worldly orthodox Protestantism to a social gospel committed to making
this world better encouraged Protestant Americans to seek abundant life
and to use expanded scientific knowledge to extend life. Social gospelers
believed that Christian citizens with the best programs at their disposal
should use politics to ensure the welfare of all. McDowell stressed the
centrality of good health to the highest civic life. The "fundamental
essentials of civilized life," she insisted during an ongoing campaign for
housing reform, included "clean air, clean food, clean streets and alleys,
and homes that are more than shelters." Such standards must become
"necessities in every city" in order to conserve "the national health and
morals" of the community.[75] In that regard the University of Chicago
Settlement provided nutrition and cooking classes, a visiting nurse program, the services of a resident physician, special eye and ear clinics,
and as long as McDowell served as head resident, the close cooperation
of the city health and sanitation departments.[76]

Health had come to be understood and pursued in a slightly different
way as well. Underlying a consumer ethos that required food, tonics, and
cosmetics to promote vigor, strength, and youth, good health was coming
to be identified with self-realization. Thus, when McDowell's successful
efforts to create a playground near her settlement produced "healthier
looking and more group-minded children," her political reform seemed
to encourage children's sense of becoming all they could become. The

ideal of health as a symbol of and means to self-realization informed an emerging political culture of progressive pluralism. "Surely this is worth fighting for," wrote Mary McDowell, "a civilization that will give every group—black and white, Jew and Gentile, people of all nations—freedom and tolerance."[77] Given this second understanding of health, it is easier to see why reformers like McDowell invested so many years and so much energy in such issues as sanitation, playgrounds, settlement house classes, and housing reform. Reformers thus endorsed the ideals of self-realization and other-direction, which were departures from Victorian expectations.

McDowell herself had departed from Victorian culture by rejecting the ideal of true womanhood. Her mother's limits had, in part, propelled her into the professional arena, and her emulation of Malcolm McDowell, Frances Willard, Jane Addams, and other public people had reinforced her professional aspirations. McDowell also began to question the church of her youth. She explained in an article prepared for *The Survey* that she "felt a longing" to know "whether or not I had religion—in reality." She confessed that while the religious education from the Methodist workers had been "a great blessing," she "could not be quite happy in that church now."[78]

Social work and social Christianity made McDowell sensitive to those around her rather than obsessed with her own soul. Years after she left Evanston to reside in the Stockyards district, she remembered that "no social climber ever desired more earnestly to be accepted by the elite than I wished to be accepted by my neighbors." Not only did she wish to get along with her neighbors, but also she wanted reassurance that her decision to be a social worker instead of a wife and mother was not a moral mistake. She gained confidence as more families in the neighborhood brought their troubles, cares, and disputes to her. During the meatpackers' strike of 1904, McDowell earned the respect and affection of trades unionists by supporting their cause and the newly founded National Women's Trade Union League.[79] Friends from the "other side of life," however, seemed to forget her. "No one except one liberal minister and one settlement woman let me know that they were thinking of me during those six weeks of storm and stress," she complained years later. She drew strength from assurances of approval from middle-class women like Jane Addams who understood her position.[80] By the end of her career, McDowell had much in common with mainstream America, in which most men and women looked to others for direction and identity.

In addition to rejecting Victorian expectations and Protestant individualism, McDowell also rejected nineteenth-century political liberalism. She and her contemporaries attacked the most virulent expressions of self-interested politics: bosses and unscrupulous politicians. When McDowell fought the open garbage dump from 1894 until well into the 1910s, for example, she discovered that the "type of politics gloriously played in city wards in the late nineties" had been responsible for the unsanitary practices. One of the aldermen in her district, who owned a brickyard, had excavated clay for his business, leaving huge holes. He then convinced the city council to pay him to dump garbage in the holes. Once the land was filled and the garbage had settled, the alderman planned to develop it for a housing project. In the meantime, "the alderman grew wealthier and more fastidious, sold his home near the garbage lands, and moved out of Packingtown to one of the lake-front districts."[81] McDowell denounced him for his greed and for raising the "death rate for children of the district" to a level higher than that of the city as a whole.[82] Americans needed "a new kind of politician," she argued, "who will respond to the call of the city's needs as the old-type politician responded to the party whip." In 1914, she urged the voters of the ward to forget about party loyalties and to protect the "welfare of all the people" in the district. Progressivism to McDowell was not the product of one party but the creation of political agents with a "social end" in view. Thus, for president, McDowell voted for the Republican candidate in 1908, the Progressive in 1912, the Democrat in 1916, and the Independent in 1924.[83] She believed in political action informed by social concern and justice.

McDowell's religious values undergirded her support of progressivism in the early years of the twentieth century. As she combatted the destructive individualism of an earlier age of politics, McDowell saw the state as the bearer of her moral as well as social vision. "I suppose all of us hold an ideal, a dream of democracy," McDowell once wrote. "To some of us it is an attitude of mind; to some it is a real religious faith."[84] McDowell's political vision merged with her religion. "My democracy and Christianity must be blended," she wrote in the margin of one of her unpublished manuscripts. "Are not both loving God with all your heart and your neighbor as if he were yourself?"[85]

McDowell discovered in her own home as well as in the stockyards district that women alone could not guard the integrity, interests, and moral virtue of a family. Economic and social pressures on both middle- and working-class mothers made it difficult for them to preserve the Victorian domestic ideal, and their lives were increasingly touched by secular agencies outside the home. As commissioner of public welfare, McDowell "sought the cooperation of all the social agencies and educational institutions" to make social religion a part of "public service."[86] Secular agencies, arms of the state, and the public servants who directed them became the watchful protectors of public morality and important supplements for family welfare. Though many, like McDowell, may have had a deep religious faith, they did not rely on religious institutions to implement their social vision. Instead, they looked to a complicated web of secular bureaucracy to assure social justice and communal welfare. In the process, McDowell and like-minded reformers participated in the transfer of moral authority from church and home to state and public servants.

Mary McDowell succeeded in making the University of Chicago Settlement an important part of the stockyards neighborhood because, as one admirer put it, she did not "stay" back of the yards, but had chosen to "live" there and learned "to say 'we' unconsciously."[87] Her religious conviction had set her on a road of questioning and investigation that led to a home among a deprived, immigrant working class on whose behalf she labored her entire career. Her professional life, however, eventually took its toll on the religious life she had hoped to revive in the Sunday classes with her father. Indeed, her work brought her to the verge of contempt for institutional religion. "I find the church very much confused today on what religion is," McDowell wrote in an essay entitled "The Settlements and Religion." In the same piece, she told of an incident that occurred when she visited England for the first time. McDowell longed to visit a cathedral because she believed she would experience "a religious emotion there never to be felt anywhere else." She toured London's East End, where she witnessed "such poverty" and "such awful sights" that she became "heartsick." Then she entered a cathedral and waited for the service to begin. "No one was there except a few tourists," she remembered, but the service went on. "I tried to worship," McDowell insisted, "I tried to be lifted up; but I did not have the religious emotion I thought I would have. *I was thinking all the time of what I had seen outside*." The poverty of London encroached on her religious experience just as the railroad workers in Pullman had disturbed her peace a decade and a half earlier. McDowell left "with a strange feeling of disappointment," and returned to the people of the stockyards and her reform.[88] Mary McDowell's faith had become embedded in Progressive social reform.

BISHOP FRANCIS JOHN MCCONNELL
Herald of a Humanized Faith

When the Methodist Episcopal Church (North) met in 1912 to determine whether the Reverend Francis John McConnell would be selected as a bishop, a number of the current bishops had reservations. For one thing, McConnell was only forty years old, a young man to assume bishopric responsibilities. Second and more interesting, he was considered to be "too cold" for the job. One bishop remarked sarcastically, "I will simply say that if a mosquito should bite him and draw blood, the mosquito would die of chill." Another of the august body added, "All that *I* will say is that if I were an ocean steamer, I would keep out of his way." A third man was more direct: Francis J. McConnell was an "iceberg."[89] Despite this widespread concern about his personality, McConnell joined the ranks of Methodist bishops in 1912 and launched a spectacular career of Protestant social action. But the society of which McConnell was becoming an influential part was much different from that in which older social gospelers like Washington Gladden and Lyman Abbott, or even Walter Rauschenbusch and Shailer Mathews, had lived. The Methodists of 1912 balked at neither the soundness of McConnell's theology nor the relative paucity of his achievements as a pastor. Instead, they complained about matters of style.

During a career that spanned a half century, Bishop Francis J. McConnell attracted the attention of both liberals and conservatives as he lobbied for industrial democracy, social security, and civil rights for Black Americans. Liberals praised him as a "democratic reformer." Conservatives branded him a dangerous radical.[90] But admirers and detractors alike agreed that McConnell took his responsibilities as minister and citizen seriously and set an example in both the religious and the political arena. Bishop McConnell provides an excellent example of the younger generation of social gospel Protestants who participated in the promotion of an evolving welfare state. He and others in his generation inherited a more fully developed social gospel and an evolving politics that altered their expectations of the ministry as well as their communicants' expectations of them. Like Robert Crunden's "ministers of reform," McConnell shared a progressive mentality with social scientists, educators, settlement workers, and politicians in the early twentieth century. But unlike them, he remained a man of the cloth.[91] Francis J. McConnell and his contemporaries helped legitimize an emerging

Bishop Francis John McConnell

welfare state as they labored to kindle enthusiasm for social gospel Protestantism.

Francis J. McConnell was born in 1871 in Trinway, Ohio, one of three sons of Israel H. and Nancy Jane Chalfont McConnell. Israel McConnell, a well-known evangelistic minister, earned his reputation as a revivalist in midwestern cities during the immediate post–Civil War years. In later life, McConnell would describe his father as "Puritanic" and "overexacting" and his mother as "profoundly religious" and a "most habitual and persistent Bible reader." The religion of both parents was "almost wholly individualistic." From Ohio the McConnells moved to Lawrence, Massachusetts, where Francis experienced his initial disaffection from the individualism of his parents. Years later he recalled that in his youth "repression was thought to be a mark of genuine religion." Sunday afternoons would find the boy with a "haunting fear" that he might not "live through till Monday morning."[92]

Although McConnell grew up in a devoutly evangelical home and joined his parents' church in 1881, a number of childhood experiences softened the rigid religious individualism of his youthful training. McConnell insisted that his parents' stories about the Civil War, for example, inspired his "youthful thinking on social issues." Furthermore, Israel tempered his stern faith with a deep love of music and enthusiasm for athletics, which kindled in his son an appreciation of the aesthetic and of team spirit. Nancy McConnell organized political support for some of her pet reforms and denounced neighbors "who didn't believe that religion had anything to do with political and social issues."[93] From her, McConnell learned that politics could provide an avenue by which religious people could reach their goal of a just society. As a student at Phillips Academy in Andover, Massachusetts, when controversy rent the Andover Theological Seminary, McConnell must have been aware of the conflict between defenders of orthodoxy and the new liberal ministry.

When McConnell worked in a textile mill in Lawrence, Massachusetts, one summer in the 1880s, he confronted "the workers' angle of view" and discovered that individual effort did not necessarily result in material success and social advancement. He learned firsthand what it meant to toil ten or eleven hours each day, something the workers would probably do for "the rest of their working lives," and he saw the need for their "Saturday-afternoon picnics" and "athletic contests," in which he was a regular participant. By the time he entered Ohio Wesleyan University in 1890, the sharpest edges of his individualism had been worn away by these experiences. While his brother Charles followed his father's theology and took a position at Boston University's School of Theology, Francis rejected their "strict legalism" and prepared for a career as a minister.[94]

The career McConnell had in mind for himself resembled neither the evangelical and personal work of his father nor the academic work of his brother. He prepared himself for an urban parish. While working on advanced degrees at Boston University and shortly after he earned his Ph.D. in 1899, McConnell served as a pastor at four churches in the greater Boston area. In 1903 he accepted a call to a Methodist church in Brooklyn, New York, where the congregation told him they wanted "two great sermons a week!" For a time, he worked hard to prepare stirring and timely sermons for Sundays and Wednesdays. At the end of a year, however, McConnell sensed that his "ministry had not made the most of its chance." And he was sure of the reason for his dissatisfaction. "I didn't know the people," he concluded. Over the next five years, McConnell completely transformed his ministry. He took a "personal interest" in the welfare of his flock, and he began to rely on young church members who were conscious of "social and economic and political problems" that confronted the church.[95] McConnell learned from experience that urban parishes required pastors who could make a broad appeal and who would address the needs of people under their care.

McConnell made the shift from an individual to a social gospel with relative ease. He grew up in an age when the older orthodoxy came under serious attack. Some of the most turbulent social and economic protests and political contests occurred during the years of his first ministries. He had studied religion and theology in institutions where controversy raged between advocates of individual and social salvation and where doubts about individualism flourished. For McConnell, the decision to accept the social gospel came less as a result of deeply felt personal anguish about individual achievement and salvation and more because it was an ascendant religious ideology. By the time McConnell became bishop in 1912, his denomination had drafted and endorsed the Social Creed of the Churches that the Federal Council of Churches had adopted in 1908. He had seen the practical results of social religion in his urban parishes. And various denominations as well as the Federal Council of Churches had erected the bureaucratic machinery for more thoroughgoing reform. In other words, the social gospel had become the chief expression of mainstream American Protestantism, and McConnell accepted it as such.

Some of his admirers, however, insist that McConnell did not adopt the social gospel until 1912. Edgar Sheffield Brightman, who celebrated the "World of Ideas" in which McConnell lived, told an audience in 1937 that McConnell "was not always a social leader." "Prior to 1912," he declared, the bishop's work fell in the category of "theology and its individual applications." His friend Harris Franklin Rall, who as a professor of systematic theology at the Garrett Biblical Institute edited a collection of essays in honor of the Methodist divine, declared that 1912 marked McConnell's "turning to definite interest in social problems."[96] Shortly after his election as bishop, McConnell accepted the presidency of the Methodist Federation for Social Service, a position that gave him practical experience in social reform at the national level. In 1912 he also agreed to deliver the Merrick Lecture at Ohio Wesleyan University, where he broke with his earlier writing on personal religion and chose social movements as the topic of one lecture. Whether McConnell became a social gospeler before 1912 or after, it is clear that acceptance of the social gospel did not result from a wrenching personal experience.

McConnell hoped to have an impact on the society in which he lived, and he chose to work in organizations like the Federal Council of Churches and the Methodist Federation for Social Service in order to do so. Under the leadership of men like Bishop McConnell, the social gospel itself was being transformed from the efforts of individual congregations into the coordinated programs of national Protestant organizations. From 1912 on, Bishop McConnell never left the realm of public affairs; he never retreated from the social gospel.

In the years of McConnell's budding activism, Americans witnessed an expansion of the role of government that not only changed the way people understood their political system but also made McConnell's kind of activism possible. The progressive ethos which laid the foundation for the welfare state that emerged more fully in the 1930s included belief in efficiency, government regulation, and the steady improvement of mankind. Beyond these goals, progressives shared a determination to do what was "right." To do what was right required the state to shoulder a wide range of responsibilities for individuals who cried out for help. Churchmen since the 1890s had helped heap an ever larger burden on the state in hopes of shoring up "defective" homes, families, and individuals. The early reforms supported by churches, especially reforms in family services, began to shift attention away from churches and toward government agencies as the purveyors of security and succor. By the 1910s, when the social gospel was at the height of its strength and popularity, Americans were beginning to expect more from their government than they had in the past.

Francis McConnell's view of vital religion as "human life at its highest and best" complemented this emerging political culture. He believed that religious conviction should not stop with itself or with the church. Christians had an obligation to "protest against political and industrial evils" in order "to guard the intellectual and moral interests of the people." McConnell realized the increasing inability of the church to act effectively on its own. In "Religion and Modern Life," he told his audience that the church is "at the mercy of social atmospheres and climates." Thus, it had become "mandatory" for Protestants to "work [their] own ideals" into the "community atmosphere" in order to "reach the public mind" and "create a demand which legislatures and other agencies of the popular will do not dare to defy or ignore."[97] In other words, churches had to engage in politics if they wanted to play a vital role in the uplift of mankind. As one of McConnell's biographers, Harris Franklin Rall, put it, the "old dualism of sacred and secular" had to give way to a realization that a "God who could not command all of life would soon have no place in any of it." Judge Hughley, another biographer, agreed. McConnell, he wrote, "virtually eliminates the line between the sacred and the secular," and at times "he tends to sanctify the secular."[98]

Not surprisingly, then, McConnell elevated citizenship to moral duty. Rather than an act of participating in community ritual or scheming for one's selfish interests, politics for the bishop was an arena of conscience and morality. Shortly after the Great War, McConnell prepared two books that articulated the dependence of Christianity on a burgeoning state. In *Democratic Christianity* (1919), McConnell affirmed the Christocentrism of the social gospel by avowing that "men prefer a God" (like Jesus Christ) who worked "in the slime and ooze of things." Such a god demanded Christian commitment to democracy and reform. The bishop also suggested that "expert leadership" created significant social change. Social gospelers should not shy away from the real problems in modern America—the "slime and ooze." Instead, he argued, they should adopt a position more in keeping with postwar consolidation of corporations, bureaucracy, and expertise. The Christian democrat, in the interest of both the church and the nation, must show his "hearty acceptance" of experts. "The expert," McConnell insisted, "must do what he knows ought to be done, in confidence that the people will at least suspend criticism until the larger results declare themselves."[99] The implication of *Democratic Christianity* was clear: social gospelers depended on the experts in governmental agencies to promote Christian and democratic interests.

Three years later, McConnell completed *Christian Citizenship* (1922), which he designed as a course of study for young people. There he argued that the "distinction between secular and sacred" had caused "much harm." While wishing to avoid a "fusion" of church and state, McConnell insisted that the two were interdependent. "What we seek today," he said, "is not formal and official connection between the larger social groups and Christianity but the sanctification of all these groups by the Christian spirit." The "Christian ideal" for the state, he argued, was the "welfare of the people." The Christian citizen thus had an obligation to participate in the political process to make the state aware of his Christian aims. McConnell even used Jesus as an example. Were he alive today, the bishop contended, "Christ would soon find his way to the offices" of reformers "striving to give men better houses, more fresh air, more healthful shop and factory ventilation."[100] Jesus, it seems, would be a lobbyist of the people in an expanding regulatory state.

American participation in World War I helped to consolidate the expanded power of the United States government. The war cemented McConnell's view of the government as provider, protector, and guardian of morality. "No institution," he wrote in *Democratic Christianity*, "will come out of this war in the same form in which it went in." The war had been about "a worldwide advance of democracy." And for McConnell democracy meant "human values, more abundant life for men, the best possible for men as men," and "enlarging human life." He insisted that after the war, American Protestants would become more and more insistent upon devotion to the "large general welfare as the true fruit of the Spirit."[101] The churches were to concern themselves with these issues rather than with individual salvation, but they would have to turn ever more frequently to the state to guarantee the enlargement of human life.

McConnell learned this lesson himself shortly after *Democratic Christianity* appeared in print. In 1919 labor strife exploded in Pennsylvania's steel mills, and within a short time the hardships caused by the strike attracted the attention of the Interchurch World Movement, an ecumenical organization promoting social service. That year, the Interchurch World Movement appointed a commission to investigate the steel strike to learn the facts of the case, to determine a fair position for clergymen, and to make recommendations for resolving the conflict. Bishop McConnell served as president of the commission. After cross-examining leaders of labor and industry, reading the U.S. Senate investigation, and compiling masses of statistics, the commission concluded that long hours and inadequate wages—not "radical" agitation—had led to the strike, and that unless working conditions were improved, the country could expect more strikes and violence in the future. On 27 June 1920, the commission sent a copy of the report to President Wilson. In the accompanying cover letter, McConnell informed the president that the commission had not found any federal agency that was "directly grappling with" the problems raised by the strikers. He warned Wilson that the Interchurch World Movement's report "ventures to suggest certain actions by the Federal Government." The commissioners offered "practical suggestions" to end "unrestricted warfare" between capital and labor and because "as Christians we can do no other."[102]

McConnell repeated again and again the widely held view that the government should serve the people and provide protection and security. The concluding recommendations of the report urged the government to establish a commission made up of laborers, employers, and statesmen to negotiate a permanent understanding between the combatants. It also included a demand for a federal investigation into violations of civil liberties and the use of labor detectives.[103] A year later when the Commission published *Public Opinion and the Steel Strike* (1921) as an adjunct to the original report, its authors were more direct: "If the twelve-hour day is bad for the country" and yet continues in practice, the commissioners wrote, "the government is to blame." By 1921, Americans expected the government to ensure the public welfare. The federation of churches took no action beyond the investigation; rather, the investigation *was* the direct action of the churches. Churches organized no relief efforts for the families of the strikers; instead, social gospelers seem to have become more or less lobbyists for a special interest. The commission petitioned the government for action and watched as its letters and reports passed from one desk to another among the "experts" in the bureaucracy of state. By 1921, telegram correspondence between the secretary of labor, W. B. Wilson, and McConnell revealed the tension between bureaucrat and "lobbyist." After the secretary's vague reply to an appeal for a mediating committee, McConnell testily told Wilson that he was "unable to determine" from his reply "whether the administration is considering any definite move toward furthering" the commissioners' recommendations. When further communication proved no more satisfactory, McConnell made his case to the Congress.[104]

McConnell's difficulties in this instance reveal a great deal about the place social gospelers found for themselves in modern American political culture. They could propose; they could even act "in cooperation" with the state in matters of general welfare, provided the state was willing; but the state always had the power of decision. It was an unequal partnership; the state itself was the final authority.

Attacks on McConnell that followed the appearance of the *Report on the Steel Strike* (1920) served in a peculiar way to advance his career. Despite a lengthy attack on the commission's report by Marshall Olds, who branded McConnell the "radical Bishop," orders for the *Report on the Steel Strike* flooded its publishers from labor unions, Sunday school classes, men's clubs, and ministers across the country.[105] One of McConnell's associates on the commission, Heber Blankenhorn, remembered years later that the report "shaped the opinion of the nation. . . . Its verdict for labor and against steel capital, became substantially the country's." McConnell—"the Bish" to his admirers among the working class—earned instant recognition and more chances to serve in national office.[106] Within the decade he served as president of the Federal Council of Churches, the People's Lobby, the Methodist Federation for Social Service, the World Fellowship of Faith, the North American Committee for the Aid of Spanish Democracy, the Board of Foreign Missions of the Methodist church, and the Religious Education Association. According to one biographer, when McConnell moved from Pittsburgh to New York City in 1928 to assume the duties of president of the Federal Council of churches, he gained "access both to Washington, through the council's lobby there, and to the New York communications media" and made his "social gospel views known nationally and internationally."[107]

In the 1930s, the bishop promoted a government-sponsored social security program. As president of the American Association for Social Security, McConnell became a lobbyist for greater federal assistance to the aged and the needy. His association educated the public about the need for the program and also guided the work of legislators. One of his colleagues, Abraham Epstein, expressed McConnell's own view when he declared in 1937: "Social security involves a profoundly religious issue. It touches the soul of man because spiritual development can be founded only upon a base of economic security. It is a highly moral question because it measures the ethical standards of a society, for nothing so well gauges the civilization of a nation as the provision it makes for its underprivileged."[108] McConnell also supported Franklin Roosevelt's "Good Neighbor" policy in Latin America and affirmed the New Deal's extension of governmental responsibility. While critics like Elizabeth Dilling, author of *The Red Network*, denounced him as a Communist, and other conservatives considered him one of the most dangerous men in the church, friends and admirers congratulated him as the architect of church-sanctioned Democratic Reformism.[109]

In *Trends in Protestant Social Idealism*, published in 1948, Judge Hughley devoted an entire chapter to McConnell. He praised the Methodist bishop for his activism in "civil rights, labor organization, social security, economic and political reforms, international agreements, race relations, [and] world peace plans," and for numerous innovations in Protestant organization. Referring to him as a "world citizen," Hughley summarized McConnell's contributions as a man of the cloth: Bishop McConnell was "an opponent of other worldly religion," "an earnest believer in the coming Kingdom on earth," and "a herald of a humanized faith."[110]

McConnell's years of political involvement made the last of these descriptions the most fitting. He had long before tried to "humanize" God when he wrote in *Democratic Christianity* that "God must be brought nearer to men not merely for the sake of men but for the sake of God Himself." Men would be the judge of God, he said. "We must have a God whom we can respect as well as love." Thus, he demanded that Christians idealize a deity who "comes close enough to the affairs of this distracted earth to feel the pressures of the burden upon men."[111] McConnell equated religion and morality with physical well-being. As he told the Hungry Club of Philadelphia in 1920 at the height of his involvement in the steel strike, "my chief business in this world is to see that human beings everywhere get a chance to be human beings."[112] In every phase of his career after 1912, he used the political system to usher in the kingdom of God—a kingdom of health, opportunity, and justice. The bishop's kingdom was also democratic—of, by, and for men and women. McConnell and the social gospel movement after the Great War, with their greater reliance on earthly institutions, humanized religious faith.

Bishop Francis J. McConnell was the pride of social gospel Protestantism. Throughout his long career, he served his fellow men through national Protestant organizations, and he attempted to meet the temporal needs of people victimized by war, unregulated industry, and depression. His efforts built on an emerging political culture of progressive reform and welfare statism, and McConnell immersed himself in the political arena. As a Christian lobbyist, the Methodist divine coaxed and prodded secular bureaucrats and politicians to do what was "right" and to shoulder greater social responsibility. His "humanized faith" included a "humanized" God and "good" legislation. Except for the source of his income, little distinguished the bishop from the host of liberal lobbyists who descended on Washington in the years following the Great War. McConnell's humanized faith, which relieved much human misery, helped the state shoulder responsibility for social conditions. By demanding more from the state, McConnell demonstrated his confidence in the power of secular, human institutions to grant security and well-being.

. . .

Lyman Abbott, Mary Eliza McDowell, and Francis John McConnell were three small actors in a very large process of change in American politics at the turn of the century. They participated in the expansion of government to address their demands for greater public assistance to those in need, better public health for the benefit of the entire community, and a general commitment to public service. Their commitment to the kingdom of God on earth helped call into being a new political culture of service, morality, and public welfare. Progressive political culture and the social gospel depended on one another for support and legitimacy. As the lives of these three people demonstrate, social gospel Protestants placed faith and confidence in the state to improve the quality of life on earth. Abbott, McDowell, and McConnell believed that Christianizing the social order would revitalize Protestantism. They never dreamed that their efforts in the political arena would undermine the church. By the 1920s, however, Bishop McConnell could complain nervously that too many Americans considered "the emblems of the nation" to be "more sacred" than the "symbols of religious faith."[113]

Lyman Abbott, like most of the older generation social gospelers, sensed the impossibility of the laissez faire liberalism and the tradition of individual responsibility. Recognizing the need for a more responsive state, Abbott anxiously proposed a shift from the "barbarism of individualism" to "fraternal government." But he had no clear conception of the parameters of the new state.

McDowell and McConnell, because they were younger and part of a different generation, placed more specific demands on the progressive governments of the 1910s and beyond. McDowell's overarching concern with sanitation and public health and McConnell's promotion of social security helped create a vast network of public agencies that provided an institutional structure for progressive political culture. All three of these spokesmen for the social gospel believed that Christianized politics would result in the coming of the kingdom of God on earth. Religious hopes lay beneath their political activism.

Yet social gospelers' political activism eventually undermined their churches. As McConnell's career indicates, the push for humane legislation to improve the quality of life in modern America produced a secular, political impact, not a Protestant one. McConnell may have been one of the guiding lights for social security legislation, for example, but the legislation itself did little to promote Christian belief or Protestant institutions, or to reinforce Protestantism in popular cultural perceptions. It was the state, not the church, that relieved misery.

Moreover, Protestant leaders, having elected to operate as political lobbyists, organized their institutions bureaucratically. Over time, the Federal Council of Churches evolved from one of the more creative, activist, and program-oriented bodies in American Christendom to a purveyor of information, coordinator of denominational activities, and lobbyist.[114] The bureaucratization of Protestantism—of which McConnell alone of the three played a significant part—provided for efficiency and political lobbying, but it could engender religious faith no better than the itinerant minister, farmer preacher, or unaffiliated churchman of the nineteenth century. If anything, it reinforced a popular conception of large-scale operations as both more efficient and less responsible. By the time McConnell took over the presidency of the Federal Council of Churches, the organization was well on its way to earning the epithet "ecclesiastical octopus" from conservative Protestants like Ernest Gordon, even as it remained the chief voice of Protestant America. Like the U.S. government, the larger the Federal Council of Churches became in response to members' demands for social involvement, the more it eluded popular control.

The careers of Abbott, McDowell, and McConnell also make it clear that the social gospel was a middle-class, "liberal" creed—it was neither radical nor revolutionary. Their willing acceptance of an ideal of self-realization cut across class lines, leaving the appearance of possibilities for anyone to advance. Interest-group politics, while legitimizing access to the political process by many different groups, did not challenge the structural disparity between the wealthy and the poor. Political activism provided comfort for the middle class in its anxieties about competition and success and corruption and gave its members the task of helping to uplift the poor, who also, in theory, benefitted from the system. But because neither social gospelers nor progressive politicians proposed any kind of structural reforms, the system that created class inequality in the first place remained intact. Self-realization in such a context could be nearly as oppressive for the working class as the self-reliance it replaced.

For McDowell and Abbott the Civil War had played a large part in shaping their political consciousness. Another war on the horizon in the 1910s crystallized and legitimized many of their treasured values. The attitudes of social gospelers toward the state informed their approach to the Great War in Europe. The social gospelers who lived to see and to survive the horror of modern total war came out of it with renewed regard for the United States and confidence in the supremacy of the social gospel. The politics of service, morality, and protection merged into a single crusade to make the world safe for democracy and to save the world from damnation. The Great War became both a religious and political mission. It helped to affirm the underlying values of the social gospel as the primary expression of American Protestantism. The war also transformed the social gospel. The Great War in Europe completed the transfer of cultural authority from Protestantism to secular institutions.

5

THE PENTECOST OF CALAMITY:

THE GREAT WAR AND THE

SOCIAL GOSPEL

Twenty-four years after Charles Monroe Sheldon took Protestant America by storm with his novel *In His Steps*, he decided it was time to reconsider the question, What would Jesus do? *In His Steps Today*, published in 1921, spoke to a postwar America that had seen "many radical changes." Written in dialogue, much like a screenplay, Sheldon's new volume promised to cause a "sensation," just as Jesus would do if he appeared on earth in the twentieth century. Sheldon addressed every aspect of American life from work to family to politics to popular culture, and he made it clear that the United States of 1921 scarcely resembled the nation of 1897, when his first volume had appeared. Industry had made "serious departures from the old order"; homes and families were "threatened by the absence of domestic service and the artificial customs that surround hotel and apartment existence"; and the war had created "a sense of international dependence." "Over all this tangle and commotion," he said, "there broods the Spirit of God." Men and women longed for a standard of conduct to govern their actions, so Sheldon tried to imagine what Jesus would do "under the present conditions that face the average man in the world." Significantly, Sheldon imagined that Jesus met modern man at the "Conference Table."[1] The Conference Table symbolized both the heroic negotiations after the war and routine corporate business. America, it would seem, had been altered by the experience of the war and by the dominance of the corporation.

Most American Protestants of the 1920s embraced the values asso-

ciated with the social gospel—service, sacrifice, love—more completely than they had before the conflict in Europe.[2] Yet the books that
now arose out of the social gospel movement, like *In His Steps Today*,
appeared to be more streamlined, more direct, less florid in style, and
less agonizing in description than books on the social gospel that appeared between the 1890s and 1914. The war had affirmed changes
that were beginning to take place in the early years of the twentieth
century, but it somehow had distilled those changes, eliminating superfluous sentiment, idealism, and effeminacy. Religion, like the society
and culture that resulted from the Great War, took on a sleeker aspect,
a more tough-minded approach, and a greater awareness of the need for
expertise, interdependence, and results.

In His Steps Today and other postwar writings by American Protestants affirmed a gospel of efficient social salvation, led by experts in
social service, that was less interested in issues of social class. The
transformed social gospel featured cooperation, service, brotherhood in
the kingdom of God, and abundance for all. It sought results in the
secular world of the state, the corporation, and the laboratory instead of
in a revitalized church or Christian settlement house. The war had
burned off all but the most essential aspects of modern Protestantism;
what remained was bound inextricably to a crusading nation that had
just "won" the war and to the industrial and organizational might that
had made the victory possible. The connections between sacred and
secular America made in the years of social and cultural transformation
merged into a single national faith in teamwork, self-realization, public
service, and Americanism. Class differences, oppression, and injustice remained, but many social gospelers preferred to see a new era
of cooperation, abundance, and common purpose. Their new faith relied on the authority of secular institutions: it scarcely appeared to be
religious at all.

Most social gospelers did not initially favor the war. Modern total
war threatened to destroy all of their hopes for a brotherly kingdom of
God on earth. America's entry into the war in Europe nearly killed
Walter Rauschenbusch. He received threats against himself and his
family because he refused to support America's decision to fight. Other
ministers opposed the conflict despite an effective propaganda campaign designed to stir up enthusiasm for the war. These adamant pacifists later earned the scorn of conservatives, who labeled them "reds"
and "anti-American." The Federal Council of Churches eventually renamed its Committee on War the Committee on Peace and International

Relations to derail any notion that American Protestant churches supported war. Some ministers even believed that if America entered the
war, it would be because churches had failed to prevent war madness
from taking over the people. As late as November 1918, for example,
Samuel Zane Batten criticized his fellow clerics for failing to prevent
the war by refusing to preach against the greed and evil that caused it.
The Great War represented for some idealistic churchmen the end of
social hopes.

Disillusionment did not prevail, however. Even Batten, whose
jeremiad of 1918 decried the ineffectiveness of his colleagues, insisted
in the same article that the war offered American Protestants a chance
to "usher in a new day." "Churches must keep alive in men the hope of
the Kingdom of God," he wrote, "and inspire men to arise and seek that
kingdom."[3] This view of the war as a challenge and a crusade dominated most Protestant circles, even those who did not favor it at first.
Protestants began to see an opportunity to extend their vision of social
salvation beyond the borders of the United States. Some, like Harry
Emerson Fosdick, saw it as a grand opportunity to save world society
and promoted America's entry into the fray. Fosdick saw no point in
coyly waiting to be drawn into the fight—especially since we had already identified the forces of good and the forces of evil. George Herron, though no longer residing in the United States, agreed with Fosdick, and he, too, urged Americans to enter the war. Though not
pushing the United States to declare war, Shailer Mathews, as president of the Federal Council of Churches, encouraged ministers associated with that organization to use "every spiritual persuasion" to inspire
a willingness to "sacrifice" for and "serve" their "brothers and sisters"
across the ocean in their moment of "distress" and "measureless adversity."[4] Social gospelers' appeals to succor the victims of war used language common in their prewar calls for reform. They urged their audiences to serve others, to make sacrifices, and to remain committed to
the kingdom of God.

Whether for or against the European war, American Protestants
realized that the conflagration overseas represented a momentous event
in Western history. They recognized, even as they tried to back away
from it, that the war had resulted from more than a foolhardy flash of
arms at Sarajevo. Many knew that America would probably become
involved before it was over. Many writers—religious and secular—
made it plain that great moral issues hung in the balance in France.
One such author, Owen Wister, famous for his novel *The Virginian*

(1902) and his celebrated friendship with Theodore Roosevelt, finished writing *The Pentecost of Calamity* in 1915. In it he urged the United States to take its place among the responsible nations of the world. Though not formally a social gospeler, Wister, the son of an upper-class Philadelphia family, longed for a rejuvenation of American character and a revitalization of American institutions—hopes shared by social gospelers.

In 1915, Wister worried about America's "national soul." Europeans had discovered that "you cannot pay too high for the finding and keeping of your own soul," while Americans "have yet to find our greater selves," he wrote in *The Pentecost of Calamity*. In a direct jab at Protestants' social hopes, Wister concluded his book by prophesying that "our talk about the brotherhood of man [might] progress from rhetoric toward realization" if the United States would but recognize its duty to save the world from German barbarism and itself from moral bankruptcy.[5] Shortly after the appearance of Wister's book, the first American soldiers embarked on a mission to make the world safe for democracy. The curious title of Wister's book, like America's participation in the war, portended both the descent of the holy spirit on faithful Americans as well as their descent into the madness of destruction. The war promised both spiritual renewal and disaster. As some social gospelers eventually discovered, the war signaled a pentecost of calamity for their creed as well.

· · ·

At first, however, most observers saw the war as a challenge to Protestantism. One of Walter Rauschenbusch's friends and a committed supporter of social reform, John D. Rockefeller, Jr., wrote "The Christian Church: What of its Future?" for the *Saturday Evening Post* in the early months of 1918. Like many Christians, he had been shocked by a war that "presented to our vision a picture so horrible it hardly seemed that it could be true." The heir to the Rockefeller fortune insisted that eventually "another picture" presented itself—one in which "millions of men and women . . . are exemplifying in their daily lives . . . characteristics and qualities which command the admiration of the world." Their "spirit of self-sacrifice" and "unselfishness" were eloquent testimony of the power of social Christianity in the world. Shailer Mathews argued that after their initial "shock and disbelief," Americans' eyes gradually "cleared to see the real meaning of the war." "Self-sacrifice in the interest of making permanent the achievement of ideals," he declared, "is the most idealistic service a man or a nation can render the world." Harry Fosdick believed that the war—the "present crisis"—was a "challenge." No matter how horrible war proved to be, Americans had to discover that it was worth dying for the soul of the nation. Bishop Francis J. McConnell believed that the war, though ghastly, advanced the cause of democracy and presented a challenge to social gospelers. "Modern war," he argued, "makes so little of the individual" that the "strictly personal" in religion was less important than "regard for the 'cause'" and "devotion to the large general welfare."6 Thus some workers in the church saw in the Great War a chance to advance their views of Christianity.

Once America sent troops, almost all social gospel writers agreed that the battle in Europe would transform American belief and behavior once it was over. "The peoples who have passed through the fires of battle," predicted Francis McConnell in 1919, "will never turn back to the former day," and "no institution will come out of this war in the same form in which it went in." After having spent a month with the YMCA preparing to speak to troops, the Reverend Archibald T. Robertson, a professor of New Testament interpretation at the Southern Baptist Theological Seminary, wrote that the war completely changed all aspects of life. "The old world passed away when Belgium took her stand in front of the Kaiser's hosts," Robertson wrote in *The New Citizenship* (1919). "Modern History began on that day. Everything is in the crucible."7 And the Great War would leave nothing unaltered. Herbert Willett, editor of the *Christian Century*, wrote that "the social customs and economic habits" of the "established order of the world" had "crumbled" in this "new time." Governmental decisions that would have "shocked an earlier generation" are now "accepted as commonplace." And "religious factors" were also "reshaping themselves" from "denominationalism" and "tradition" to the "forces of progress."8 The president of Chicago's Theological Seminary, Ozora S. Davis, spoke more specifically about the effect of war on religion in an article for *Biblical World*. "A new era of religion is coming," he contended, that "will contain far more of the element of human fellowship and patient tolerance than has ever been known on the earth." Edward Scribner Ames agreed with Davis. In 1918 he wrote, "The war has become an abyss of fire and death between the past and the future." Ames hailed the advent of the "new orthodoxy," social gospel Protestantism, "the religion of democracy."9

By the time the peace treaties had been signed, it was clear that these early prophets of change had been correct. American life and belief had been transformed by war. Americans had seen their government marshal tools and men for the vast undertaking. Mass production, massed troops, and mass annihilaton had wrought the victory "over there." The War Industries Board coordinated the various sectors of the economy into an efficient operation. Large companies rose to the challenge of outfitting, arming, and transporting American soldiers. McConnell's observation that war "makes little of the individual" held true for more than men in the trenches. Teamwork on the home front, at work, and in scientific laboratories, as well as on the battlefront, created conditions for victory. The war effort at home and the campaign abroad required interdependence and espirit de corps. Moreover, the drive for efficiency required specialists and experts. Trained soldiers, researchers, medics, and producers executed the war and elevated in the minds of citizens the ideal of professional expertise. It was also a war that was packaged and sold to wary Americans. The Creel Committee's propaganda and promotional campaign used familiar techniques of advertising that played on the need to be part of the group and the longing for security. Such tactics became even more prevalent at the war's end. All dimensions of life in the United States were transformed.

The new society and culture of postwar America did not materialize out of thin air, however. Rather, they resulted from a consolidation of tendencies that had emerged before 1914 and crystallized during the war. Progressive politics, an incorporating economy, cooperation and teamwork among laborers, and a social gospel based on the coming Kingdom passed through the crucible of war and became the associative state, corporate liberalism, management and expertise, and a social gospel based on efficient social service that dominated the 1920s. Social gospelers' reforming spirit became incorporated in a war effort that ultimately affirmed the legitimacy of the order they had challenged in the 1890s and early 1900s. At every step along the way, ministers helped define the changes and participated in the alteration of social relations and cultural forms. The war brought about the ultimate demise of Victorianism and the triumph of the social gospel. In the aftermath of victory, the social gospel was part of a different dominant culture.[10]

• • •

Probably the most widely noticed change was that churches in mainstream Protestant denominations were less defensive about their social perspective. The war had demonstrated what social gospelers long had believed: men and religion in the twentieth century had to have social concerns. Protestants associated with the social gospel movement gained their newfound confidence from conversations with soldiers. Ozora Davis, for example, remembered a talk with Lieutenant Pat O'Brien, who told him that the war had altered his religious experience. "I was what I suppose you would call an individualist," O'Brien confided, "I thought chiefly of *my* fun, *my* happiness, *my* pleasures." But the war gave him a more "serious" perspective on life, and he had become "more sensitive to suffering in others," which translated into a "new feeling about religion"—a social feeling.[11] Another officer told his chaplain, who was a friend of Harry Emerson Fosdick, "The reason I don't like religion, padre, is that it's such a selfish thing. It simply threatens sinners with hell and promises comforts to the good." His testimony convinced Fosdick that the only religion that would move Americans after the war would be a religion of social justice, interdependence, and fraternity.[12] Another chaplain reported that most of the soldiers he had seen in France "live partly by faith in a good God," but their religion was social rather than individual. "They have very lax ideas about drunkenness and sexual irregularity," he told Sherwood Eddy, "but they have very strict ideas about the sacredness of social obligations with the groups to which they belong."[13] The war had exposed the limits of an individual, self-seeking kind of religion. If men were to be saved, it would be by social rather than individual means.

During the war, American Protestants learned the importance of cooperation, which social gospelers had been preaching for decades. The need to work together for a common end came home with force as soldiers worked together in the trenches and as workers labored in concert at home. When Francis McConnell prepared *Christian Citizenship* (1922) for young Methodists, he reminded them that the social gospel emphasized the "importance of those duties which men can only perform together." A generation of men just returned from war understood when he went on to say, "There must be cooperation."[14]

But most people understood the word "cooperation" in new ways after the war. Of the several definitions attached to the word by groups with differing political agendas, the bureaucratic and commercial definition seemed to assume greater prominence after the war. Appeals to brotherhood and social harmony did not disappear, but "cooperation" was often used in the context of institutional organization. The need for cooperation was often accompanied by a demand for "efficiency," "organization," and "centralization" of authority. For example, Charles Jefferson used "cooperation" and "coordination" synonymously in *Old*

Truths and New Facts: Christian Life and Thinking as Modified by the Great War (1918). He believed that the war provided "valuable hints" on organizing the social gospel in the postwar world. "We must grasp the principles of cooperation," he wrote. "There must be a coordination of all our movements if the enterprise is not to crumble and break down."[15] Similarly, Harry Emerson Fosdick believed that the war had impressed on Protestants the need for efficient service. Men and women in the "new World" after the war "will look on inefficiency as a sin," he argued in *The Meaning of Service* (1920). They would also redefine their efforts to reform society. In the hardened language of postwar America, Fosdick declared, "usefulness is not a matter of heart alone but of head, not of kind intention but of efficient skill; slovenliness is wickedness and escapable ineptitude is treachery; no man's benevolent feeling can cover from condemnation his avoidable fumbling of a noble task." After the massive coordination necessary to execute the war and social-gospel-inspired war relief, earlier definitions of cooperation as harmony and "sweet reasonableness" gave way to a commitment to efficient organization.[16]

Henry Frederick Cope decided that the only way to learn the new meaning of cooperation was to present it in a new Sunday school. In 1919, he finished writing *The School in the Modern Church*, which extolled the "task of training lives" for "efficiency." The Sunday school no longer could rest content with producing competent biblical scholars. Rather, he argued, "it seeks to develop boys and girls who can pass the tests that the school, the street, business, social relations, and daily work put on them." Cope urged Sunday school directors to plan team games to promote "social training" and "team cooperation." Another even more important key to helping young people accept the terms of social organization and efficiency was an "educated, adequately trained leadership" and a "trained, competent laity." Teacher training, therefore, became a central fact of the new Sunday schools, for there, as in other church activities, the minister required men and women with "trained and expert power."[17]

Francis McConnell echoed Cope's remarks. In *Democratic Christianity* (1919), he, too, affirmed the importance of expertise for administration of social services. "Democracy is not safe if it begins to disparage the expert," he wrote. "The church leader must be expert in knowledge and expert in skill."[18] The social gospel seemed to be shifting from an expansive invitation to all Christians to serve society to a more hard-nosed recruitment of experts. Social gospelers after the war wanted results efficiently, and the war had taught them that experts could deliver.

The social gospelers' insistence on coordination of specialists, efficiency, and results mirrored similar developments in industry and stemmed in part from a growing disenchantment with the frills of sentiment. As one minister noted, the soldiers in France cut through all the folderol of religion and accepted only the "bare essentials." Whether in church or in the secular arena, men after the war wanted no-nonsense, effective results.

.   .   .

Postwar ministers' attention to these war-hardened men worked a subtle but unmistakable change in the character of their ministries. Before the war they had merged feminine and masculine virtues. The "feminine" virtues of service, sacrifice, and love remained central components of the masculine arsenal of values after 1919, but social gospelers spoke with greater confidence to what they believed would be a male audience and approached that audience with a language that appealed to earlier conceptions of manliness as rugged and ambitious. The social gospel, instead of serving as a counterpoint to corporate power, promised to deliver through corporate means a secure basis of manly identity and achievement.

Indeed, Protestantism after the war spoke more directly to men than it had in the immediate prewar years. While the number of women writers in the social gospel movement never had been large, few, if any of them, had much to say about the agony of war, and some joined movements for World Peace. Their experience, largely limited to the home front, excluded them from the formative associations with efficient organization, expert leadership, and the tough-minded demand for results. It is small wonder that few women wrote influential works on the postwar social gospel. What *is* remarkable is their loyalty to an expression of Protestantism that was spoken so directly to men. Perhaps the prominence of terms like service and self-sacrifice provided a common vocabulary to which they could apply their own definitions. Perhaps the public women, who cared most about social service, had become sufficiently hardened by their professional careers in governmental and corporate social services that the masculine terms did not sound altogether unfamiliar. Mass culture bombarded both men and women with symbols of manly achievement. Perhaps merely the dominant cultural endorsement of masculine effectiveness convinced both men and women of the efficacy of manliness in Protestantism. In any event, Protestant churches after the war made obvious overtures to men by promising a kind of heroic enterprise that paralleled the war experience.

Henry Cope linked the new manliness and the drive for efficiency more consciously than most social gospelers after the war. In *The School in the Modern Church*, he wrote enthusiastically that "the regeneration of humanity" and "the reconstruction of society" after the war created "a man's work for a man in the church and a full-sized task for every man." He argued that "men are ready to answer the call for heroic service." But the task before Americans in the 1920s demanded "a new type of heroism"—one that was "technically trained and efficient." Charles Macfarland told the readers of "The Minister and Democracy" to "get hold of *men*. Never mind so much about the women, you will get them anyway without trying, and at any rate you will get them if you get their husbands and brothers." He went on to remind the new recruits that they did more than serve and preach: they made the church and the gospel effective. When Richard Beall Niese advised Protestants in the mid-1920s to use newspapers for advertising their churches, he lectured them on the need to appeal to men. "The biggest men in the country today are proud to proclaim their faith in the Nazarene—and they do so without a blush or a stammer."[19]

What had erased the blush and calmed the stammer? A Protestant campaign that appealed to "millions of big, red-blooded men" had transformed churches from "a place only for women and children" to "a community of men's Bible classes" and "weekly men's luncheons" where men "gather around the table and have an hour of fellowship" and where "campaigns for building standard Sunday schools are planned."[20] In other words, heroic manliness stood just a step away from the corporate board of efficient planning. Protestant appeals to men used language associated with the war—heroism and efficiency. These appeals also outlined an agenda of social service that was aggressive, organized, and challenging. Consequently, men could transfer the methods of their workplaces into the realm of the church without fear of profaning a sacred task and without subjecting themselves to the values or mode of behavior they associated with women in the church.

· · ·

The results that Protestant reformers demanded had changed as well. Social gospelers after 1918 worked to create conditions that would allow everyone to achieve the most out of life and realize his full potential. Immediately following the war, for example, Edward Scribner Ames insisted that churches would have to do things differently in postwar America. He thought that churches should create social conditions in which individual Christians could develop their talents, because "the chief end of man is to grow." In order to promote individual growth, Ames advocated a revamped worship service that minimized the "penitence and self-abasement" that "prostrate" men before an almighty ruler. "Quite a different attitude is felt when religious ceremonials are . . . concerned with the creative and expanding life of mankind," he wrote. "Now they appear as contributing to the realization of that larger life and to its fuller appreciation, and enjoyment." The church became, in Ames's words, "a house of aspiration, a refuge of security, a center of genuine companionship and of ideal intimations." Therefore, the church developed social "policies" in the decade of the 1920s designed to help the individual "realize his human possibilities."[21]

This social gospel emphasis on self-realization, of course, had been evolving in the decades spanning the turn of the century. Mutual observation and affirmation had been guiding an anxious generation for years. But the unembarrassed and enthusiastic embrace of self-realization in works by ministers after 1919 suggests once again that this goal had consolidated under new social conditions during the war. The kind of family relations that sustained the quest for self-realization had become commonplace by the 1920s. Companionate families with youthful, indulgent parents and expressive children represented the ideal.

In *In His Steps Today*, Charles Sheldon's parental characters responded to Jesus' question, "Are you afraid of your children?" as follows: "We have probably followed the line of least resistance in matters of conduct, of amusement and the choice of expenses and companionship. If that is what you mean by being afraid of our children, we have probably avoided making our children obey what has really been the best course in our own minds, but we have not wanted to oppose our children's wishes." The father gave his boy a new car, for instance, because he did not want his friend-son "to get mad at him."[22] Parents had become companions rather than figures of authority, and they wanted their children to get along well in society, in school, in their careers.

The legitimation of the companionate family also found its way into postwar theological discussions of God the father. The "immanent" God of the social gospel, who reflected the distance between Victorian fathers and their children, gave way to the "limited" God of the 1920s. According to Bishop McConnell the modern God was bent on "winning" the "respect and love" of his children and had to prove that he was "worthy of the free service of men." He went on to say that modern American Protestants "must have a God whom we can respect as well as love, and who respects as well as loves us."[23] Like modern parents, God had lost authority over his children's lives and had to earn their attention and affection.

As Sheldon's example illustrates, families reinforced another underlying basis of self-realization after the First World War: consumerism. Father gave the boy a car because his son "said that so many boys had cars."[24] Consumer products after the war helped men and women improve their appearance and hygiene and accustomed them to a new standard of personal presentation. Consuming permitted people to take part in an activity that their society believed to be valuable. Buying a car because others had one suggests the importance of fitting in with the group and its standards of behaving and owning. So powerful had the consumer ethos become that advertising and access to mass culture became important parts of the churches' plans to spread the social gospel. As McConnell confessed in the 1920s, "To a greater degree than we are willing to admit, we [of the Protestant churches] are at the mercy of . . . public opinion." Thus, the principal way to gain public attention with a creed of social salvation lay in "control of news sources or magazine columns or book-publishing houses." It had become "mandatory" for social gospelers to employ mass media.[25] In *Democratic Christianity* the Methodist bishop linked this consumer mentality to the experience of war and warned churchmen to deliver whatever they advertised. "The soldier," he told them, "wants straightforward dealing. . . . He will come to a straight preaching service, if that is what he is asked to attend. But if prayers are 'sprung' at the close of a picture-show he may get up and go out[,] as he ought."[26] The soldier-consumer—and eventually simply the consumer—reigned supreme in McConnell's vision of postwar America. Edward Scribner Ames assured readers of *The New Orthodoxy* (1918) that worldliness and abundance were parts of the wonderful opportunities available to men and women to expand their lives. Thus the "worldling"—"gaily dressed," "artistic," "convivial and human"— once despised by "the puritan," in modern times "isn't so bad." In fact, he was in "deeper accord with Jesus," Ames averred, than were the old Puritans.[27]

. . .

One of the successful manuals on church advertising during the war years featured examples of effective display copy for ministers as fledgling advertisers. In *Church Advertising: Its Why and How* (1917), W.

B. Ashley urged Protestant pastors to strike "the timely note in a striking way." To accompany his argument, Ashley displayed a poster entitled "Preparedness Best Insured by Religion." In the center of the poster was a picture of a huge twelve-inch gun on a naval destroyer aimed directly over the reader's shoulder, guarding the viewer against some unseen enemy. The caption beneath the picture read "Guardians of Uncle Sam's Coast."[28] Were the churches that advertised or the twelve-inch guns the "guardians" of America? In 1917 the war blurred the issue, and advertising helped meld faith in church with faith in the U.S. government to provide protection and security to its citizens.

Woodrow Wilson's "Message to the American People" delivered on 15 April 1917, a little over a week after the United States declared war on Germany, contributed to a fusion of social gospel values and a protective state. After assuring Americans that the government was "putting our navy upon an effective war footing" and equipping "a great army" in order to defend the nation, the president called for a national commitment to "the great task" of "future peace and security of the world." "We must realize to the full how great the task is," Wilson told Americans in language more than vaguely reminiscent of social gospel sermons, "and how many things, how many kinds and elements of capacity and service and self-sacrifice it involves." Wilson called for devotion in the very terms social gospelers had been using to urge people to embrace their creed and their agenda for social reform. But in the case of war, Wilson challenged citizens to serve and to sacrifice themselves to "supply ships," "to keep the looms and manufactories" of Europe in raw materials, and to provide clothing and ammunition to the nations with whom "we are cooperating." And in keeping with a dawning comprehension of a more "realistic" definition of cooperation, Wilson demanded greater productivity, efficiency, and effective results. All enterprises "must be more economically managed and better adapted to the particular requirements of our task" than they had been in the past. He asked farmers to produce abundant foodstuffs in the interest of "cooperation." Men of the railways had the responsibility of preventing "obstruction," "inefficiency," or "slackening power" in the movement of material. "The manufacturer does not need to be told, I hope, that the nation looks to him to speed and perfect every process." Finally, Wilson combined the language of corporate efficiency with the social gospel crusade when he proclaimed the formation of a "great national, a great international, service army" made up of men and women at home, a "notable and honored host engaged in the service of the nation and the world, the efficient friends and saviors of free men everywhere."[29] Work in the war effort on behalf of the government promised spiritual reward. In a single powerful speech, Pres. Woodrow Wilson fused social gospel ideas, a benevolent and protective state, and the corporate ethos into a national creed. Like the church advertisers, he left unclear whether religious, political, or economic forces held the key to that faith.

Wilson and church advertisers were not alone in fusing religion and politics during and after the war. Other social gospelers celebrated the emergence of a government that proffered security and order at a time of uncertainty and chaos. The state, as caretaker of the public welfare, had shouldered responsibility for its citizens by defending the nation during wartime and by sponsoring regulatory legislation and agencies to ensure that each man and woman had at his or her disposal the tools to strive for success in modern America. The "new state" offered personal fulfillment through bureaucratic means. Unlike the liberal state of the nineteenth century, which left individuals to their own devices, the associative state that emerged out of progressivism theoretically offered each individual the chance to become whatever he or she might, at the same time that it offered bureaucratic supports against disaster.

In 1922 Samuel Zane Batten predicted a wonderful future for the nation if democracy, as he defined it, prevailed. To Batten, democracy was "the confession of brotherhood in political relations" and "confidence in the downmost man and a regard for his personality. So far as democracy is true to itself and its origin, it believes . . . that the highest goods of life are for all men; and so it seeks to bring these goods within reach of every man."[30] Whether the U.S. government in the 1920s fulfilled Batten's hopes is open to question. But his sentiment expressed an expectation of government that was shared by others in the movement. In the early twenties, social gospelers helped lay the groundwork for a welfare state that came into being in the 1930s and beyond. They also agreed with Vernon Kellogg, who in 1918 hailed Herbert Hoover as the political ideal of the future. Sensitive to human suffering, as he demonstrated in his coordination of the Belgium War Relief, Hoover submerged sentiment in efficiently organized programs. Hoover was committed to social service in a coolheaded, dispassionate manner.[31]

If Hoover was the prototype for future politicians, Woodrow Wilson inspired loyalty and adoration from social gospelers as the symbol of American faith during the dark years of war. For example, Algernon Sydney Crapsey, a social gospeler from Rochester, New York, and author of *International Republicanism* (1918), praised the president for having attained "sublime heights of unselfish statesmanship" in order to "serve the peace and safety of the world."[32] Wilson led Americans in the fight for justice in Europe and salvation of the world. In fact, social gospelers described an American crusade led by Wilson, a national faith articulated by the president, and civil religion. Books such as *Germanism and the American Crusade* (1918), *If America Fail: Our National Mission and Our Possible Future* (1922), *The New Horizon of State and Church* (1918), and *Democratic Christianity* (1919) bore the unmistakable marks of a religion shaped by confidence in an inspired state.

In *Germanism and the American Crusade*, for instance, George Herron proclaimed: "The iron of God has gone deeply into the American soul, and in the strength thereof has America gone forth, and gone forth never to retreat. Either [Germany] utterly and at once repents, or America will march forth for Germany's military and imperial destruction."[33] Herron left no doubt that the Great War was a war for redemption, but he made it equally clear that *America*, with the help of God, was the redeemer. Worldwide social salvation would come at the hands of the United States. Samuel Zane Batten equated the United States with social religion. "America is not a country merely, not primarily a form of government," he wrote in *If America Fail*. "America is a gospel, an ideal, a faith, a spirit, a state of heart, a set of principles, a trinity of ideas, an interpretation of the kingdom of God, and far-off goal of history."[34] During the war years and immediately afterwards, social gospelers confessed their faith in the nation as well as in the social gospel.

In the process, social gospelers helped promote the secular forces that would succeed them as figures of authority, as sources of comfort and personal well-being, and as guarantors of justice. In his celebration of the "new world consciousness," William H. P. Faunce, theologian and president of Brown University, lauded the invention of "wireless telegraphy, the aeroplane, the submarine," and the telephone, which he believed would result in "the transformation of the social order," something he and his colleagues in the social gospel had attempted for decades. "Every inventor," he went on to say in *The New Horizon of State and Church*, "is an unconscious worker in the field of ethics and society." Bishop McConnell praised a religion that provided the "highest and best for men" and also praised the "trained expert who seeks out the ways to realize the human ideals." Edward Ames looked to religion and science as the twin pillars of hope for postwar America: religion to provide the spirit, science the results. A nation, not a religion, dedicated to social welfare and social reform would pave the way for self-realization. George

Herron wrote in 1917 that part of the "American crusade" was to become a state that "provides for the realization of [the citizen's] selfhood in the joyous service of his fellows."[35] The state, not the church, promoted service and promised fulfillment.

.   .   .

The Great War in Europe proved to be a pentecost of calamity for the social gospel. In the spirit of Pentecost, the conflict itself bestowed on the social gospel the blessings of legitimacy and supremacy in mainstream Protestantism. As the terms and forms of the social gospel emerged from the transforming experiences of war, they became the starting point for most Protestants, and vital institutions like the Federal Council of Churches, social service commissions, and the YMCA promised to move forward in bureaucratic perpetuity. The war consolidated the outward institutional and creedal forms of social gospel Protestantism.

While the war sealed the victory of such social gospel forms and values as service, sacrifice, and cooperation, it also proved calamitous to the religious faith that social gospelers had set out to revitalize. A gospel that featured an "immanent" God, then reduced him to a "limited" God, was but paces away from mourning the death of God as some Americans soon did. When the kingdom of God arrived by way of city hall, as Washington Gladden had suggested, or through the scientific laboratory, as Edward Ames predicted, something besides religion had captured American imagination and faith.

The social gospel's liberal faith in progress, improvement, and fulfillment, and its endorsement of science, economic organization, and an extended state in the moment of crisis led its proponents into the arms of secular authority. Most social gospelers quickly and overwhelmingly buried their worst doubts in self-congratulation for the resiliency of their gospel. Bishop McConnell rued the fact that in the 1920s "the emblems of the nation" had become "more sacred" than the "symbols of religious faith," but he also went on to make a career of democratic reformism in the associative state of the 1920s and the New Deal of the 1930s.[36] Those who asked if science had overtaken religion in the 1920s celebrated the advances in medicine and nutrition for which they believed their social activism was partly responsible. In the 1920s, the social gospel lived, but it was expressed, practiced, and understood in different ways.

When George Davis Herron, Harry Emerson Fosdick, and Edward Scribner Ames saw the storm clouds gather in Europe in the 1910s, their first thoughts went to the social gospel. All three had found purpose in their lives when they accepted the social gospel, and all of them defended it against criticism—even Herron, who was deposed from the Congregational ministry. When the dust of war finally settled, each had the social gospel to which he could cling, but they all had participated in a process that altered religious life and that advanced the institutions of secular America. Herron's experience highlights the tension between the aspirations of a social gospeler from the 1890s and the social and cultural consequences of the Great War. His life illuminates the war's effect on social gospel ideas. Both Fosdick and Ames became spokesmen for the new social gospel. Fosdick spoke to men at the front during the war and reached a wide radio audience afterwards. Ames summarized the "new orthodoxy" in 1918 as he witnessed the impact of war on all aspects of American life. Social hopes informed the response of all three men to the Great War, and that conflict helped transform their ideas on the social gospel.

GEORGE DAVIS HERRON
The Defeat in the Victory

In 1921, George Davis Herron prepared his final statement about the Great War in Europe. He had written other books on the war during and immediately following the conflict, but this book stood out from the others as a personal, anguished account of the events of 1918 and 1919. He dedicated his book to all who "still strive for the redemption of the nations." He remembered that as a socialist he had opposed any kind of militarism and at first had protested against American involvement in the European squabble. But as the perniciousness of "Germanism" became clear to him Herron believed that America's entry into the war was essential for a "Christly world-order." "I did not doubt," he wrote seven years after the fighting first had begun, "the war would issue in a world delivered from many ancient wrongs, in a democratic redemption and federation of the nations, and in a high and happy transmutation of the whole relational life of man."[37]

Herron earnestly believed that Woodrow Wilson had seen the war as a crusade to save the nations of the world from tyranny and damnation and that this war, while vile and destructive, would give credence to the social gospel for which Herron and others had labored for many years. In *Woodrow Wilson and the World's Peace*, written in 1917, Herron noted that the president held an "ideal" of "universal communism of production and distribution, with a common and unfettered freedom as regards

George Davis Herron

the right of each individual to choose the way in which he shall go, and grow, and give himself." Wilson believed in the Sermon on the Mount as the "ultimate construction of mankind," and he hoped to awaken America to her "national selfhood and calling."[38] Finally, Herron thought that Wilson, "a colossal Christian apostle," would make the world into the "kingdom of God." When the staggering number of casualties yielded only stronger capitalism, heightened nationalism, and continued hardships for many, Herron concluded that in the end the Great War had undermined the ideals for which Americans had fought. Herron saw defeat in the victory.

In a sense, Herron was correct. The Great War legitimized a social gospel, but not the social gospel that Herron and his colleagues had first articulated in the 1890s. The transformed social gospel that emerged after the war upheld corporate order, therapeutic social relations, and self-realization. Part of Herron's obsession with the Great War may have come from his recognition of dimensions of the "new" social gospel in his own beliefs. The shrillness of his critique betrays an inchoate under-standing of his own participation in the transformation of the social gospel. Perhaps he could see at some level how a creed that denounced individual responsibility for success and salvation ("redemption of the nations"), that argued for improved, harmonious social relations ("trans-mutation of the whole relational life of man"), and greater economic incorporation ("communism of production and distribution"), and that awakened the nation to its "calling" provided important cultural, psy-chological, and moral support for the kind of order that emerged.

But the consumer capitalism that bloomed after the Great War was not what social gospelers like George Herron intended. He had hoped that the conflict would usher in a "Christly world-order" or the kingdom of God. Like Americans in the war, social gospelers had won. But in winning legitimacy for their creed, they helped to affirm the process of corporate development that in part had given rise to their critiques in the first place. Herron realized that the war had ushered in a new order, and that, in ways he did not intend, he had been partially responsible for the defeat in the victory. A closer examination of George Davis Herron's checkered career reveals a tragic figure striving to revitalize the faith of his ancestors. Caught up in the momentum of his own spectacular rise to national renown followed by years of public disgrace, Herron found in the Great War a chance to rekindle both his social and religious dream and confidence in his leadership as a spokesman of reform. Herron found private as well as public defeat in the aftermath of the First World War.

Anyone who knew the Herron family in Montezuma, Indiana, in the 1860s probably never would have guessed that the only son of William and Isabella Davis Herron would achieve any sort of fame as a leader. Humble toilers and sternly pious people, the Herrons could offer their child few material advantages. Their poverty denied him a formal educa-tion in the public schools, and illness isolated the child at home with a fanatically righteous, invalid mother. Like Hannah in the Bible, who dedicated her son Samuel to the service of Jehovah, Isabella Herron gave God a child "consecrated to his service." A young George Herron re-ported in the early 1890s that "she received me as from God and gave me back to God as her free-will offering. She besought God to keep me upon the alter of a perfect sacrifice in the service of his Christ and her Re-deemer."[39] Given his frequent illnesses and the peculiarly intense rela-tionship with his mother, Herron had few friends his own age and re-ceived most of his education from his father instead of from the public schools. With few advantages, poor health, and little but spiritual support from his parents, the young Hoosier did not show promise as a social or political or cultural leader.

Though steeped in the evangelical tradition and the special calling of his parents, George Herron found it difficult to determine his niche in the world and to succeed as an individual. While still in his teens, he entered a local printing office and worked under what he considered "depraved and sinful conditions."[40] In 1879, he decided to pursue a more formal education in hopes of discovering a more compelling life work. He entered the preparatory division of Ripon College in Wisconsin. Once again, however, ill health and financial difficulties contributed to an unimpressive performance and his withdrawal from the institution after about two years. For a time, he worked on the local Ripon newspaper. Then in 1883 he married Mary Everhard, a daughter of a prominent physician. With his new bride Herron moved to St. Paul, where he hoped to launch a career in literature and journalism. Instead of taking up the pen, however, Herron, under the sway of a mighty religious experience, entered the Congregational ministry.

Events leading up to his entry into the ministry reveal much about his later articulation of the social gospel. In 1883, the year of his marriage and the year he set out to find a career in St. Paul, George Herron experienced a dramatic emotional religious conversion. In his own words, he "groped in the horror of darkness which settles upon a soul when it knows that there is no sound thing in it, and that it merits nothing but eternal death and endless night." Failures and indecision in the previous two years probably compounded anxiety over his inability to live up to his mother's promise to God. He claimed that Jonathan Edward's Enfield sermon was "the only thing real enough to answer my experience."[41] So he writhed in lonely anguish and despair until God lifted him up and planted his feet "on the rock of salvation."

Despite his allusions to Calvinist orthodoxy, Herron's experiences seem to have resulted from late-nineteenth-century anxieties about inner direction and individual purpose at a time when both were hard to achieve. For despite his lonely struggle for peace, he found the writings of men like F. D. Maurice, Henry George, and Giuseppe Mazzini—all social messages—convincing and compelling. After seven years in the ministry, speaking to congregations from the perspective of his individual spiritual experience, Herron took Protestant America by storm in 1890 with a powerful social gospel message. Because many members of his congregation had experienced the same problems with the Victorian code in a changing America, they drew near to this messenger from God and propelled him into the national spotlight. Within a few years, George Herron received more attention and publicity than any other social gospeler in America.

Herron's sermons and books in the 1890s all carried the same message. As he wrote in *The Christian State* in 1895, "The civilization that now builds upon the assumption that men are antagonistic, and not members of one social body, is fundamentally anarchical—against the divine course of things."[42] He eschewed the competitive individualism of the nineteenth century and proposed instead cooperation, social salvation, and a commitment to the kingdom of God. His critique targeted individual competition in the economic arena, selfish rivalry between denominations in the ecclesiastical realm, and liberal self-interest in politics. He embraced the concept of brotherhood as a key to social responsibility and social justice, and like many of his colleagues, he incorporated "feminine" virtues of service, sacrifice, and nurture into his religious creed. If every person would be his "brother's keeper," he argued, the social ills that beset the nation and the private disappointments that frustrated striving individuals eventually would disappear. *Between Caesar and Jesus* (1899), *The Christian State*, and *The New Redemption* (1893) laid the groundwork of his social gospel and became the basis of his phenomenal popularity and success in the decade of social turmoil.

In 1891, Herron addressed an association of Congregational ministers in Minneapolis, where he delivered a sermon entitled "The Message of Jesus to Men of Wealth," a passionate appeal for social responsibility and applied Christianity, and a scathing denunciation of the ill-gotten gains of the wealthy. Within months of delivering this powerful sermon, Herron received numerous invitations to speak in public lectures and to leave his tiny parish in Lake City, Minnesota. When he accepted the call of a large church in Burlington, Iowa, he met an independently wealthy widow, who found the young minister's message appealing and decided to support him in any endeavor he chose.

Mrs. E. D. Rand endowed a chair of Christianity at Iowa College in Grinnell, which enabled the college to establish an innovative department of applied Christianity in which they offered Herron a position. Packed classrooms gave him confidence in the message he had to offer, and after the appearance of his book *Between Caesar and Jesus*, outsiders reinforced his sense of purpose. One New York critic wrote: "Dr. Herron, like a prophet—a speaker of God that he is—does not argue, he appeals to one's moral nature; he pleads, he commands."[43] Herron joined

George A. Gates, president of Iowa College, on the staff of Gates's journal *The Kingdom*, serving as associate editor and finding a forum for his social gospel. In the Kingdom movement, Herron became acquainted with some of the most prominent and influential Protestants in America as they exchanged ideas and critiques in regular seminars and conferences. In addition to the Kingdom movement, Herron participated in the National Christian Citizens' League, the Union Reform League, and the National Social Reform Union.

Herron won support outside the academy when farm problems in the 1890s made his support of populist politics attractive to beleaguered Iowa farmers. Iowa Populists wanted him to run for Congress or governor on their party's ticket, and while he chose to remain aloof from politics, he commended party members for the "profound religious feeling" that "permeated" their organization. He predicted that a "revival of faith in Christ" would come from their heroic efforts.[44] In the mid-1890s, Herron stood on the verge of winning wider influence in his profession, among his students, and in the community at large.

The decade that brought Herron unexpected success and influence also brought his demise. As he became more deeply involved in God's work off-campus, Herron neglected his duties at Iowa College. After the first year, eager students turned away in disappointment from the professor's courses in applied Christianity because he frequently left the instruction to advanced students or to President Gates. Within a short time, enrollments in his courses dropped off, and resentment against him grew. The highest-paid member of the faculty, Herron seemed to be doing very little at the college. Herron took long trips to recover from the frequent illnesses that continued to plague him, at the expense of his responsibilities to the college. Because of these professional shortcomings, the board of trustees for Iowa College began to voice serious doubts about this unconventional man. Complaints mounted, and in 1899, Herron officially resigned.

Support for the social gospeler completely collapsed when the community learned of a grave private indiscretion. Herron began to see Mrs. E. D. Rand's daughter Carrie and spent more time with her than with his growing family. The Rands, mother and daughter, kept a room for him in their home, where he rested between classes, and the three of them took European cruises together. Members of the Iowa College faculty, already dissatisfied with Herron's occasional abandonment of teaching responsibilities, repeated a remark from one of Herron's children, who was reported to have said, "We don't have meat for dinner any more because

Papa has his dinner at Aunt Carrie's."[45] In 1901, Herron returned from a vacation with Carrie Rand and asked his wife of eighteen years for a divorce. Within two months of the divorce, he married Rand in a "socialist" ceremony in which "each chose the other as companion" to avoid "all coercive institutions."[46] Shortly thereafter, the Congregational church deposed him. Much of the admiration of and support for Herron that had marked his early career disappeared. The college, church, and community all scorned him. Not long after his remarriage, a cowed George Herron emigrated to Italy and with his new wife and mother-in-law settled into a comfortable estate outside Fiesole.

According to Robert Crunden, Herron's fall from public grace served to reinforce his sense of kinship to Jesus. As the 1890s drew to a close, Herron wrote about Jesus in ways that reflected his own experience. He wrote of Christ, for example, that "no one ever so hungered for human sympathy as Jesus" and "no one was so misunderstood—even down to the present day—by his own disciples, his own church." Herron might have felt that these sentiments applied to his own life as well. One friend and supporter, the Reverend William T. Brown, made the comparison between Herron and Jesus more explicit, noting both men's devotion to selfless love and social welfare. Brown insisted that Herron's life had been "one long crucifixion" and that his character throughout the ordeal had been "divine."[47] Crunden's assessment undoubtedly is correct, and in light of subsequent events, Herron's identification with the Messiah probably intensified the nagging sense of guilt about this mother's pledge to God and his mission to man.

Crunden also notes that Herron felt equally at home with Populists, Progressives, and Socialists in the 1890s and 1900s. Herron exhorted American citizens to vote for the reform tickets of one of the three parties. This ideological eclecticism reveals one of the weaknesses of social gospelers' reform impulse. Their lack of focus made them a target of cooptation by dominant American culture. Though they stood outside the mainstream, criticizing and advocating reform, eventually their shifting political loyalties helped deny them a consciousness of purpose and allowed them to be incorporated by the system they had hoped to change. Herron became a self-proclaimed socialist and referred to both communism and socialism in his program of reform, which would indicate a basic disenchantment with liberal America. But at bottom, he seems to have wanted what many other Americans wanted during those troubled times: "human sympathy," a state devoted to "public service," and an economy based on "cooperation" and "opportunity."[48] Aside from his personal entanglements, Herron had been popular because many Americans identified spiritually with Jesus and because the professor of applied Christianity pinpointed many of their longings in *fin de siècle* America.

Because of his personal humiliation and disgrace, however, Herron spent the next fifteen years outside the United States. He became a socialist and qualified his support of traditional Christianity. Yet Herron's years in the "wilderness" of Europe could not erase the fame he once had known nor his aspirations for renewed influence in his native land. Thus, the approach of war signaled something besides destruction and death to Herron. It promised to provide him a forum for recovering a measure of his public stature and for legitimizing his message of social salvation. Herron's keen interest in the Great War prompted him to break a fifteen-year silence in the United States with a cluster of books about "Germanism," America's role in the conflict, and the prospect of international peace. The messenger of God felt compelled once again to speak out to direct the American people toward salvation.

From his first book about the war to his last, Herron equated the conflict with affirmation of the social gospel. In *The Menace of Peace*, written in 1916, before America's entry into the war, Herron declared that the meaning of the war lay in the choices before the people of the Western world. "History is deciding," he wrote in the opening pages, "whether the will that proceeds from mutual love, from an affection that is collective and fraternal, or the will of sheer mechanic might, shall be the power that finally and commonly prevails." The former he called the "will to love" and its opposite, the "will to power." Herron viewed the war as a struggle between the will to love, "cooperation," "common growth," "equal opportunity," "social goodness," and "spiritual gladness" on one side and the will to power, "individual procedure," "power improved by the strength of the right hand of a master class," and "sheer mechanic might" on the other. Herron naturally prayed that the collective forces would prevail. Indeed, Herron believed that France was "sacrificing her sons for Germany as well as for herself," and that some Germans realized that their defeat by the lovers of freedom was their "only hope of salvation."[49] In true social gospel fashion, the nations of Europe arrayed against Germany sacrificed themselves to serve their posterity and to save the souls of the German people. According to Herron, war in 1917 was a religious crusade.

It came as no surprise, therefore, when the following year, after the United States declared war on Germany and her allies, George Herron

wrote a book entitled *Germanism and the American Crusade*. From the
very first page, Herron wrote ebulliently of America's participation in the
war "for the purpose of cleaning up the world, and of ridding it of war and
Germanism forever." Writing from Italy, the social gospeler identified
with the Yanks. "When we did perceive the catastrophe and the crisis it
had precipitated," he wrote, "we began to feel, very soon, that unto us
was amazingly given the divine chance of closing up the old world and its
political methods; and that it furthermore rested with us to lay living
foundations for a world wherein should be none but democratic and
cooperative peoples." The highly charged sense of religious mission
stands out unmistakably in this text. Americans had a "divine chance" to
save the world. Rescued from the clutches of Germanism, Americans, as
God's agents on earth, could institute democracy and cooperation. Later
in the book, Herron explained that Americans "will now play one of
God's great games" with a consciousness of "world-mission," "righteous
judgement," and "creative purpose" that come from Christ.[50] For Herron
the war presented a two-sided opportunity—a chance for the United
States to save the world with a vital social vision and a chance for George
Herron to inspire that vision and to recapture the spiritual and moral
influence he had lost.

In order for the United States to make the most of this opportunity,
Herron suggested in *Germanism and the American Crusade* that Americans needed revivalists and a plan for redemption. Herron avowed that
"Germanism and Americanism cannot stay together in the same world."
But instead of emphasizing military might, Herron chose instead to
demand "repentance." The war, in the expatriot's mind, was a giant
revival. He and the Yanks were exhorters, and the Germans were sinners. The significance of this position lies in Herron's faith in ideas and
in rational persuasion. Though primarily considered "activists," progressives like Herron nonetheless demonstrated an abiding confidence
in the necessity of ideological and spiritual regeneration. They believed
that if they somehow could change their opponents' minds, an improved
world would appear. The better world that Herron envisioned featured
"spiritual and social inquiry and adventure." "American youths," he
explained, "were preparing to make war on the unknown; to wring from
nature her secrets; to find out the truth about the kingdom of heaven; to
make the world a free and decent habitation, an equal invocation and
opportunity, a place of brave and abundant and beauteous life, for all the
sons and daughters of men."[51] What Herron wanted resembled the kind
of culture and society that was beginning to emerge in the United States:

one based on scientific inquiry, consumer abundance, and interdependence for a comfortable life.

By the time the armistice was signed in November 1918, Herron had managed to win the confidence of Woodrow Wilson and worked as a special emissary to the Germans. He convinced the Germans that Wilson would enforce conditions favorable to Germany and persuaded Kurt Eisner to advocate the acknowledgement of war guilt so as to get better terms. When the Russian Revolution threatened to impede the peace settlement, a conference at Prinkipo was organized to work out some arrangement with Russia. Wilson sent George Herron as one of two representatives to that meeting.[52]

An eager propagandist, Herron had written extensively in Europe of Wilson's "new freedom" and Fourteen Points and his commitment to social justice and the salvation of Germany. He had regained a large measure of his former influence and significance. Herron knew that his was a voice to be heeded, and he saw himself as one of the president's right-hand men. As he wrote in 1921, "Upon my faith in Wilson's fidelity to the faith he had confessed, I built myself a new and pinnacled house of hope for humanity" and also found a "reason for being alive."[53] Both were dashed by the events at Versailles.

When the terms of the peace became known, Herron's disappointment could not have been greater. He later recalled that an incident in Paris portended disaster weeks before the outcome had become final. Herron owned a cane he had gotten on a trip to the "holy land" of Syria. The cane, carved from an olive tree not far from Jerusalem, symbolized his mission of peace. He told his sixteen-year-old son, "I am going to Paris to set up the kingdom of heaven, and this staff from the country of Jesus is a symbol of my purpose." His son warned him not to let the other "peacemakers" break it. Upon reaching the conference, Herron met a military attache and an economic adviser, both of whom pushed past him and slammed the door on his cane. It broke in several places. "Curiously and instantly," he remembered, "fell also my faith, as unsupporting as my shattered stick—a faith so incredibly naive, retrospectively looked at, as to make me doubtful if ever I should have been allowed to leave my mother's knee."[54]

The peace negotiations left Wilson in a minority position, the Germans demoralized and punished, and Herron scorned by Germans, radicals, and conservatives alike. The Prussians, Bavarians, Bolsheviks, and American press all hated him, and he was left with little to do but retreat to his estate in Fiesole. His final book on the war, *The Defeat in the Victory* (1921), was intended to be "photographic of the present psychological plight of such as gave to Wilson's early gospel and leadership an active and even apostolic trust." It was written in the "troubled hours snatched from futile, but . . . faithful service." All he had wanted was "the privilege of serving" and "seeing mankind started upon a nobler and happier history." Instead of "collective righteousness" and "international brotherhood," however, the war and its peace brought "greedy and savage and lawless" treaties, "dishonesties," "primitive revenge," and "capitalist modernity."[55] Though victorious on the battlefield, the Allies tasted defeat in the terms of peace.

By the 1920s Herron realized that the war had resulted in an important victory: destruction of the old order. "Faith in the old world has gone," he insisted, and "belief in the fraudulency and incompetence of current social and governmental organization is now generally and irrevocably active."[56] The brutality of competition and individualism, liberal self-interested politics, and oppressive institutions of Victorian culture had been shattered by the Great War. So in one sense, the social gospel had not met with defeat after all. The problem was that a society based on cooperation and interdependence, abundance, and human sympathy was not the utopian kingdom of God on earth that he and others had imagined it would be. It was instead a consumer capitalist society, with shallow social relations, and unrivaled material wealth. Furthermore, instead of making all capitalists into Christians, as Herron had exhorted in the 1890s, the war and its victorious social gospel seemed to have made Christians into consumer capitalists. Americans' faith seemed to rest in the tools of commerce, science, and the state to provide security and comfort.

The Defeat in the Victory was the last book George Herron wrote. Discredited by his role in the Prinkipo conference and the Treaty of Versailles, Herron could not return to his native land. He remained in his adopted homeland and invested great hopes in the creation of a Christlike state in that country. Three years after his last book appeared, George Herron died. The events of Herron's life help explain how many a young Protestant in the late nineteenth century grasped the social gospel as a mooring post in a sea of vast uncertainty. His experiences also show, albeit in exaggerated form, how the social gospel sprang from personal sources and how the quest for social justice coincided with a quest for identity and purpose. Most importantly, however, George Herron makes plain the strength of the social gospel in the postwar world. He understood in an inchoate way that the war did not defeat the social gospel, but that a victorious social gospel resulted in a triumphant secular culture as well.

Not all social gospelers perceived defeat in the aftermath of the world war. Some were inspired to examine the social gospel anew in the clarified postwar atmosphere of efficiency and heroism. Harry Emerson Fosdick rose to the challenge of war and in its wake found a new vitality in his ministry. Fosdick's life illustrates how the war influenced social gospelers and their ideas and how they adapted the social gospel to conditions in postwar America.

HARRY EMERSON FOSDICK
The Challenge of the Present Crisis

Of the more than forty books that Harry Emerson Fosdick wrote during his long career in the ministry, he regretted only one. *The Challenge of the Present Crisis* appeared in 1918 as a "defense of war." More than two thousand copies of it sold in the United States, and a British press printed a special edition for its market across the Atlantic. The book propelled Fosdick into the YMCA crusade in France, and his work in this effort won him national recognition and fame as one of the best preachers in the United States.[57] The book won for the middle-aged minister one of the most thrilling and authentic experiences of his life: survival in the trenches of the Great War in Europe. But after another world war and a police action, the Reverend Fosdick remembered with embarrassment his attempt to "back up and even idealize the war." As he wrote in his autobiography, *The Living of These Days*, published in 1956, "I was never more sincere in my life than when I wrote it, but I was wrong," and "I now repudiate it."[58] Like a burr on his conscience, *The Challenge of the Present Crisis* reminded Fosdick of his ardent support of war.

The Challenge of the Present Crisis was part of a growing literature by religious men in America who had begun to view the Great War as a chance to save the world. The final words of the book were both a call to arms and an affirmation of social salvation. "He must have a callous soul who can pass through times like these and not hear a voice, whose call a man must answer, or else lose his soul," he wrote. "Your country needs *you*. The Kingdom of God on earth needs *you*. The cause of Christ is hard bestead and righteousness is having a heavy battle in the earth—they need *you*."[59] One can almost see the long, crooked finger of Uncle Sam pointing down relentlessly from a recruiting poster at some sturdy farm boy, stiffening his determination to whip the Huns. Fosdick promised even more than Uncle Sam. Instead of mere military victory, the Baptist assured his listeners that salvation and righteousness would be theirs as well. And, according to Fosdick, the war would change many aspects of American life. "The whole course of mankind's increasing interdependence," he insisted, "indicates that in this war we are paying the heavy price for the upward climb toward solidarity. We are fighting the war on the way up, not on the way down. Give man time and he yet will learn to handle the new relationships for fraternity and not for war."[60] The "new relationships" of which he spoke were improved communication, cooperation at work and among nations, and social faith.

Fosdick's most recent biographer, Robert M. Miller, notes that "one rather desperately misses even the thinnest vein of irony in Fosdick's war commentary."[61] The minister reported the gruesome events of war as earnestly as he did the remarks and experiences of the men who witnessed them. Perhaps the reason for this lack of irony lies in the personal meaning of the war for Fosdick. The war marked a turning point in his life and career. In his autobiography, Fosdick noted that upon his return to the United States he picked up where he left off at home "as though nothing had happened." "But," he conceded, "something had." His preaching before the war, he admitted, "never had had the drive that it had afterward."[62] He became one of the leading spokesmen for modernism when the Fundamentalists launched their attack in the 1920s. Fosdick also emerged as the principal proponent of "muscular Christianity," an emphasis that saved Protestantism from returning to the stern orthodoxy of the nineteenth century at the same time that it rescued manliness from the clutches of a "feminized" culture. Fosdick's career illustrates how the war challenged social gospel ministers to make their message a part of the postwar creed and, as representatives of a new social faith, to assume effective leadership in the society that consolidated after the war. His life also shows how the social gospelers' experience during and after the war prepared them for the postwar secular culture.

Born in 1878, Harry Emerson Fosdick grew up in the deeply religious home of his parents, Frank Sheldon and Amy Weaver Fosdick.[63] His father, a schoolteacher, expected his children to attend services and devotions regularly, and religion seems to have constituted a large part of Fosdick's childhood. He, his mother, and his siblings attended a Baptist church while his father led the singing in a Congregational church to earn extra money for the family. Fosdick and his father spent most

Harry Emerson Fosdick

Sundays discussing the differences between the ministers at the two churches, one of whom was conservative and the other liberal. At the age of seven, young Fosdick decided to join the family church and to dedicate his life to Christian service. After earning a bachelor's degree from Colgate University, he earned a B.D. from Union Theological Seminary in 1904. While still working on his divinity degree, Fosdick volunteered to toil among New York City's outcasts at the Mariners' Temple Mission in the Bowery. As soon as he was ordained, he began preaching in the First Baptist Church in Montclair, New Jersey.

Despite his dedication to Christianity, Fosdick did not embrace religion without considerable torment. His decision as a seven-year-old to become a Christian came at a time of personal trauma. That year his father's meager income as a public school teacher forced the family to move from a comfortable home on Pennsylvania Street in Buffalo to a rather shabby home on Prospect Avenue. The same year, Amy Fosdick suffered a debilitating nervous breakdown. Before she recovered her health she had to be removed to a home in the country, where she received constant attention. The three Fosdick children were deposited in different relatives' households until she was well enough to care for them again. His mother's illness and separation from him were not the only reasons for the boy's serious interest in religion. A sister died of diphtheria, and the family expected Harry to succumb to the disease as well. The nearness and reality of death and the kind of religion commonly taught in churches in the 1880s made religion a vital, albeit frightening, subject to Fosdick.

Indeed, Fosdick associated many unpleasant memories with churches and orthodox Protestantism. As an old man, he recalled the "deplorable" effect that "fire-and-brimstone preaching" had on him. "I vividly recall weeping at night for fear of going to hell," he wrote in 1956, "with my mystified and baffled mother trying to comfort me."[64] More than one evangelical minister convinced him that simple pleasures— cider drinking, the Virginia reel, and the theater—were unpardonable sins. He missed his only chance to see Edwin Booth, the great Shakespearean actor, because he feared eternal damnation if he went to Booth's performance of *Hamlet*. Excerpts from books owned by the Fosdick children show that despite their parents' "sanity" regarding religion, the children nevertheless were exposed to "books of monstrous morality." One of these books warned children who "behave wickedly to their parents" that God "punishes them by letting them die while they are young, and sending their souls to hell." It is possible that Fosdick considered his mother's illness and separation from him a result of some wickedness on his part and his own brush with death a sign of God's displeasure.[65] In any event, Fosdick suffered in agony over the torments of hell and accepted religion at a time when he was most impressionable and insecure. Years later, during World War I, Fosdick confessed his "hidden anger" at the church of his youth for its "wretched play upon my selfish fears and selfish hopes."[66]

By the time the young New Yorker entered Union Theological Seminary in 1901, social religion was an important part of the seminary's curriculum. It would have been difficult for Fosdick to escape the social gospel of Gladden, Strong, Rauschenbusch, and Mathews; the last two had risen to prominence in Fosdick's denomination. Much of his "revolt against orthodoxy" had taken place during his undergraduate days at Colgate. Independent reading reinforced the process of questioning that began in his college courses. By the beginning of his second year of college study, his friends found him "a disturbing upsetter of the saints" who questioned and doubted everything to do with religious faith. Within two years, Fosdick surprised them by announcing that he wanted to become a preacher. He had decided to make a Kierkegaardian leap of faith and to dismiss as unimportant the strict legalism of nineteenth-century Protestantism. Fosdick began his theological studies with an open mind at a time when the "new theology was well under way." The social religion he learned at the seminary, combined with his work in the Mariners' Temple a year later, brought Fosdick irrevocably into the camp of the social gospel. His seminary work "emancipated" him from "the old, hidebound orthodoxies."[67]

Illness and renewed financial trouble arose once more as Fosdick began his course of study at Union Theological Seminary in 1901, however. Having drained precious family resources to earn his bachelor's degree and begin preparation for the ministry, Fosdick hoped to make his own way, in true Victorian fashion, in the exciting city. "On his toes with excitement" as he faced the "greatest opportunity" and "stiffest competition" of his life, Fosdick plunged into his new surroundings and work with spirited determination to make the most of his chance. In addition to his regular course of study, he ministered to the "forgotten men" who lived in the "raw filth, poverty, and degradation of the Bowery." He "worked without respite" and before long suffered a severe nervous breakdown. At first he hoped that a weekend in Worcester with his fiancée would cure him, but instead he "went from bad to worse." Fosdick went back to Buffalo "a humiliated nervous wreck, returning to be an emotional and financial burden" to his family. In the days that followed, Fosdick experienced the "hell of neurotic agony." "After months of perdition," the family physician sent him to a sanitarium for a rest cure, and Fosdick shrank in shame, knowing that he "should have been on his own" but instead was "eating deeper and deeper into the family's capacity to borrow money at the bank." After four months, he had recovered sufficiently to visit his fiancée, whose father, seeing that the young man was still "nervously ragged," sent him to Europe for six weeks, where he finally made a full recovery.[68]

The entire crisis from beginning to end exposed to Fosdick the limitations of individual endeavor. Competition with the students and faculty at Union Theological Seminary, witnessing the outcasts of industrial competition in the Bowery, and his family's financial hardships in spite of hard work and frugality—all drove home the insufficiency of individual competition and responsibility. "The technique I had habitually relied upon—marshaling my wit and my volition and going strenuously after want I wanted—petered completely out," he wrote in his autobiography. "I, who had thought myself strong, found myself beaten, unable to cope not only with outward circumstances but even with myself."[69] The experience confirmed his faith in the social gospel, but it also left him feeling uneasy. For though he had been spared a lonely conversion, Fosdick continued to long for some way to succeed as an individual and to feel the surge of manliness he assumed would come with success. In 1904 Harry Emerson Fosdick graduated from Union Theological Seminary and began his ministry in Montclair, New Jersey.

Fosdick began at once to reform the orthodox worship service in his new parish. He opened the communion table to anyone who wished to partake, whether Baptist or not. He hoped to make the services and the congregation as ecumenical as possible, in the spirit of church unity that had become increasingly popular in the early twentieth century. In addition, he began to preach liberal sermons. While still at Montclair, the young minister wrote his first books and articles. Some, like *The Second Mile* (1908), were little more than expanded sermons. *The Manhood of the Master* (1913), however, contributed to a growing body of literature about Jesus. Like Walter Rauschenbusch, who at about this time declared that Jesus was a "man's man," Fosdick's volume contributed to the effort to rescue Jesus from limp-wristed androgyny. *The Manhood of the Master* also helped legitimize the domestic values of service, sacrifice, and nurture for Christian men. After seven years at Montclair, Fosdick added teaching to his preaching duties, offering courses in homiletics at Union Theological Seminary. Four years later he was named the Morris K. Jessup Professor of Practical Theology, a position he retained until 1934.[70]

From 1915 to 1919, Harry Emerson Fosdick did not have time for a regular parish—he was too involved with war work. Up to this time, Fosdick had earned a measure of respect for his preaching, teaching, and writing. He had begun to attract the attention of Protestant leaders across the nation as a powerful spokesman of the social gospel. The war, however, seemed to elicit more from Fosdick than mere patriotism. It was, in his words, both a "challenge" and a "crisis," and he threw himself into it. Perhaps the war gave Fosdick a chance to proclaim his independence at the same time that he furthered the social gospel. He confessed in 1919 that the Great War "resurrected" old "wrath" against the church from which he had revolted. In an article for the *Atlantic Monthly* near the end of the war, he remembered: "As a lad, I was frightened half to death because I feared to go to hell! At nine, I suffered tragic torments because I thought I had committed the unpardonable sin, and so was 'lost.' All through my youth I perjured my soul almost beyond redemption." When soldiers in France complained about the "negativeness" of the church,

Fosdick heartily agreed, remembering ridiculous laws against "everything that a normal boy wants to do."[71] The war, he hoped, would demolish the orthodoxy that had oppressed him as a boy. The war thus would save the world and redeem the man.

Harry Fosdick did much more than preach an occasional sermon in support of the conflict, however. He took the lead in arousing a martial spirit in the United States long before the *Lusitania* sank. When President Wilson ran for reelection on the platform "He kept us out of war," Fosdick scolded Wilson's opponent, Charles Evans Hughes, for not promising to take America into the conflict. He stumped New York State with a "team" of speakers, "whipping up the enthusiasm of great audiences to get into the fight." When the YMCA organized an expedition to France and sent men to speak to American troops, Fosdick was included on their list of "itinerant speakers." At one point during this tour his sermons were so bellicose that one man in the audience later told the Baptist, "Everyone was so inspired by what you said that all would have eagerly torn into the enemy barehanded, had they been able to come in contact with them."[72] Fosdick spent four months in Great Britain, France, and Belgium, often at or near the front. He proved his own courage while he boosted the morale of the troops and convinced them that their combat was part of a holy cause.

If the war left an indelible mark on Fosdick's character and ministry, it had an equally great effect on the social gospel. The cover of *The Challenge of the Present Crisis* (1917) featured a mailed hand wreathed by a crown of thorns, presumably to suggest that Jesus endorsed the fighting in Europe. Fosdick assured his readers that the war affirmed social Christianity. "Only a little while ago many were telling us that Christianity had nothing to do with social questions, that it was a gospel of salvation for the individual out of the wreckage of a ruined world," he declared early in the book. "Now we are told that Christianity has failed because it has not stopped war! It is confessed, then, that Christianity does have something to do with social questions, that it will be judged rightly not alone by what it does for individuals but by what it makes of the world in which individuals must live." He urged the orthodox to take their "old faiths" into the "trenches, the hospitals, the desolated homes of Europe" and find out how inadequate they had become.[73] Social hopes alone could satisfy the demands of those situations. He believed that greater intimacy in the world had led to the conflict, but that it would also be the basis of the new order once peace was restored. Only social religion would satisfy people living in an interdependent society.

His experiences in the trenches with Allied soldiers convinced Fosdick that the war represented an important watershed in the history of civilization. "Nothing is going through this fire," he wrote in the *Atlantic Monthly,* "without becoming malleable, or, becoming malleable, can resist the pressure of remoulding circumstance." And no peacetime minister ever had enjoyed the opportunity to speak about the social gospel to such a large cross-section of Americans. American soldiers had gone to France to "save the world," he said, and they learned that "innermost salvation" comes only through "social sacrifice." The experience of war stripped away all but the bare essentials of religion. And in 1919 the bare essentials included "service," "sacrifice," "courage," "unconquerable cheer," and "fidelity to comrades." "They want a fairer, more fraternal world to show for their travail," Fosdick reported.[74] He predicted a postwar world dominated by cooperation at the workplace, brotherliness in social relations, the idealization of service in the state, and the social gospel in religion.

The social gospel, however, bore only faint resemblance to the idealistic gospel of Walter Rauschenbusch, Washington Gladden, and Josiah Strong before the war. In the heat of destruction, sentimentality, naive faith in goodness and progress, and feminine charity evaporated, leaving behind a hardened tough-mindedness that required fearless leadership, belief in great causes, and, above all, manliness. Fosdick warned his peers in the ministerial fraternity that their churches would have to get a "type of Christianity" that "real men" would find worthwhile to accept. He reported that many soldiers worried that the proscription against various forms of amusement and entertainment threatened to "emasculate" the church. Soldiers and postwar Protestants demanded "courage," "fortitude," and "perfect willingness to die for their causes." Fosdick believed that no organization dominated by idealistic women would interest them, for with the soldiers, "only manhood matters." Like an army, social gospel Protestants would have to plan, coordinate, and execute their reforms efficiently. "They went out, boys," Fosdick warned Americans at home of their brave sons and husbands; "they will come back like the Judgement Day."[75]

The Great War in Europe gave Fosdick some of the most thrilling experiences of his life, and he, too, returned to the United States like the "Judgement Day." He claimed that his preaching never had been better, and he accepted a call to the First Presbyterian Church in New York City as part of an ecumenical experiment. After his first year, Fosdick expanded his ministry by taking advantage of the new technology of radio.

Beginning in the 1920s, Fosdick prepared and delivered weekly radio sermons that reached thousands of unchurched Americans across the country.[76] When the "war" between fundamentalists and modernists heated up in the mid-1920s, Fosdick found himself in the middle of the controversy, defending modernism against the anachronistic attacks of conservative Protestants. The liberals and social gospelers, he remembered, eventually won the battle. Fosdick, however, became a casualty of the conflict when the Presbyterians decided in 1925 that their experiment in ecumenicity required a less combative pastor. Returning to his own denomination, Fosdick accepted a call to the Park Avenue Baptist Church in New York on the condition that the congregation move to a less wealthy neighborhood and build a new church dedicated to community service. The congregation agreed to his request, and in 1931 they and their pastor opened the Riverside Church, behind whose pulpit Fosdick remained until his retirement in 1946. All of his efforts after World War I radiated his determination to defend the new social religion.

Despite the vigor with which Fosdick undertook his enterprises after the war, even he could not escape a troubling sense that the war had undermined the moral authority of churches. Toughened by war, he had become enough of a realist to recognize the darker side of civil religion after the war. In 1925, in a sermon to the League of Nations in Geneva, Fosdick admitted that Americans had made the nation the "supreme object of devotion." Indeed, he added, "they know no higher God; they really worship Caesar." The war had "helped" his country "to identify religion and patriotism." His bellicosity had helped lead Americans into a Protestant crusade, but patriots had returned to worship the nation that had made them men and that had emerged victorious from battle. The "center of loyalty" in the "religious life of the people," Fosdick noted, "has increasingly become the nation."[77] Two years later in the Park Avenue Church Fosdick rued "the breakdown of traditional standards of right and wrong." Since the war, young people asked what authority could define moral behavior for them. Again Fosdick concluded that Protestantism had failed to "retain its grip on the consciences of youth." Fosdick proposed "good taste" as a way to "create within [the child] a high opinion of his life" and make him "loyal to the royal" in himself.[78] Fosdick's social gospel was a gospel of self-realization.

Harry Emerson Fosdick came to maturity at a time when the social gospel was on the rise. Because of the particular circumstances of his youth, he nonetheless wrestled with the oppressive demands of orthodox Protestantism and became a potent defender of the social gospel. The

Great War in Europe became a front for his battle to win self-respect as well as an arena for social salvation. His support of the war resulted from personal experiences, and his affirmation of social gospel Protestantism came out of the social and cultural experiences of war. He participated in a transformation of the social gospel into "muscular Christianity" and into a gospel of tough-minded, efficient service.

Like Fosdick, Edward Scribner Ames enthusiastically hailed the social gospel and the advances in medicine and technology that resulted from war. Ames melded even more completely than Fosdick the sacred and secular forces for social reform. When Ames published *The New Orthodoxy* in 1918, he summarized the most important beliefs of American Protestantism—beliefs that were emerging from the war.

EDWARD SCRIBNER AMES
The New Orthodoxy

In 1918, Edward Scribner Ames articulated what he believed were the common beliefs of twentieth-century Christians in a book he entitled *The New Orthodoxy*. In its opening pages, he made the startling claim that future historians may "regard Protestantism as coming to its close with the end of the nineteenth century as a vital, ascending type of religion." Ames explained: "In that century several of the most characteristic principles of Protestantism were undermined by a larger knowledge of history and science. Protestantism was individualistic; the new order is social. It assumed the infallibility of the Bible, and that is no longer tenable. It exalted authority, and now there is no legitimate authority except that of experience." Protestantism, Ames believed, had given way to a "new orthodoxy" based on "the natural and the social sciences." As he wrote in the preface, "This book seeks to present in simple terms a view of religion consistent with the mental habits of those trained in the sciences, in the professions, and in the expert direction of practical affairs."[79]

Ames called the new orthodoxy "social Christianity" and "the religion of democracy." It included the most important aspects of the social gospel. He believed that it had been evolving for two decades as a result of "the inventions, the discoveries, the revolutionary achievements in democracy, in education, in the arts, in industry, and in religion." One event, however, brought this ferment to a head: the world war. "The great war," Ames insisted, "has already written in blood and tears the end of

Edward Scribner Ames

the old and the beginning of the new." The war in Europe helped consolidate the social gospel in the United States.[80]

Unlike earlier works on the social gospel, Ames's book did not defend social Christianity against anticipated criticism. Ames articulated with confidence ideas that once had caused a storm of controversy. In 1918, Ames believed that social concern, Christocentric theology, the kingdom of God on earth, and the scientific ethos were parts of the new accepted wisdom that was legitimized by the experience of war. The war quickened the social gospel. Ames and his contemporaries also discovered that the Great War transformed it.

Edward Scribner Ames, one of the younger generation of social gospelers, was the youngest of four children born to Lucius Bowles and Adaline Scribner Ames. Near the end of the Civil War, Lucius Ames learned about the Disciples of Christ, joined the church, and became a minister, to the chagrin of his "deeply religious Calvinistic" family. As a Disciples minister, he moved frequently throughout the Midwest. In 1870, when Edward was born, the Ames family lived in Eau Claire, Wisconsin, but they moved six more times before Lucius Ames retired from the ministry. Edward Ames later confided that he decided to remain in one church for forty years "to make up for all the moving my father did." Both his father and his father's adopted religion, however, helped pave the way for Ames's embrace of the social gospel. The older man maintained a "mood of piety" in his home and church, but he also encouraged "hospitality," "comradeship," and "friendliness" in the practice of a religion that "bound people together." Though he demanded individual piety from his children, Lucius Ames insisted that they care about others. Moreover, Edward Ames never found his father's behavior capricious or tyrannical. His father seemed to be "a guarantee of safety against all." Unlike many other men and women of his generation, Edward Ames knew and loved his father, and the two were fast friends.[81]

Ames underwent a conversion experience at the age of twelve, which, he remembered, gave him "a new comradeship" with his father. Ames took pride in his baseball skills and in the team spirit that pervaded his childhood religion and play. A child of more modern times, Ames craved excitement, novelty, and abundance. He enjoyed the thrill of adventure novels, the novelty of visiting relatives in Chicago and seeing a polar bear in Union Park, and the fascinating spectacle of life on the Mississippi River when he lived in Davenport, Iowa. He associated religion with abundance, as his "unanswered prayer" for a pony attests. His youthful money-making enterprises reflected the changing social arena in which he lived. Ames found it fun to sell goods, and he eventually worked himself into a position as general agent for a bookselling firm with workers beneath him who performed most of the labor. He remembered fondly that he "learned the reward and satisfaction" of "receiving a commission from the labor of other fellows."[82] Ames acknowledged the need for interdependence at work, at play, on his debating team at Drake University, and eventually, in his ministry.

Ames began his ministry as an advocate of the social gospel after receiving a progressive education in the 1880s and 1890s. After graduating from Drake University in Iowa at the age of 19, Ames earned a divinity degree from Yale in 1892 and a Ph.D. from the University of Chicago in 1895. He taught religion and philosophy at Butler College in Indiana until 1900, when the University of Chicago invited him to offer a course in philosophy. He remained in Chicago as pastor of the Disciples of Christ church in Hyde Park for the next forty years. The narrowly individualistic view of orthodox Protestantism held no fascination for him. He insisted in his autobiography that he had been "sympathetic to the social gospel" from the beginning.[83]

In 1902, after he had been at the Hyde Park church for nearly two

years, Ames decided to make a personal confession of faith to his parishioners. He declared his independence from "devitalized orthodoxy" and
then redefined the major categories of Protestant experience. Salvation
for Ames was the "conscious participation" in "this boundless, holy life,
rather than the escape from the consequences of original sin and the fall
of man." Salvation was a "life process" that led to the "realization of the
natural power of the soul." Thus, heaven was not an ethereal realm in
another dimension; rather, "participation in the divine life" was "here
and now." Likewise, hell was a "failure to attain this realization of one's
powers" and the "suffering" and "torture" that usually surrounded un-
fulfilled men and women. Finally, Ames proclaimed Jesus, not God, as
the primary "object of faith" because he "inspires men to the highest
spiritual life."[84] Ames's confession of faith incorporated the immediacy,
Christocentrism, and soothing qualities of the social gospel into a personal statement of belief. It became the basis of his ministry in Hyde
Park.

Reactions from church members to Ames's 1902 sermon were mixed.
One man reassured Ames that the message "was not new to me," while
one of the deacons admitted that "it wasn't as bad as I feared it would be."
Ames overheard one woman exclaim, "Well, what do you think of that!"
But by far the most typical response echoed the man who was heard to
say, "Oh, I don't know. It doesn't hurt me, and it does him so much good
to say it."[85] In short, Ames's declaration of faith in the social gospel
received mixed reviews from people unaccustomed to thinking about
theology. But his programs, which also reflected the social gospel, received hearty support in the years that followed, and through these
programs, Ames helped to legitimize the faith he confessed in 1902 and
made the social gospel the official creed of his congregation.

Ames's programs addressed the needs of people living in the greater
Chicago area. In 1907, for example, Ames invited the church to work
with the Chicago Fund, which coordinated a wide range of social agencies from the Bureau of Charity to the American Home-Finding Association. Two years later the Hyde Park congregation was participating in
school extension work, a children's home and aid society, a boys' club, a
society of social hygiene, a visiting nurse program, the Municipal Voters'
League, and the University of Chicago Settlement. The church invited
local reformers like Graham Taylor, Mary McDowell, Jane Addams, and
Charles R. Henderson to speak, and it opened a library to educate
parishioners in the social ideals of religion. Finally, the Hyde Park
church established a "benevolence budget" separate from the operating

budget and a "social service council" that made possible further efforts at reform. In 1915 during Social Service Week, the church sponsored a dramatic performance by the Little Theatre that they advertised as an effort to "emphasize the religious character of social work and the social interests of religion." Yet another project involved financing a missionary's work in China. Unlike the rigid proselytizers of old, Ames and his congregation sponsored "new missionaries" who took seriously "the welfare of human beings, physically and psychologically," and who brought their beneficiaries the "knowledge and social order which are basic for an intelligent meaning of the 'spiritual' life."[86] Even the "imperialism" of missionary work took on a social cast. In all of these projects, Ames found firm support from the men and women who attended his church. He discovered in the years before the Great War a steady growth of interest, involvement, and commitment to the social gospel.

Nevertheless, even Edward Ames's work met certain obstacles along the way. While he had experienced individual conversion in the context of pleasant social fellowship and had moved on comfortably and easily to social salvation, Ames found that it was not so easy to convince the members of the church "to believe in themselves" and to "throw off the long-standing idea that man is evil." Despite their willingness to support social service agencies, some of the saints of the Hyde Park church doubted the credibility of "self-realization" for salvation. Ames reminded his congregation that "conditions of efficiency" and "laws of health" made good people "better saints." His repeated message of efficiency, organization, service, and self-realization combined with the social upheaval of the 1890s and 1900s—which gave a "clearer and more poignant realization of the tragedies and horrors existing in the world"—gradually influenced the members to disavow their confining orthodoxy. At a time of great anxiety for many middle-class American Protestants, Ames's belief that "the ideals of the social worker" were beginning to replace the image of the pious individual provided comfort to those who pursued a profession instead of an individual enterprise.[87] Ames ultimately overcame the obstacles to belief in the social gospel by providing comfort to the middle class and by telling them that their efforts on behalf of those less fortunate than themselves sanctified their professions and their teamwork.

Ames's "personal work" probably did much to accustom his parishioners to the social gospel. For Ames, a key attraction of the social gospel lay in its power to ease anxieties and to affirm individuals' strengths. As he told his congregation, "A cup of cold water given in the name of

brotherhood would save the soul of the *giver*." The social gospel that
Ames preached and practiced eased people's fears of not belonging in a
corporate world, of not getting along with others on whom they depended
for identity, meaning, and approval. At the funeral of one church member, the widow approached Ames with a question about her husband's
immortality. "The best thing to do," he told her, sensing her anguish
about her own mortality, "is to make the most of this life, in a true sense,
and trust God for the rest." Her reply reveals the extent to which she had
become dependent on her minister's personal work. "That is what I
believe, too," she confided, "but I wanted to have you say it to me right
here and now. It is truly a comfort." Ames also believed that the importance of Jesus lay in his lessons of sympathy and forgiveness, which
"attuned him to his fellow men." In his pastoral work Ames tried to
reassure his members of their worth and to show them that he cared.[88]

Religion at the Hyde Park Disciples of Christ church also was compatible with consumer society. The church's decision to construct a new
building revealed some of the connections between the social gospel and
consumerism. In 1911, Ames announced in *The Messenger*, his church's
official periodical, that if two hundred people attended services six
weeks in a row, he would organize a fund-raising committee for a new
church. Six weeks later, he congratulated the congregation on their
"many new friends" and agreed to start a building fund. "This experiment has proved that we can get good audiences at our present location,
and it has shown that the method of getting them is to stir up our own
members," he wrote.[89]

The key phrases here are "good audiences," "present location," and
"to stir up our own members." Like theaters, movie houses, and other
establishments of entertainment, the Hyde Park church hoped to attract
"good audiences" interested in the church's program. It was not enough
to minister to people; instead, the church required a steady, dependable
clientele to succeed. Another important consideration was the efficacy of
the "present location." Such a concern reflected the pervasive worry
among businesses of all kinds that their location would hinder rather
than promote trade. Churches also seemed to consider their place in the
city as one key to their success or failure. Finally, the focus on stirring up
current members suggests an even more insidious influence of consumerism on religious life. Building a church represented a reward to
regular worshipers. Ames and his congregation apparently believed that
the promise of a material reward would stir the members to action—
indeed, he praised them for soliciting "new friends" in order to get the

church. Ames did not mention the benefits of the new church building to social work or to spiritual life. The new edifice would simply provide more comfortable accommodations for people who labored to drum up more "business" for the church.

In other contexts as well, Ames demonstrated his adoption of the terms of commerce in his ministry. When he spoke of social service, for example, he insisted that the "value of the deed"—like the value of many consumer items—could be "measured by the way the doer thinks and feels about it." Feelings about an act or an item were as important as their actual efficacy or utility. And when Ames regarded Jesus as the god of modern man, he argued that the Carpenter of Nazareth would probably "talk in terms of radios and telephones, of automobiles and airplanes, of stocks and bonds, of political conventions and movies and bestsellers, of Hollywood and Wall Street."[90] Jesus would be a man in tune with the instruments of mass culture.

By the time Europe exploded in conflict in 1914, Ames had succeeded, by and large, in popularizing the social gospel in his church in Hyde Park. The church's Social Service Council and the Chicago Fund ministered to the unemployed, the ill, the homeless, and the impoverished of Chicago, and the pastor had introduced his congregation to new doctrines and ideas. Their minister's social gospel made sense in corporate America, put them at ease personally, made them feel approved and worthwhile, and provided services efficiently to those in greatest need. Any lingering doubts that may have troubled the Disciples on the eve of America's involvement in the Great War probably were dispelled in the years immediately following the carnage of World War I. The war itself helped to legitimize the social gospel of Edward Scribner Ames. It also served to transform Ames's Protestantism.

The war had dragged on for four years when Edward Scribner Ames began writing *The New Orthodoxy* (1918). In his introduction, Ames wrote that the "opening years of the twentieth century" had begun "one of the most important epochs in history" and had ushered in a "consciousness of progress and of new developments" in all aspects of American life. The war, he believed, crystallized those changes. Recognizing that the war represented a great divide separating one understanding of religion from another, Ames devoted considerable attention to a contrast of before and after. According to Ames, nineteenth-century Protestantism was "static," "perfectionist," and "apart from life, from the state, and from practical affairs." It "despised and feared" the world. By contrast, the new orthodoxy was "dynamic," in search of "improvement," "integral with life in all its forms," and "specialized and made concrete by the peculiar duties and relations given to each person." It "loves the natural [world] especially in its service of social ideals." He also noted that Jesus, once "unreal and remote," had become "human" and God had drawn near to men "at the risk of seeming finite." Finally the personal ideal of "the good man," "serene and at peace, withdrawn from the common struggle," had given way to a new ideal, "a man sinewy and full of courage, working in the midst of human tasks, clear-headed and good-natured, conscious of far horizons."[91] Ames saw a complete dissolution of the faith of his father and grandfather and the emergence of a religion compatible with the postwar world.

The New Orthodoxy offered a streamlined, clarified social gospel for postwar America. Throughout the book, three essential dimensions appeared repeatedly: corporate organization, a team spirit, and science. The gospel of social salvation and social service, refracted by the experience of war, became an efficient, rational, manly creed that fitted men and women for the world of Babbitt in the 1920s. The war made it a religion of experts, friends, and science.

The great war demanded expertise and coordination of men and materiel. In the economic arena, it had consolidated a corporate order that was in nascent form at the onset of the conflict. It had served as a catalyst furthering developments in specialization and organization in government and business. As Ames put it, "In the emergency, which the war has created, a degree of consolidation and unification has been attained which would have required decades or centuries to achieve otherwise." The consequence for religion was "the necessity of cooperation" among church members and between churches, social settlements, public schools, and boards of health. Society after the war insisted upon cooperation and the "closer supervision of private affairs, of individual property, and of business."[92]

"Cooperation" had always been a key word in social gospel publications. But "cooperation" in Ames's text connoted something slightly different from the loving interaction and mutual assistance envisioned by the first generation of Protestants to embrace the social gospel. It referred to a complex organization of specialists working in tandem toward a common goal. In Ames's model, cooperation required experts. In fact, a few years later in a famous "letter to God," Ames remarked to the Almighty, "Your best representatives are . . . scientists . . . and inventors and experts," because they "labor for better knowledge, for more justice, for world peace, and for any interest which promises improvement and enlargement for our lives."[93] These specialists had contributed to the war effort in laboratories, on the War Industries Board, in factories, and on the battlefield. In Ames's *New Orthodoxy* and in other postwar works by social gospelers such expertise and coordination of disparate functions gained both legitimacy and religious content. According to Ames, corporate order could save society.

Social relations within this new corporate order also took on religious significance for Ames. The war showed Americans how fragile life is and how dependent on others men and women had become. The "terrible strain and confusion of the present war," he wrote, make the "enrichment and enlargement of human life" a "more attractive goal" for modern Protestants. "The religious life . . . involves one's own personality, the personality of others, and of God," he declared in *The New Orthodoxy*. "The conditions for growth of personality lie in the give and take of the interaction of many individuals." "Love of our fellow men" even found its way into the hearts of businessmen, who demonstrated a "sense of friendliness" for their workers by adopting "better methods for the protection" of employees.[94] Ames believed that the war cemented into the social structure an ethos of friendliness, other-direction, and mutual support and approval among men and women.

Social relations described by Ames were also firmly set in the emerging order of leisure and consumption. Ames referred to the "drama" of religious life in which "every man takes his role in the action by virtue of his nature and his relation to his fellows." No "sharp lines" separated "the audience and the performers." Everyone watched and acted simultaneously and learned from others who they were. The corporation symbolized not only the appropriate arena for entering into these pleasant and rewarding relations but also made possible the media for homogenizing the nation and easing social strains. In this regard, the war had transformed the meaning of democracy. Older social gospelers had waged war against corporate exploitation of workers and against indifference to human suffering. In *The New Orthodoxy* Ames argued that "travel and communication and the movies enable even the plainest citizen to enter into intimate understanding with the classes and conditions which have hitherto been inaccessible to him."[95] After the war, Ames equated consumerism and democracy.

For Ames, the war affirmed the ideal of self-realization. In the midst of war, he wrote that the "dream of the present" was a "free society" that furnished "all its members the greatest possible power of intelligence, and will, and sympathy, and capacity for social cooperation and progress." Ames believed that the "function of the church" was to make possible the "ideal of a free and growing brotherhood of mankind."[96] Thus, the new orthodoxy of the social gospel was much less concerned with salvation—individual or social—than with fulfillment. In *The Church at Work in the Modern World* (1935), Ames returned to the theme of self-realization, explaining that "it is impossible longer [*sic*] to draw a line between the sacred and the secular in a way which limits the religious concern to the ceremonials. Whatever affects the realization of the best life for men, women, and children must be taken into account. Every individual stands in the midst of a wide-reaching complex of social and physical conditions which affect his well-being, and which must be included within any serious attempt to help him realize his human possibilities." He went on the describe religious people as men and women who believe in life and its "capacity for yielding larger and finer satisfactions."[97] Self-realization as personal growth provided important psychological support for capitalist commitment to expansion and incorporation. Social gospelers like Ames underlined that support as well.

Self-realization and coordination of experts linked postwar religion and the modern corporate order. Religion provided moral legitimacy to these dimensions of modernity as they and the social gospel emerged after the First World War. One other product of the war gained affirmation from both wartime experience and the new orthodoxy: faith in science. Science and religion understandably had been at odds for centuries because of the empiricism of science and the belief in religion in spite of empirical evidence. As late as the end of the nineteenth century, the use of the historical method by biblical scholars had prompted accusations of apostasy and heresy and had created rifts in schools of theology between those who accepted "higher criticism" and those who remained true to the inerrancy of the Bible.

The warm embrace of science by Ames and other social gospelers may appear, at first glance, to be peculiar. Yet, in a consolidating corporate order with an emphasis on self-realization, and a religious commitment to health, well-being, and expertise, the apparent inconsistency makes sense. Scientists in chemical laboratories, medical practice, and munitions factories had helped "save the world." They made possible greater comfort, good health, and peace. Thus, when Edward Ames paused to reflect on the Great War in his autobiography, he concluded that in order to avoid such massive destruction in the future, Protestant men and women should pursue science. "In spite of wars and the ensuing depression," he wrote sometime in the 1930s, "the scientists have kept on with their patient, enthusiastic collaboration in the search for truth about many things." They invented the products that improved common life: "better and cheaper clothing," "better means of health," "better and safer transportation," and "more comfortable beds and better cooking stoves."[98] People could depend on scientists to improve their lives. In *The Church at Work*, Ames suggested that ministers devote part of their time in sermons to stories of "a new scientific discovery which promises to eradicate some dread disease." Such a theme was religious because it "renews trust in life" and contributes to health.[99] Ames believed that American Protestants were determined to make their lives richer and fuller of meaning. As he remarked in *The New Orthodoxy*, the sentiment of nineteenth-century Protestantism could be summed up in the hymn "I'm But a Stranger Here; Heaven Is My Home." In postwar America a new hymn captured the modern spirit: "We Are Builders of That City."[100]

After the war, Ames continued to serve the parish in Hyde Park and wrote one of his most influential books, *Religion*, in 1929. He remained in the Hyde Park pulpit until 1940 but continued working in the Disciples' Divinity House for five years and edited the *Scroll*, his congregation's quarterly publication, for another eleven years. Though he remained active in church affairs until he reached his eighties, Ames spent many of his later years relaxing in the old family home near Lake Michigan. The social gospel he had spread during his active ministry helped him get as much as possible out of life. Edward Scribner Ames held steadfastly to the social gospel he had embraced as a young man and to the new orthodoxy that emerged out of the First World War. "Christianity," he wrote in his theological autobiography, "now faces the alternative of becoming a religion of this world or of having no appeal to this age."[101] As his work demonstrates, the social gospel *had* become a religion of this world—a religion of experts, organization, and science.

. . .

The Great War in Europe was a pentecost of calamity for the social gospel, but it did not mark an abrupt departure from the recent past. All of the values and tendencies that emerged in postwar America and in the social gospel of the 1920s had been part of the Protestant social gospel that took shape at the turn of the century. The war merely heightened, intensified, and distilled the values of service, sacrifice, love, and the kingdom of God, creating from the 1910s a creed for the 1920s. As a chaplain explained to Sherwood Eddy in 1918, most of the soldiers had been "hardened" by war, "though," he hastened to add, "not necessarily in a bad sense."[102] Social gospelers believed that soldiers longed for a religion that spoke more directly to their experience, and they, also affected by war, subtly altered the meanings of their gospel. The social gospel did not vanish in the disillusionment of the "lost generation." Harry Fosdick and Edward Ames espoused it throughout their long careers. But the war had exposed and magnified the intertwining of Protestantism and secular culture that had begun decades before the war. Thus, in spite of the more highly publicized Fundamentalist efforts to restore repressive control on American society in the jazz age, the social gospel became the chief expression of mainstream Protestantism in the twentieth century, and it depended on popular faith in secular institutions.

Indeed, the Great War and Protestant responses to it showed how dependent social gospelers had become on secular institutions of government. The war strengthened the bond between the social gospel and the state. Social gospelers blurred the mission of the state with their commitment to the kingdom of God and created a single national crusade with the blessing of the church. Once national symbols became sacred symbols, the transfer of adoration and faith was not far behind. Though religious leaders may have meant that America was God's instrument, a generation of Americans accustomed to tangible results must have found more to trust in the armed force, effective organization, and success of the nation than in the invisible force of God. American civil religion— faith in the nation—grew, and social gospelers helped cement the bond between the people and their nation. In so doing, they facilitated the burgeoning authority of the state and of science in American culture.

Because both the social gospel and modern culture resulted from the same vast process of change in the late nineteenth century—the same disenchantment with Victorianism and liberal society—they shared common points of departure, perspective, and values. The war helped to showcase the connections and interdependence between American Protestantism and secular culture. Churchmen insisted that they offered something different to their communicants, but the shrillness with which they made their claims in the 1920s suggests at the very least a disturbing sense that their voices had gotten lost in the clamor of modern civilization. When the *Literary Digest* reported on the "kind of religion soldiers want," it recorded the words of a chaplain who warned churchmen at home that soldiers lived in "sheer fear" of "public opinion." "They would rather be in fashion than be right," he declared.[103] From a handful of avant-garde critics in the 1880s and 1890s, the social gospel movement had become, by the 1920s, the "fashion" in Protestant America.

Edward Scribner Ames believed that religion had to become part of the world in order to retain its hold on the American imagination. Harry Emerson Fosdick saw the war as a challenge to his beliefs, and he worked all the harder to ensure their survival in the postwar era. George Herron, of course, saw defeat in the victory for the United States and for the social gospel. As all three men and their colleagues in the social gospel movement show, faith in general did not disappear, but people's experience of religion was different after the Great War. Secular beliefs and institutions assumed greater importance in their culture. People found in work a source of reward; in family, emotional comfort; in politics, security and abundance; and in the nation, a symbol to be adored. For many, the social gospel laid the ideological and moral foundation for these social and cultural changes.

As the United States passed through the crucible of war, the nineteenth-century trappings of its culture fell away. Purveyors of American culture, including social gospelers, had challenged the oppressiveness of Victorian culture since the turn of the century, but a full-blown alternative to it did not appear until after the Great War. The assault on Victorian culture by writers, artists, advertisers, and men of the cloth destroyed the Protestant roots of cultural life in the United States and left in its place a powerful consuming ethos. Social gospelers participated in that process. Reforming zeal, which drove men and women to attack Victorian values and the economic institutions that had evolved out of them, eventually gave way to enthusiastic support for secular values. The Great War helped affirm the social gospel as a mainstream expression of Protestantism in America. But by the time Americans went to war, the social gospel had been drained of its early spirit and much of its Protestantism.

6

A Consuming Faith: The Social Gospel and Modern American Culture

As middle-class Americans entered the 1920s, they aspired, at least in the North, to companionship in family life and interdependence and efficiency in the economy. They were bombarded by messages concerning direction and goals from the mass media and advertisers. They demanded a government willing to serve its citizens and intervene in times of disaster. Americans had passed through the crucible of war to find that the social norms and cultural imperatives that had been taking shape in the prewar decades had become fixtures of twentieth-century American life.

Social gospelers had been advocates of many of the changes Americans experienced in 1920. They had helped redefine the work ethic and family relations. They had employed advertising to broaden the appeal of social gospel ideas and to reach the mass of unchurched Americans. In their own way, social gospelers had contributed to the movement of progressive reform that had created a socially responsible state. They had anointed that state for a holy mission to save the world when war erupted in Europe. Social gospelers had articulated these beliefs and taken such action in the hope of maintaining the vitality and influence of Protestantism in America. They had hoped to Christianize the economy, the politics, and the social institutions of the country.

But the culture of the 1920s turned out to be configured differently. Protestant belief was no longer at the core of American culture. With their focus on the improvement of society in the here and now, social gospelers had helped lay the ideological and moral foundations of a society and culture dominated by secular institutions, standards, and values. The evolution of the social gospel and of American culture occurred simultaneously, each influencing the nature of change in the other. By 1920 the message of the social gospel had helped create and legitimize a new culture in the United States that effectively marginalized historical Protestantism. Social gospelers, in their effort to be part of the changing culture they served, adopted the secular language, methods, and standards of commerce in their religious belief and practices. The success of the social gospel writers in articulating a new social understanding of work, family, and the polity also had the ultimate effect of undermining its originating religious impulse.

The attractiveness of a consumer culture in the United States was in part due to middle-class Americans' longing for objective reality, emotional intensity, and personal security. The cultural affirmation of youth and the emphasis on immediate psychic and material rewards resulted from Americans' impatience with deferred, ethereal promises and found expression in such widely divergent impulses as modernism and antimodernism, literary realism, and spectator sports. Cultural spokesmen—literati, artists, and increasingly, advertisers—were responding to their own yearnings when they proposed new cultural forms that undercut deferred gratification, faith in the unseen, and self-control. What they may not have realized, however, was that the very act of consuming—that is, participating in and being a part of a consumer culture—became an act of faith, faith in the messages of corporate and scientific experts and in the ability of commodities and therapeutic professionals to advance a general process of social identification and self-realization.

The postwar affirmation of modern culture by American Protestants was the culmination of a process that began in the late nineteenth century. Like changes in work, family, private life, and politics, the transformation of culture and the social gospel after the Great War represented the consolidation of trends that had appeared much earlier. The years before the war hold the keys to understanding the absorption of the social gospel by modern culture in the 1920s. Social gospelers' embrace of consumer culture in the decade of Babbitt must be understood as the outcome of serious attempts to address the deficiencies of Victorian culture. Yet in breaking loose of those limiting cultural codes, the social gospelers became vulnerable to incorporation by the language, methods, and authority of consumer culture.

When Protestants faced challenges to their world view from science, industrialization, immigration, and social change in the late nineteenth century, they wanted to establish their presence as a potent force in the community. In the last two decades of the century, many congregations built new church buildings in the hope of asserting their existence as a vital counterpoint to the secular world. In Lexington, Missouri, for instance, all eleven churches in the small Missouri River city built new structures between 1880 and 1900. Even the Second Baptist Church, 75 percent of whose members were unemployed because of the depression of the mid-1890s, erected a new edifice in 1894 to offer evidence to the community that their church thrived in the midst of adversity. Perhaps they wanted to convince themselves. Churches in large cities also began constructing new towers of faith. The Broadway Tabernacle in New York City, built in 1905, rose eight stories above the vast entertainment district of the huge metropolis. The Reverend Charles E. Jefferson planned it, and the congregation, according to one member, "felt we had to get it." Another New York minister, the Reverend Christian Reisner, told his congregation, "I want to turn this hole-in-the-ground church into a mighty institution." He wanted to make the Broadway Temple a "real" force to be believed and embraced by American Protestants.[1]

In addition to building massive churches, American Protestants also began to search for a "real" god to allay their doubts.[2] Faith in Jesus, encouraged in large part because of changes in family life and tension between generations, emerged also because of a longing for religious authenticity. God, the unknown and unseen power in the universe, shrank in importance compared to his Son, the man who had lived on earth. In response to a survey on how to make religion a more vital force in women's lives, Mrs. H. R. Chamberlain of Toledo, Ohio, told the questioner that Protestants should make "Christ more real and indispensable." Another respondent, Mrs. F. H. Sheets of Evanston, Illinois, agreed. "Christ," she wrote, "will bring a real 'feeling' to disciples."[3] In 1925, the Reverend Walter Russell Bowie of Grace Church in New York City wrote *The Inescapable Christ*, which spoke of modern Americans' "desire for reality" and of the ability of Protestantism in the twentieth century to "stand the wear and tear of our actual world." In the following pages he urged people to fight for Christianization of business and politics and to promote "brotherhood" and peace.[4] Bowie believed that Jesus and the social gospel could provide assurance and a sense of purpose in an uncertain world.

·   ·   ·

The example of Jesus as a man of the people who worked among the lowly and downtrodden inspired another alternative to cultural upheaval: social reform. American Protestants articulated social service programs, politics for relief of suffering, and in 1908 a Social Creed of the Churches in order to feel connected to the real, daily struggle of life. The Reverend Charles Brown, dean of the Yale Divinity School, explained that middle-class Protestants were participating in reform because "people want to see life, to know life, and to possess life. It is the universal quest." To create the kingdom of God through reform was "personal," "visible," and "present as a moral achievement." A journalist, William Shepherd, reported that the Reverend Christian Reisner's social gospel in New York City was "a religion for you, for today, to help you in helping the world and thus escape having your own life useless."[5] Social gospel reform brought real material and spiritual comfort to impoverished and exploited Americans. It also promised to rescue middle-class American Protestants from the stifling isolation of individual faith and deliver them to the reassuring atmosphere of the city, the tenement, and reform.

Thus, reform inspired by the social gospel plunged middle-class American Protestants into the world of misery and woe buried in the tenements and slums of urban America. What began as a quest to recover connections to the authentic world of work and travail ended quite often in a tangle of powerful feelings that gave evidence of life. As a Ph.D. student at the University of Chicago wrote in 1914 in his dissertation, "Doing for others enriches the emotional life." William Hutchins interviewed dozens of Sunday-school children who took part in their churches' social service programs and found that the social gospel intensified their feelings. "It gives happiness to one's self to do for others," reported one eighteen-year-old boy. "One feels better afterward," insisted another. Two younger children told Hutchins, "We feel happier after doing such work," and "I felt awful happy." Erwin L. Shaver, a social gospel author who wrote extensively for the University of Chicago Press under the direction of Dean Shailer Mathews, asserted that young Protestants were "anxious" to engage in reform that demanded "clear thinking and vigorous action." He believed that the "experience" would be "one of rich discovery and lasting satisfaction."[6]

As often as Protestants found "happiness" and "lasting satisfaction" they found themselves repelled by the filth of poverty. Overcoming the repulsion, however, was a source of satisfaction. Henry Cope, author of *The Friendly Life* (1909) and other social gospel pamphlets, wrote that "our factories, our streets, all our complex life" can be an "energizing place," as long as one "forgets that the beggar is dirty and decrepit, unwholesome and repulsive" and "sees only the opportunity to serve." The "proof" of Christian social reform, Cope insisted, is the "love of the unlovely." Robert Coyle declared that the needs of the "masses of humanity" continued to be as "great and imperative" in the twentieth century as they were when Jesus "ate with publicans and sinners." The social gospel, he told audiences in Oakland, California, in the early 1900s, was "not pleasant" and "not easy," but it promised great reward. One worker wrote to Coyle that "what we want is that Christians should come down and love us." To which Coyle exclaimed, "What an appeal!"[7] Sympathy could yield a feeling of struggle, of usefulness, and of affection. Thus, much social gospel reform benefitted the givers as much as the recipients of charity. It made them feel useful.

                              .   .   .

Newspapers and other media soon became the natural allies of middle-class Protestant reformers. Muckraking exposés of injustice, corruption, and exploitation prompted Protestant crusades for social justice. When the leaders of the Men and Religion Forward Movement prepared their final report in 1912, they devoted an entire volume to "the church and the press." They emphasized that the "newspaper men" knew "the facts—the honeycombing influences at work in democracy eating away the fiber of our national character." They encouraged "the newspapers and the churches" to work together to usher in "a new earth wherein dwelleth righteousness." Since a "keen regard for social conditions" impelled both newspapermen and social gospelers into the slums, they shared a "common obligation" to seek social justice and would "find themselves rubbing shoulder to shoulder in the same street of life," according to the Men and Religion Forward Movement. In the early 1920s, the editor of the *Nashville Tennessean* decided to help churches use the newspaper more effectively "in the service for the master." In *The Newspaper and Religious Publicity* (1925), Richard Beall Niese declared simply, "There is no greater agency known to mankind today for the spreading of the teachings of Christ Jesus than the daily press."[8] Protestants and journalists united to reform American society.

The alliance was not an equal one. Protestants soon began to realize that daily exposés of unsavory conditions in urban America helped strengthen the power of the newspaper to shape American beliefs and values. The leaders of the Men and Religion Forward Movement, for example, noted that "there is no force in the world today more potent and far reaching" than the force of newspapers. "It is a force that goes into men's homes and dictates to them what they shall eat and wear, where they shall travel and how they shall act; that moulds the course of their lives; that influences their politics and their religion."[9] The Reverend Charles Fleischer, who led worship services on the Boston Commons to reach a wide variety of people, was even more direct. To fail to use newspapers was a refusal to realize that "organized religion has practically lost its 'authoritative' place in society."[10] The voice of the faceless reporter, editor, or wire service carried farther in American culture than the voice of the church. Protestants may have uncovered corruption and advocated reform, but newspapers legitimized their findings by printing them. By allying with newspapers, social gospelers did precisely what made sense in a mass society.

Social gospelers' involvement with newspapers also introduced them to the power of advertising. Advertising promised to bring the message of the church to the unchurched and to inform potential clients of the social services available in the churches. As early as 1908 one social gospeler prepared a primer on church advertising. Soon others joined the Association of Advertisers of the World. There they presented papers and sought advice for more effective promotion of their churches. One member, the Reverend Roy B. Guild, who served as a secretary of the Federal Council of Churches and worked in the Men and Religion Forward Movement, insisted that developing a "department of advertising" would reinforce the churches' ability to "serve." Accordingly, when the Men and Religion Forward Movement held a meeting at Carnegie Hall in 1912, a "great electric sign" flashed the message of the evening: "I am my brother's keeper."[11] Others, like the Reverend Daniel E. Weigle of Philadelphia, experimented with advertising techniques at the local level. Weigle's Friendly Church in the City of Brotherly Love sported giant electric lights that spelled out its name and outlined a cross atop the massive house of worship. Membership had tripled, money for programs of service had doubled, and Weigle proudly concluded, "It pays to advertise."[12] The Reverend Daniel Hoffman Martin of New York City recognized in 1916 that while church services once had provided "the wildest excitement of the week," now "the Church bell must compete with the breakfast bell, the telephone bell, the door bell, and the locomotive bell of the Sunday excursion train." In order to survive in a consumer capitalist society, he concluded that ministers "must advertise" to "command a hearing" and "to hold a congregation."[13]

Christian Reisner's ministry offers an example of the development of ties between the social gospel and advertising. In the early 1900s, Reisner ministered to a large Methodist church in Denver, Colorado. Like many ministers of his day, he wanted to offer effective programs of reform and service. In *Workable Plans for Wide-Awake Churches* (1906) Reisner noted that "the attitude of religion toward the world has altered." In the past, ministers "had nothing to say about dirty faces, bare backs, empty stomachs," but now his church offered expanded services, "the practical application of religion to every-day affairs," and "social cures" rather than "formal creeds." In *Social Plans for Young People*, he tried to instill in teenagers some of the ideals of the social gospel. By encouraging a strong youth program, Reisner hoped to make "brotherliness" and "social joy" the primary objects of Protestant religion. In both cases, Reisner insisted that advertising would promote the interests of the social gospel. Accordingly, Reisner advertised—on the streets, on the church, in the newspapers—and thousands flocked to his door.[14]

In the late 1910s, the Coloradoan's success attracted national attention. One of the largest Methodist congregations in New York City called Reisner to be their pastor. Within months of arriving at the Broadway Temple, Reisner realized that his efforts in Denver would not suffice in a city of entertainment, sports, amusement, and vice. He decided to adjust his method to the challenge. "I want to build up at least one more great church," he told a journalist in the early 1920s.[15] In order to attract the attention and command the respect of the multitudes, Reisner built a four-million-dollar "skyscraper" church with a thirty-foot lighted cross atop hundreds of apartments, offices, and sanctuary. He built a church whose "bells and steeples" stood out among the "greatest business structures on the skyline of an American city" and which thus kept "people from forgetting" the social gospel.[16]

To Christian Reisner, being a minister required dedication to the ideal of the social gospel. Religion, he wrote, "isn't a garden of rest; it's a field of service where your spiritual muscles are always in use. It isn't a place of sighing sacrifice; it's a place where you must do things for men, at great cost to yourself, taking your pay in the good coin of your God's quiet 'well done.'"[17] Yet the very terms in which Reisner spoke of his religion in the 1920s suggest that his foray into the field of advertising had affected him and had shaped the social gospel of his ministry. Certainly any reader of his *Church Publicity* (1913) would be hard pressed to locate the historical boundary between commerce and religion. Reisner, and many religious leaders who followed his experiments with advertising techniques, were largely erasing that boundary. At least indirectly they were giving religious support to the legitimation of the rapidly developing consumer culture.

During and immediately following the Great War, social gospelers aggressively promoted church advertising. It was in these years that they spoke of their message in specifically commercial terms. For example, the Reverend Tom Sykes, a general secretary of the Brotherhood movement, told an advertising convention after the war that "anything daring, heroic, unselfish" appeals to American Protestants. If the "church advertises a salvation" of safety, he argued, no one will respond, but if it "announces salvation through risk, and danger, and sacrifice, there will be no lack of volunteers." He urged fellow social gospelers to use skill in the "art of suggestion" to "stimulate interest and awaken wonder" in church members.[18] Sykes's address is revealing because it employed terms such as "heroic," "daring," "sacrifice," and "volunteers" that spoke to the war experience as well as to a commitment to social justice. Using the "art of suggestion," however, placed emphasis on the form rather than the content of the message. In other words, Sykes's formula for success required that the rhetoric of the secular be taken over by the sacred.

Other church advertisers similarly commingled the social gospel and consumerism. In *Handbook for Church Advertising* (1921), for example, Francis Case insisted that churches should employ the personal approach that had become popular in secular sales pitches. "Give your church advertising such a personality," Case suggested, "that people will be as glad to see it as they would be to meet a friend."[19] Others shared his approach. Frederick T. Keeney, a pastor of the Methodist Episcopal Church in Syracuse, New York, believed that the minister who prepared ads "must have 'pep' as well as piety; he must know the times in which he lives and be able to find the shortest and surest way through the eye to the mind and heart."[20] An advertising consultant, W. P. Hotchkin, encouraged churchmen to employ the same kinds of ads used by car companies. "The millions of people who have bought automobiles," he declared, "have not paid big prices because they were tempted to possess a complicated machinery, that would cost a lot of money to maintain in active service. They have been overwhelmed with desire to enjoy the open road, to feel the car speeding under them, to get out into the country, to have a quick, easy way to visit friends. And they have been finally stimulated to the purchase by seeing the pleasures that others realized in owning automobiles. So it is with religion."[21]

. . .

Not only ads but also the church services displayed attention to the media and the standards of secular culture. "We have no right to make the Sunday evening service dry, sombre, formal, cold, and all but repugnant," declared Christian Reisner in 1917. "In this modern day people must be entertained. They will go into despair and suicide if laugh [sic], fellowship and bright thoughts are not furnished them." Or as the editor of the *Christian Herald*, Graham Patterson, put it, ministers' jobs included showing "interestingly that Christianity is something to *like*—not just something to believe!"[22] A few years earlier, John Collier had made a case for using movies to bring people to the social gospel. Since motion pictures hold "sway in this country," he argued, churches should use them. If they wanted to gain strength, Collier insisted, churches should strive to be as "gracious as the saloon, as lively and as rhythmic as the dance hall and as profound as the motion picture hall."[23] Christian Reisner used films "to create an atmosphere for the sermon to follow," and the Reverend Chester C. Marshall of the Metro Temple in New York City agreed that "for a service on reform, or along the lines of social service, there is no more powerful adjunct than an appropriate picture."[24] Reisner, Marshall, Collier, and others realized that reaching Americans with a message of social justice, reform, and service required a medium that would literally attract their attention away from other pursuits. They spoke the language of mass culture because it was available to them and because both mass culture and religion were responding to deeply felt human needs.[25]

Between 1914 and 1918, the movie industry assumed a prominent place in American popular culture.[26] Not surprisingly, the manuals on church advertising began to incorporate the terms of Hollywood. Ernest Eugene Elliott, for example, saw the preacher as a "star performer," "leading man," and "maker or breaker of the local enterprise." A graduate of a school of church advertising established by the Kansas City Church Federation in 1917, Elliott advised his readers that if their minister had "personality," they should "capitalize it." If he does not, Elliott continued, then "manufacture it and then compel him to make good." He also urged the creation of a good "program"; a strong "supporting cast" of musicians, Sunday-school teachers, and social agencies;

and a favorable auditorium. "The stage must be set," he reminded his audience, "or the affair cannot succeed."[27] Most churches began to print "programs" for their Sunday services, and many ministers began to refer to their listeners as an "audience" rather than a congregation. Charles Jefferson, the pastor of the Broadway Tabernacle in New York City, earned the respect of most men in his profession primarily because he enjoyed the "longest run" on the Great White Way.[28]

The First Methodist Episcopal Church in Sioux City, Iowa, under the direction of the Reverend Earl Hoon, succeeded in melding entertainment and social service. Hoon made religion "attractive" by securing the best "sermon, music, athletics, social services, education, and a deep spirituality" that "money can buy." He boasted about his "full line-up" of programs, services, and social events at a church that featured a gymnasium, a swimming pool, a bowling alley, racket courts, and a "moving picture outfit" in addition to its sanctuary and Sunday-school classrooms. Hoon took greatest pride in his church's social services. The First Methodist Episcopal Church provided emergency loans, groceries, medical services, clothes, ambulance service, and free embalming for funerals. It was an employment agency and a rental agency, and it even had nurses, doctors, and detectives on the staff available to those in need. "People love a church like that!" Hoon exclaimed. What made all this social service possible? Sunday evening services "scintillating with light, cheer, every window shining" and attractive programs made "people come by the thousands." The social gospel in Sioux City was brought to its congregation by sponsors of the most entertaining shows "money could buy."[29]

· · ·

If the language of films and mass culture could evoke a sense of immediate gratification for anxious Protestants, an equally powerful cultural tool for social gospel Protestants was baseball. Social gospel ministers used it as a tool to "win" young men and boys to the cause of Jesus, the "captain" of the team. In the 1910s, social gospelers asked the boys of summer to endorse religion. For example, Christian Reisner invited members of the New York Giants to a special service one year when they were about to win the pennant. He distributed ads for the service in the Giants' ballpark, and he attended a week of games to be thoroughly conversant with the game and its lingo. On the night of the service, several "conspicuous players" agreed to give testimonials about their religion. Hundreds of men packed the church, and "a number . . . were secured for membership."[30] The power of mass spectator sports and a revitalized religion merged in a single act of faith and loyalty.

Both films and baseball appealed to Americans' embrace of youth and vigor. Frozen images of youth on the diamond or silent screen became ideals toward which young and old alike began to strive. As Protestants increasingly incorporated motion pictures and sports into their presentation of the social gospel, their theological concentration on this world rather than the next complemented the growing obsession with youth in consumer culture. For instance, social gospelers' portrayal of Jesus as a likable, active reformer fed the cultural longing for eternal youth. Jesus, killed as a young man at the peak of his physical and mental development, stood suspended in time, the ever-powerful, ever-youthful champion of justice.

Advice literature by social gospelers responded to this quest for an image of youth. In the *Threshold of Manhood* (1909), William Dawson exclaimed that "the world belongs to its youth." In a passage that used Jesus to inspire youthful zeal, Dawson told his readers that "the great Captain of souls looks on you, the young, the strong, the eager, whose hearts are all athrob with forceful impulses and passions, and cries 'Will ye also be my disciple?'" After the war, ministers spoke more directly about the inspiring example of youth. W. N. Bayless of Cleveland advised fellow churchmen to advertise "to keep abreast of modern times" and to keep themselves "alive." "To keep alive, keep modern," he wrote. "Men are finding to-day the essential value of keeping young mentally as well as physically and one of the best ways is to keep receptive to new ideas."[31] Advertising the church—like using movies, referring to baseball, and following Jesus—promised youth.

· · ·

While very real cultural fears lay beneath the social gospelers' strategies for reviving American Protestantism, the emerging culture of consumption began to define the meaning of the social gospel and to make it a commodity. In ways that the enthusiastic corps of social gospelers and church advertisers never realized, their campaigns to spread the social gospel subordinated their faith and practice to secular culture and secular standards. Their religion became one of a myriad commodities artfully presented by advertisers with corporate sanction. The social gospel became less a statement of faith than an act of obedience to images, voices, and authority that rested elsewhere. That is not to say that social gospelers believed their message any less in the 1920s than in the 1890s or in 1908, but rather that its appeal depended upon emotions, images, and experience that placed faith in immediate satisfaction of wants. The social gospel had become one of many commodities that people could use to realize their full potential.[32]

Indeed, images that paralleled "spending" came to be associated with character by some social gospel writers. In 1910, Christian Reisner advised ministers who wanted to be "preacher-persuaders" to "spend" themselves in order to succeed. "Surely we can afford to spend and be spent as personal persuaders if by it we may win disciples, and so speed the coming of the Kingdom." A few years later when Norman Richardson examined the religious education of adolescents, he encouraged careful management of health and diet as essential for being an effective social Christian. His interest in exercise, regularity, proper rest, and health care represented an obsession with the importance of the life of the body in a culture of youth, where religion showed little regard for an afterlife, and where the mode of social relations was based on therapeutic interaction. But apart from these, Richardson's instruction to adolescents to believe the "KYBO adage—keep your bowels open" suggests yet another layer of "spending" that psychologically had come to be associated with well-being. In addition to regularity, Richardson advised young people to "keep open the channel of expression." Refusing to restrain bodily functions and self-disclosure promised the ideal "social" person, who best could carry out social gospel programs. Bishop Charles D. Williams of the Protestant Episcopal church told a reporter in the early 1920s that "selfishness, the direct effort to *save* your life, is paganism. Spend your life, your soul, your self—that is the very fundamental of Christian experience."[33] Spending promised salvation in the social gospel.

The Reverend John Muyskens, pastor of the First Presbyterian Church in Red Bank, New Jersey, considered "adept in awakening" his local community to the powerful presence of his church, praised the power of buying. "Before it will be possible for us as leaders in the church to sell our religion to others it is supremely important that we buy it for ourselves and thus make the world realize that we mean business," he declared. "You cannot sell an article to any one else until you have first sold it to yourself. But when the man whom you are seeking to interest in your 'goods' sees that your 'goods' are a part of you, you will be successful in your salesmanship. He cannot help but buy. You are only selling yourself, and everyone knows that personality is the hardest of all things to resist and the richest treasure of life." In addition to the fervor of Muyskens's plea, it is striking how often he used words such as "goods," "selling," and "buying." "Personality" also played a central role in his pitch. Muyskens's comments illuminate the altered social and cultural universe of the 1920s. "Personality" and "advertising" defined individuals in a way that "character" and "creed" had in an earlier era.[34]

Considering the similarities between consumerism and the language used by social gospelers, it comes as small surprise that some modern Protestants like John Lee Mahin would call different denominations "different brands of an article" that could be "merchandized" and "exploited" for optimum use. W. R. Hotchkin, former advertising manager for John Wanamaker and later an advisor to church advertisers, compared churches to "any other distributor of a commodity." After all, he told churchmen, both "churches and commerce" must "appeal to the desires of human nature," and each must try to get "its commodities into general use." L. J. Birney, dean of Boston University's School of Theology, considered it a promoter's dream to have "something" that millions of Americans needed but had not begun to use or had quit using.[35] Every author of a manual on church advertising repeated the same axiom: churches should convince people that Protestantism had something they needed.

As advocates of church advertising deepened their commitment to publicity campaigns for spreading the social gospel, they began to place increasing confidence in experts. Since the turn of the century, American ministers had hoped to present a "specialized" face to a world that valued experts trained in particular fields. This new arena of publicity therefore called for someone especially prepared to carry it out. Not only did ministers consult manuals prepared by leaders in the field of advertising, but they often hired assistants or private companies to handle the work. When Charles Stelzle left the Presbyterian ministry, for example, he opened his own advertising company, which specialized in religious and civic promotion. Ernest Eugene Elliott advised churches not to leave advertising to the preacher. "He is busy," he argued in *How to Advertise a Church* (1920). "Furthermore, the average preacher is not an advertising specialist." Speaking for laymen, the journalist William Shepherd declared, "We insist on experts, men who act on convictions and what they believe to be incontrovertible knowledge."[36] Edward Scribner Ames went one step further. After the Great War in Europe, Ames cast about for new "forms of constructive cooperation" in a world torn by bloodshed and strife. He looked first to scientists whose "search for truth" would make life better. "The vast majority of the fruits of science," he wrote in his autobiography, "are for the advantage of common life, for better and cheaper clothing, for better means of health, for better and safer transportation, for more comfortable beds and cooking stoves."[37] Ames, a theologian of the social gospel, believed that science, once the enemy of religion, could restore well-being and faith.

What were the implications of the chain of developments that enmeshed the social gospel in the tangle of advertising? Those most deeply involved in employing marketing techniques pondered the question. When Francis Case began to write the *Handbook of Church Advertising*, he received a letter from Lupton A. Wilkinson, an advertising manager of the Baptist Forward Movement, who wrote: "The church has come to the point where *it must ask itself* . . . why other institutions and other influences have more hold on the daily life of millions, even of millions who rate themselves Christians, than the church itself." Case's response showed how dependent Protestants had become on mass culture by the 1920s. A "valuable by-product of advertising for the church," Case contended, "is the authority or recognition which it is accorded by the public at large. Many a church has earned and paid for prestige while others, less courageous and vigorous, have looked on in envy." He believed that religion depended on popularity for its perpetuation and had become a minor star in a constellation of cultural examples. As Case put it, "Just as people are interested in knowing what any man in the public eye, be he movie hero or Presidential candidate, thinks on certain subjects, so are they ready to listen when the opinion of an eminently successful church is expressed or when its detailed projects are heralded."[38] Churches and the social gospel no longer commanded respect by virtue of their existence as moral counterpoints to secular materialism. Rather, they were bound by the same rules that governed consumer capitalism.

In his later collection of essays, *Advertising the Church* (1925), Francis Case included an article by James R. Joy, editor of the *Christian Advocate*, an influential Methodist journal and an organ for the social gospel. Joy proclaimed: "The modern advertising agent needs no defense. He is perplexed humanity's universal guide, counselor, and friend." Joy, a man who actively promoted the reunification of the northern and southern Methodist churches, declared his faith in something besides religion to give him strength as he went on:

> To the advertising agent we owe our choice of the clothes we wear, the razor that scrapes and the soap that saves our faces, the toothbrush and the paste that lies flat upon it, and it is not his fault if the hairs of our heads are "going! going!! gone!!!" He has helped

us to a dainty breakfast of oranges, cereal, self-raising cakes and coffee—or its substitute for "there's a reason!" Fortunately (or otherwise) it does not pay the bootlegger to advertise, yet your reminders will not let us perish of thirst. You help us to pick out our automobile (and its tires), our route by rail or water, and the inn where we take our ease. For our leisure hours you have put the right golf club in our hands and the proper ball at our feet—alas you cannot help our swing! You do your best to put tobacco to our lips, and if not comfort us with alcohol, you bring us phonographs, player-pianos and radio outfits, and all the while you ply our jaws with the chewing gum whose "flavor lasts."

"Who could get anywhere in the maze of everyday life without your direction?" he concluded. "At every choice I have come to—except mother, wife, and heaven—you have halted me with your captivating propositions, faced me with the opinion of 'the man who owns one,' and led me to an informed decision, where otherwise I should have groped in darkness or taken the first article that was offered."[39]

Despite the unmistakably ironic tone of Joy's remarks and despite his disclaimer that the adman did not choose his religion, this "grateful" affirmation of advertising was delivered to "enforce" the "value" of church advertising. It is a stunning affirmation of consumer culture's reach and influence and an equally astonishing statement of faith in the guiding hand of advertising. The advertiser, his products, and presumably the benevolent corporation that produced them eased fears of being improperly clad and nourished or inadequately stimulated, and gave direction to and validation of choices made in the marketplace. At each critical juncture of one's life, consumer products solved problems, endorsements replaced reasoned analysis, and recitation of popular slogans united speaker and audience in common awareness of popular culture. Social gospelers placed their faith in culture and consuming. They presented religion as a partner in the culture of abundance.

. . .

Yet for all the hoopla over church advertising in the 1920s, for all the enthusiasm for "muscular Christianity" and efficient, scientific reform, the transformation of American culture did not come without personal anguish and private disappointment. Victorian youths could not eradicate from their lives the values, traditions, and beliefs handed down by parents and other respected elders. Because Protestantism lay so close to the heart of Victorian culture, cultural doubts often raised ultimate fears not easily confronted, even less easily allayed. The choices young Protestants had to make in the late nineteenth and early twentieth centuries involved more than the selection of one "brand" over another. Rather, they involved the formation of identity and the search for meaning for their lives. Cultural quest and religious quest merged into a single search for certainty and purpose.

The accommodations social gospelers made with modern culture arose out of deeply felt cultural anxiety. Social gospelers like Charles Sheldon, Charles Stelzle, and Charles Jefferson, who endorsed various aspects of the secular culture around them, wanted to make life better for people in their communities. They nevertheless advanced dimensions of secular life. Charles Sheldon's novel *In His Steps* was a bestseller in 1897. Charles Jefferson's success on Broadway was in part a result of his respect for drama and entertainment. Charles Stelzle became the head of an advertising company. All three tried to live up to the expectations of their Victorian families and searched frantically for connections to a real world. They did not discard the cultural baggage of their youth, but they transformed it in ways that made it almost unrecognizable by the end of their careers. Their own obsessions with youth, fame, and promotion sprang both from the Victorian past of individual achievement and from their modern present of mass consumption. These obsessions testify to the powerful attraction of consumer culture. None of them saw fully how his efforts at promoting the social gospel reinforced secular culture.

CHARLES MONROE SHELDON
"Youth, it's your innings!"

Charles Monroe Sheldon was obsessed with youth. At the age of sixty-eight, Sheldon closed his autobiography with a tribute to "two old friends": old age and death. In his effort to make the two more acceptable to a generation of Americans living for the moment in the tumult of the jazz age, Sheldon found himself returning again and again to the attractions of youth. "Listen to me," his friend, old age, advised, "You have had your day. Why hang around where you are not needed or at least wanted? . . . You have had your turn. Let up. . . . Relax. Enjoy leisure. . . . It is Youth's turn." As a Protestant, Sheldon should not have been troubled by old age and death. Were not salvation and eternal life

Charles Monroe Sheldon (right) and his father,
Stewart Sheldon

after death the objects of faith? Yet Sheldon could not face with equanimity the prospect of aging and dying. "I do not like the idea of Youth
shoving me off the bench where I have been sitting so long," Sheldon
confessed. He grudgingly agreed to "catch" his "breath" before he retired to a land "where youth is eternal." Yet even this reference to heaven
incorporated a vision of young, sturdy vigor into the meaning of eternal
bliss. Sheldon betrayed a deep anxiety about the process of growing old
even as he proclaimed to the generation that succeeded his own, "Youth,
it's your innings! Go to it, and beat the old 'un, if you can!"[40] As he
passed into obscurity, the venerable social gospeler clung to the promise
of youth.

As a young man, Charles Sheldon had been a favorite of Protestants
in the United States and around the world. His novel *In His Steps*, which
was published in 1897, reached millions of readers in twenty different

languages and established him firmly in the social gospel movement. As the author of a novel that advised modern Americans to ask "What would Jesus do" as they made day-to-day decisions, Sheldon took his own counsel and operated a Christian daily in 1900, addressed workingmen's issues in Topeka, Kansas, participated in a national campaign of prohibition, and continued to write didactic novels about the social gospel and Christian reform as he believed Jesus would have done. In his heyday Charles Sheldon did as much as any other minister in the social gospel movement to popularize ideas first articulated in more scholarly works by Washington Gladden, Josiah Strong, and Walter Rauschenbusch. He helped make the social gospel accessible to Protestant America.

As an important cultural spokesman, however, Charles Sheldon conveyed a message that was grounded in part in the Victorian culture of his childhood and in part in an emerging culture of youth and consumption. Interested in making religion vital and real in the new century by embracing the social gospel, Charles Sheldon did not realize fully the extent to which his message and his methods contributed to the formation of a culture based on consumption and youth. His anguish in the mid-1920s suggests that he tried to cling to Victorian culture even though modern culture held him ever more firmly in its grip.

As Charles Sheldon approached adolescence on a farm in South Dakota, cultural uncertainty played no part in his development. Born in 1857 in Wellsville, New York, Charles Sheldon was the younger of two sons of Sarah Ward and Stewart Sheldon. Sheldon's father, a Congregational minister and missionary pioneer, moved his family from New York through various congregations in the Midwest and eventually, in 1867, settled on a farm near Yankton, South Dakota. As one of his biographers reported, "Sheldon fondly recalled his adolescent years on the farm, with its hard work, self-reliance, close family life, and clear-cut moral verities."[41] The elder Sheldon steeped his family in Victorian values of hard work, self-control, and individual achievement. Stewart Sheldon led the family in daily devotions; then he and his sons worked diligently on the farm. His youngest son later remarked, "We never questioned his authority." Though religion was a part of the texture of everyday life for the Sheldons, the individual conversion experience played a particularly important role. Attending church and behaving decorously did not satisfy Sarah and Stewart Sheldon's demand for personal piety. Both parents had "serious talks" with their children about repentance and salvation, and in the winter of 1877 they took their youngest son to "protracted meetings" conducted by Sarah's brother, Joseph Ward, until he professed religion. His parents were "supremely happy" when their son joined the ranks of saved believers.[42]

Through much of the rest of his youth, while he prepared for the ministry, and in the early years of his parish work, Charles Sheldon displayed complete confidence in the power of hard work and individual striving to achieve success. Hampered by the sporadic and limited quality of his education on the prairie, Sheldon redoubled his intellectual efforts once he entered Phillips Academy in Andover, Massachusetts, in 1877. In order to pay for his room, board, and tuition, Sheldon took several part-time jobs. Between jobs he worked on his lessons, making up intellectual ground he had not covered in Yankton Academy. He went from Andover to Brown University for a bachelor's degree and then returned to the Theological Seminary in Andover, working his way through each institution. When he finished his course at the seminary, Sheldon proudly reported that he had "no debts nor anything else in the way of future service in any church."[43] He had succeeded by his own effort.

When he began his first job at Waterbury, Vermont, Sheldon brought with him the Victorian cultural baggage of his childhood and college years. He viewed the New England community and his parish as arenas of individual endeavor. During the first few months of his tenure at Waterbury, he "entered into" a "church rivalry" with the Methodists of the town. He spent an enormous amount of creative energy "trying to get all the town to come and hear me preach," he remembered, "and making all the friends I could for the purpose of making the 'Congo' church popular." Sheldon lured the Methodists' talented organist away from that congregation with the promise of a higher salary, which he paid from his own funds. He also entered the "field" of "wholesome amusements" by establishing a reading club that attracted both Congregational and Methodist young people. In an effort to win friends who lived on Main Street, Sheldon devised a sprinkling system that would control the dust that normally clouded up on blustery New England days. He burst with pride in his own accomplishment when the sprinkling wagon made its "triumphal progress" down Main Street, settling the dust and insuring the increasing popularity and prosperity of his church and himself.[44] Sheldon stood as an inspiring exemplar of Victorian achievement.

In the same years, the young minister hinted at a vague dissatisfaction with accepted order and authority and with rigid self-control. For example, while he never questioned the authority of his father, he did not always turn to him for direction and inspiration. His uncle, Joseph Ward, appears to have been his primary guide and confidant and was, by Sheldon's own admission, his "man hero." His uncle taught the school that Sheldon attended in Yankton, and Joseph Ward had presided at Sheldon's conversion. Following his uncle's example, young Sheldon went to Phillips Academy and then to Brown University. Sheldon had even accompanied his uncle to Dakota before his parents and brother decided to move there. At the very least, Joseph Ward compromised and weakened Stewart Sheldon's paternal authority over his son.[45]

In addition to questioning his father's authority, Sheldon also registered some annoyance with the sameness of life on the Dakota prairie. Unrelieved toil and limited entertainment may have been conducive to discipline and steadiness, but they were also boring. Sheldon remembered only a couple of adventures that broke the routine of farm work. Thus, when he went east for his education, Sheldon experienced for the first time cultural diversity and a plethora of entertaining diversions that whetted his appetite for more. Upon graduating from the seminary, Sheldon used the balance of his savings to spend two months in England. He had come to crave something more than work, study, and individual piety.

Perhaps the greatest challenge to Sheldon's Victorian upbringing came in the late 1880s and early 1890s shortly after he accepted a call to the Central Congregational Church in Topeka, Kansas. Thousands of men lost their jobs as a result of the economic downturn of 1890, and Sheldon worried because he had been sheltered from the workers' struggle for dignity and a livelihood. He complained of the "isolation of the preacher" from the "great world of labor" and from the harsh tests of manhood. "What did I know of it except the little experience I had had on a farm as a boy?" he asked as he began his new ministry. He felt "remote" from the "working masses" and wondered how to "ease" his own "mental unrest." He undertook an experiment to recapture a sense of "reality" by donning some worn-out clothes and hitting the streets of Topeka to look for work. For a week he tramped from one business to the next hoping to get a job. As the days wore on, Sheldon admitted that his experiment had become "somehow real." When he saw men at work he began to feel the weight of personal failure, and he concluded that "the getting and holding of a job had come to seem . . . the very apex of success in life." A foreman at the railyard finally allowed Sheldon to shovel snow off the railroad tracks, and the middle-class minister rejoiced at being "a part of the world's labor." He returned home "well satisfied" with his quest for "reality."[46]

Sheldon's experiment was a powerful indictment of the life he had led to that point and the values that had informed his existence. He became disillusioned with the concept of individual responsibility in a world over which individuals could exert little control. He doubted the power of self-control to restore a sense of vital involvement in the world of work. Self-denial became for Sheldon the tragic symbol of individual failure rather than a virtue of patience. After his unsuccessful search for re-munerative labor, Sheldon became an outspoken advocate of social gos-pel reform. He wanted to revitalize Protestant culture. Two beneficiaries stood to gain from his social gospel: the poor men and women who sank into squalor through no fault of their own and the middle-class Ameri-cans who suffered from a troubled recognition of their own softness in corporate America.

From the 1890s until the end of his active career, Charles Sheldon wrote stories and novels to ease his "mental unrest" about the state of cultural confusion. The stories, prepared for his Sunday evening meet-ings with young people, almost always returned to the same theme: middle-class Protestant life had become unreal, and work among the victims of industrial development promised to restore a sense of "con-nectedness." As Paul Boyer put it in his reappraisal of *In His Steps*, the "fear" that "looms just below the surface of the novel" was that the middle class was "losing its sense of cohesion and common purpose" and was "seriously threatened with disintegration."[47] *In His Steps* (1897), *The Crucifixion of Philip Strong* (1894), *Robert Hardy's Seven Days* (1893), and *The Reformer* (1902) were among the best known of Sheldon's works. Set in medium-sized cities and inhabited primarily by earnest young Protestants of the middle class, Sheldon's novels explore the characters' lack of awareness of "real" social conditions, their guilt when they discover poverty, and their attempts to recover feelings of vitality and meaning. In other words, each novel is a restatement of Sheldon's own experience in Topeka. While the novels demanded individual commit-ment to reform, they generally exposed the limitations of Victorian indi-vidualism. And while they praised the disciplined will of the earnest protagonists, the novels also revealed the attractions of uncontrolled emotion.

The Crucifixion of Philip Strong, for example, pitted a "tall, pale-faced, resolute and loving preacher" against the unrepentant members of

the Milton Calvary Church, whose fortunes had been made from factories, unhealthful tenements, and unregulated saloons.[48] In ideal
nineteenth-century fashion, the Reverend Strong speaks in rigid moral
terms. He praises good and denounces evil as he makes a personal
commitment to righteousness. But before long he discovers the shameful
social and economic conditions of Milton and begins a series of sermons
on the social responsibilities of American Protestants. These lectures
exact a great emotional cost. For though he shrinks from the unhealthful
environment of the city, Strong also grows physically ill when he attacks
it. He is attracted to and repulsed by the denizens of Milton's slums. A
personal encounter with an unnamed "Brother Man," for instance, stirs
deep feelings of guilt about his own comfortable life as the minister of
Calvary Church. Within weeks of his meeting with this representative of
the underworld of "real" struggle and deprivation, Strong and his wife
give up their comfortable parsonage in exchange for a small house in the
tenement district. Daily visits to the sick and dying, the unemployed,
and the outcast infuse Strong's ministry with purpose and ease his guilt.
The conflict between his Victorian background and his situation in industrial America undermines Strong's faith in individual achievement
and endeavor.

Strong's iron self-control meets the same fate as his individualism.
At the outset, the pale young man "controlled his voice and his manner"
as he "drove the truth home" about economic conditions in the industrial
town.[49] He offered his critique in measured tones and with a calm that
belied the passionate outrage he felt inside. By the end of a year in
Milton, Strong had changed. When he rose to address his congregation
for what proved to be the last time, his "intense love of the people . . .
surged into him uncontrollably. It swept away all other things. He no
longer sought to justify his ways; he seemed bent on revealing to men the
mighty love of Christ for them and the world. His lip trembled, his voice
shook with the yearning of his soul for the people, and his frame quivered
with longing."[50] In an excessive emotional display, Strong won the loyalty and commitment of his congregation when quiet reason had failed.
Feeling had become as "real" as acting in the world. And for many in
Strong's middle-class congregation, feeling would be as close as they
came to the urban underworld.

The cultural message of *The Crucifixion of Philip Strong* was ambiguous. Cherishing Victorian domesticity, individualism, and self-control,
the protagonist nonetheless affirmed social responsibility, the indulgence of one's feelings, and the need for church or state interference

in the homes of the wretched. This novel and others by Sheldon paved the way for a culture of intense feeling and immediate gratification that had begun to emerge in the closing years of the nineteenth century, even while Sheldon hoped to reinvigorate the culture of his youth. Sheldon's simple stories legitimized the yearning for authenticity that lay at the bottom of Americans' drive to consume well-being and that buttressed efforts to perpetuate youth. Sheldon's reforming zeal, which found expression in his ministry as well as in his novels, propelled him into an embrace of this life, an emphasis on ushering in the Kingdom of God on earth, and a kind of presentism that pervaded the entire social gospel movement. Without fully realizing what was happening, Sheldon found himself swept along by the force of his writing and by people's responses to it into an acceptance of modern culture.

During the 1890s, when Sheldon penned many of his stories, his private life diverged from the Victorian code. While still in Waterbury, Vermont, Sheldon met a woman who flaunted her disregard for the ideal of the "true woman" and who moved him as no other woman ever had in the past. Mary Abby Merriam met the serious young minister while she was visiting her grandmother in 1887. Viewing her granddaughter as an "impetuous young girl" whose curly brown hair was "not always in perfect order," Mary Merriam's grandmother warned her not to trifle with the minister's affections. But when Mary Merriam first met her future husband that summer, she noticed immediately that Charles Sheldon had "the figure of an athlete" and that he was strikingly handsome. She admired his "dark hair, blue eyes, good chin, firm and strong," and she was amused by his "rather awkward" behavior around women. Charles Sheldon attracted the stylish young woman not with his earnest preaching nor with his effort to build the church, but with his youth, strength, and vigor. When he met Mary Merriam, Sheldon broke a year-long rule not to go riding with any young women. Four years later the two were married. Mary Merriam Sheldon became what she considered an ideal minister's wife: "plump and smiling" with "excellent taste in dress," and Sheldon did what he could to retain his athletic figure and youthful good looks in order to please his wife.[51] As the first family of the Central Congregational Church in Topeka, Kansas, the Sheldons charmed the community for thirty years with their youthful enthusiasm and pleasing appearances. His lovely wife further complicated Sheldon's once-clear commitment to Victorian culture. She introduced him to a culture of youth and consumption that valued vitality and physical attractiveness more than character.

Sheldon participated in the emerging modern culture in other equally inadvertent ways. His decision to run a Christian newspaper in Topeka in 1900, for example, acquainted him with team effort, interdependence, and the world of advertising and mass media. When he took over the *Daily Capital* to run it for one week as Jesus would have run it, Sheldon found that simply by refusing to print stories about prize fights, crime, vice, and scandals, he could not keep "modern" influences out of the enterprise. Front men organized a subscription drive that guaranteed economic success for the week of newspapers. After a couple of nearly sleepless nights, Sheldon learned that he alone could not make all of the editorial decisions, and he eventually trusted those under him to use their best judgment. Newspaper reporters invaded Topeka to "scoop" the story of a Christian daily. And advertisers flooded the *Capital*'s business office with requests for space in the most widely read paper that week. Sheldon suspended the advertising agreements with local businessmen and filled their columns with advertising copy from nationally known companies. Thus, even though Sheldon hoped to set an example of Christian responsibility in the newspaper business, he allowed a vast array of impersonal corporations to peddle their products in his Christian daily. He also discovered the power of the newspaper itself. When reporters for other publications printed twisted and false accounts of his experience, Sheldon learned that people believed them. "'It was in the paper,' they say. 'Must be so.'" he wrote.[52] By 1900 the newspaper as an influential medium already had assumed authority over the American reading public.

Sheldon's participation in the national prohibition campaign of 1914 and 1915 ironically showed how far down the road to modern culture his embrace of the social gospel had brought him. He joined the "Flying Squadron," an organization of singers, speakers, and ministers that crisscrossed the nation to build support for prohibition. Unlike the dour prohibitionists of the nineteenth century, the Flying Squadron provided "exciting and interesting speaking programs." The Squadron required a carefully planned itinerary, a team of press agents to handle advance advertising, and the cooperation of the railroad to make all connections. It was an extravaganza of modern efficiency and mass marketing. Sheldon helped organize this "succession of prohibition meetings, non-sectarian, non-political but at the same time so interesting and unusual that a whole town or city would be attracted to them, in spite of the hackneyed word 'prohibition.'"[53] The key words here are "unusual" and "attracted."

By 1915 Sheldon had become aware of the need for novelty in addressing American consumers, and the prohibition campaign succeeded because it was out of the ordinary. And Sheldon had begun to realize that attracting audiences had become an essential part of any religious program. Religion and religious reform were commodities that had to make an appeal for support and participation. Sheldon's charming anecdote about one of the Flying Squadron's singers, who accidentally fell in a baptismal tank and was kidded for being a "wet," also revealed the subtly changing cultural milieu of the United States in the mid-1910s. The embarrassed performer hurried back to his hotel room to change clothes, then returned amid congratulations for being a "good sport" and performed to the "delight of the audience." His good-natured extra effort paid off when he and the other musicians "received more enthusiastic applause than the two speakers together."[54] Being a "good sport," not a studied speaker, won support for the movement.

By the mid-1910s, Sheldon had become a beloved representative of the social gospel. He had used his pulpit to promote greater social responsibility. He had tried to set an example of responsible journalism with his Christian daily in 1900, and he offered an alternative to punitive police work when, as temporary police commissioner of Topeka, he chose officers who would act as "missionaries" on the streets. A popular speaker, Sheldon traveled around the country as a "minister-at-large" during the late 1910s, spreading his version of the social gospel to prohibitionists, graduating classes, civic groups, and religious gatherings. Part of his great appeal lay in the simplicity of his message and its ties to the familiar modes of consumer culture. Sheldon encouraged therapeutic social relations, abundance, and youth, and he implied that these formed the base of his religion in the twentieth century.

Sheldon's most eloquent merging of the social gospel and consumer culture appeared in *The Mere Man and His Problems*, published in 1924. Assuming the role of one of "the great unadvertised number of American men," Sheldon provided religious advice to men and women beset by the daily challenges of life in the 1920s. In the book, he affirmed an ethic of leisure, the power of consumption, and the centrality of being nice, all of which undergirded both consumer culture and Protestantism. One chapter explored moral choices on the links; another showcased the family's deliberations over buying a car. The book culminated in the Mere Man's religious creed, which was barely distinguishable from the message in most secular advice literature. The creed undeniably reflected aspects of the social gospel; its theology was Christocentric, and its object was social justice. But the language Sheldon chose to convey the social gospel betrayed its origins in the undemanding realm of secular culture. "Human kindness" and "love of little children" passed as synonyms for social justice. The mere man worshiped Jesus because he was "a very *real* person" and a "world hero," and God, because he would "never do any human being an injustice."[55] Sheldon's religion in the 1920s placed men and women squarely in the middle of the universe and insisted that human needs were paramount and would be met by others, by material things, and even by the Godhead. By investing this self-centered behavior with religious import, Sheldon helped to legitimize what Americans were encouraged by secular culture to do: to seek personal satisfaction.

Later books carried further what Sheldon first stated in *The Mere Man and His Problems*. In 1929, for instance, he wrote that "life on all sides, life abundantly is the minister's business."[56] If the title alone did not convey the message, *Let's Talk It Over* served throughout as a reminder of the importance of human interaction. In it he argued that ministers had to make religion "a part of human growth."[57] A year later, *What Did Jesus Really Teach?* announced that "religion is a practical and everyday thing, belonging to the life that now is, and salvation is a real and everyday thing." The God who reigned over this universe, Sheldon promised, "will do all in his power to see that his children have happiness and abundant life."[58] One cannot help but wonder how conscious he was of his own part in the demystification of religion when he declared on the opening page of *What Did Jesus Really Teach?*: "Much of our so-called religious life in this world is lacking in depth and sincerity."[59]

Sheldon's obsession with youth must be understood in the context of his growing attachment to personal satisfaction and the abundant life. "The physical let-down that goes with approaching old age is one of the factors that makes it dreadful," Sheldon confessed. He determined to keep his "bodily machine in good working order as long as possible." He planned on "staving off Old Age" by keeping busy and active. As he began to age, Sheldon took greater pains with his appearance to give the illusion of youth. He took up walking and playing horse shoes for exercise, watched his diet, and always tried to give "the impression" that he had an "important engagement" even when he had none.[60] Charles Sheldon considered "physical pleasure and power" as well as comforting associations to be the apex of religious life—a summit shared with consumer culture. Using the popular imagery of baseball, Sheldon suggested that youth was entitled to action on the field and that older folks should occupy their "seat on the bleachers." To the "onlooker," the spectator, the consumer, came peace.[61] As Charles Sheldon closed the book on a forty-year career, he uncertainly made peace with modern consumer culture.

CHARLES STELZLE

A Son of the Bowery on Madison Avenue

Shortly before he died, Washington Gladden received a letter with a peculiar request from his friend Charles Stelzle. His fellow social gospeler, serving as a committee chairman for the Presbyterian Home Missionary Society, asked Gladden to write an article on some social problem "as the Church has to do with it." Gladden knew that the Presbyterian church had given Stelzle a "special mission to the working men" in 1903. Since that time, the machinist-turned-minister had reached hundreds of thousands of Americans with his social gospel message and his invitation to participate in a revitalized religion of social salvation. Coming from the working man's preacher, however, Stelzle's letter must have seemed incongruous. He asked Gladden to write so that the "propaganda idea" would not be "too much in evidence," and he explained that the object was "to make the newspaper reader feel that he must be interested" in the matter whether he was or not and whether he was in the church or out.[62] Charles Stelzle wanted the old man of the social gospel to sell his creed to unsuspecting consumers.

Charles Stelzle's life and career provide important clues for understanding the transfer of cultural authority from religion to commerce in the early twentieth century. Stelzle was, as historians have written, the "apostle to labor," but he was also a pioneer in church advertising. The latter role was not a dramatic departure from the former. Rather, it grew out of the necessity for social gospelers to reach the unchurched masses. As they made innovations in the appeal of Protestantism, however, social gospelers like Charles Stelzle inadvertently bolstered the corporate ethos. If they did not themselves become major figures in corporate enterprise, they helped affirm the legitimacy and power of mass marketing. They began to commodify their religion. Stelzle, the "union preacher" who wanted "to give the sons of other poor men a better chance than he himself enjoyed," spent a career making religious faith a part of upward mobility.[63] The "Son of the Bowery" who made it on Madison

Avenue ultimately conferred on a secular consumer culture the power to provide social justice and personal well-being.

Though he called himself a "son of the Bowery," Stelzle did not immediately reflect the working-class values of his neighbors. Born in 1869, Stelzle was the oldest child and only son of John Stelzle, a poor brewer from Germany. His mother, Dora Uhlendorf Stelzle, the daughter of a prosperous baker in Germany, earned extra money for her young family by sewing cloaks for a Lower East Side sweater. John Stelzle's lack of business acumen kept the family from rising out of poverty, and his death in the late 1870s submerged them more fully in the working class. Yet Dora did not permit her children to fall into a pattern of hard work, hard play, and hard drinking typical of many neighbors. She instilled in them the values of hard work, self-control, and individual responsibility—values she had learned from her middle-class Protestant family in Germany. While Dora Stelzle wanted her children to get an education, to rise above manual labor, and to become self-reliant, however, she had to face the fact that without her son's wages the family could not long survive. When her father offered to educate the boy in one of Germany's fine universities, she insisted that Charles remain in New York City. Stelzle later reported that he regretted at the time not being allowed to go.[64] In 1880, Stelzle quit school and went to work full time.

It took Stelzle a while to become conscious of the plight of working men. He began working part-time at a tobacco factory as an eight-year-old. At the end of each week, he gave his meager wages to his mother for groceries or safekeeping. Later, he took a position in a sweatshop where artificial flowers were made. As the only "man" in a shop of about seventy-five workers, he spent much of his time killing the rats that swarmed all over the shop floor, manfully protecting his co-workers. He could preserve in his mind the ideal of a "true gentleman" at the same time that he brought wages home to his mother. Not until he apprenticed as a machinist did Stelzle begin to shed the Victorian individualism of his youth and to realize the need for unity, cooperation, and collective responsibility. An eager, disciplined worker, Stelzle surpassed the demands placed on him by the managers of R. Hoe & Company, a printing press manufacturer. Hoping to distinguish himself in the eyes of his employer and in Horatio Alger fashion rise out of his poverty, he took on a dangerous special order and risked his life to break the record for producing an enormous printing cylinder. Instead of the company's praise and appreciation, however, Stelzle earned the scorn of his fellow work-

Charles Stelzle

men when the manager lowered the standard piece rate for all workers. His individual effort resulted in lower wages and the disdain of the men on the floor. Disappointed and embarrassed, Stelzle finally recognized the limited value of individual drive in industrial America. He supported efforts to form a union that would restrain workers like himself, and he served as assistant secretary of the mutual benefit society the workers created for insurance.

At the same time that he worked industriously in factory and shop, young Stelzle sought to escape the strictures of a Victorian code whenever he could. Because of the burden of working for a living from the time he was eight, Stelzle tried to relieve the sameness of his youth with quests for adventure and excitement. The Marble Cemetery, for example, held "a peculiar fascination" for the lad. He worshiped the famous New Yorkers buried there. He especially idealized Adam and Noah Brown, who built ships for Commodore Perry's fleet that sailed into strange and distant lands. He also paid homage to John Ericsson, who built the *Monitor*. St. Mark's Church cemetery also inspired awe because A. T. Stewart, one of the city's merchant princes, had been buried there and later removed by graveyard thieves. "What a source of mysterious possibilities this story was to us boys!" he later exclaimed. "Nothing that St. Mark's ever did was big enough to overshadow the story of the ghouls who robbed the graveyard."[65] It was not the program of the churches that inspired him. Rather, it was the commercial men who lay buried in the churches' cemeteries and the powerful, abundant world they represented that captured Stelzle's imagination.

Believing death to be the ultimate experience, Stelzle frequently placed his own life in danger to get "as much real excitement out of life" as possible. He swam from an East Side dock "in violation of the law, and in peril of my life," dodging ferries and the "dangerous eddies" they created. He and his friends once constructed a lifelike dummy to throw in front of a horse car to simulate the horror of death and to watch "the driver frantically pull rein."[66] One Fourth of July, Stelzle gathered powder from spent and broken firecrackers to make one "glorious blaze." He climbed to the roof of his tenement, set fire to the powder, and then reeled backward as he caught "the full force" of the explosion in his face. Left an invalid for two months without funds for dime novels and without access to a lending library, the bandaged boy turned to the Bible for entertainment.[67]

Stelzle did not explain in his autobiography how or why he became interested in religion. He remarked early in his life story that the cross on the steeple of a nearby chapel appealed to his adolescent "religious imagination." The fascination, however, lay not in the reminder of a mystical power in the universe, but rather, that the cross "could be seen for blocks against the deep night sky." He accompanied his mother to an East Side mission but never underwent a conversion experience. For a time, he belonged to a boys' club run by St. Mark's Church. The first evidence of a consistent commitment to a church came when he was twenty-one. At the end of his apprenticeship in the machine shop, Stelzle became an elder in the Presbyterian church. Within four years he enrolled in the Moody Bible Institute to prepare for the ministry. From 1893 on, Stelzle moved from one downtown mission to another, making an appeal to newsboys, bootblacks, and working people. In 1903 after only three years as an ordained minister, Charles Stelzle received a "special mission to workingmen" from the Board of Home Missions of the Presbyterian church.[68] Stelzle's name became synonymous with the social gospel among laborers.

Perhaps the practical assistance the Stelzles received at the hands of the Hope Mission they attended influenced Stelzle's later conception of the social gospel. As a minister prominent in the social gospel movement, he helped form boys' clubs like the one to which he had belonged as a child, to keep youngsters involved in constructive social activities. He supported labor unions and urged the Presbyterian church to lend its support to workingmen's issues. The missions and churches with which Stelzle became affiliated were institutional churches. Their social clubs, gymnasiums, reading rooms, and other services ministered to the practical as well as the spiritual needs of his congregations. Stelzle made every effort to improve the conditions of his neighborhood to pave the way for social salvation. In 1908, Charles Stelzle had been unable to contain himself when Frank Mason North delivered his report "The Church and Modern Industry," which became the basis of the Social Creed of the Churches. He called it the "greatest paper on this subject" he ever had heard.[69] In 1915, he issued *The Call of the New Day to the Old Church*, in which he insisted that the "men of today" should "express their religious aspirations in their own way," not in the manner of "another generation."[70] Stelzle clearly belonged to the generation of the social gospel. His way was that of the social gospel.

His way was also that of a burgeoning consumer culture. As an "apostle to labor," Stelzle drew heavily on the issues and interests that had punctuated the monotony of his youth in order to succeed in his ministry. He went on speaking tours and wrote popular tracts to "translate the church" to laborers and to "translate the labor movement" to the church. Special programs, shop and union meetings, and private talks with workingmen broke the numbing routine of work for the laborers and gave them a living example of someone who had escaped a life of drudgery. Stelzle appealed to workers' hope for something more satisfying than years of endless toil for an impersonal company. The church, he told them in *Messages to Workingmen* (1906), had "a vital interest in the 'here and now' as well as in the 'hereafter.'" He told workingmen that one important part of the "here and now" was entertainment. Churches remained "open every night and nearly all day," Stelzle reminded them, providing "concert courses and lecture series, free dispensary and savings bank, serving school and cooking classes, boys' clubs and reading rooms, men's clubs and library, music classes and women's clubs, and everything else that is helpful and inspiring—so far as their means will permit and the community demands."[71] As Stelzle saw it, the church, like businesses, provided services that their "consumers" demanded; they gave workers the diversity they needed.

When he opened the Labor Temple in 1910, Stelzle carried the commingled values of the social gospel and consumer culture into the religious venture. The Labor Temple of New York City became the show-case of Stelzle's brand of the social gospel. Having been true to his scattered working-class missions for seven years, Stelzle petitioned the Presbyterians for a viable downtown congregation. He earned an appointment to a church in New York City that the presbytery otherwise would have disbanded. Stelzle agreed to run the church as an experiment for two years. Within a block of New York City's downtown amusements, the Labor Temple elicited little faith or hope from most long-time churchmen. Stelzle nonetheless rose to the challenge by using the language, methods, and message of mass culture to attract workers to the church. He competed with movie marquees by erecting an electric sign made of letters two feet square. "In addition," he reported in his autobiography, "four large bulletin boards, two on each street, were studded with electric lights and announced in big letters what was going on in the Temple."[72] Stelzle decided to draw working-class audiences simply by outshining his competition.

From the beginning, Stelzle defined his mission in terms of commercial amusement. He took pride in the "number of features" the Labor Temple offered. On Sundays, for example, he boasted that the Temple "ran continuous 'bills'" as it addressed the "everyday problems and life" of its communicants. Instead of speaking to a congregation, Stelzle thought of his worshipers as an "audience," and he considered it quite an accomplishment when he retained his audience through all parts of the service, which he called a "program." Describing the program at the temple in 1926, he insisted that it was as "diversified as a radio program nowadays." In another context Stelzle wrote that the church had been "placed in the position of a solicitor—an advertiser—who must so attractively and so convincingly present his proposition, that it will appeal to those who have a perfect right to buy, or not to buy."[73] Stelzle's gospel was an item to market, and the temple was his spiritual marketplace.

The hundreds of thousands of workers who crowded in to see Stelzle's bill during the two-year experiment apparently were not disappointed that they had forgone the music halls and movie theaters on Broadway. The son of the Bowery admitted that he "studied the methods of motion-picture houses and vaudeville theaters" to discover the reason for their immense popularity. He hoped to introduce "life and snappiness into the program" at the temple. Following the lead of irreverent vaudevillians, Stelzle kept the "acts" in his program moving along. He dared not leave any time between sermon and anthem, or anthem and movie, lest he lose some of his audience before he invited them to join the church and before he had collected the offering. "It was contrived," he explained, "that almost at the snap of the finger the curtain was pulled to one side, the lights were turned up, and the choir burst forth into an inspiring song. I was on my feet before the choir had finished the song, and with a studied gesture—differing according to the occasion and the audience—I prevented a pell-mell movement toward the big front door."[74] Stelzle promised and delivered fast-paced entertainment, and workers came time and again to see his show.

The pastor of the Labor Temple offered two principal reasons for his success. First, he took no chance that his congregation was unaware of the church's program. Stelzle advertised. As early as 1907, the missionary to the working class had advocated the use of various promotional techniques so that "the man on the street and the people in the homes" would come to church and participate in social gospel programs. In *Christianity's Storm Center* (1907), Stelzle impressed on his readers the importance of widespread publicity. He urged the use of admission cards, announcements, huge billboards and signs, gospel wagons, notices in streetcars, messages in the amusement columns of the local newspaper, photographs and newsstories, and candle-illuminated, muslin-covered wagons bearing notices of meeting times and places of special worship services. The church is in "one of the most crucial periods in her history," the social gospeler wrote, and the only way for the church to minister to those in need was to give the church and its programs high visibility.[75]

Stelzle's second secret for success was his refusal to employ standard religious material in his program. He turned his back on the better-than-life characters who inhabited the world of nineteenth-century religious tracts. Stelzle saw a need and a demand for "reality." So he showed films such as *Kelly the Cop*, featuring a protagonist who performed "a real man's job as a policeman" and who tackled the problems Stelzle's viewers knew in a personal way. He shied away from the "impossible characters," too good to be true, who were featured in the "average religious film."[76] Stelzle's worship programs used modern forms of expression in every available medium to speak to social problems. He satisfied his congregation's cry for justice and their outspoken yearning for diversion in a carefully planned religious program.

Stelzle nevertheless remained firmly in the social gospel movement in American Protestantism. His methods aside, the working-class man of the cloth made numerous services available to people who were often ignored by the majority of American Protestants. The simple pledge he asked of his congregation at the Labor Temple—"I accept the purpose of Jesus. I will help bring in the Kingdom of God"—committed new members to a social creed and a Christocentric theology. Because of his accomplishments in New York City, the Federal Council of Churches consulted him frequently for advice on the development of the Social Service Committee. They asked him to speak on more than one occasion at their annual conferences. And when the Men and Religion Forward Movement gathered momentum in its crusade to interest men and boys in responsible church work, its leaders called on Charles Stelzle to chair the Social Service Department. Stelzle gave the workers to whom he ministered the dignity that others in the movement often denied. Workers were not pitiable objects of reform but people, like himself, who needed understanding.[77] "Let us talk less about 'helping,' about 'service,'" he wrote in *The Church and Labor* (1910), "and let us think more about 'exchange'; for that is what it is—the exchange of our abilities, our contributions. He who teaches his brother a great truth, himself learns another."[78]

The concept of "exchange," however useful in elevating to a higher plane the relationship between "the masses and the classes," suggested that everyone had something to sell or to trade. It meant that the social gospel of Stelzle and his colleagues represented a commodity to be "exchanged" for the financial and spiritual support of the people who came to the church. Therein lay the tension in Stelzle's ministry. Determined as a social gospeler to usher in the kingdom of God by addressing the problems of people here and now, Stelzle also joined commercial men in satisfying popular wants as quickly as possible. As conscious as he was of the exploitation of laborers by large-scale firms, Stelzle nevertheless embraced the methods of the corporation as the most efficient for "winning" converts and supporters. He ultimately showed great faith in the power of consuming in a mass market. Responding to the advice of unknown, unseen experts, trusting in the verities of science and technology, and hearing the persuasive opinion of the herd promised security and well-being once obtained from religion. The locus of cultural authority had shifted—from the unseen God of the universe to the unknown expert in the corporation, from the arbitrary laws of Jehovah to the predictable laws of science, from the emotional testimony of faith by saints to the paid testimonials by influential twentieth-century men and women. "I believe" came as much from a scientific random sample of satisfied churchgoers, it seemed, as from the heart.

By 1912, Stelzle's experiment at the Labor Temple came to an end.

His methods had proved more effective with the urban working class than anything the Presbyterians had ever tried. Thousands of new members joined the Labor Temple. Revenues soared. The presbytery had every reason to continue the program with their full support. Stelzle's success, however, proved to be his undoing. For when the church finance department saw the bottom-line success of the New York mission to the working class, its chiefs reduced Stelzle's already meager budget. The old conservative administration, which plagued other Presbyterian congregations Stelzle had served, surfaced again in 1913. Having seen the results of modern methods, the Presbyterians nonetheless chose to appropriate the money to other projects that could not support themselves. Their fiscal cautiousness cost them their chief representative among prominent social gospelers. When Stelzle learned of the budget cuts, he tendered his resignation and embarked on his third career. Charles Stelzle opened a church advertising agency in New York City.

What may appear to be a glaring inconsistency proved to be but a new mission for the energetic social gospeler. His pique with the Presbyterian administrators resulted from their unwillingness to further the social gospel with the methods he had demonstrated. Stelzle himself and the hundreds of clients he served never imagined that an advertising agency could be considered incongruous in the social gospel movement. "How can men be expected to go to a church of which they have not heard," he asked his readers in *Principles of Successful Church Advertising* (1908), "and how can they feel that that church has the message which they need, unless this fact has been repeatedly made plain to them?"[79] Stelzle knew that he had obtained commitments to the social gospel more effectively at the Labor Temple by using advertisement than most of his colleagues achieved in a career without it. So in the interest of the social gospel and the kingdom of God, Stelzle pioneered in a new field of endeavor.

As he had done in both of his previous careers, Stelzle worked with abandon at the advertising business. He opened an office in New York City and handled clients who came to him for help. During World War I, the Red Cross hired him to prepare a publicity campaign for them in Washington, D.C. Because of the campaign's success, Stelzle found that after the war, other patriotic and community organizations called on him to direct their promotional campaigns.[80] He eagerly added their names to his list of regular customers. In 1908, Stelzle had published one of the handbooks on church advertising studied by modern ministers in many denominations. *Principles of Successful Church Advertising* contained the secrets of Stelzle's success. It also explains how an effort to revitalize American Protestantism succeeded in affirming the authority of the secular corporation.

His primer on church advertising actually betrayed Stelzle's firm grasp of the anxieties and concerns that beset modern middle-class Americans. He did not make his appeal to the unchurched masses when he wrote the book. Instead, he showed ministers and professionals in the middle class how to increase church membership, collections, and Christian influence in the nation. He spoke to men and women who were addressing their own uncertainty about self and personal direction, about teamwork and responsibility, and about unrestrained participation in the abundance of consumer capitalism. Stelzle invoked a vocabulary that was becoming familiar to modern Americans: the authoritative voice of the expert. "Cultivate the feeling that the church speaks with warrant concerning the subjects which are being advertised," he declared, and Protestants "will accept pretty nearly whatever comes from such a source, because they have confidence in it."[81] His object continued to be "helping men toward Christ and the Church," but he reached his goal with a "constant freshness of appeal," "sensational advertising," and manipulation of "emotions."[82] Stelzle wanted to make people *feel* the reality and intensity of religion.

Stelzle made his most powerful appeal to men. Capitalizing on their obsession with a manly identity of youth and vigor, which would become even more pronounced after the Great War, Stelzle created ads designed to lead men to the church, where they could learn "the best type of manhood." He scoffed at old programs and old activities that none but the tired and decrepit wanted to support. In their stead, Stelzle offered an energetic campaign of "efficiently organized" community work. Men's activities included working with boys and speaking in factories. "In carrying on this work we do not need a great deal of money," he contended. "It is rather a question of flesh and blood—real red blood, too." And like many successful advertisers, Stelzle made the message personal. "We need the sort of men who can do things," he went on, "and who do them because they like to do them. Are you that kind of man?"[83] The question promised to reinforce an image of virility and versatility to the man who responded in the affirmative.

Stelzle also urged men in the church to harness "the hearty, masculine voice" to persuade others to join. Conscious of modern Americans' longing to belong, to fit in, and to take their signals from those around them, Stelzle declared that most people are "obedient servants" who need to be "led" by others. "The direct command" promised results because the American "admires the strong virile element." "'Do it now,'" he explained, "has become a favorite motto in many offices, and the phrase has undoubtedly influenced many a man to prompt and immediate action." The son of the Bowery strongly advised against "appearing to be doing the 'dear brother' act," however. The authoritative voice of the advertiser had to make a "personal" appeal but could not "presume upon his brief and limited acquaintance." He thought that churches should give men and women the direction they craved without letting them know they had been manipulated and guided.[84]

One other aspect of Stelzle's church advertising plan displayed a shrewd understanding of an emerging modern culture: religion was like a game. Stelzle evoked the spirit of teamwork and competitive endeavor with "winning" language. More than a decade earlier, Stelzle had advised American Protestants in *Boys of the Street: How to Win Them* (1904) that "fair play and cooperation" in the Sunday school classroom would build "the average boy's character" and "win" him to the church. In 1915, Stelzle used a more subtle approach. He spoke of thriving churches as "successful advertisers" who knew they would "win" even before they actually had won. He encouraged churchmen to write about their organizations in such a way that people would want to take part. "No one likes to be identified with a losing proposition," Stelzle told readers, many of whom probably had become spectator fans of successful professional teams. "That the church is winning out must therefore be made very plain in one's advertising."[85]

Finally, the concept of winning served one other purpose: clergymen could take advantage of the "bandwagon effect." Stelzle told ministers to consult their audiences to find out why they had chosen their church. "What has won them," he confided, "will win others." He made it clear that religion was like a product to be marketed so that people could consume it. A consumer survey of the neighborhood of the church would reveal the "talking points" that preachers could use later to convince the unchurched to buy. The object of advertising a church, Stelzle declared, was to "create a desire, convince of need, and decide for action." In the matter of consuming, Stelzle let down his guard further than on anything else. He flatly stated that churches were "businesses" and "solicitors" that had to convince American Protestants that they had something valuable to offer.[86]

In the end, Stelzle's church advertising business pivoted on some of the same points as a secular advertising agency. Both relied on the illusion of need, the voice of authority, and the power of consuming to provide a sense of participating in a community practice. For Stelzle, commodifying religion made it recognizable and attractive. Consuming religion, like any other packaged good, restored a sense of well-being. The problem, however, was that religion was no more or less powerful than anything else on the market. "The Church has no monopoly of Christianity; it is in sharp competition with other forces, which insist that they have a right to speak with as much authority as the Church," Stelzle admitted. "There is no particular authority vested in the Church."[87] Stelzle recognized that even a revitalized faith could be little more than a season's sensation, a fast-moving article.

Charles Stelzle lived out the remainder of his life as an advertising agent in New York City. He died in 1941 after a long illness. The point of telling his story is not to condemn a social gospeler turned marketer, but to understand the ease with which the transfer of authority from religion to corporation could be made. Charles Stelzle earned the affectionate names "apostle to labor" and "union preacher" because he cared enough about working people to force a conservative denomination to give him a special appointment to serve their needs. In his zeal to speak to the widest possible audience, however, Stelzle became caught up in the power of advertising. When the son of the Bowery arrived on Madison Avenue, the social gospel had become a consuming faith.

CHARLES E. JEFFERSON

Thirty Years on Broadway

In 1934, shortly before he died, Charles E. Jefferson preached a sermon in New York City. An old man, Jefferson lacked much of the spark and vitality that had marked his oratorical style as a young preacher in the Broadway Tabernacle. A long-time admirer, who sat in the congregation that evening, noted that "his powers had waned, and the one-time Jefferson was no more." Frederick K. Stamm had become a minister partly because he was inspired by the powerful pastor of the Broadway Tabernacle. At the close of the sermon, Stamm offered to drive his idol home for a chance to be near the "greatest American preacher" in the twentieth century. On the way, the two ministers spoke of the older man's books and many accomplishments. When Stamm told Jefferson that *The Building of the Church* (1910) had been his favorite, Jefferson replied, "Everyone says the same thing." As Stamm became more com-

Charles E. Jefferson

fortable with the old preacher, he began to ask some personal questions:

> "Are you doing any preaching these days?" Stamm asked.
> "No," Jefferson replied.
> "Doing any writing?"
> "No, I wrote all I knew long ago."
> "What do you do?"
> "Oh, sit around the house reading the newspaper and
>   listening to the radio all day."[88]

The man who had preached for thirty years on Broadway spent his twilight years absorbed in mass culture.

By all accounts, Charles Jefferson was one of the most impressive speakers ever to stand behind an American pulpit. His admirer and chief biographer, Frederick Stamm, considered him a "modern prophet of God" who "never preached a poor sermon" in his halcyon days in New York City. Stamm was not alone in his regard for the minister of Broadway. Edgar Jones included Jefferson among "the royalty of the pulpit" in 1951 and included testimonies from numerous prominent ministers who praised Jefferson's strength, "poise," and "graciousness." According to the Reverend Roger Eddy Treat, for example, Jefferson had been "one of the greatest of the American preachers throughout all the years of his ministry at the Broadway Tabernacle." Jones himself declared that Jefferson was "the most envied of American preachers," whose fellow clergymen looked upon him with "awe and admiration." When William Shepherd wrote biographical sketches of the eleven best preachers in 1924, Charles Jefferson was among them.[89] Jefferson's thirty-year tenure in the Broadway Tabernacle testifies to his immense popularity among communicants as well.

Considering his obscurity in the last quarter of the twentieth century, however, we must wonder what accounted for his fame and popularity from 1900 to 1930. Though he called himself a social gospeler, his accomplishments in that movement seem small compared to the work done by ministers in urban institutional churches. Theology written by Walter Rauschenbusch, Shailer Mathews, Washington Gladden, or Edward Scribner Ames easily dwarfed Jefferson's banal collections of sermons and advice literature. His main claim to fame appears to lie in his talents as a communicator. As one historian has put it, Charles Jefferson interpreted Protestant faith "in terms which a generation affected by scientific, evolutionary, and progressive thought" could understand.[90] Charles Jefferson, sensitive to the cultural crisis of *fin-de-siècle* America, attempted both to shore up older Victorian values and to adapt them to the twentieth century. He also helped establish an emerging culture of youth, leisure, and consumption.

As a boy growing up in Cambridge, Ohio, in the 1860s and 1870s, Charles Jefferson had a proper Victorian childhood. His mother, Ella Sachett Jefferson, had come to the United States from the English Isle of Guernsey. His father, Dr. Milton Jefferson, was a dentist who had moved to Ohio from Virginia. The Jeffersons enjoyed a comfortable living in the years following the Civil War. As devout Methodists, they raised their three children in the church and educated their oldest child and only son at Ohio Wesleyan University. After receiving a degree in 1882, Jefferson secured a position as superintendent of public schools in Worthington, Ohio, but his parents had grander ambitions for their son. Two years after leaving Ohio Wesleyan, Jefferson enrolled in Harvard Law School "in response to the wishes of his family."[91] For a time, he worked tirelessly at learning law. But before a year was out, the young man sensed that something was missing in his life.

By the time Jefferson had graduated from Ohio Wesleyan, he had rejected much of the Methodist creed of his youth. He regarded ministers as "an inferior set" and looked down on the church as "a belated institution." Christianity, he believed, was rapidly becoming "obsolete." The young Ohioan's idols included Thomas Huxley and Herbert Spencer, from whom he undoubtedly gained his appreciation of evolution and his secular faith in human progress. He confronted, in his college days, the troubling doctrines of science that undermined the religious faith of his childhood. But he did not abandon all of the lessons of his youth. He still felt compelled to work hard to achieve individual success. His class-mates at Harvard saw in him an up-and-coming lawyer and statesman. Jefferson had internalized his parents' advice and culture, and he was determined to seek his fortune in Boston. He went, however, with "a bundle of doubts" about religion.[92] Before long, his doubts overtook his capacity for hard work and left the young man floundering about for a profession as well as a creed.

Sometime during his first months in Boston, Jefferson began attend-ing two or three church services each Sunday, partly for the sport of watching Boston's famous preachers perform, and partly in a genuine quest for faith. He rarely attended the same church more than once. The one exception was Phillips Brooks's Trinity Church. Rev. Brooks spoke with an elegance, force, and clarity that demanded attention and re-spect. Jefferson eagerly gave both. After hearing only a few sermons, Jefferson became obsessed with Brooks. His work at the law school fell off, and his interest in law nearly disappeared. He longed to know as much about the Boston divine as he could learn. Years after the fact he wrote, "I longed to tell everybody about him."[93]

Phillips Brooks probably never realized the effect he had had upon the youthful midwesterner who haunted his church each Sunday. Jeffer-son abandoned the Methodism of his parents and attended the Episcopal church of Phillips Brooks. Not suspecting the younger man's tortured quest for purpose and moral equanimity, Brooks granted a rather casual interview and encouraged Jefferson to come to him if he ever had a more specific matter he would like to discuss. Jefferson, overwhelmed by the "personality and presence" of Trinity Church's pastor, made an impor-tant decision that day. He left Harvard and enrolled in the Boston Univer-sity School of Theology. In 1887 Charles Jefferson focused his energy, talent, and determination on a career in the ministry.

While Jefferson's dedication to the ministry had come in large part from a Victorian commitment to hard work and individual achievement, his slavish emulation of Phillips Brooks heralded the arrival of changing cultural standards. For while he wanted to do a great work in his life, he wanted even more to be noticed. He enjoyed popularity and approval. From the moment he began working in his first parish in Chelsea, Massachusetts, until he answered the call of a church in New York City, Jefferson labored tirelessly to win popularity. *The History of the Broadway Tabernacle* reports that he succeeded in every phase of his career to earn a good reputation. While he was in seminary, locals considered him "one of the brilliant young men in Boston," and later in Chelsea, his congregation "greatly admired" the young man and his work.[94]

Jefferson's work eventually became other people's entertainment and Sunday leisure. Over the years, he came to place great importance on delivering eloquent and engaging sermons. His success came to depend on the theater habit that he often decried and on the appeal of mass entertainment. "As one who continued to draw crowds twice every Sunday for over thirty years," writes one of Jefferson's biographers, "he was often spoken of as the man who had the longest run on Broadway."[95] Jefferson's message and style contributed to the formation and legitimation of modern secular culture.

Charles Jefferson, of course, did not perceive his pulpit in the Broadway church as a stage nor his tenure as a "long run." Rather, he viewed his work as a cultural mission. Describing the thirty years he lived in New York City as "a time of stress and storm," the divine recognized that "changes in the realm of thought" had been "widespread and revolutionary." In addition to the advent of higher criticism, which radically altered the way men and women viewed the Bible, the new psychology, other new philosophies, and conflicts between fundamentalists and modernists had rocked the basis of religious faith. "The whole intellectual world," he insisted in 1930, "has been shaken to its foundations."[96] His mission was to make religion seem convincing to those who were lost in doubt.

Jefferson himself had been assailed by doubts as a young man and had begun to feel that religion was somehow unreal and disconnected from modern material existence. The doubts that overtook the young Harvard law student in the 1880s probably did not vanish immediately, even under the influence of Rev. Brooks. As Jefferson explained of himself in *Thirty Years on Broadway* (1930), "Because of his painful experience as a young man in working his way into a living and rational faith, his heart has been singularly sympathetic with all minds that are struggling with doubts."[97] It could have been in part to make religion seem more majestic and more concrete that Jefferson persuaded his congregation in 1905 to remain downtown and to build a magnificent "skyscraper" church. The new Broadway Tabernacle at the corner of Broadway and Fifty-sixth, with its administrative offices, office space for rent, and Sunday school classrooms reaching toward heaven, was the first of its kind in a city that has since become famous for its skyline. The church thus attracted attention, inspired awe, and stood as a symbol of the "reality" and substance of modern Protestant religion.

Jefferson also felt a need to affirm the social gospel that promised to revitalize religion in the early twentieth century. All around him in New York City battles between social gospelers and orthodox Protestants raged. Dozens of settlement houses brought relief and culture to the impoverished masses that made up the city, while at the same time muckrakers discovered the shameful tenements owned by New York's Trinity Church. Institutional churches based on social responsibility and Christian commitment took over the parishes of once-fashionable downtown congregations that fled to the suburbs. Charles Stelzle's Labor Temple, for example, won wide acclaim when it appeared in 1910, only to lose some of its funding in 1913 because of conservatives among the Presbyterian leadership. Charles Jefferson believed he had a mission to the inner city of New York. Although many of his most steadfast communicants lived in Westchester County, the minister of the Broadway Tabernacle resisted the appeal of a brand new suburban church. He insisted that Protestants had a social obligation to remain on the "tumultuous and ever-changing and reputedly godless thoroughfare."[98] Jefferson brought the social gospel to the Great White Way.

The Tabernacle, however, never pretended to be an institutional church, complete with bowling alley, gymnasium, classrooms, and social clubs, though its doors were open "day and night, seven days out of every week." Its minister simply asserted that the "individual gospel is no gospel at all. Dip down into the teaching of Jesus anywhere you please, and you will find him preaching the social gospel." The social gospel that Jefferson presented to his congregation was a "friendly" gospel. He offered Christocentric theology instead of the harsh tenets of orthodox Protestantism and the angry God of old. "Christ is the one and only sufficient savior," Jefferson wrote in 1901, because under Jesus all men are "brethren" and Christ is the "teacher." Jefferson decided to build a "society of friends, a brotherhood, a family" inside his church. In that way he hoped to minister to the "poor in spirit, in courage, in faith, in social graces, in business capacity, in success, in purse, in talent, in achievement." The Broadway Tabernacle, he declared in 1901, must remain in the thick of urban life, reaching out to those of all classes who needed assistance. "If the Tabernacle becomes conservative, cautious, dainty, fastidious, timid, exclusive, belated in thought and antiquated in method, a lover of ease rather than of battle, desirous of comfort rather than of leadership, its days of usefulness are over."[99]

Jefferson's way of implementing this social gospel took various forms. Like many churches of its day, the Broadway Tabernacle under Jefferson's direction contributed liberally to "all moral reform" and to agencies that provided the material for relief to those victimized by the city and by industry.[100] The congregation also engaged in a monumental fund-raising drive to earn money for building the new church in 1905. Spending money to get the best materials for the church bound members of the congregation together. These two examples suggest a pattern that has become more prevalent in the twentieth century: spending money to solve problems. Whereas nineteenth-century reformers devoted their time to effect individual rehabilitation, many of their twentieth-century counterparts disposed of their duties primarily by giving money to professional reform agencies. Likewise, congregations in the 1800s assiduously avoided indebtedness, while churchmen in the 1900s spent large sums to build grand churches of modern design. The indifference of members of the Tabernacle to spending and temporary indebtedness might reflect their growing acceptance of loosened restrictions against consuming for pleasure and success.

Enthusiasm for consuming emerged in conjunction with the growing American concern with getting along with others. The "other-directed" personality type that had begun to take shape in the early years of the century had, after all, come to rely on the messages, products, and approval of others for a sense of identity and direction. Jefferson urged new converts to tell others of their decision to be Christians. "With others he is to live, and from others in large measure will come the strength and light of his life," Jefferson declared in 1909. Moreover, he told new members, "it is not wholesome to keep one's eye fixed upon the inner movements of the heart." When a new member joined the Tabernacle, he was the "guest of honor" at two different church socials. He would eat with his new friends in order to feel like part of the group.[101]

The closest link between the Broadway Tabernacle and the emerging culture of consumption, however, lay in the Sunday services. Like many other social gospelers, Charles Jefferson not only wanted church members to feel secure despite personal shortcomings, but he also wanted to present his message to as large an audience as possible by providing worship services that would attract into the church the crowds of disheartened who thronged Broadway. His elaborate preparation for the Sunday morning "performance" suggests that he placed the greatest faith in his ministry on the program of worship. One minister who heard and praised the New York divine wrote in 1923 that Jefferson was a man of "strength," "poise," and "serenity," who was "touched by that elusive magnetic quality so impossible to define." His scholarship and preparation, concluded Joseph Fort Newton, accounted for the "sermonic excellence" in evidence every Sunday. [102] Jefferson's all-consuming mission was public preaching.

Jefferson gave virtuoso performances every Sunday. A handsome man, he captured his audience's attention with timely sermons. On occasion he included examples from Shakespeare to permit himself the opportunity to give a dramatic reading. A popular sermon on ambition, for example, included passages from three of Shakespeare's plays. From the tone of his description of his thirty-year career in New York, Jefferson seemed to view his work as a role he was playing. Throughout the text of *Thirty Years on Broadway* (1930), he refused to use the first person, referring to himself as "The Pastor." The order of his service broke conveniently into two parts, like acts in a play. And "latecomers, pewholders and strangers alike," had to wait in the "vestibule" until the "appointed pause," when ushers seated them. Having carefully crafted a service that created a "worshipful mood," Jefferson refused to have it broken by "belated individuals."[103] Judging from the thousands of people from New York City, Westchester County, and New Jersey who associated with the Broadway Tabernacle over the years, Jefferson's style was effective.

Nevertheless, the star of the Broadway Tabernacle chafed when outsiders compared his work to that of the stage performers on the Great White Way. Although Broadway was, he admitted, a "rendezvous for shows," he did not consider his worship service one of them. He had seen "several generations of Broadway showmen come and go," but their popularity was always "short-lived," while his own "abide[d]." He sensed that part of his success depended on the theater-going habit established by members of his church. When he explained, for instance, why he chose to adopt a "conversational style" in his preaching, he acknowledged that his parishioners "have seen enough shows through the week"—they did not want more drama. He insisted that no mere showman could survive as long as he had in the middle of the theater district. "A church is here to do a *work*, not to make a *show*," Jefferson asserted in a 1929 sermon. [104]

The shrillness of Jefferson's defense of his work and mission and his refusal to acknowledge the showmanship of his service indicate the ambivalence he felt toward the conflict between Victorian individualism and modern consumerism. He scoffed at the "charming singers, famous dancers, popular actors, skillful vaudeville performers, [and] platform stars" who stirred "the town for a day" and then passed on. Yet he judged his own work by their standards: by the length of its run. "The Pastor of the Broadway Tabernacle," he wrote in the introduction to *Thirty Years on Broadway*, "has the unique distinction of being the only Congregational clergyman in the history of New York City who has ever filled a pulpit on Broadway for more than thirty years."[105]

Jefferson also judged other ministers by the standards of the stage. Charles G. Finney, the renowned revivalist of Victorian America and designer of the original Broadway Church, had "cared more for acoustics than for aesthetics," according to Jefferson, and had helped to make the church a "popular" auditorium. Jefferson praised his immediate predecessor, Dr. William Taylor, who, he said, "would have made an actor of consummate power" with his "great body, great head, great neck, great voice."[106] His attacks on the flighty quality of stage stars, who captured the attention of patrons for a while and then left before returning for a new run, bore some autobiographical weight. Jefferson himself attributed much of his success in the Tabernacle to a generous congregation that paid for his vacations every summer. He spent three months each year traveling in the United States and abroad. By the end of his tenure, he had visited all the states of the union and all the states of Continental Europe. "The Pastor of the Tabernacle would have become sterile and stale long ago," he declared in his autobiography, "had it not been for his wide travels." His own life resembled that of a celebrated thespian. Finally, despite his insistence that worship services were not shows, Jefferson scolded fellow Christians who did not "put forth sufficient energy to make religion entertaining."[107]

Jefferson's ambivalence also might have been fueled by the direction he had taken the social gospel. He, like many other social gospelers, became fascinated with the life of Jesus and wrote a book about it, entitled *The Character of Jesus* (1908). The very categories Jefferson chose for characterizing the man of Galilee betray his assumption of modern articles of cultural faith. For instance, Jefferson admired Jesus' "poise" that "wooes and wins the heart," and his "originality," which promised to restore "sparkle" and "zest" in a "drab world." Jesus displayed characteristics that made him "popular" and "attractive" to twentieth-century American Protestants. Jefferson concluded that Jesus was a "great man" because "men who stood nearest to him were charmed and swayed by his loveliness. He was full of grace and truth. He had a charm about him which wooed and fascinated. Children liked him, boys sang for him, publicans hung upon him."[108]

Besides his twentieth-century portrayal of the Nazarene, Jefferson offered messages compatible with an emerging culture of leisure and consumption. His popular sermon on ambition turned on the notion of pleasing the crowd. He compared human striving for purpose and right-eousness with efforts of popular sports figures. "The athletic world," he told his audience, "throbs and sparkles with energy." Thousands of people traveled great distances to watch others perform and to excel. Thus, every man should do his best for some team so others can "see a victory." And Jefferson lauded man's power. Forgetting for a moment the omnipotent Jehovah of his youth, Jefferson declared in the same sermon that "man is the King of the earth and he has no rest till he gets the whole of it under his feet." The key to man's strength, however, lay hidden not in faith but in "the realm of scientific research."[109] In the end, the message of the great communicator sparkled with the language of enter-tainment and legitimated a transfer of faith from the boundless power of God to the convincing and verifiable strength of science.

Charles Jefferson set the standard for an entire generation of Ameri-can Protestant ministers. His power of elocution and enormous popu-larity in New York City brought him praise and fame across the nation. By the end of his career, the pastor of the Broadway Tabernacle easily could have mistaken adulation for Victorian achievement and poise for self-control. He had become so attuned to the pulse of the Great White Way that he no longer denied his embrace of modern culture. When Jefferson left his radio and newspaper for the last time, that night in 1934, he spoke to a generation whose faith lay in the power of consump-tion and of science to grant well-being. Charles Jefferson probably never realized how fully he had participated in the affirmation of that modern faith.

. . .

Charles Sheldon, Charles Stelzle, and Charles Jefferson, having themselves sensed the strain in Victorian culture, responded to the cultural crisis of the late nineteenth century by trying to infuse religion with fresh life and meaning. In so doing they used the language of consumer culture that was increasingly available to them. Their efforts to regenerate American faith thus incorporated terms of secular culture into religion. And as social religion gained appeal in the stories that celebrated youth, in advertising, and in the techniques of mass enter-tainment, culture absorbed and gained authority from that religion.

Sheldon, Stelzle, and Jefferson all contributed to an acceptance by American Protestants who listened to them of the instruments and media of mass culture as providing a sense of identity, place, belonging, acceptance, and well-being. What began as an attempt to rejuvenate Protestant culture ended as a celebration and embrace of consumer culture.

All three men wanted to influence other men. They longed to imbue men and boys with youthful manliness, red-blooded masculinity, and manly courage. The terms of twentieth-century manly character and religious morality included heroic sacrifice, unselfish service, and heartfelt emotion. They were terms associated in an earlier century with femininity. Sheldon, Stelzle, and Jefferson, as cultural spokesmen, legitimated and transformed the feminization of American culture that, according to Ann Douglas, took shape in the nineteenth century. Twentieth-century consumer culture—which had its roots in the liberal Protestantism, the domestic novels, and the feminized literature and ministry of the nineteenth century that Douglas describes—became something quite different. As Sheldon, Stelzle, and Jefferson demonstrated, consumer culture was challenging enough to attract and inspire red-blooded American men. Using the language of sacrifice, service, and love, purveyors of religion and of culture could appeal simultaneously to men and women.

Probably the most powerful attraction of the Protestant social gospel was its demand for "reality." While a deeply felt cultural anxiety prompted a quest for concrete, reassuring faith, the consequence of that quest was denial of faith. For to see and feel contradicted the spiritual acceptance of an unseen power in the universe. Faith, in part, implies trust without tangible evidence. Beyond that, the demand for concrete religion and evident feeling left American Protestants to doubt the value of future reward and punishment and made them more demanding of immediate results. Social reform drew their attention to the concerns of this world and to their own feelings of usefulness and purpose. When men and women felt good about reform, they became more deeply ensnared in the tangle of therapeutic relations that undergirded the emerging secular culture and that granted a new, if sometimes uneasy, personal peace.

All three men saw their missions in the terms of mass culture. While they continued to hope that social gospel religion could influence American society and culture, Sheldon, Stelzle, and Jefferson sought legitimacy for their religion in secular culture. Sheldon's reform had to offer youth and vigor or, he believed, lose its audience. Stelzle thought that advertising represented the last best hope for reaching the otherwise uninterested masses. Jefferson required attendance, attention, and accolades for satisfaction. Sheldon, Stelzle, and Jefferson bolstered consumer culture. Their religion testified to the power of consuming to produce psychic comfort and economic and cultural ease. In the end, consuming gave Americans the identity, comfort, and direction for which they yearned. Social religion became one with this new culture of consumption. As Stelzle realized, it no longer stood as the authority even on matters of philanthropy and spiritual fulfillment. Religion had become but one more commodity packaged and presented to a mass society.

The close ties between business and religion in the 1920s should not come as a surprise considering the prewar evolution of the economy and social gospelers' reformulation of the work ethic and salvation. Social gospelers had been borrowing the terms and model of commerce and corporation for decades, even as they worked to inspire progressive reform. Later, they used the methods of advertising and adopted the mentality of salesmanship in order to spread their ideas and to reach the unchurched. These actions, in and of themselves, may or may not have been significant, but as time passed, the practice of religion, the presentation of religious ideas and beliefs, and the imagery on which churchmen depended bore a striking resemblance to practices, ideas, and images in the dominant culture. Eventually, churchmen urged each other to live up to such standards as timeliness, novelty, wide appeal, and efficiency. In so doing, Protestants endorsed these standards of success. They helped give legitimacy to values and ideals that underlay consumer culture.

· · ·

The social gospel incorporated a broad spectrum of social concerns. Having been articulated by men and women who observed and experienced the disruption caused by industrial capitalism, the social gospel arose from and spoke to concerns about family cohesiveness, the meaning of work, the relationship between social classes in a democracy, and the appropriate role for the state in an industrialized society. From the beginning, social gospelers considered their religious beliefs relevant to the world around them. They set out to ameliorate the harsh conditions in inner-city neighborhoods. But the social gospel was always more than a program to help an exploited urban working class. It was written by and for the middle class as well.

The social gospel was bound up in a dramatic cultural transformation. The conditions that drove Protestants in the late nineteenth century to reconsider their religious beliefs and practices also challenged the dominant Victorian culture. Consequently, as members of families, as "workers," as citizens, and as purveyors of culture, social gospelers addressed both spiritual and cultural concerns. Their efforts contributed to the reordering of American cultural life, and their lives and work show how a modern, secular culture grew out of Protestant-based Victorian cultural assumptions.

Although social gospel Protestantism and American culture were evolving and influencing one another in the late nineteenth and early twentieth centuries, it took a crisis to consolidate the reordering. World War I seems to have been that critical moment. Social gospelers believed that the war was a turning point in Western civilization, and the social gospel was a part of the "new orthodoxy" after the war. Yet after the war the social gospel increasingly incorporated the language and techniques of commerce, which had also galvanized during the conflict. It was after the Great War that the implications of earlier reconsiderations of family, work, and politics became clear. For the original redefinitions prepared the ground for a culture based on immediate gratification, material comfort, and group orientation as well as for a gospel of social salvation. After the war, the intertwining of religion and culture became evident. Protestants in the social gospel tradition increasingly relied on the standards of business, entertainment, and the state to evaluate their religious efforts. They assumed that churches spoke with authority only insofar as they measured up to secular standards of expertise, efficiency, and entertainment.

By the 1920s, attention to commercial standards altered the experience of religion. To offer the best social programs that money can buy (in the words of the Reverend Earl Hoon), suggests that social justice and social salvation could be achieved through consuming. The presentation of social gospel activities in attractive advertisements and the attempt to appeal to a wide audience through radio programs and special church services also imply that religion was being commodified. The promise of abundant life and the shift in emphasis away from the afterlife contributed to frustration with deferred gratification. The immediacy of the social gospel undergirded an ethos of consumption. Striving for youth and novelty reflected emerging cultural assumptions but revised the traditional Protestant focus on the blessings of heaven and the unchanging standards of morality. In these ways social gospelers offered religious experience, spiritual enrichment, and social responsibility to audiences and consumers as if they were in a marketplace.

Commitment to social responsibility did not flag after the Great War.

Social gospelers continued to sponsor social service commissions, to advocate social-welfare legislation, and to seek collective answers to social problems. They believed they were creating a living faith and never perceived themselves as anything less than men and women of God. They should not be mistaken as tools of business interests. Nevertheless, they contributed in the 1910s and 1920s to the consolidation of new values and ideals in American culture. Their ideas and actions made it easier for Protestant Americans to embrace a secular culture in which Protestantism was not prominently featured. The social gospel contributed to the reorientation of American culture that validated abundance, consumption, and self-realization. Social gospelers, reformers though they were, created, not a critique of modern capitalism, but rather a consuming faith in the material abundance it promised.

NOTES

CHAPTER 1   AMERICAN PROTESTANTISM AT A CROSSROADS

1. Walter Rauschenbusch, *Christianizing the Social Order* (New York, Macmillan, 1912), vii, 6, 7, 10.

2. The following books illustrate the intensifying interest in matters related to the "social question" in the late nineteenth century: Washington Gladden, *Applied Christianity* (Boston: Houghton Mifflin, 1886); Josiah Strong, *The New Era* (New York: Baker & Taylor, 1893); George Davis Herron, *The New Redemption* (New York: T. Y. Crowell, 1893); Washington Gladden, *Social Salvation* (Boston: Houghton Mifflin, 1902); and Walter Rauschenbusch, *Christianity and the Social Crisis* (New York: Macmillan, 1907). For a discussion of Straton's and other conservatives' interest in social reform, see Ferenc Szasz, "The Progressive Clergy and the Kingdom of God," *Mid-America: An Historical Review* 55 (January 1973): 12–15. Szasz cites a passage from Straton's *Gardens of Life* (1921): "The minister and the Church of Christ are traitors to their trust, they are recreant to their duty, unless they cry aloud and spare not—unless they battle heroically against such evils as unjust wages, especially to women workers, child labor, and the hell-black social evil, lawlessness, and the awful shame and disgrace of the liquor traffic!"

3. Authors responsible for painting this standard picture of the social gospel include Charles Hopkins, *The Rise of the Social Gospel in American Protestantism, 1865–1915* (New Haven: Yale Univ. Press, 1940); Aaron Abell, *The Urban Impact on American Protestantism, 1865–1900* (Cambridge: Harvard Univ. Press, 1943); Robert Handy, *The Social Gospel in America, 1870–1920* (New York: Oxford Univ. Press, 1966); Henry May, *Protestant Churches in Industrial America* (New York: Harper, 1949); Ronald White, *The Social Gospel* (Philadelphia: Temple Univ. Press, 1976); and Jacob Dorn, *Washington Gladden: Prophet of the Social Gospel* (Columbus: Ohio State Univ. Press, 1968). Dorn's book and the following works all suggest how pervasive the social gospel had become by the early twentieth century: Dores Sharpe, *Walter Rauschenbusch* (New

York: Macmillan 1942); Howard Wilson, *Mary McDowell, Neighbor* (Chicago: Univ. of Chicago Press, 1928); George B. Nash, III, "Charles Stelzle: Apostle to Labor," *Labor History* 11 (Spring 1970): 151–74; Robert Crunden, *Ministers of Reform: The Progressives' Achievement in American Civilization, 1889–1920* (New York: Basic Books, 1982); John P. McDowell, *The Social Gospel in the South: The Woman's Home Mission Movement in the Methodist Episcopal Church, South, 1886–1939* (Baton Rouge: Louisiana State Univ. Press, 1982); William Hutchison, "Cultural Strain and Protestant Liberalism," *American Historical Review* 76 (April 1971): 386–411; idem, *The Modernist Impulse in American Protestantism* (New York: Oxford Univ. Press, 1982); and Szasz, "The Progressive Clergy," 3–20. Hutchison and Crunden both discuss the midwestern, middle-class backgrounds of many of the social gospelers. Caroline Bartlett Crane's People's Church in Kalamazoo, Michigan, is the subject of "One Woman's Civic Service in Kalamazoo," *Delineator* 73 (June 1909): 767–68. Charles Sheldon, better known for writing *In His Steps*, practiced the social gospel in Topeka, Kansas. Churches in Lexington, Missouri, joined together in the 1890s to meet the needs of men and women—church members and nonmembers alike—during the prolonged coal mine strike. See Susan Curtis Mernitz, "Church, Class, and Community: The Impact of Industrialization on Lexington, Missouri, 1870–1900" (M. A. thesis, Univ. of Missouri, 1981). The Reverend Earl Hoon told the story of his church in Sioux City, Iowa, in Francis Case, *Advertising the Church* (New York: Abingdon Press, 1925).

4. Abell, *The Urban Impact on American Protestantism*, presents the best look at the institutional church movement. For a specific example of an institutional church, read about the People's Church in Kalamazoo, Michigan, under the direction of the Reverend Caroline Bartlett Crane in "One Woman's Civil Service in Kalamazoo," 767–68; and "Story of an Institutional Church in a Small City," *Charities* 14 (6 May 1905): 723–31. For a discussion of the Social Creed of the Churches see Dorn, *Washington Gladden*; Elias Sanford, *The Origin and History of the Federal Council of the Churches of Christ in America* (Hartford, Conn.: S. S. Scranton, 1916); "Report of the Church and Modern Industry," *Christian Advocate*, 24 December 1908, 2139; Harry Ward, *Social Creed of the Churches* (New York: Eaton & Mains, 1912); and Creighton Lacy, *Frank Mason North: His Social and Ecumenical Mission* (Nashville: Abingdon Press, 1967). Charles Stelzle was commonly associated with the social gospel and the labor movement, and one of his colleagues, Charles Macfarland, settled some labor disputes in Massachusetts before he became general secretary of the Federal Council of Churches. William Bliss, who had a parish in South Boston at the same time that he compiled *The Encyclopedia of Social Reform*, was recruited by the local Labor party to run for lieutenant governor. Mary McDowell in Chicago helped women organize a union in the early 1900s. See William T. Ellis, "A Union Preacher," *Outlook* 95 (13 August 1910): 838–42; Nash, "Charles Stelzle: Apostle to Labor"; Charles Macfarland, *Across the Years* (New York: Macmillan, 1936); William Bliss, *The Encyclopedia of Social Reform* (New York: Funk & Wagnalls, 1897); Lea Taylor, "The Social Settlement and Civic Responsibility: The Life Work of Mary McDowell and Graham Taylor," *Social Service Review* 28 (March 1954): 31–40; "For a National Investigation of Women," *Independent* 62 (3 January 1907): 24–25; and "The Religious Faith of One Social Worker," *Survey* 60 (April 1928): 40–43.

5. Rauschenbusch, *Christianizing the Social Order*, 19–20, 14. The New York–based Association Press published a multivolume report of the activities of the move-

ment in 1912 in a series called Messages of the Men and Religion Forward Movement. Volumes entitled *Boys' Work in the Local Church* and *The Church and the Press* are just two of the reports in the series.

6. For examples of didactic novels written by social gospelers see, by Charles Sheldon, *In His Steps* (Chicago: Advance, 1897), *The Crucifixion of Philip Strong* (New York: Street & Smith, 1899), *Robert Hardy's Seven Days* (Chicago: Advance, 1899), *The Reformer* (Chicago: Advance, 1902), and *The Spirit's Power* (Cleveland: F. M. Barton, 1906); and by Elizabeth Stuart Phelps Ward, *Friends: A Duet* (Boston: Houghton Mifflin, 1881), *A Singular Life* (Boston: Houghton Mifflin, 1894), and *The Story of Jesus Christ: An Interpretation* (London: Sampson, Low, Marston & Co., 1897). Henry Cope worked for many years in the Religious Education Association. The following books by Cope outline the revolutionary changes in Sunday school literature in the early twentieth century: *The Modern Sunday School* (New York: Revell, 1907), *Ten Years' Progress in Religious Education* (Chicago: Harmegines & Howell, 1913), *The School in the Modern Church* (New York: Doran, 1919), and *Education for Democracy* (New York: Macmillan, 1920). The University of Chicago Press, at the urging of Shailer Mathews, printed a number of new teaching materials: these included Herbert Gates, *The Life of Jesus* (1908); Shailer Mathews, *The Message of Jesus to Our Modern Life* (1915); Erwin L. Shaver, *A Christian Education* (1927); idem, *Christianizing our Community* (1927); and Isaac Burgess, *A Teacher's Manual for the Life of Jesus Christ* (1927). See also Norman Richardson, *The Religious Education of Adolescents* (New York: Abingdon Press, 1918), and an anonymous article, "Religious Education and Social Duty," *Biblical World* 33 (April 1909): 19–22.

7. Walter Rauschenbusch, *A Theology of the Social Gospel* (New York: Macmillan, 1917); Shailer Mathews, *The Faith of Modernism* (New York: Macmillan, 1924); and Edward Scribner Ames, *The New Orthodoxy* (Chicago: Univ. of Chicago Press, 1918), are the principal formal discussions of religious belief. Other works, of course, reflected the shift in theology even though they did not pretend to be theological tracts. The best known of the works that preceded the theology are Josiah Strong, *My Religion in Everyday Life* (New York: Baker & Taylor, 1910); Washington Gladden, *Social Salvation* (Boston: Houghton Mifflin, 1902); idem, *Applied Christianity*; and Charles Stelzle, *Christianity's Storm Center* (New York: Revell, 1907). For a general discussion of religious thought at the turn of the century see Hutchison, *The Modernist Impulse in American Protestantism;* Williston Walker, *A History of the Christian Church* (New York: Scribner's 1970); James Turner, *Without God, Without Creed* (Baltimore: Johns Hopkins Univ. Press, 1984); William R. Miller, *Contemporary American Protestant Thought: 1900–1970* (New York: Bobbs-Merrill, 1973); William McLoughlin, *Revivals, Awakenings, and Reform: An Essay on Religion and Social Change in America, 1607–1977* (Chicago: Univ. of Chicago Press, 1978); and Paul Carter, *The Spiritual Crisis in the Gilded Age* (DeKalb: Northern Illinois Univ. Press, 1971).

8. A number of scholars have identified the period between 1880 and 1920 as one of transition from Victorianism to modern culture and have explored the social, cultural, and private aspects of those changes. A complete listing of the tremendous work that has been done would constitute a lengthy bibliographic essay. I offer a more modest citation that includes a number of important and suggestive recent works: Herbert Gutman, *Work, Culture, and Society in Industrializing America* (New York: Vintage, 1976); Alfred Chandler, *The Visible Hand: The Managerial Revolution in American*

Business (Cambridge: Harvard Univ. Press, 1977); Alfred Chandler et al., *The Changing Economic Order* (New York: Harcourt, Brace & World, 1968); Louis Galambos, *Competition and Cooperation* (Baltimore: Johns Hopkins Press, 1966); Harry Braverman, *Labor and Monopoly Capital: The Degradation of Work in the Twentieth Century* (New York: Monthly Review Press, 1974); James Gilbert, *Work without Salvation: American Intellectuals and Industrial Alienation, 1880–1910* (Baltimore: Johns Hopkins Univ. Press, 1977); Daniel Rodgers, *The Work Ethic in Industrial America, 1850–1920* (Chicago: Univ. of Chicago Press, 1974); James R. Green, *The World of the Worker: Labor in Twentieth-Century America* (New York: Hill & Wang, 1980); and David Montgomery, "Herbert Gutman's Nineteenth-Century America: A Review Essay," *Labor History* 19 (Summer 1978): 16–29. All of these works explore the changed patterns of economic life, from the reorganization of capital to the experience of the shop floor. Taken together, they illuminate the emergence of a corporate order that, while evolving out of the market capitalism of the early nineteenth century, had developed into a system that undermined many of the values that had called it into being. Works such as Stephan Thernstrom, *Poverty and Progress: Social Mobility in a Nineteenth-Century City* (Cambridge: Harvard Univ. Press, 1964); Howard Chudacoff, *Mobile Americans: Residential and Social Mobility in Omaha, 1880–1920* (New York: Oxford, 1972); Clyde Griffen, *Natives and Newcomers: The Ordering of Opportunity in Mid-Nineteenth-Century Poughkeepsie* (Cambridge: Harvard Univ. Press, 1978); and Edward Pessen, "The Equalitarian Myth and the American Social Reality," *American Historical Review* 76 (1971): 989–1035, examine some of the private effects of the evolution of capitalism. Christopher Lasch, *Haven in a Heartless World* (New York: Basic Books, 1977); Richard Sennett, *Families against the City* (Cambridge: Harvard Univ. Press, 1970); Elaine May, *Great Expectations: Marriage and Divorce in Post-Victorian America* (Chicago: Univ. of Chicago Press, 1980); and Christopher Lasch, "The Family and History" and "The Emotions of Family Life," *New York Review of Books*, 27 November 1975, deepen our understanding of changes in family life that were tied to broader economic and cultural change. Several writers point to the cultural crisis of *fin-de-siècle* America and Americans' attempt to reinterpret the categories of meaning for their lives: Ann Douglas, *The Feminization of American Culture* (New York: Knopf, 1977); Jackson Lears, *No Place of Grace* (New York: Pantheon, 1981); Alan Trachtenberg, *The Incorporation of America* (New York: Hill & Wang, 1982); Philip Rieff, *The Triumph of the Therapeutic* (New York: Harper, 1966); John Higham, "The Reorientation of American Culture in the 1890s," in *Writing American History: Essays on Modern Scholarship* (Bloomington: Indiana Univ. Press, 1970); and Warren Susman, *Culture as History: The Transformation of American Society in the Twentieth Century* (New York: Pantheon, 1973). The consumer culture they identify grew out of the complex interplay between public demands and private doubts and served to reinforce the economic and social structure that was developing. The political culture of progressivism also resulted from these massive changes, as the following works suggest: Crunden, *Ministers of Reform;* James Weinstein, *The Corporate Ideal in the Liberal State* (Boston: Beacon, 1968); David P. Thelen, *The New Citizenship: Origins of Progressivism in Wisconsin, 1885–1900* (Columbia: Univ. of Missouri Press, 1972); Michael McGerr, *The Decline of Popular Politics: The American North, 1865–1928* (New York: Oxford Univ. Press, 1986); Clyde Griffen, "The Progressive Ethos," in Stanley Coben and Lorman Ratner, eds.,

The Development of an American Culture (Englewood Cliffs: Prentice-Hall, 1970); and Robert Kelley, "Ideology and Political Culture from Jefferson to Nixon," *American Historical Review* 82 (June 1977): 531–62.

9. For discussions of American reform in the antebellum years and its characteristic individualistic vision, see David Rothman, *The Discovery of the Asylum: Social Order and Disorder in the New Republic* (Boston: Little, Brown, 1971); David Brion Davis, *Antebellum Reform* (New York: Harper & Row, 1967); Ronald Walters, *American Reformers, 1815–1860* (New York: Hill & Wang, 1978); and Lois Banner, "Religious Benevolence and Social Control: A Critique of an Interpretation," *Journal of American History* 60 (June 1973): 23–41. Jane Addams, Mary Eliza McDowell, and Walter Rauschenbusch specifically mention their parents' involvement in reform or community life. See Addams, *Twenty Years at Hull House* (New York: Macmillan, 1910); McDowell, "The Religious Faith of One Social Worker," *Survey* 60 (April 1928): 40–43; and Rauschenbusch, *Leben und Wirken von August Rauschenbusch Angefangen von ihm selbst, vollendet, und herausgegeben von seinem Sohne Walther Rauschenbusch* (Cassel, Germany: J. G. Oncken Nachfolger, 1901). For secondary works linking antebellum reform and later social activism see Charles C. Cole, *The Social Ideas of the Northern Evangelists, 1826–1860* (New York: Columbia Univ. Press, 1954); Timothy Smith, *Revivalism and Social Reform: American Protestantism on the Eve of the Civil War* (Baltimore: Johns Hopkins Press, 1957); and Anne Rose, *Transcendentalism as a Social Movement, 1830–1850* (New Haven: Yale Univ. Press, 1981).

10. Rauschenbusch, *Christianizing the Social Order*, 19.

11. Ibid., 10.

12. See David Kennedy, *Over Here: The First World War and American Society* (New York: Oxford Univ. Press, 1980).

13. In recent years a number of works have explored the various dimensions of this emerging culture of consumption. Inspired in part by Philip Rieff's *Triumph of the Therapeutic* (New York: Harper & Row, 1966) and David Riesman's *Lonely Crowd* (New Haven: Yale Univ. Press, 1950), both of which discussed America's changing social relations and evolving cultural values in the modern period, these more recent examinations of consumer culture explore the new ways people learned the cultural messages of their society, the emphasis on immediate gratification, and some of the contradictions this emerging cultural system raised. See Jackson Lears and Richard Wightman Fox, *The Culture of Consumption: Critical Essays in American History, 1880–1980* (New York: Pantheon, 1983); Roland Marchand, *Advertising the American Dream: Making Way for Modernity, 1920–1940* (Berkeley and Los Angeles: Univ. of California Press, 1985); Daniel Horowitz, *The Morality of Spending: Attitudes toward the Consumer Society in America, 1875–1940* (Baltimore: Johns Hopkins Univ. Press, 1985); Susman, *Culture as History*; Higham, "The Reorientation of American Culture in the 1890s"; Coben and Ratner, *The Development of an American Culture*; Douglas, *The Feminization of American Culture*; and Leo Ribuffo, "Jesus Christ as Business Statesman: Bruce Barton and the Selling of Corporate Capitalism," *American Quarterly* 33 (Summer 1981): 206–31. For specific discussions of the important place of leisure in this consumer culture see Lewis A. Erenberg, *Steppin' Out: New York Nightlife and the Transformation of American Culture, 1890–1930* (Chicago: Univ. of Chicago Press, 1981); Lary May, *Screening Out the Past: The Birth of Mass Culture and the Motion*

Picture Industry (Chicago: Univ. of Chicago Press, 1980); and John F. Kasson, *Amusing the Millions: Coney Island at the Turn of the Century* (New York: Hill & Wang, 1978).

14. Charles Fiske, *The Confessions of a Puzzled Parson and Other Pleas for Reality* (New York: Scribner's, 1928); Caroline Miles Hill, *Mary McDowell and Municipal Housekeeping* (Chicago: Millar, 1938); Ames, *The New Orthodoxy*; and Rev. Earl Hoon of Sioux City, Iowa, in Francis H. Case, *Advertising the Church* (New York: Abingdon, 1925).

15. Quoted in Alan Trachtenberg, *Critics of Culture: Literature and Society in the Early Twentieth Century* (New York: Wiley & Sons, 1976), 4.

CHAPTER 2   WORK AND SALVATION IN CORPORATE AMERICA

1. North's speech, and responses to it, are printed in Elias Sanford, *The Origin and History of the Federal Council of Churches* (Hartford, Conn.: Scranton, 1916), 494–503. For biographical information on North and his plain style of speaking, see Creighton Lacy, *Frank Mason North: His Social and Ecumenical Mission* (Nashville: Abingdon, 1967).

2. "Report of the Church and Modern Industry," *Christian Advocate*, 24 December 1908, 2139. Elias Sanford also recorded the responses to North's speech in *Origin and History*, 256–57, as did Shailer Mathews in *New Faith for Old* (New York: Macmillan, 1936), 121.

3. Jacob Dorn in *Washington Gladden: A Prophet of the Social Gospel* (Columbus: Ohio State Univ. Press, 1968) and Creighton Lacy in *Frank Mason North* both insist that the passage of the Social Creed marked the acceptance by Protestant America of the social gospel. Protestants in the early twentieth century enthusiastically supported the Social Creed and asked that a pamphlet be prepared by a special committee explaining its origin and content. Harry Ward and a half dozen others collaborated on *Social Creed of the Churches* (New York: Eaton & Mains, 1912), which was distributed to thousands of classes, clubs, and study groups in the thirty-three denominations that endorsed it. Its widespread popularity sprang in part from the fact that several denominations had written and adopted parts of it before it was presented to the Federal Council of Churches. See Charles Stedman Macfarland, *The Churches of Christ in Council* (New York: Missionary Education Movement, 1917).

4. Sanford, *Origin and History*, 257.

5. While the idea of doing good works to be saved has been considered heretical by different groups of Christians throughout the centuries, including predestinarian Puritans, there is no question that work and salvation were linked in practice by many Protestants in America. Discussions of the Protestant work ethic suggest that doing hard, disciplined, productive·work was seen as a way to glorify God and an answer to a holy calling. According to Michael Walzer, the discipline of work as well as other aspects of the Puritans' regimen were a source of order to men and women living in the midst of disorder. See Walzer's "Puritanism as a Revolutionary Ideology" in Alden T. Vaughan and Francis J. Bremer, eds., *Puritan New England: Essays on Religion, Society, and Culture* (New York: St. Martin's Press, 1977), 19–42; and Max Weber's classic work, *The Protestant Ethic and the Spirit of Capitalism* (New York: Scribner's, 1958). In the American experience, Paul Boyer and Stephen Nissenbaum's discussion of the Salem witchcraft trials shows how Putnam women accused their neighbors of witchcraft when social

and economic changes undermined their prosperity and hard work. Paul Johnson's account of the revivals of the Second Great Awakening in Rochester, New York, in the early nineteenth century demonstrates that industry and sobriety were considered to be evidence of Christian commitment. Shopkeepers, who were the first converts, wanted to bring the revivals to the workers, so that they, too, could find peace and happiness in their lives. Worldly success sprang from diligence, temperance, and discipline, they believed, and the commitment to individual responsibility for one's own moral state reinforced that behavior with the moral force of religion. Looking at the condition of work in the late nineteenth century, James Gilbert showed how American intellectuals despaired that work was not the ennobling activity it once had been. The work ethic, as Daniel Rodgers sees it, became problematic because of changed conditions of work, and that change had profound religious and cultural significance. Between the late seventeenth and early twentieth centuries Americans' view of work and salvation changed, the link between the two becoming looser as time passed and as people like Benjamin Franklin urged people to work simply to become prosperous. But the link remained intact, so that by the end of the nineteenth century, American intellectuals, social critics, and ministers felt a sense of loss. See Paul Boyer and Stephen Nissenbaum, *Salem Possessed* (Cambridge: Harvard Univ. Press, 1974); Paul Johnson, *A Shopkeeper's Millennium* (New York: Hill and Wang, 1978); James Gilbert, *Work without Salvation* (Baltimore: Johns Hopkins Univ. Press, 1977); Daniel Rodgers, *The Work Ethic in Industrial America, 1850–1920* (Chicago: Univ. of Chicago Press, 1974); James Henretta, *The Evolution of American Society, 1700–1815* (Lexington, Mass.: D. C. Heath, 1973); and Jackson Lears, "From Salvation to Self-Realization," in Jackson Lears and Richard Wightman Fox, *The Culture of Consumption* (New York: Pantheon, 1983).

6. Walter Rauschenbusch, *Christianity and the Social Crisis* (New York: Macmillan, 1907), 234.

7. Washington Gladden, "The Labor Question," *Century* 32 (June 1886): 328.

8. Edward A. Ross, "The Near Future of American Society," *Independent* 58 (25 May 1905): 1155; H. A. Atkinson, *Men and Things* (New York: Missionary Education Movement, 1918), 191–92. Atkinson was one of the collaborators with Harry Ward in *Social Creed of the Churches*. He also was the secretary of the Social Service Department of the Congregational Churches and an associate secretary of the Commission on the Churches and Social Service of the Federal Council of Churches.

9. Harry Ward, *Social Creed of the Churches*, 13.

10. Rodgers, *Work Ethic in Industrial America*; Harry Braverman, *Labor and Monopoly Capitalism* (New York: Monthly Review Press, 1974); Herbert Gutman, *Work, Culture, and Society in Industrializing America* (New York: Vintage, 1976); and David Montgomery, "Gutman's Nineteenth-Century America: Review Essay," *Labor History* 19 (Summer 1978): 416–29, explore the changes in the nature and organization of work in the late nineteenth and early twentieth centuries. Rodgers examines the transformation of the work ethic in the years between 1850 and 1920 and shows how the compulsion to work continued, but lost its religious significance. Work was carried out in a context of an emerging youthful culture of play and leisure: work became the means to enjoy the fruits of consumer capitalism. Harry Braverman focuses his attention on the degradation of work in the twentieth century, the narrowing or loss of skills resulting from the infinite division of labor. While his work is an important study of the alienating drudgery of modern work, certain correctives are necessary to keep the issue of work and meaning in

perspective. David Brody's study *Steelworkers in America* (New York: Harper, 1960) and various essays by Herbert Gutman in *Work, Culture, and Society* suggest that workers clung tenaciously to certain rules governing the shop floor. They tried to resist attempts to break down union control of shop organization and definition of the process of production with slowdowns, sabotage, strikes, union rules, and fines. Montgomery's essay balances Braverman's and Gutman's points of view by suggesting the adaptability of American workers. Workers, he points out, were neither unerringly resistant nor completely degraded; they adopted some modern practices at the same time that they clung to some older definitions of work. Studies of success literature and rags-to-riches mythology also suggest that success for everyone, not just for a submerged working class, had become problematic. Even for the upper classes, success seemed to have less to do with talent, perseverance, individual initiative, and hard work, and much more to do with the accident of birth, inheritance, and family connections. See Gabriel Kolko, "Brahmins and Businessmen," in Kurt Wolff, ed., *Critical Spirit: Essays in Honor of Herbert Marcuse* (Boston: Beacon, 1967); John Cawelti, *Apostles of the Self-Made Man* (Chicago: Univ. of Chicago Press, 1965); and Irvin Wyllie, *The Self-Made Man in America* (New Brunswick, N.J.: Rutgers Univ. Press, 1954).

11. Lacy, *Frank Mason North;* Dores Sharpe, *Walter Rauschenbusch* (New York: Macmillan, 1942); Jacob Dorn, *Washington Gladden* (Columbus: Ohio State Univ. Press, 1968); Robert Crunden, *Ministers of Reform* (New York: Basic Books, 1982); and Christopher Lasch, *The New Radicalism* (New York: Vintage, 1965), offer biographies of a generation of middle-class Protestants searching for meaning in work. Autobiographies by Jane Addams, *Twenty Years at Hull House* (New York: Macmillan, 1910); Washington Gladden, *Recollections* (Boston: Houghton Mifflin, 1909); Charles Stelzle, *A Son of the Bowery* (New York: Doran, 1924); and Charles Macfarland, *Across the Years* (New York: Macmillan, 1936), record the anguish of individuals trying to find meaningful life work.

12. Washington Gladden, *Tools and the Man* (Boston: Houghton Mifflin, 1893), 122; Josiah Strong, *The New Era* (New York: Baker & Taylor, 1893), 165, 8; Rauschenbusch, *Christianity and the Social Crisis*, 265.

13. Gladden, *Tools and the Man*, 176; Rauschenbusch, *Christianity and the Social Crisis*, 271.

14. Charles Stelzle, *Gospel of Labor* (New York: Revell, 1912), 11; Strong, *The New Era*, 300.

15. Henry Cope, *The School in the Modern Church* (New York: Doran, 1919), 93–94, 145–47; E. L. Shaver, *A Christian's Recreation* (Chicago: Univ. of Chicago Press, 1925), 29–30; Herbert Gates on recreation in Shaver, *A Christian's Recreation*, 35.

16. Gilbert, *Work without Salvation;* Alan Trachtenberg, *The Incorporation of America* (New York: Hill & Wang, 1982); Rodgers, *Work Ethic in Industrial America*. Historians of leisure offer clues to modern avenues to reward for otherwise unrewarding toil; see John F. Kasson, *Amusing the Millions* (New York: Hill & Wang, 1978); and Roy Rosenzweig, *Eight Hours for What We Will* (New York: Cambridge Univ. Press, 1983). Studs Terkel's *Working* (New York: Avon, 1972), a collection of statements from late-twentieth-century workers, demonstrates the creative adaptations many modern workers have made to their jobs. While certain aspects of their jobs rob them of control, most reported something about their work that interested or challenged them. Still, with few exceptions, work is a means to enjoying life, not really the essence of being.

17. Ward, *Social Creed of the Churches*, 70; Harry Munro, *Agencies for Religious*

Education of Adolescents (St. Louis: Bethany Press, 1925), 62–63; Hugh Hartshorne, *Childhood and Character*, in Shaver, *A Christian's Recreation*, 27; Shaver, *A Christian's Recreation*, 1.

18. Atkinson, *Men and Things*, 7; William Norman Hutchins, "Social Service in Religious Education" (Ph.D. diss., Univ. of Chicago, 1914), 126.

19. Henry Cope, *The Friendly Life* (New York: Revell, 1909), 7–8; Gladden, *Recollections*, 429; Gladden, "Educational Value of Good Work," Commencement Address, Ohio State University, 1910, pp. 6–7, in Washington Gladden Papers, Ohio State Historical Society, Columbus; Shailer Mathews, *The Message of Jesus to Our Modern Life* (Chicago: Univ. of Chicago Press, 1915), 90; Mathews, *New Faith for Old*, 136.

20. Paul Boyer alerts historians of modern American culture to the longing for "reality," connectedness to work, and the struggle for life in the late nineteenth century in *"In His Steps:* A Reappraisal," *American Quarterly* 23 (Spring 1971): 60–78. *In His Steps* and most of Sheldon's other novels, as well as novels by Elizabeth Stuart Phelps Ward and other Christian reform novelists, explore the personal dimensions of middle-class reform. When the action centers on the reformer rather than on his work and the people among whom he works, one wonders whose salvation the novelist is reporting.

21. Charles Sheldon, *The Reformer* (Chicago: Advance Publ. Co., 1902), 159.

22. Edward A. Ross, "The Near Future of American Society," *The Independent* 58 (25 July 1905): 1157.

23. Gladden, *Tools and the Man*, 238; Gladden, "The Labor Question," 104–5; Cope, *The School in the Modern Church*, 208–9; Henry Cope, *Ten Years' Progress in Religious Education* (Chicago: Harmegines & Howell, 1913), 5. For a discussion of medievalism in turn-of-the-century Anglo-American culture, see Jackson Lears, *No Place of Grace* (New York: Pantheon, 1981).

24. William De Witt Hyde, ed., *Vocations* (Boston: Hyde, 1911), 1:xvii, xxvii; Ernest Poole, "Cowboys of the Sky," ibid., 51–63; C. M. Keys, "The Railroad Conquest of the Mountains," ibid., 14; Ray Stannard Baker, "Casting a Great Lens," ibid., 176. See all of volume 1, on mechanical arts; as well as George A. Gordon, "The Claims of the Ministry," ibid., 5:308, 324; and Hyde, Preface, ibid., 7:xv. Throughout the ten volumes of this work, all of the large fields, from "hand" work to "brain" work, are described in terms of heroic endeavor and intense emotional reward—the new reasons for work. The volumes in the series are (1) *Mechanical Arts*, (2) *Homemaking*, (3) *Farm and Forest*, (4) *Business*, (5) *Professions*, (6) *Public Service*, (7) *Education*, (8) *Literature*, (9) *Public Entertainment*, and (10) *Fine Arts*.

25. Atkinson, *Men and Things*, 6; E. L. Shaver, *Christianizing the Community* (Chicago: Univ. of Chicago Press, 1927), vii; Mathews, *The Faith of Modernism* (New York: Macmillan, 1924), 91; Washington Gladden, *Rights and Duties* (Ann Arbor: Univ. of Michigan Board of Regents, 1902), p. 2 of text (unnumbered).

26. Ida M. Tarbell, *The Business of Being a Woman* (c. 1912; New York: Macmillan, 1921), ch. 1; Charlotte Perkins Gilman, *His Religion and Hers* (New York: Century, 1923), 290; Elizabeth Stuart Phelps Ward, *Doctor Zay* (Boston: Houghton Mifflin, 1882), 231.

27. For sensitive treatments of the problem of identity formation and women in the late nineteenth century, see Jean Strouse, *Alice James: A Biography* (Boston: Houghton Mifflin, 1980); Mary A. Hill, *Charlotte Perkins Gilman: The Making of a Radical Feminist, 1860–1896* (Philadelphia: Temple Univ. Press, 1980); Allen F. Davis, *Ameri-*

can Heroine: The Life and Legend of Jane Addams (New York: Oxford Univ. Press, 1973); and Christopher Lasch, *The New Radicalism in America, 1889–1963* (New York: Vintage, 1965).

28. Ellen Key, *Renaissance of Motherhood* (New York: Putnam's 1914); Ida Tarbell, *Business of Being a Woman*, 27; *Women's Citizenship*, 1913 issue, which explored women's commitment to their "larger home"; *Boys Work in the Local Church*, Messages of the Men and Religion Forward Movement, vol. 5 (New York: Association Press, 1912), 89, 96, 98–99; Josiah Strong, *The Challenge of the City* (New York: Young People's Missionary Movement, 1907). Research on advertisement has revealed the growing dependence on experts and on others in advertisements. See Lears and Fox, *Culture of Consumption*.

29. "The Story of an Institutional Church," *Charities* 14 (6 May 1905): 728.

30. Edward S. Martin, *The Unrest of Women* (New York: Appleton, 1915), 3–4.

31. Elizabeth Stuart Phelps Ward, *Friends: A Duet* (Boston: Houghton Mifflin, 1881), 45–46.

32. Franklin W. Johnson, *The Problems of Boyhood* (Chicago: Univ. of Chicago Press, 1914), 4.

33. Stelzle, *Gospel of Labor*, 12.

34. Gladden explained the uproar caused by his discussion of amusements with the Congregational young people's society on the flyleaf of *Amusements: Their Uses and Their Abuses* (North Adams, Mass.: Robinson, 1866). He also included the letter signed by twenty-seven laymen that urged him to publish his work in an effort to still the troubled waters. Gladden includes a brief reference to the event in *Recollections*. The letter from "Clericus" to Washington Gladden, 5 April 1867, is part of the Washington Gladden Papers (WGP) in the Ohio Historical Society (OHS) on microfilm edition (mf) roll 1, frame 273.

35. Gladden, *Amusements*, 5–7, 22, and passim.

36. Washington Gladden, *From the Hub to the Hudson* (Boston: New England News Co., 1869), iv.

37. John Faris, *Reapers of His Harvest* (Philadelphia: Westminster Press, 1915), 70–71. This short essay focuses on Gladden's struggle with the meaning of work and how that struggle informed the social gospel, for which he was largely responsible. For a superb biography of Gladden see Jacob Dorn's *Washington Gladden: A Prophet of the Social Gospel*. Harry Elwood Starr gives a brief synopsis of his life and career in "Washington Gladden," *Dictionary of American Biography* (hereafter *DAB*), 7:325.

38. Gladden, *Recollections*, 59.

39. Washington Gladden, "Onward," *Williams Quarterly* 6 (August 1858): 15–16, in WGP, OHS, mf r. 51, fr. 190.

40. Amanda Williams to Washington Gladden, 2 April 1859, WGP, OHS, mf r. 1, fr. 133.

41. Washington Gladden to his family, 1859, WGP, OHS, mf r. 1, fr. 182. Gladden's *Recollections;* Faris, *Reapers of His Harvest;* and the *DAB* are the three principal sources of information about Gladden's life.

42. Hattie Hamilton to Washington Gladden, 12 May 1858, in Dorn, *Washington Gladden*, 25. Photographs of Jennie Cohoon in the Gladden Papers show an extraordinarily plain woman. Though hundreds of people sent their condolences to Gladden at the time of her death, Gladden himself left no written tribute and mentions little about her

in his autobiography. She seemed to have been overshadowed by his career and accomplishments.

43. Washington Gladden, "Fifty Years in the Ministry," WGP, OHS, box 436, no. 10.

44. Gladden, *Recollections*, 114.

45. Gladden, "Fifty Years in the Ministry," 5.

46. Gladden, *Recollections*, 114.

47. Dorn, *Washington Gladden*, 26.

48. I run the risk of carrying symbolism of the Civil War and Gladden's moves too far, but the connections seem highly suggestive. Gladden's state of mind, combined with his perception of the war, may have bred discomfort with particular places—made them difficult to confront daily. His letter of resignation is in WGP, OHS, mf r. 51, fr. 1075–77.

49. Gladden, *Recollections*, 182.

50. Gladden to Henry C. Brown, WGP, OHS, mf r. 1, fr. 425.

51. Gladden, *Recollections*, 268, 273. Gladden never found complete satisfaction in the ministry. Parish duties did not absorb his energy. He dabbled in politics, continued to publish, made numerous tours, and organized and joined dozens of committees, associations, and boards for reform. He also continued to be defensive about his work and himself, as an incident in 1886 illustrates. In that year he published *Applied Christianity* and advocated a social gospel that would balance "self-interest" and "benevolence." The *Congregational Quarterly* accused him of lacking "manly" resolve by remaining in the church instead of acting outside of it as a reformer. Gladden's testy retort, which appeared in the same journal, spoke tellingly of his recurring bouts of insecurity: "I speak for nobody but myself, but I happen to know that I am not alone in my opinions, nor in my determination to stand by them. There are quite a number of us who have no wish for controversy, but who do believe to some extent in the manly art of self-defense, and we shall not be posted as sneaks in the 'Congregational Quarterly' without mildly protesting. If by refusing to go straight over to infidelity, we must lose the respect of the editor of the 'Quarterly,' so be it; we shall try not to lose our own self-respect."

52. Gladden, *Tools and the Man*, 30.

53. Washington Gladden, *Social Salvation* (Boston: Houghton Mifflin, 1902), 13.

54. I am following a historiographical path well-lighted by historians Ann Douglas, Jackson Lears, and Daniel Rodgers. Other scholars whose insights inform this essay include David Riesman, *The Lonely Crowd* (New Haven: Yale Univ. Press, 1950), and Philip Rieff, *Triumph of the Therapeutic* (New York: Harper & Row, 1966), who explore the emergence and nature of modern social relations in a corporate, consumer, mass society. Janet F. Fishburn also suggests an interesting influence of "feminine" values on social gospel thinkers. Her observation that many social gospelers were fatherless emphasizes the important influence of mothers' values on their development. Service, sacrifice, and love—the triad of social gospel values—sprang from Victorian values associated with women. See Fishburn, *The Fatherhood of God and the Victorian Family* (Philadelphia: Fortress Press, 1981).

55. Gladden, *Applied Christianity*, 14, 28–29.

56. Gladden, *Tools and the Man*, 234, and idem, *The Labor Question* (Boston: Pilgrim Press, 1911), 141–42.

57. Gladden, *Social Salvation*, 7, 10, 14.

58. Gladden, *Recollections*, 253.

59. Gladden, *The Labor Question*, 112–13.

60. Gladden, *Tools and the Man*, 30.

61. Gladden, "Educational Value of Good Work," 16.

62. Washington Gladden, "The Past," in *Organized Labor and Capital* (Philadelphia: Jacobs, 1904), 62–63.

63. Washington Gladden, *The Church and Modern Life* (Boston: Houghton Mifflin, 1908), 219–20.

64. Washington Gladden, "The Relation of Corporations to Public Morals," *Bibliotheca Sacra* 52 (October 1895): 619–20.

65. Gladden, *Social Salvation*, 2–3.

66. Gladden, *Recollections*, 298.

67. Gladden, *The Church and Modern Life*, 221.

68. Mathews, *New Faith for Old*, 20.

69. Bernard Meland, "Shailer Mathews," *DAB*, S-3: 514–16; *Dictionary of American Religious Biography*; Mathews, *New Faith for Old*; and Miles Krumbine, *Process of Religion* (New York: Macmillan, 1933), are the chief sources of information about Mathews's life.

70. Ernest Gordon, *An Ecclesiastical Octopus* (Boston: Fellowship Press, 1948), 14–15; William R. Hutchison, *The Modernist Impulse in American Protestantism* (New York: Oxford, 1982), 275.

71. Krumbine, *Process of Religion*, 4.

72. Mathews, *New Faith for Old*, 10–13.

73. Ibid., ch. 1; Meland, "Shailer Mathews," 514–16.

74. Krumbine, *Process of Religion*, 4–5.

75. Mathews, *New Faith for Old*, 37.

76. Ibid., 127.

77. Ibid., 39, 50–51.

78. Ibid., v.

79. Ibid., 10, 101, 147–48.

80. Ibid., 93, 101.

81. Shailer Mathews, *Scientific Management in the Churches* (Chicago: Univ. of Chicago Press, 1912), v–vi. Compare Frederick Winslow Taylor's *Principles of Scientific Management* (New York: Harper, 1911) with Mathews's *Scientific Management in the Churches*.

82. Mathews, *Scientific Management in the Churches*, 50, 26.

83. Ibid., 25–34.

84. Ibid., 35.

85. Ibid., 32, 57–58.

86. Mathews, *The Message of Jesus to Our Modern Life*, 26, 90.

87. Shailer Mathews, *The Making of Tomorrow* (New York: Eaton & Mains, 1913), 40–43.

88. Mathews, *What Religion Does for Personality* (Chicago: American Institute for Sacred Literature, 1932), v, 6, 134–35.

89. Ibid., 13, 130, 134–35.

90. Mathews, *New Faith for Old*, 297; idem, *The Message of Jesus to Our Modern Life*, 39; idem, *New Faith for Old*, 299.

91. Mathews, *Scientific Management in the Churches*, 19–21.

92. Mathews, *New Faith for Old*, 86–87.

93. Ibid., 103.

94. Krumbine, *Process of Religion*, 12.

95. "Caroline Bartlett Crane of Kalamazoo: Minister to Municipalities," *American Review of Reviews* 42 (October 1910): 485–87.

96. P. U. Kellogg, "Sketch of Caroline Bartlett Crane," *American Magazine* 69 (December 1909): 174.

97. The biographical sketch that follows is based on the following articles: "Caroline Bartlett Crane of Kalamazoo," 486–87; Kellogg, "Sketch of Caroline Bartlett Crane"; "Story of an Institutional Church in a Small City," *Charities* 14 (6 May 1905): 723–32; "Portrait: Caroline Bartlett Crane," *Delineator* 64 (October 1904): 632; Mabel Potter Daggett, "One Woman's Civic Service in Kalamazoo," *Delineator* 73 (June 1909): 767–68; "Public Housekeeper," *Hampton's* 26 (January 1911): 117–18; Sarah Comstock, "Public Housekeeper," in Hyde, *Vocations*, 6:114; and an entry in *Notable American Women*.

98. Kellogg, "Sketch of Caroline Bartlett Crane," 174.

99. "Caroline Bartlett Crane of Kalamazoo"; Daggett, "One Woman's Civic Service in Kalamazoo"; *Notable American Women*; and Comstock, "Public Housekeeper."

100. Daggett, "One Woman's Civic Service in Kalamazoo," 767.

101. *Notable American Women*, 401.

102. "Public Housekeeper," 117–18.

103. Daggett, "One Woman's Civic Service in Kalamazoo," 767.

104. Ibid., 819.

105. "Story of an Institutional Church," 728.

106. Comstock, "Public Housekeeper," 114–15.

107. Daggett, "One Woman's Civic Service in Kalamazoo," 768.

108. Caroline Bartlett Crane, *Everyman's House* (Garden City: Doubleday, Page & Co., 1925), 2, 69, 76. Crane's reliance on experts is particularly remarkable in that she believed that advertising was education. She praised stove companies for informing women of modern alternatives to their old woodstove-cooking.

109. Ibid., 128–29.

110. Ibid., 108; "U.S. Inspected and Passed," *Survey* 30 (September 1913): 695–98.

CHAPTER 3   AMERICAN FAMILIES AND THE SOCIAL GOSPEL

1. Josiah Strong, *The Challenge of the City* (New York: Young People's Missionary Movement, 1907), 53–54, 104, 131, 144.

2. Ibid., 210, 274.

3. Earl Hoon in Francis Case, ed., *Advertising the Church* (New York: Abingdon Press, 1925), 129.

4. In a three-part review essay published in the *New York Review of Books*, 13 November 1975, 33, Christopher Lasch explains the complicated connections between

family, society, and the individual that provide the basis of my argument. I quote in full because Lasch's language unravels that which is so easy to tangle:

> If reproducing culture were simply a matter of formal instruction and discipline, it could be left to the schools. But it also requires that culture be embedded in personality. Socialization makes the individual want to do what he has to do; and the family is the agency to which society entrusts this complex and delicate task.
>
> Of all institutions, the family is the most resistant to change. Given its importance, however, changes in its size and structure, in its emotional organization, and in its relations with the outside world must have enormous impact on the development of personality. Changes in character structure, in turn, accompany or underlie changes in economic and political life. The development of capitalism and the rise of the state reverberate in the individual's inner being.

5. For discussions of nineteenth-century American families see Nancy Cott, *Bonds of Womanhood* (New Haven: Yale Univ. Press, 1977); Stephen Mintz, *A Prison of Expectations* (New York: New York Univ. Press, 1983); Mary Ryan, *Cradle of the Middle Class* (New York: Cambridge Univ. Press, 1981); Kathryn Sklar, *Catharine Beecher* (New Haven: Yale Univ. Press, 1973); and Paul Johnson, *A Shopkeeper's Millennium* (New York: Hill & Wang, 1978). Autobiographies are also revealing; see, e.g., E. S. P. Ward, *Austin Phelps: A Memoir* (New York: Scribner's, 1891); Walter Rauschenbusch, *Leben und Wirken von August Rauschenbusch* (Cassell, Germany: Oncken Nachfolger, GmbH, 1901); and P. T. Barnum, *Struggles and Triumphs* (New York: Viking Penguin, 1981).

6. Shailer Mathews, *New Faith for Old* (New York: Macmillan, 1936), 11–12; Dores Sharpe, *Walter Rauschenbusch* (New York: Macmillan, 1942), 24–45; Francis McConnell, *By the Way* (New York: Abingdon, 1952), 23–36, 57; Paul Boyer, "Charles Monroe Sheldon" *Dictionary of American Biography*, S-4: 740

7. For works on the late-nineteenth and early-twentieth-century family see Christopher Lasch, *Havens in a Heartless World* (New York: Basic Books, 1977); Richard Sennett, *Families against the City* (Cambridge: Harvard Univ. Press, 1970); Elaine May, *Great Expectations: Marriage and Divorce in Post-Victorian America* (Chicago: Univ. of Chicago Press, 1980); and Ann Douglas, *The Feminization of American Culture* (New York: Knopf, 1977). Testimony from the social gospelers themselves includes memories of mothers who were talented writers or who became involved in local reform or charity. Elizabeth Stuart Phelps's mother was a writer, for example, whose devotion to her career cut into her time with the family. Washington Gladden's mother was a schoolteacher who resumed classroom duties when her husband died suddenly and unexpectedly in the 1840s. Josiah Strong saw institutional churches take over a number of functions once performed by families; he interpreted the change as evidence of the social mission of the church.

8. For full discussions of Gladden, Mathews, and Crane, see Chapter 2, above. Phelps and Macfarland are discussed later in this chapter. See Chapter 4 for Abbott, Chapter 5 for Herron, and Chapter 6 for Jefferson. For others mentioned in this paragraph, see Creighton Lacy, *Frank Mason North: His Social and Ecumenical Mission* (Nashville: Abingdon, 1967); Charles Fiske, *The Confessions of a Puzzled Parson and Other Pleas for Reality* (New York: Scribner's, 1928), 197–200; Charlotte Perkins Gilman, *The Living of Charlotte Perkins Gilman* (New York: Appleton-Century, 1935); and Jane Addams, *Twenty Years at Hull House* (New York: Macmillan, 1910).

9. Charlotte Perkins Gilman, *His Religion and Hers* (New York: Century, 1923), 290. See also Jean Strouse, *Alice James: A Biography* (Boston: Houghton Mifflin, 1980), and Elizabeth Clough Peabody, *Lives Worth Living* (Chicago: Univ. of Chicago Press, 1915).

10. Charles Stelzle, *A Son of the Bowery* (New York: Doran, 1926), 30–31.

11. Charles M. Sheldon, *New Opportunities in Old Professions* (Chicago: Ulrich, 1899), 10.

12. Harry Emerson Fosdick, "The Trenches and the Churches at Home," *Atlantic Monthly* 123 (January 1919): 27.

13. Walter Rauschenbusch to John S. Phillips, 24 May 1909, Walter Rauschenbusch Papers, American Baptist Historical Society, Rochester, New York, Box 39 (hereafter WRP, ABHS); Rauschenbusch, *Christianizing the Social Order* (New York: Macmillan, 1912), ch. 1.

14. Shailer Mathews, *The Individual and the Social Gospel* (New York: Missionary Education Movement, 1914), 12–13.

15. Charles Stelzle, *Boys of the Street: How to Win Them* (New York: Revell, 1904), 13.

16. Clarence Barbour, *Making Religion Efficient* (New York: Association Press, 1912), 29–30.

17. *Boys' Work in the Local Church*, Messages of the Men and Religion Forward Movement, vol. 5 (New York: Association Press, 1912), 95–96.

18. Henry Cope, *Ten Years' Progress in Religious Education* (Chicago: Harmegines & Howell, 1913), 19.

19. Norman Richardson, *Religious Education of Adolescents* (New York: Abingdon, 1918), iv, 58–61.

20. Harry Munro, *Agencies for the Religious Education of Adolescents* (St. Louis: Bethany Press, 1925), 62.

21. Quoted by Jaroslav Pelikan, *Jesus through the Centuries* (New Haven: Yale Univ. Press, 1985), 2.

22. Galley proof of an article entitled "Jesus and the Social Problems of Our Age," WRP, ABHS, box 41; Sharpe, *Walter Rauschenbusch*, 322.

23. Washington Gladden, *Tools and the Man* (Boston: Houghton Mifflin, 1893), 38; Charles Macfarland, *Spiritual Culture and Social Service* (New York: Revell, 1912), 23.

24. Josiah Strong, *The Times and Young Men* (New York: Baker & Taylor, 1901), 45–46.

25. Among the lives of Christ were the following: Lyman Abbott, *Jesus of Nazareth* (New York: Harper, 1869); Frederic W. Farrar, *The Life of Christ* (New York: World, 1874); Harriet Beecher Stowe, *In the Footsteps of the Master* (New York: Ford, 1877); DeWitt Talmage, *From Manger to Throne* (Philadelphia: Historical Publ. Co., 1890); George Gordon, *The Christ of To-Day* (Boston: Houghton Mifflin, 1896); Shailer Mathews and Ernest Burton, *The Life of Christ* (Chicago: Univ. of Chicago Press, 1901); George Wendling, *The Man of Galilee* (Washington, D.C.: Olcott, 1907); Herbert Gates, *The Life of Jesus* (Chicago: Univ. of Chicago Press, 1908); Charles Jefferson, *The Character of Jesus* (New York: Crowell, 1908); Francis G. Peabody, *Jesus Christ and the Christian Character* (New York: Macmillan, 1908); E. S. Ames, *The Divinity of Christ* (Chicago: New Christian Century, 1911); Herbert Willett, *The Call of the Christ* (New York: Revell, 1912); H. E. Fosdick, *The Manhood of the Master* (New York: Association Press, 1913); Bouck White, *The Call of the Carpenter* (c. 1911; Garden City: Doubleday, 1914); G. W.

Fiske, *Jesus' Ideals of Living* (New York: Abingdon, 1922); Bruce Barton, *The Man Nobody Knows* (Indianapolis: Bobbs-Merrill, 1925); Robert Norwood, *The Man Who Dared to Be God* (New York: Scribner's, 1929); Walter Denny, *The Career and Significance of Jesus* (New York: Nelson, 1934); Thomas Hughes, *The Manliness of Christ* (Boston: Houghton Mifflin, n.d.). These books represent only a partial list of the hundreds of books that began to appear on the life of Jesus at the turn of the century and into the 1920s. I cite these because they represent the gradual change in the way American Protestants handled their subject.

D. F. Strauss, a pioneer in higher criticism, wrote an early theological treatment of the life of Jesus attempting to discern which of the gospel accounts could be trusted for an accurate story. See Williston Walker, *A History of the Christian Church*, 3d ed. (New York: Scribner, 1970). Charles M. Sheldon's *In His Steps* (Chicago: Advance, 1897) and Paul Boyer's entry for Sheldon in the *Dictionary of American Biography* also explore the pervasive interest in Jesus' life.

26. Robert Coyle said much the same thing about the carpenter of Nazareth. "Jesus Christ, the Prince of the Highest, became our Elder Brother, the Great Servant of the erring, sinning sons of men." See *Workingmen and the Church* (Chicago: Winona, 1903), 59. See also White, *Call of the Carpenter*, 340, 289–90. Several authors discuss the emergence of a new hymnody in the United States. The best and most complete account is Sandra Sizer, *Gospel Hymns and Social Religion* (Philadelphia: Temple Univ. Press, 1978). See also Douglas, *The Feminization of American Culture*, and Henry Cope, *One Hundred Hymns You Ought to Know* (New York: Revell, 1906).

Cope's one hundred hymns "which may be counted of greatest worth and force on account of their power for spiritual nurture, for character determination" included only three by the great hymn-writer, Isaac Watts—"Oh God Our Help in Ages Past," "Messiah's Kingdom," and "The Wondrous Cross"—three of the gentlest and most sentimental ones penned by Watts. Of the master hymn-writer Cope wrote, probably as an explanation for the dearth of Watts's works, "He wrote some of the worst doggerel that children have ever been forced to learn." Probably the worst part of Watts's doggerel to Cope was its early eighteenth-century Edwardsian Protestant sensibility.

27. Talmage, *From Manger to Throne*, 217–18. See also Herbert Gutman, "Protestantism and the American Labor Movement: The Christian Spirit in the Gilded Age," in *Work, Culture, and Society in Industrializing America* (New York: Vintage, 1966), 79–117.

28. White, *Call of the Carpenter*, 312.

29. Herbert Gates, *The Life of Jesus* (1906); Mary Austin, *The Man Jesus* (New York: Harper & Bros., 1915); George Wendling, *The Man of Galilee* (1907); Herbert Willett, *The Call of the Christ* (1912); Burgess, *The Life of Jesus: Teacher's Manual*; Mathews, *New Faith for Old*, 123–24.

30. Fosdick, *The Manhood of the Master*, 161.

31. Richard Niese, *The Newspaper and Religious Publicity* (New York: Doran, 1925), 15–16.

32. Charles Stelzle, *Principles of Successful Church Advertising* (New York: Revell, 1908), 56–57.

33. Rolf Lunden, *Business and Religion in the American 1920s* (Westport, Conn.: Greenwood, 1988). See Chapter 6 below. The following books show evidence of both the

social gospel and commercial interest: Stelzle, *Principles of Successful Church Advertising;* Clarence Barbour, ed., *Making Religion Efficient;* W. B. Ashley, *Church Advertising: Its Why and How* (Philadelphia: Lippincott, 1917); Francis Case, *Advertising the Church* and *Handbook of Church Advertising* (New York: Abingdon, 1921); Ernest Eugene Elliott, *How to Advertise a Church* (New York: Doran, 1920); Christian Reisner, *Church Publicity* (Cincinnati: Methodist Book Concern, 1913), and *The Preacher-Persuader* (New York: Eaton & Mains, 1910); Shailer Mathews, *Scientific Management in the Churches* (Chicago: Univ. of Chicago Press, 1912); and Charles E. Jefferson, *Thirty Years on Broadway* (New York: Libien Press, 1930).

34. Frederick Anderson, *Man of Nazareth* (New York: Macmillan, 1920), viii, 22; Fiske, *Jesus' Ideals of Living,* 3; Jones, *The Life of Christ,* 9; Charles Fiske and Burton Easton, *The Real Jesus: What He Taught, What He Did, Who He Was* (New York: Harper, 1929), 73; Barton, *The Man Nobody Knows;* Denny, *The Career and Significance of Jesus;* Norwood, *The Man Who Dared to Be God.*

35. Henry Cope, *The Friendly Life* (New York: Revell, 1909), 50; William Dawson, *Threshold of Manhood* (New York: Revell, 1909), 242.

36. Josiah Strong, *My Religion in Everyday Life* (New York: Baker & Taylor, 1910), 44.

37. Lyman Abbott, *What Christianity Means to Me* (New York: Macmillan, 1921), 5–10; Sharpe, *Walter Rauschenbusch,* 322.

38. *Boys' Work,* 5–6.

39. Richardson, *Religious Education of Adolescents,* iv, 58–61; Macfarland, *Across the Years;* Walter Rauschenbusch to Hilmar Rauschenbusch, 1 May 1917, WRP, ABHS, box 50.

40. Elizabeth Stuart Phelps, *Chapters from a Life* (Boston: Houghton Mifflin, 1896), 53.

41. Ibid., 277. My analysis attempts to place Phelps in a context of late-nineteenth-century family and religious life. Most recent studies have viewed her as a troubled early feminist whose life illustrates the obstacles to complete autonomy for women in *fin de siècle* America. The following biographies provide additional personal information about Phelps, more thorough discussions of her major novels, and a more thoroughly feminist interpretation of her life: Mary A. Bennett, *Elizabeth Stuart Phelps* (Philadelphia: Univ. of Pennsylvania Press, 1939); Carol Farley Kessler, *Elizabeth Stuart Phelps* (Boston: Twayne, 1982); Susan Coultrap-McQuin, "Elizabeth Stuart Phelps: The Cultural Context of a Nineteenth-Century Professional Writer" (Ph.D. diss., Univ. of Iowa, 1979); Lori Kelly, "'Oh the Poor Women!': A Study of the Works of Elizabeth Stuart Phelps" (Ph.D. diss., Univ. of North Carolina, 1979).

42. Information about Phelps's life comes from Elizabeth Deering Hanscom, "Elizabeth Stuart Phelps Ward," *Dictionary of American Biography,* 19: 417; her autobiography, *Chapters from a Life;* Sheldon's *Charles M. Sheldon: His Life Story* (New York: Doran, 1925); and her papers in the Boston Public Library and the Andover (Mass.) Historical Society.

43. Phelps, *Chapters,* 54.

44. Austin Phelps's testimony in *The Last Leaf from Sunnyside* (Boston: Phillips, Sampson, 1854) and an article about young Elizabeth (née Mary Gray Phelps) in one of the Andover newspapers, a clipping of which is available in the Andover Historical

Society, provide the main outlines of the Phelps family life in the 1840s and early 1850s. Elizabeth includes her conviction about her mother's premature death in *Chapters,* and it is mentioned by nearly all her biographers.

45. Phelps, *Chapters;* Austin Phelps, *Last Leaf;* newspaper clippings, especially an article on Mary Johnson Phelps and one from the *Boston Herald* entitled "Elizabeth Stuart Phelps Personally" in Elizabeth Stuart Phelps Papers (ESPP), Andover Historical Society (AHS), Andover, Mass.

46. Ward, *Austin Phelps,* 10, 28, 37, and passim.

47. Ibid., 40.

48. Ibid., 138.

49. See ESPP, AHS; Phelps, *Chapters,* ch. 3.

50. Ward, *Austin Phelps,* 157. When the Andover Seminary was wracked by theological debates in the late nineteenth century, Austin Phelps defended the legitimacy of orthodoxy. He refused to accept the notion of salvation for the unrepentant, and he resisted the liberal theology that shaped some of the universalist assumptions of his daughter. Phelps's description of her father during the theological debates captures both her respect for her father as well as her acknowledgement of his weakness. She described him as "the man gray in the service of an ancient and honorable faith" who lifted "a trembling hand to protect" it. See *Chapters,* 53–54.

51. Ward, *Austin Phelps,* 126, 128.

52. Ibid., 278. In an attempt to obscure the fact that the last group of letters were written to her, Phelps gave as the subtitle "Letters to one of his children." For the others she had written "Letters to Francis" and "Letters to Stuart," so there was little doubt who "one of his children" was. Since Elizabeth compiled and completed the memoir, it is significant that she would choose the particular letters that appeared.

53. Van Wyck Brooks, *A New England Summer* (New York: E. P. Dutton, 1940), 80–82, 314, 411.

54. Elizabeth Stuart Phelps, *The Gates Ajar,* (Boston: Fields, Osgood, 1868), 184.

55. Mary Angela Bennett reports in her biography, *Elizabeth Stuart Phelps,* p. 1, that Austin Phelps considered his daughter guilty of heresy. Phelps discusses the response to *The Gates Ajar* at length in her autobiography and includes samples of the letters she received from readers across the country. See chapter 6, "And Still the Gates Ajar," in *Chapters,* 110–30.

56. Phelps summarized the reaction to *The Gates Ajar* as follows:

> The young author of the "Gates Ajar" was only put to the question. Heresy was her crime, and atrocity her name. She had outraged the church. She had blasphemed its sanctities. She had taken live coals from the altar in her impious hand. The sacrilege was too serious to be dismissed with cold contempt. Opinion battled about that poor little tale, as if it had held the power to overthrow the church and state and family.
>
> It was an irreverent book—it was a devout book. It was a strong book—it was a weak book. It was a religious book—it was an immoral book. (I have forgotten just why; in fact, I think I never knew.) It was a good book—it was a bad book. It was calculated to comfort the comfortless—it was calculated to lead the impressionable astray. It was an accession to Christian literature—it was a disgrace to the religious antecedents of the author, and so on, and so forth. (*Chapters,* 119.)

57. Elizabeth Stuart Phelps, *Gypsy Breynton* (Boston: Graves & Young, 1868), 254, 18.

58. Elizabeth Stuart Phelps, *Friends: A Duet* (Boston: Houghton Mifflin, 1881), 163.

59. Elizabeth Stuart Phelps, *A Singular Life* (Boston: Houghton Mifflin, 1894), 264–65.

60. Henry Wadsworth Longfellow to Elizabeth Stuart Phelps, ESPP, Boston Public Library (BPL).

61. At about the same time of her courtship, Elizabeth Stuart Phelps wrote a humorous piece called *Burglars in Paradise*. Though Corona, the protagonist, sets traps for thieves, she is not prepared for the old lover who steals back into her life near the end of the story to wrest from her the independence she had struggled to gain. He already had taken her youthful dream of marriage and motherhood by leaving her in the lurch years earlier, and now, when she can no longer bear children, he returns to take her autonomy. Elizabeth Phelps's description of the anxiety Corona feels about setting up her own household echoes her own anxiety at the prospect of marrying Ward. In startling and suggestive (though undoubtedly unconscious) sexual imagery, she wrote of Corona: "How should she get any rain, if she *had* a hogshead? How could she keep house till she had a clothes-post? And how could she get a clothes-post till she had begun to keep house? Night after night she dreamed of hogsheads and clothes-posts. She waked cold with her efforts to plant the clothes-post in the parlor carpet, and weak with the attempt to set a lunch-table for sixteen upon the slippery surface of the hogshead. Her mind became a frightful chaos of household detail." *Burglars in Paradise* (Boston: Houghton Mifflin, 1886), 43. Of her own impending marriage she wrote: "The first delicate sheath of ice upon the top of the hogshead of rain water which had always been my thermometer at the chalet, and told me when it was time to go back to my father's house, called me to Andover Hill no more. The Old Maid's Paradise was closed that year forever." *Chapters*, 242.

62. Phelps, *Chapters*, 243. The two collaborations were *The Master of the Magicians* and *Come Forth*. Among the books Phelps wrote on her own during these years is one entitled *Confessions of a Wife*, written under the pseudonym Mary Adams. The following passage, which characterizes much of the tortured prose in the volume, suggests the depth of her unhappiness and confusion:

> "I am thought to be quite a proper person, like other well-bred girls and the curious thing is that the savage in me never breaks out in improper ways, but only smolders, and sharpens knives, and thinks things, and hums war-cries under its breath—and carries chiffon sunshades, and wears twelve-button gloves and satin slippers or embroidered Mayflowers all the while. And nothing could prove it so well as the fact that my hand and my brain are writing this sentence, putting words together decently and in order, while I have fled into a pathless place and hidden from myself. If [my husband] were here this minute, searching my soul with his splendid eyes, that man could never find me. I cannot find myself. There is no trail. (Mary Adams, *Confessions of a Wife* [New York: Century, 1902], 34–35.)

63. Phelps, *Chapters*, 213; see chapter 10, "Gloucester," ibid., 198–220.

64. Elizabeth Stuart Phelps to Mrs. Lothrop, 23 July 1890, and Phelps to Miss Gould, 28 October 1892, in Edwin Bacon, *Literary Pilgrimages in New England*, ESPP, BPL.

65. Most of the short stories of *The Empty House* (Boston: Houghton Mifflin, 1910) dealt with death. But oddly, none of the deaths was "real." Either the person was brought back to life, feigned death, imagined death, or returned after having been believed dead. Phelps no longer thought about death as a continuation of life. These last stories seemed to be denials of death and celebrations of life.

66. Rauschenbusch to a member of his church, 16 February 1897, WRP, ABHS, box 23.

67. Ray Stannard Baker, "The New Evangelism," *The Independent* 56 (12 May 1904): 1055–61.

68. Rauschenbusch, *Leben und Wirken*.

69. Information about Rauschenbusch's life comes from Harry F. Ward, "Walter Rauschenbusch," *DAB*, 15:392; *the Dictionary of American Religious Biography*; Sharpe, *Walter Rauschenbusch*; and WRP, ABHS.

70. F. W. C. Meyer to Mrs. James (Winifred Rauschenbusch) Rorty, 17 September 1929, WRP, ABHS, box 39.

71. Sharpe, *Walter Rauschenbusch*, 38.

72. Rauschenbusch, *Leben und Wirken*, 216.

73. Ibid., 210.

74. Ibid., 208, 223.

75. See ibid. and Sharpe, *Walter Rauschenbusch*.

76. Sharpe, *Walter Rauschenbusch*, 41.

77. Rauschenbusch, *Leben und Wirken*, 249–50; Walter Rauschenbusch to Ford Munson, 27 May 1883, WRP, ABHS, box 23.

78. Sharpe, *Walter Rauschenbusch*, 41.

79. Ibid., 35, 39, 58.

80. Sharpe, *Walter Rauschenbusch*, 25–26; Rauschenbusch to Pauline Rauschenbusch, 10 September 1894, WRP, ABHS, box 38. Other letters in the same location convey his troubled concern about impotence.

81. Sharpe, *Walter Rauschenbusch*, 43.

82. Rauschenbusch, *Leben und Wirken*, 228–29.

83. Sharpe, *Walter Rauschenbusch*, 57. See the following for discussions of Rauschenbusch's ministry in New York: Ernest Trice Thompson, *Changing Emphases in American Preaching* (Philadelphia: Westminster, 1943), 183–221; Paul L. Higgins, *Preachers of Power* (New York: Vantage, 1950), 59–71; and Robert G. Torbet, *The Baptist Ministry Then and Now* (Philadelphia: Judson Press, 1952), 57.

84. Rauschenbusch to John S. Phillips, 24 May 1909, WRP, ABHS, box 39. See also Rauschenbusch to Dr. Barnes, 10 May 1918, WRP, ABHS, box 39.

85. For an account of the Brotherhood of the Kingdom, see Sharpe, *Walter Rauschenbusch*, ch. 7.

86. Galley proof of "Jesus and the Social Problems of our Age," WRP, ABHS, box 41.

87. Rauschenbusch, "Religion and the Great Unrest" (sermon), 1913–16, WRP, ABHS, box 41.

88. From *A Theology for the Social Gospel* (New York: Macmillan, 1917), quoted in Sharpe, *Walter Rauschenbusch*, 335.

89. Sharpe, *Walter Rauschenbusch*, 342.

90. Ibid., 72.

91. Walter Rauschenbusch to Hilmar Rauschenbusch, 1 May 1917, WRP, ABHS, box 50.

92. Walter Rauschenbusch to Pauline Rauschenbusch, 13 September 1894, WRP, ABHS, box 41.

93. Pauline Rauschenbusch to Walter Rauschenbusch, 16 May 1915, WRP, ABHS, box 37; document dated 31 March 1918 on details of Rauschenbusch's estate, WRP, ABHS, box 39; Sharpe, *Walter Rauschenbusch*, 164. Rauschenbusch became more sensitive to the role of fathers in the twentieth century as he struggled to provide guidance and a good example for his children while permitting them great latitude in their lives. In 1917 he was asked to address the graduating class at Simmons College on the subject of "the issues of life." Rauschenbusch decided to "put in a good word for fathers," whom he believed were maligned by popular cultural media. Too often fathers were portrayed as stumblers and bumblers, who provided money for the family to live but were otherwise laughable. He reminded his youthful audience of the reality of the twentieth century: fathers had to leave their children every day in order to serve them. See "The Issues of Life," a commencement address delivered in Harvard Church, Brookline, Mass., 11 June 1917, in *Simmons Quarterly* 7 (July 1917): 1–9.

94. Sharpe, *Rauschenbusch*, 377; Walter Rauschenbusch to Brother Curtis, 24 March 1915, WRP, ABHS, box 32; Rauschenbusch to Prof. John W. Buckham, 11 June 1916, WRP, ABHS, box 39. Rauschenbusch seems to have been especially sensitive to other people's responses to him. In one of his letters to his wife shortly after they were married, he wrote in desperately embarrassed tones about his unstylish "long coat" that excited "much attention" in New York City and that prompted his attempt to dress so he "wouldn't be noticed." "As long as you are around, you support it," he wrote Pauline Rauschenbusch in an anguish far out of proportion to the social error, "but now—," and then he bought a short coat. Rauschenbusch to Pauline Rauschenbusch, 23 June 1895, WRP, ABHS, box 41.

95. Sharpe, *Rauschenbusch*, 448.

96. Rauschenbusch, "Religion and the Great Unrest."

97. Charles S. Macfarland, *Across the Years* (New York: Macmillan, 1936), 313–14.

98. Ibid., 10.

99. Ibid., 6, 5.

100. See chapter 1, "Nineteenth-Century Boston, 1866–1884," ibid., 1–23.

101. Macfarland, *Across the Years*, 343.

102. Charles S. Macfarland, *Christian Ministry and the Social Order* (New Haven: Yale Univ. Press, 1913), 119–120.

103. Macfarland, *Across the Years*, 26.

104. Ibid., 319.

105. Ibid., 324.

106. Ibid., 330.

107. Ibid., 322.

108. Ibid., 115; Macfarland, "The Part and Place of the Church and the Ministry in the Realization of Democracy," in *Christian Ministry and the Social Order*, 41.

109. Macfarland, *Across the Years*, 323–28.

110. Charles S. Macfarland, *The Churches of Christ in Council* (New York: Missionary Education Movement, 1917), 1:160, 181–84.

111. Charles S. Macfarland, *Spiritual Culture and Social Service* (New York: Revell, 1912), 188.

112. Macfarland, *Christian Ministry and the Social Order*, 32.

113. Macfarland, *Across the Years*, 115.

114. See chapter 14, "Daughters of the American Revolution Discover a Revolutionary Daughter," in Macfarland, *Across the Years*, 232-57.

115. Macfarland, *The Churches of Christ in Council*, 1:160, 181-84.

116. Macfarland, "The Opportunity of the Minister in Relation to Industrial Organization," in *Christian Ministry and the Social Order*, 119-20.

117. On the Macfarland children, see Macfarland, *Across the Years*, 325.

CHAPTER 4   MINISTERS AND THE BULLY PULPIT

1. Walter Rauschenbusch, *Christianity and the Social Crisis* (c. 1907; New York: Macmillan, 1915), 255.

2. Washington Gladden, *Recollections* (Boston: Houghton Mifflin, 1909), 389-93.

3. See Robert Wiebe, *Search for Order*, (New York: Hill & Wang, 1967); James Weinstein, *Corporate Ideal in the Liberal State* (Boston: Beacon, 1968); Charles Forcey, *Crossroads of Liberalism* (New York: Oxford Univ. Press, 1961); David Kennedy, "Overview: The Progressive Era," *The Historian* 37 (May 1975): 453-68; Clyde Griffen, "The Progressive Ethos," in Stanley Coben and Lorman Ratner, eds., *The Development of an American Culture* (Englewood Cliffs, N.J.: Prentice-Hall, 1970); Robert Kelley, "Ideology and Political Culture from Jefferson to Nixon," *American Historical Review* 82 (June 1977): 531-62; John M. Blum, *Woodrow Wilson and the Politics of Morality* (Boston: Little, Brown, 1956).

4. Washington Gladden, *Christianity and Socialism* (New York: Eaton & Mains, 1905), 243-44; Samuel Zane Batten, *The Social Task of Christianity* (New York: Revell, 1911), 112; C. R. Henderson, "The Church and Political Action," *The Chautauquan* 37 (August 1903): 435.

5. Shailer Mathews, "A Religion for Democracy," *The Independent* 86 (10 April 1916): 53; Paul M. Strayer, "Jesus and Modern Civic Life," *Biblical World* 36 (December 1910): 392.

6. Woodrow Wilson, *The Religious Ideals of a President* (Allahabad, India: Allahabad Mission Press, 1914), 8-9, 14-15.

7. Josiah Strong, *Our Country* (New York: Baker & Taylor, 1886); idem, *The Times and Young Men* (New York: Baker & Taylor, 1901), 110-11.

8. Charles Brown, "The Supreme Need of the Modern Churches," *Outlook* 82 (21 April 1906): 880; Charles R. Henderson, "Social Duties," *Biblical World* 30 (July 1907): 21. For G. W. Plunkitt's definition of "good graft" see William L. Riordon, *Plunkitt of Tammany Hall*, repr. ed. (New York: E. P. Dutton, 1963), 9-14.

9. Josiah Strong, *The New Era* (New York: Baker & Taylor, 1893), 331; Gladden, *Recollections*, 381.

10. Theodore Roosevelt, *The Conservation of Womanhood and Childhood* (New York: Funk & Wagnalls, 1912), 53-54.

11. Biographical information on W. D. P. Bliss comes from W. J. Ghent, "W. D. P. Bliss," *DAB*, 1:377-78; and Bliss, *Encyclopedia of Social Reform* (New York: Funk & Wagnalls, 1897), 122, 211-12.

12. Batten, *Social Task of Christianity*, 194; idem, *The New Citizenship* (Philadelphia: Union Press, 1898), 249.

13. Josiah Strong, *Our World* (Garden City: Doubleday, 1913), 1:274–75.

14. Washington Gladden, *Tools and the Man* (Boston: Houghton Mifflin, 1893), 290–91; Shailer Mathews, *The Message of Jesus to Our Modern Life* (Chicago: Univ. of Chicago Press, 1915), 77.

15. Batten, *Social Task of Christianity*, 112, 148.

16. Roosevelt, *Conservation of Womanhood and Childhood*, 42; Edward A. Ross, "The Near Future of American Society," *The Independent* 58 (25 May 1905): 1155.

17. I rely on the definition and explanation of the term "domestication" provided by Paula Baker in "The Domestication of Politics: Women and American Political Society, 1780–1920," *American Historical Review* 89 (June 1984): 620–47.

18. Strong, *The New Era*, 191–94, 183; Gladden, *Tools and the Man*, 288, 288–94.

19. Lyman Abbott, *America in the Making* (New Haven: Yale Univ. Press, 1911), 49.

20. Walter Rauschenbusch, *Christianizing the Social Order* (New York: Macmillan, 1912), 3–5; "Religious Education and Social Duty," *Biblical World* 33 (April 1909): 222; Batten, *Social Task of Christianity*, 68–69.

21. Imogen Oakley and Lucretia Blankenburg, "The Ideal City," *Woman Citizen's Library* 9 (1913): 2211–55; Howard Wilson, *Mary McDowell, Neighbor* (Chicago: Univ. of Chicago Press, 1928), 210.

22. Strong, *The Times and Young Men*, 111.

23. Paul Strayer, "Jesus and Modern Civic Life," 392.

24. Ibid.

25. Brown, "Supreme Need of the Modern Churches," 880.

26. Jane Addams, "Why Women Are Concerned with the Larger Citizenship," *Woman Citizen's Library* 9 (1913): 2141.

27. Rauschenbusch, *Christianity and the Social Crisis*, 285.

28. Various studies in urban history speak of the expansion of sanitation and health services in response to epidemics in the nineteenth century. Charles Rosenberg, *The Cholera Years* (Chicago: Univ. of Chicago Press, 1962), for example, traces the evolving attitude toward disease and public responsibility in the nineteenth century until a "gospel of public health" took shape. For discussions of health care see Judith Walzer Leavitt, *Brought to Bed: Childbearing in America, 1750–1950* (New York: Oxford Univ. Press, 1986), and John S. Haller, Jr., *American Medicine in Transition, 1840–1910* (Urbana: Univ. of Illinois Press, 1981).

29. Rauschenbusch, *Christianity and the Social Crisis*, 205–6.

30. Gladden, *Christianity and Socialism*, 236–37.

31. Batten, *Social Task of Christianity*, 9–10. Biographical details come from *Who Was Who in America*.

32. Batten, *The Christian State* (Boston: Griffith & Rowland, 1909), 383–84, 437; Batten, *Social Task of Christianity*, 145.

33. Lyman Abbott, *The Rights of Man* (Boston: Houghton Mifflin, 1901), 206; Rauschenbusch, *Christianity and the Social Crisis*, 241–42; Harold Shepheard, *Jesus and Politics* (New York: E. P. Dutton, 1915), xvii–xviii.

34. For discussions of progressivism see Daniel Rodgers, "In Search of Progressivism," *Reviews in American History* 10 (December 1982): 113–32; David Kennedy, "Overview: The Progressive Era" *The Historian* 37 (May 1975): 453–68; John D. Buenker et

al., *Progressivism* (Cambridge, Mass.: Schenkman Publishing Co., 1977); and Robert Wiebe, *The Search for Order* (New York: Hill & Wang, 1967). Kenneth S. Mernitz, "Prosperity at a Price" (Ph.D. diss., Univ. of Missouri, 1983), discusses the part played by the Bureau of Mines in attempting to disseminate information to small and medium-size companies that aspired to make their enterprises competitive with the likes of Standard Oil. Charles Rosenberg, in *No Other Gods* (Baltimore: Johns Hopkins Univ. Press, 1976), makes a similar argument for the Department of Agriculture. See Jackson Lears and Richard Wightman Fox, eds., *The Culture of Consumption* (New York: Pantheon, 1983), for essays on the pervasiveness of consumer culture and the attraction of experts in that culture. For a discussion of the professionalization of politics see Michael McGerr, *The Decline of Popular Politics* (New York: Oxford Univ. Press, 1986). George Juergens, *News from the White House* (Chicago: Univ. of Chicago Press, 1981), chronicles the emergence of presidential attention to mass media beginning with Theodore Roosevelt.

35. Charles Stedman Macfarland, *The Churches of Christ in Council* (New York: Missionary Education Movement, 1917), 157, 164, 198, 268, 269.

36. Ellis Hawley is responsible for the term "associative state." See "Herbert Hoover and the Vision of Associative State," *Journal of American History* 61 (June 1974): 116–40.

37. Rauschenbusch, *Christianizing the Social Order*, 6.

38. Theodore Roosevelt, *Americanism in Religion* (Chicago: Blakely & Oswald, 1908), 17–18.

39. Shailer Mathews, "Will the State Displace the Church?" *Biblical World* 30 (August 1907): 83.

40. Paul Strayer, "Jesus and Modern Civic Life," *Biblical World* 36 (December 1910): 388.

41. Batten, *Social Task of Christianity*, 27–28.

42. Lyman Abbott, *Reminiscences* (Boston: Houghton Mifflin, 1923), 420–21.

43. Abbott's *Reminiscences* and Howard Allen Bridgmon, "Lyman Abbott," *DAB*, 1:24, provide most of the biographical information for this sketch.

44. Abbott, *Reminiscences*, 23–40, 61–64, 93.

45. Janet F. Fishburn, *The Fatherhood of God and the Victorian Family* (Philadelphia: Fortress, 1981), makes this point about Lyman Abbott, among others, in the social gospel movement.

46. Lyman Abbott, *What Christianity Means to Me* (New York: Macmillan, 1921), 5–10.

47. Ibid., 185–86.

48. Abbott, *Reminiscences*, 15–16, 20–21.

49. Abbott, *What Christianity Means to Me*, 4–5.

50. Abbott, *Reminiscences*, 18.

51. Ibid., 113–114, 123.

52. Ibid., 21, 123, 133, 135, 296, 243.

53. Ibid., 338–39.

54. Ibid., 362–64.

55. Ibid., 431.

56. Lyman Abbott, *Duty and Destiny* (Brooklyn: Brown, 1898), 2, 12, 16, 19–20.

57. Abbott, *The Rights of Man*, 281, 333–34, 206, 195.

58. Abbott, *Reminiscences*, 442.

59. Ibid., 444.

60. Abbott, *America in the Making*, 49.

61. Biographical information on Mary McDowell is from Howard Wilson, *Mary McDowell, Neighbor* (Chicago: Univ. of Chicago Press, 1928); Mary McDowell, "The Religious Faith of One Social Worker," *Survey* 60 (April 1928): 40–43; and Louise C. Wade, "Mary McDowell," in *Notable American Women*, 2:462–64; Louise C. Wade, "Mary Eliza McDowell," *DAB*, S-2:407–9.

62. Howard Wilson, *Mary McDowell*, 13.

63. McDowell, "Religious Faith," 40–42.

64. Ibid., 40.

65. Wilson, *Mary McDowell*, 9, 15–17; *Notable American Women*, 2:462.

66. Wilson, *Mary McDowell*, 21.

67. Quoted ibid., 45–46.

68. Mary McDowell, *The University of Chicago Settlement* (Chicago: n.p., 1901), 24; idem, "Religious Faith," 42.

69. Wilson, *Mary McDowell*, 220.

70. McDowell, "Religious Faith," 60.

71. Graham Taylor's tribute to McDowell in Caroline Hill, *Mary McDowell and Municipal Housekeeping* (Chicago: Millar, 1938), x.

72. Wilson, *Mary McDowell*, vii.

73. A point also made by Paula Baker in "The Domestication of Politics," 620–47.

74. Mary McDowell, "City Waste," in Hill, *Mary McDowell*, 7.

75. Hill, *Mary McDowell*, 67.

76. McDowell, "The Activities of the University of Chicago Settlement," *University Record* 12 (January 1908): 111–15.

77. McDowell, "Religious Faith," 60.

78. Ibid., 40; Wilson, *Mary McDowell*, 215.

79. *Notable American Women*, 2:463.

80. McDowell, "Religious Faith," p. 43.

81. Wilson, *Mary McDowell*, 143.

82. Hill, *Mary McDowell*, 2.

83. Wilson, *Mary McDowell*, 187, 189, 191.

84. Hill, *Mary McDowell*, 108.

85. Wilson, *Mary McDowell*, 216.

86. McDowell, "Religious Faith," 59.

87. Editorial in *Unity* (Chicago), 11 August 1904.

88. McDowell, "The Settlements and Religion," in Wilson, *Mary McDowell*, 215.

89. Francis J. McConnell, *By the Way* (New York: Abingdon-Cokesbury, 1952), 128.

90. Judge Neal Hughley, *Trends in Protestant Social Idealism* (New York: King's Crown Press, 1948); Harris Franklin Rall, *Religion and Public Affairs* (New York: Macmillan, 1937); and Donald Meyer, *Protestant Search for Political Realism* (Berkeley and Los Angeles: Univ. of California Press, 1960), all see McConnell as a moderate democratic reformer. Marshall Olds, *Analysis of the Interchurch World Movement Report on the Steel Strike* (New York: Putnam's, 1923), and Elizabeth Dilling, *The Red Network* (Kenilworth, Ill.: private printing, 1934), see him as a radical.

91. Crunden argues that ministers of reform turned to politics for the pulpit and for a

place of authority. Robert Crunden, *Ministers of Reform* (New York: Basic Books, 1982). As the example of McConnell shows, ministers themselves contributed to the notion of a bankrupt sacred pulpit.

92. McConnell, *By the Way,* 23, 27, 56; Paul Carter, "Francis John McConnell" *DAB,* S-5:445.

93. McConnell, *By the Way,* 21, 208–9.

94. Ibid., 209; Carter, "Francis John McConnell," 445.

95. McConnell, *By the Way,* 113.

96. Rall, *Religion and Public Affairs,* 162, 5.

97. Francis J. McConnell, "Religion and Modern Life," in *Creative Intelligence and Modern Life* (Boulder: Univ. of Colorado Press, 1928), 6–8, 18–19.

98. Rall, *Religion and Public Affairs,* 6–7; Hughley, *Trends in Protestant Social Idealism,* 85.

99. Francis J. McConnell, *Democratic Christianity* (New York: Macmillan, 1919), 33.

100. Francis J. McConnell, *Christian Citizenship* (New York: Methodist Book Concern, 1922), 9, 15, 43.

101. McConnell, *Democratic Christianity,* v, 48, 86.

102. Interchurch World Movement, *Report on the Steel Strike* (New York: Harcourt, Brace & Howe, 1920), iii.

103. Ibid., 18.

104. Interchurch World Movement, *Public Opinion and the Steel Strike* (New York: Harcourt Brace & Co., 1921), 324–30.

105. Olds, *Analysis of the Report of the Steel Strike,* 409–10; Philip Ensley, "The Interchurch World Movement and the Steel Strike of 1919," *Labor History* 13 (Spring 1972): 226–27.

106. Rall, *Religion and Public Affairs,* 33–34.

107. Carter, "McConnell," 445–46. See also Rall, *Religion and Public Affairs;* Hughley, *Trends in Protestant Social Idealism;* and Dilling, *The Red Network.*

108. Abraham Epstein, "Labor Struggle," in Rall, *Religion and Public Affairs,* 87.

109. Hughley coined the phrase "Democratic Reformism" in his book *Trends in Protestant Social Idealism,* using it for the title of a chapter on McConnell.

110. Ibid., 55.

111. McConnell, *Democratic Christianity,* 2, 5, 9.

112. Ensley, "The Interchurch World Movement," 227.

113. McConnell, "Religion and Modern Life," in *Creative Intelligence,* 19–20.

114. Donald K. Gorrell, *The Age of Social Responsibility* (Macon, Ga.: Mercer Univ. Press, 1988), 321–37.

CHAPTER 5   THE PENTECOST OF CALAMITY

1. Charles M. Sheldon, *In His Steps Today* (New York: Revell, 1921), 5–7.

2. Donald K. Gorrell, *The Age of Social Responsibility* (Macon: Mercer Univ. Press, 1988). Fundamentalists' attacks on modernism were based on cultural and class differences, but many fundamentalists accepted some of the same terms and most of the methods of mass appeal and advertising that social gospelers used. In fact, some of the fundamentalists were the first to experiment with "modern" methods of evangelism.

3. Samuel Zane Batten, "Moral Meaning of War," *Biblical World* 52 (November 1918): 279.

4. Harry Emerson Fosdick, *The Challenge of the Present Crisis* (New York: Association Press, 1917); idem, *The Living of These Days* (New York: Harper & Row, 1956); George Herron, *The Menace of Peace* (New York: Kennerley, 1917); Charles Stedman Macfarland, *Churches of Christ in Council* (New York: Missionary Education Movement, 1917), 230.

5. Owen Wister, *The Pentecost of Calamity* (c. 1915; New York: Macmillan, 1916), 148, 145, 140–41.

6. John D. Rockefeller, Jr., *The Christian Church: What of Its Future?* (New York: n.p., 1918), reprinted from the *Saturday Evening Post* (9 February 1918), 3–4; Shailer Mathews, "Religion and War," *Biblical World* 52 (September 1918): 176; Francis J. McConnell, *Democratic Christianity* (New York: Macmillan, 1919), 86.

7. Ibid., vii; A. T. Robertson, *The New Citizenship* (New York: Revell, 1919), 8.

8. Herbert L. Willett is quoted in "A Call to Repentance" *Literary Digest* 59 (30 November 1918): 30.

9. Ozora S. Davis, "Preaching in a World at War," *Biblical World* 45 (September 1918): 251; Edward Scribner Ames, *The New Orthodoxy* (Chicago: Univ. of Chicago Press, 1918), 2, 10.

10. David Kennedy, *Over Here: The First World War and American Society* (New York: Oxford Univ. Press, 1980); Robert Wiebe, *The Search for Order* (New York: Hill & Wang, 1967); Charles Forcey, *Crossroads of Liberalism* (New York: Oxford Univ. Press, 1961).

11. Davis, "Preaching in a World at War," 250.

12. Harry Emerson Fosdick, "The Trenches and the Church at Home," *Atlantic Monthly* 123 (January 1919): 26–31.

13. "Kind of Religion Soldiers Want to Hear," *Literary Digest* 59 (5 October 1918): 30.

14. Francis J. McConnell, *Christian Citizenship* (New York: Methodist Book Concern, 1922), 11–12.

15. Charles Jefferson, *Old Truths and New Facts: Christian Life and Thinking as Modified by the Great War* (New York: Revell, 1918), 212–13.

16. Harry Emerson Fosdick, *The Meaning of Service* (New York: Association Press, 1920), 157–58. The following books also reflect the new definition of "cooperation": Francis J. McConnell, *Church Finance and Social Ethics* (New York: Macmillan, 1920), 2; Shailer Mathews, *New Faith For Old* (New York: Macmillan, 1936), 208; Edward Scribner Ames, *Beyond Theology* (Chicago: Univ. of Chicago Press, 1959), 147.

17. Henry Frederick Cope, *The School in the Modern Church* (New York: Doran, 1919), 89, 145, 216, 217.

18. Francis J. McConnell, *Democratic Christianity* (New York: Macmillan, 1919), 33–34.

19. Cope, *The School in the Modern Church*, 208–9; Charles Macfarland, "The Ministry and Democracy," in *Christian Ministry and the Social Order* (New Haven: Yale Univ. Press, 1913), 35–43; Richard Beall Niese, *The Newspaper and Religious Publicity* (New York: Doran, 1925), 15.

20. Niese, *The Newspaper and Religious Publicity*, 15–16.

21. Edward Scribner Ames, *The Church at Work in the Modern World* (Chicago: Univ. of Chicago Press, 1935), 81, 90, 99–100.

22. Sheldon, *In His Steps Today*, 166–67. Sheldon found in a survey of Americans in 1921 that 75 percent of the parents polled expressed sentiments similar to the father depicted in his novel.

23. McConnell, *Democratic Christianity*, 2, 9.

24. Sheldon, *In His Steps Today*, 167.

25. Francis J. McConnell, "Religion and Modern Life," in *Creative Intelligence and Modern Life* (Boulder: Univ. of Colorado Press, 1928), 6–7.

26. McConnell, *Democratic Christianity*, 81.

27. Ames, *The New Orthodoxy*, 43–44.

28. W. B. Ashley, *Church Advertising: Its Why and How* (Philadelphia: Lippincott, 1917), 132.

29. Woodrow Wilson, "President's Message to the American People," 15 April 1917, in Woodrow Wilson, *Why We Are at War* (New York: Harper & Row, 1917), 71–79.

30. Samuel Zane Batten, *If America Fail: Our National Mission and Our Possible Future* (Boston: Judson Press, 1922), 162.

31. Vernon Kellogg, "Herbert Hoover as Individual and Type," *Atlantic Monthly* 121 (March 1918): 375–84.

32. Algernon Sydney Crapsey, *International Republicanism* (Philadelphia: Society for Ethical Culture, 1918), 36–37.

33. George Herron, *Germanism and the American Crusade* (New York: Kennerley, 1918), 29–30. Herron italicized this entire passage in his book.

34. Batten, *If America Fail*, 20–21.

35. William H. P. Faunce, *The New Horizon of State and Church* (New York: Macmillan, 1918), 14; McConnell, "Religion and Modern Life," 19–20; Herron, *Germanism and the American Crusade*, 35.

36. McConnell, "Religion and Modern Life," 19.

37. George Herron, *The Defeat in the Victory* (London: Palmer, 1921), xv.

38. George Herron, *Woodrow Wilson and the World's Peace* (New York: Kennerley, 1917), 75, 77.

39. Robert Crunden, *Ministers of Reform* (New York: Basic Books, 1982), 41. I rely on Crunden's essay on Herron for most of the details of Herron's strange life and career. Biographical information is also available in Clara Millard Smertenko, "George Davis Herron," *DAB*, 8:594.

40. Crunden, *Ministers of Reform*, 42.

41. Ibid.

42. George Herron, *The Christian State* (New York: T. Y. Crowell, 1895), 19.

43. Quoted in "George Davis Herron" in *National Cyclopedia of American Biography*, 9:277.

44. Herron is quoted in Crunden, *Ministers of Reform*, 46.

45. Crunden, *Ministers of Reform*, 47.

46. Smertenko, "George Davis Herron," 594.

47. Crunden, *Ministers of Reform*, 49–50.

48. Ibid. Herron proclaimed his belief in cooperation in *The Christian State*, and he admitted his loyalty to socialism in *The Defeat in the Victory*, xi–xiii.

49. George Herron, *The Menace of Peace* (New York: Kennerley, 1917), 16, 88.

50. Herron, *Germanism and the American Crusade*, 23, 25–27, 31.

51. Ibid., 27, 29–30.

52. Smertenko, "George Davis Herron," 594; Christopher Lasch, *American Liberals and the Russian Revolution* (New York: McGraw-Hill, 1962), 173–88.

53. Herron, *The Defeat in the Victory,* xiv.

54. Ibid., 161.

55. Ibid., ix–x, 2–3.

56. Ibid., 4–5.

57. The entry "Harry Emerson Fosdick" in the *National Cyclopedia of American Biography,* as well as Robert M. Miller, *Harry Emerson Fosdick* (New York: Oxford, 1984) and Fosdick's own autobiography, give ample evidence of his prominence in the twentieth-century Protestant ministry.

58. Harry Emerson Fosdick, *The Living of These Days* (New York: Harper & Row, 1956), 121.

59. Harry Emerson Fosdick, *The Challenge of the Present Crisis* (New York: Association Press, 1917), 86–87.

60. Ibid., 11.

61. Miller, *Harry Emerson Fosdick,* 79.

62. Fosdick, *The Living of These Days,* 132.

63. I rely almost exclusively on Fosdick's autobiography, *The Living of These Days,* for the details of his life and career.

64. Ibid., 36.

65. Miller, *Harry Emerson Fosdick,* 8.

66. Harry Emerson Fosdick, "The Trenches and the Churches at Home," *Atlantic Monthly* 123 (January 1919): 27.

67. Fosdick, *The Living of These Days,* 63, 77.

68. Ibid., 70.

69. Ibid., 70–75.

70. Harry Emerson Fosdick, *The Second Mile* (New York: YMCA Press, 1908); idem, *The Manhood of the Master* (New York: Association Press, 1913); "Harry Emerson Fosdick," *National Cyclopedia of American Biography.*

71. Fosdick, "The Trenches and the Churches at Home," 27.

72. Fosdick, *The Living of These Days,* 122–23.

73. Fosdick, *The Challenge of the Present Crisis,* 16–17, 7.

74. Fosdick, "The Trenches and the Churches at Home," 22, 31.

75. Ibid., 24, 31, 32.

76. "Harry Emerson Fosdick," *National Cyclopedia of American Biography.*

77. Harry Emerson Fosdick, *A Christian Conscience about War,* a sermon delivered at the League of Nations Assembly Service at the Cathedral at Geneva, 13 September 1925 (New York: n.p., 1925), 10, 11.

78. Harry Emerson Fosdick, *Good Taste,* a sermon delivered at the Park Avenue Baptist Church, New York, 16 January 1927 (New York: n.p., 1927), 5–7. Fosdick got the phrase "loyal to the royal in thyself" from Lord Tennyson.

79. Ames, *The New Orthodoxy,* 10, vi.

80. Ibid., 1.

81. Ames, *Beyond Theology,* 1–7. I rely almost exclusively on Ames's autobiography for the details of his life and career. For a brief sketch of his life see Richard M. Pope, "Edward Scribner Ames," *DAB,* S-6:13–14.

82. Ames, *Beyond Theology,* 6–15.

83. Ibid., 109.

84. Ibid., 76–81

85. Ibid., 77–78.

86. Ibid., 106, 111–14.

87. Ibid., 116–17.

88. Ibid., 185, 136.

89. Ibid., 142.

90. Ibid., 185, 186.

91. Ames, *The New Orthodoxy*, 10, 91–93.

92. Ibid., 124.

93. Edward Scribner Ames, *Letters to God and the Devil* (New York: Harper, 1933), 7–8.

94. Ames, *The New Orthodoxy*, 20–21, 32–33, 89.

95. Ibid., 110–11, 23–24.

96. Ibid., 103.

97. Ames, *The Church at Work*, 90, 99–100.

98. Ames, *Beyond Theology*, 127.

99. Ames, *The Church at Work*, 92.

100. Ames, *The New Orthodoxy*, 126.

101. Ames, *Beyond Theology*, vii.

102. Sherwood Eddy quoted in "The Kind of Religion Soldiers Want," *Literary Digest* 59 (5 October 1918): 30.

103. Ibid.

CHAPTER 6   A CONSUMING FAITH

1. Susan Curtis Mernitz, "Church, Class, and Community: The Impact of Industrialization in Lexington, Missouri, 1870–1900" (M.A. thesis, Univ. of Missouri, 1981); William Shepherd, *Great Preachers* (New York: Revell, 1924), 129, 113.

2. Alfred Kazin, *On Native Grounds* (New York: Harcourt, Brace & World, 1942); Larzer Ziff, *The American 1890s* (New York: Viking, 1966); and Eric Sundquist, *American Realism* (Baltimore: Johns Hopkins Univ. Press, 1982), explore the drive for realism in American literature at the turn of the century. Garff Wilson, *Three Hundred Years of American Theater* (Englewood Cliffs: Prentice-Hall, 1973), and Benjamin McArthur, *Actors and American Culture, 1880–1920* (Philadelphia: Temple Univ. Press, 1984), note the same shift in American theater—a shift from the clear moral choices of the melodrama to the details and ambiguity of dramatic realism. Philip V. Scarpino, *Social Change and Environmental Quality* (Columbia: Univ. of Missouri Press, 1985); Sylvia McGrath, "Giant Telescopic Lens" (Paper delivered at the Mississippi Valley History Conference in Omaha, 1983); Alan Trachtenberg, *Brooklyn Bridge, Fact and Symbol* (New York: Oxford Univ. Press, 1965); and Joseph Corn, *Winged Gospel* (New York: Oxford Univ. Press, 1983), all suggest the importance of technology in American society. Wonderful technologies represented gods. See also Jackson Lears, *No Place of Grace* (New York: Pantheon, 1981), and Alan Trachtenberg, *The Incorporation of America* (New York: Hill & Wang, 1982).

3. Christian Reisner, *Disciple Winners* (New York: Abingdon, 1930), 36, 102.

4. Walter R. Bowie, *The Inescapable Christ* (New York: Scribner's, 1925), 4, 168. Another example of this dependence on the reality of Jesus is *The Real Jesus* (New York: Harper, 1929) by Charles Fiske and Burton Easton.

5. Charles Brown, *The Quest of Life* (Boston: Pilgrim, 1912), 3, 13–14; Shepherd, *Great Preachers*, 108–9.

6. William Norman Hutchins, "Social Service in Religious Education" (Ph.D. diss., Univ. of Chicago, 1914), 130–31; Erwin L. Shaver, *Christianizing Our Community* (Chicago: Univ. of Chicago Press, 1927), 2.

7. Henry Cope, *The Friendly Life* (New York: Revell, 1909), 26–28; Robert Coyle, *Workingmen and the Church* (Chicago: Winona, 1903), 49–50, 53.

8. *The Church and the Press*, Messages of the Men and Religion Forward Movement, vol. 7 (New York: Association Press, 1912), 10–11; Richard Beall Niese, *Newspapers and Religious Publicity* (New York: Doran, 1925), vii, 37. For additional evidence of the impact of media on churches, see Harry Ward, *Social Creed of the Churches* (New York: Eaton & Mains, 1912), 39, 68, and Francis Case, *Handbook of Church Advertising* (New York: Abingdon, 1921), 60.

9. *The Church and the Press*, p. 67.

10. Charles Fleischer, "Publicity and the Minister's Message," in William Ashley, *Church Advertising: Its Why and How* (Philadelphia: Lippincott, 1917), 198.

11. Charles Stelzle, *Principles of Successful Church Advertising* (New York: Revell, 1908); Roy B. Guild, in Francis Case, *Advertising the Church* (New York: Abingdon, 1925), 15–16, 142.

12. The story about Daniel Weigle appears in the caption of a photograph of the brightly lit Friendly Church that serves as the frontispiece to Ashley, *Church Advertising*.

13. Daniel H. Martin, "Advertising and Modern Times," in Ashley, *Church Advertising*, 166.

14. Christian Reisner, *Workable Plans for Wide-Awake Churches* (Cincinnati: Jennings & Graham, 1906), 10–11; idem, *Social Plans for Young People* (Cincinnati: Jennings & Graham, 1908), 6–7, 13. For information on Reisner's ministry see Shepherd, *Great Preachers*, 108–13; Case, *Advertising the Church*, 18–19, 136–37; and Ashley, *Church Advertising*, 61–67. Other books by Reisner include *Preacher-Persuader* (New York: Eaton & Mains, 1910); *Disciple Winners* (Cincinnati: Abingdon Press, 1930); and *Church Publicity* (Cincinnati: Methodist Book Concern, 1913).

15. Reisner is quoted in Shepherd, *Great Preachers*, 112–13. Reisner tells of the inadequacy of his Denver style in New York City in "Special Sunday Night Attractions," in Ashley, *Church Advertising*, 53–54.

16. Shepherd, *Great Preachers*, 113.

17. Reisner, quoted in ibid., 108.

18. Sykes quoted in Case, *Advertising the Church*, 64–65.

19. Case, *Handbook of Church Advertising*, 29.

20. Frederick T. Keeney, "Preparing the Copy," in Ashley, *Church Advertising*, 41. For a similar view see Christian Reisner, "Special Sunday Night Attractions," 66–67.

21. W. R. Hotchkin, "The Dynamics of Church Advertising," in Ashley, *Church Advertising*, 83–84.

22. Reisner, "Special Sunday Night Attractions," 65–67; Graham Patterson quoted in Case, *Advertising the Church*, 56.

23. John Collier, *Motion Pictures and the Social Center: An Address before the First National Conference on Civic and Social Center Development at Madison, Wisconsin, October, 1911* (Madison: n.p., 1911), 5–7.

24. Reisner, "Special Sunday Night Attractions," 61–62; Chester Marshall quoted in Ashley, *Church Advertising*, 191. For additional evidence of the melding of religion and mass entertainment see Willard Price, "Making Religious Information Appetizing," in Ashley, *Church Advertising*, 148–49.

25. Neil Postman traces an important shift in public discourse from the written word to the image. He argues, in terms reminiscent of Marshall McLuhan, that the modern media for public discourse—telegraph, photograph, and later radio, television, and motion pictures—have assaulted the seriousness of public discussions by promoting reliance on visual images and by creating a demand for "instant" information. Because social gospelers embraced these new technologies for mass communication, they participated in the transformation of public discourse that Postman described. See *Amusing Ourselves to Death* (New York: Penguin Books, 1985).

26. In *Screening Out the Past: The Birth of Mass Culture and the Motion Picture Industry,* Lary May suggests that the American movie industry "took off" between 1914 and 1918.

27. Ernest E. Elliott, *How to Advertise a Church* (New York: Doran, 1920), 46–47.

28. Robert T. Handy, "Charles E. Jefferson," *DAB* S-2:345. For references to audiences and programs, see W. C. Skath, *Building the Congregation* (Cincinnati: Methodist Book Concern, 1919), 26; Christian Reisner, in Case, *Advertising the Church*, 9; and Edward S. Ames, *Beyond Theology* (Chicago: Univ. of Chicago Press, 1959), 142.

29. Hoon quoted in Case, *Advertising the Church*, 129.

30. Reisner, "Special Sunday Night Attractions," 56–57.

31. William Dawson, *The Threshold of Manhood* (New York: Revell, 1909), 47; W. N. Bayless quoted in Case, *Advertising the Church*, 34.

32. Rolf Lunden, *Business and Religion in the American 1920s* (Westport, Conn: Greenwood, 1988), demonstrates many connections between churchmen and businessmen in the 1920s. He does not trace the historical roots of those connections, nor does he limit his discussion to social gospelers.

33. Reisner, *Preacher-Persuader*, 66; Norman Richardson, *Religious Education of Adolescents* (New York: Abingdon, 1918), 27, 38; Shepherd, *Great Preachers*, 66.

34. Muyskens quoted in Case, *Advertising the Church*, 159–60. Muyskens's viewpoint would seem to be in agreement with the argument made by Warren Susman in "'Personality' and the Making of Twentieth-Century Culture," in John Higham and Paul Conkin, *New Directions in American Intellectual History* (Baltimore: Johns Hopkins Univ. Press, 1979).

35. John L. Mahin, "Preacher as a Salesman," W. R. Hotchkin, "Dynamics of Church Advertising," and L. J. Birney, "Why the World Needs Our Goods," all in Ashley, *Church Advertising*, 184, 79, 13.

36. Elliott, *How to Advertise a Church*, 41; Shepherd, *Great Preachers*, 85.

37. Edward S. Ames, *Beyond Theology*, 127.

38. Case, *Handbook of Church Advertising*, 183, 165–66.

39. Joy, quoted in Case, *Advertising the Church*, 134–35.

40. Sheldon, *Sheldon: His Life Story*, 294–95.

41. Paul Boyer, "Charles Monroe Sheldon," *DAB*, S-4:740.

42. Sheldon, *Sheldon: His Life Story,* 24, 37–38.

43. Ibid., 62–63.

44. Ibid., 69–70.

45. Ibid., 34.

46. Ibid., 81–89.

47. Paul Boyer, "*In His Steps:* A Reappraisal," *American Quarterly* 23 (Spring 1971): 63.

48. Charles M. Sheldon, *The Crucifixion of Philip Strong* (New York: Street & Smith, 1899), 29.

49. Ibid.

50. Ibid., 259.

51. Sheldon, *Sheldon: His Life Story,* 277–80.

52. Ibid., 123. Sheldon devoted an entire chapter to his Christian daily.

53. Ibid., 145. Sheldon also devoted a chapter to his adventures with the Flying Squadron.

54. Ibid., 158.

55. Charles M. Sheldon, *The Mere Man and His Problems* (New York: Revell, 1924), 188, 189, 193, 196.

56. Sheldon's *Let's Talk It Over: The Biggest Business in the World* (Elgin, Ill.: David C. Cook Publishing Co., 1929), 36; and *What Did Jesus Really Teach?* (Topeka: Capper Publications, 1930), both later works, reflect both his Victorian roots and his accommodation with modernity.

57. Sheldon, *Let's Talk It Over,* 29.

58. Sheldon, *What Did Jesus Really Teach?* 50, 61.

59. Ibid., 1.

60. Sheldon, *Sheldon: His Life Story,* 220, 294.

61. Ibid., pp. 294–295.

62. Charles Stelzle to Washington Gladden, 8 December 1909, WGP, OHS, microfilm ed. roll 8, frame 992. Gladden's reply to Stelzle's letter was not available, so I cannot say whether or not he fulfilled Stelzle's request.

63. George Nash, "Charles Stelzle: Apostle to Labor," *Labor History* 11 (Spring 1970): 151–74; William Ellis, "Union Preacher," *Outlook* 95 (13 August 1910): 842.

64. Charles Stelzle, *A Son of the Bowery* (New York: Doran, 1926), 30. For a brief sketch see Robert Handy, "Charles Stelzle," *DAB,* S-3:733–35.

65. Stelzle, *A Son of the Bowery,* 14, 19.

66. Ibid., 16.

67. Ibid., 35.

68. Ibid., 19; Charles Stelzle, *Boys of the Street: How to Win Them* (New York: Revell, 1904); Handy, "Charles Stelzle."

69. Elias Sanford, *Origins and History of the Federal Council of Churches* (Hartford, Conn.: Scranton, 1916), 256–57.

70. Charles Stelzle, *The Call of the New Day to the Old Church* (New York: Revell, 1915), 5.

71. Handy, "Charles Stelzle," 733; Charles Stelzle, *Messages to Workingmen* (New York: Revell, 1906), 105–6.

72. Stelzle, *A Son of the Bowery,* 121.

73. Ibid., 124–25; Stelzle, *Principles of Successful Church Advertising,* 12.

74. Stelzle, *A Son of the Bowery*, 125.

75. Charles Stelzle, *Christianity's Storm Center* (New York: Revell, 1907), 224–25, 17.

76. Stelzle, *A Son of the Bowery*, 124.

77. Ibid., 130; Handy, "Charles Stelzle"; Donald K. Gorell, *The Age of Social Responsibility* (Macon: Mercer Univ. Press, 1988), 148–52, 157–58, 219–22, 235–37.

78. Charles Stelzle, *The Church and Labor* (Boston: Houghton Mifflin, 1910), 91–92.

79. Stelzle, *Principles of Successful Church Advertising*, 11.

80. Handy, "Charles Stelzle." Stelzle also worked on the staff of the Federal Council of Churches. See Gorrell, *The Age of Social Responsibility*, 219–22, 235–37.

81. Stelzle, *Principles of Successful Church Advertising*, 41–44.

82. Ibid., 33, 22, 25.

83. Ibid., 11, 56–57.

84. Ibid., 44.

85. Stelzle, *Boys of the Street*, 23; idem, *Principles of Successful Church Advertising*, 39.

86. Stelzle, *Principles of Successful Church Advertising*, 36–37, 12.

87. Ibid., 12, 13.

88. Frederick K. Stamm, *The Best of Charles E. Jefferson* (New York: Crowell, 1960), 2.

89. Ibid., 1; Edgar Jones, *The Royalty of the Pulpit* (Freeport, N.Y.: Books for Libraries, 1951), 73, 69; Shepherd, *Great Preachers*.

90. Robert Handy, "Charles E. Jefferson," *DAB* S-2:344.

91. Ibid.

92. Stamm, *The Best of Charles E. Jefferson*, 3.

93. Ibid., 4.

94. *The History of the Broadway Tabernacle* is quoted in ibid., 3.

95. Handy, "Charles E. Jefferson," 344.

96. Charles E. Jefferson, *Thirty Years on Broadway* (New York: Libien Press, 1930), 5.

97. Ibid., 36.

98. Ibid., 3.

99. Ibid., 10, 15, 16; Stamm, *Best of Charles E. Jefferson*, 9; Charles E. Jefferson, *The Broadway Tabernacle of the Past and Future* (New York: n.p., 1901), 36, 42, 44.

100. Jefferson, *The Broadway Tabernacle*, 37.

101. Charles E. Jefferson, *The Next Step* (New York: YMCA Press, 1909), 8, 26; Jefferson, *Thirty Years on Broadway*, 31.

102. Joseph Fort Newton quoted in Jones, *The Royalty of the Pulpit*, 70.

103. Charles E. Jefferson, *Ambition* (New York: n.p., 1913), 5–6; idem, *Thirty Years on Broadway*, 38, 42.

104. Jefferson, *Thirty Years on Broadway*, 38, 42; Stamm, *The Best of Charles E. Jefferson*, 2.

105. Jefferson, *Thirty Years on Broadway*, 3.

106. Jefferson, *The Broadway Tabernacle*, 9, 11, 20.

107. Jefferson, *Thirty Years on Broadway*, 7; idem, *Ambition*, 19.

108. Charles E. Jefferson, *The Character of Jesus* (New York: Crowell, 1908), 92, 103, 351.

109. Jefferson, *Ambition*, 8–12.

INDEX

Abbott, Lyman, 2, 76, 176–78; Austin and Benjamin Abbott (brothers), 149–50; childhood, 148–51; *Christian Union*, 147, 152; Civil War, 151; *Cone Cut Corners*, 149; conversion, 150; democracy, 147; on God, 86, 150; individualism, 150–51; on Jesus, 86, 150; life and career, 147–56; marriage to Abby Francis Hamlin, 151–52; *The Outlook*, 146, 149, 152, 153, 155; at Plymouth Church, Brooklyn, 153; on politics, 138, 155–56; public health, 142; *The Rights of Man*, 154; on Spanish-American War (1898), 153–54; *What Christianity Means to Me*, 86, 150

Addams, Jane, 76, 139, 156–57, 160, 161, 164, 218

Advertising, 10, 124; Association of Advertisers of the World, 233; Charles Stedman Macfarland, Jr., 125; and the church, 190–91, 233–36, 238, 239–42, 260, 262–65; cultural authority, 33, 229, 238, 263–65, 274–75; language of, 11, 238–39, 259, 274, 277; and reform, 55, 228; and war, 191–92; and women, 67

Ames, Edward Scribner, 194, 226, 227, 267; childhood, 216–17; *The Church at*

Work in the Modern World, 224, 225; conversion, 217, 219; at Hyde Park, 217–21; on Jesus, 218, 220, 221, 222; life and career, 217–25; *The New Orthodoxy*, 190, 215–16, 221–22, 223, 225; reform, 218–19, 221; *Religion*, 225; science, 11, 193, 194, 215, 222–23, 224–25, 240–41; and World War I, 183, 188–89, 195, 221–24

Anderson, Frederick, 85

Andover Theological Seminary: and Austin Phelps, 89, 90, 91–92; and Charles Sheldon, 246

Ashley, W. B., *Church Advertising: Its Why and How*, 190–91

Atkinson, Henry A.: on labor, 20–21, 26; on salvation, 31

Baker, Ray Stannard, on scientists and labor, 30

Barbour, Clarence, *Making Religion Efficient*, 79

Bartlett, Caroline Julia. *See* Crane, Caroline Julia Bartlett

Barton, Bruce, 82, 85

Baseball: as character ideal, 24–25, 238; compared to religion, 11, 244, 253–54; Washington Gladden's model of social

Ward, Elizabeth Stuart Phelps (*cont.*)
  Herbert Dickinson Ward, 99–100; re-
  form, 99–100, 127; relationship with
  Austin Phelps, 88–90, 92–94; *A Singu-
  lar Life*, 96, 97–98, 100; *The Story of
  Avis*, 96–97; *The Story of Jesus Christ*,
  81, 97, 100; social gospel literature, 4;
  women and work, 32, 98
Watts, Isaac, 82, 151
Weigle, Daniel E., 233
White, Bouck, *The Call of the Carpenter*,
  83
White, William Allen, 124
Wilkinson, Lupton A., 241
Willard, Frances, 160, 164
Willett, Herbert, 183
Williams, Charles D., 239
Williams, Leighton, 109
Wilson, Woodrow, 132, 142, 143; election
  (1912), 15; politics and religion, 131,
  173; and progressivism, 129–30; and
  World War I, 191–93, 195–96, 204,
  212
Wister, Owen: *The Pentecost of Calamity*,
  182; *The Virginian*, 181
Women: domestic ideal and "true woman,"
  31, 61, 66, 68, 74, 101, 164; "new
  woman," 59, 61, 68; public housekeep-
  ing, 32, 138, 157; and reform, 138,

161–66, 187; and work, 31–34, 60–61,
  65–66, 70–71
Women's Christian Temperance Union, 160
Work: heroic effort, 29–30; meaning for individuals, 12–13, 16, 18, 19, 30, 35,
  45, 53–54, 69–71; and Protestantism,
  18–19; and religious reform, 16–19, 48;
  and salvation, 25, 56; work ethic, 20,
  22, 30, 35
Working class, 2, 4, 7, 169; and churches,
  5, 19–21, 158; class warfare, 13, 17,
  19, 173; families, 72–73, 78–79, 88,
  127, 249–50; in literature, 27–28; social gospelers' interest in, 19–24, 69,
  73–74, 134–35, 156–57, 160–62, 166,
  223, 247–48; steel strike (1919), 173–
  74
World War I: effect on Protestantism, 10,
  13, 146, 178–80, 183–95, 212–13,
  227, 235; as agent of social change, 10,
  12, 173, 178, 180, 183–84, 202, 205,
  207, 215–16, 221–22, 228, 277; and
  Charles Macfarland, 123; and Walter
  Rauschenbusch, 113–14, 180; Charles
  Stelzle and advertising, 262; the war effort, 184, 223; War Industries Board,
  184, 223

YMCA, 1, 194, 212

New Studies in American Intellectual and Cultural History
Thomas Bender, Series Editor

Library of Congress Cataloging-in-Publication Data

Curtis, Susan, 1956–
    A consuming faith : the social gospel and modern American culture
/ Susan Curtis.
        p.   cm. — (New studies in American intellectual and cultural
history)
    Includes bibliographical references and index.
    ISBN 0-8018-4167-4 (alk. paper)
    1. United States—Church history—19th century.   2. United States—
Church history—20th century.   3. Social gospel.   4. Protestant
churches—United States—Clergy—Biography.   5. Social reformers—
United States—Biography.   I. Title.   II. Series.
BR525.C87   1991
277.3'082—dc20   90-28696

DATE DUE

JUN 07 1998		
AUG 08 2007		